Library of
Davidson College

CAMBRIDGE CLASSICAL STUDIES
General editors: M.I.Finley, E.J.Kenney, G.E.L.Owen

THE SELEUCID ARMY
Organization and Tactics in the Great Campaigns

THE SELEUCID ARMY

ORGANIZATION AND TACTICS IN THE GREAT CAMPAIGNS

BEZALEL BAR-KOCHVA
Lecturer in Hellenistic and Ancient Jewish History
Tel-Aviv University

CAMBRIDGE UNIVERSITY PRESS
Cambridge
London:New York:Melbourne

Published by the Syndics of the Cambridge University Press
The Pitt Building, Trumpington Street, Cambridge CB2 1RP
Bentley House, 200 Euston Road, London NW1 2DB
32 East 57th Street, New York, NY 10022, USA
296 Beaconsfield Parade, Middle Park, Melbourne 3206, Australia

© Faculty of Classics, University of Cambridge 1976

ISBN: 0 521 20667 7

First published 1976

Printed in Great Britain
at the University Printing House, Cambridge
(Euan Phillips, University Printer)

TO MY WIFE, BEENA

CONTENTS

Acknowledgements ix Abbreviations xi Introduction p1

PART I: ORGANIZATION

1. The numerical strength of the Seleucid armies p7
2. Sources of manpower p20
   1. The military settlements p20
   2. The national contingents p48
3. The regular army p54
   1. Heavy infantry p54
   2. Cavalry p67
   3. Elephants and chariots p75
4. The command - king, stratēgoi and other officers p85
5. Training and discipline p94

PART II: THE ARMY IN ACTION

6. Seleucus I at Ipsus (301 B.C.) p105
7. Against Demetrius at Cyrrhestica (285 B.C.) p111
8. The victory over Molon (220 B.C.) p117
9. The storming of the Porphyrion pass (218 B.C.) p124
10. The battle of Raphia (217 B.C.) p128
11. The crossing of the Elburz range (210 B.C.) p142
12. The battle of Panion (200 B.C.) p146
13. The defence of Thermopylae (191 B.C.) p158
14. The battle of Magnesia (190 B.C.) p163
15. The march to Beith-Zacharia (162 B.C.) p174
16. Bacchides against Judas Maccabaeus at Elasa (160 B.C.) p184

Conclusion p201
Notes p207
Bibliography p277
Addenda p295
Index p301

MAPS

1	The campaign of 301 B.C.	106
2	The Amanus and Cyrrhestica	113
3	Cyrrhus	115
4	Antiochus' expedition against Molon	118
5	The battlefield against Molon	120
6	The battlefield of Porphyrion	125
7	The battlefield of Raphia	130
8	Raphia: disposition of the troops	at end
9	The Elburz	143
10	The Fifth Syrian War	147
11	The battlefield of Panion	at end
12	Thermopylae	159
13	The battlefield of Magnesia	164
14	Magnesia: disposition of the troops	at end
15	The battlefield of Beith-Zacharia	178
16	Bacchides' expedition to Judaea	190
17	The battlefield of Elasa	200

ACKNOWLEDGEMENTS

This book has been revised from the thesis which I submitted for the Ph.D. degree at Cambridge University in the summer of 1972. My work was made possible by a grant from Tel Aviv University and the Memorial Foundation for Jewish Culture. The field work in Greece, Turkey and the Middle East was supported by awards from the Faculty of Classics at Cambridge University and Gonville and Caius College. To all these I owe my thanks.

I find it a very pleasant duty to express my deep gratitude to my supervisor, Mr G.T. Griffith of Gonville and Caius College, who generously devoted to me endless hours of discussion. Although the responsibility for faults and misjudgements rests solely with myself, I owe a great deal to his constructive criticism, and more than one of his ideas and remarks found their way into the book. I hope it can be construed as a not too inadequate return for his efforts and patience.

My appreciation extends to my examiners, Professor M.I. Finley of Jesus College, Cambridge, and Professor H.W. Parke of Trinity College, Dublin, for suggesting considerable improvements, and to the former for recommending publication of the book in Cambridge Classical Studies and guiding its transition from thesis to book; to Professor S. Perlman, Professor S. Simonsohn and Professor Z. Yaabetz of Tel Aviv University, whose initiative enabled me to have leisure and facilities to complete this book; and finally to my teacher, guide and mentor, Professor J. Efron of Tel Aviv University, whose acuteness and extensive knowledge in Classics and Judaism provided valuable stimulation and guidance throughout the years.

I owe most to my wife, to whom this book is dedicated. She provided not only encouragement and help, but also the astringent criticism of a legal mind. Our constant discussions of almost every point made the process of writing more of a pleasure than an author has any right to expect.

Tel-Aviv   B.B.
September 1973

ABBREVIATIONS

AA   Archaeologischer Anzeiger
Abh. Bay. Akad - Abhandlungen der Bayerischen Akademie der Wissenschaften. Phil.-hist. Abteilung
AJA   American Journal of Archaeology
AJP   American Journal of Philology
AM   Mitteilungen des deutschen archäologischen Instituts, Athenische Abteilung
AS   Ancient Society
BCH   Bulletin de Correspondance hellénique
BJPES Bulletin of the Jewish Palestine Exploration Society
Boll. di Fil. Class. - Bolletino di filologia classica
Bull. Soc. arch. Alex. - Bulletin de la Société archéologique d'Alexandrie
CAH   Cambridge Ancient History
CIJ   Frey,J.B. Corpus Inscriptionum Judaicarum. Rome, 1936-1952
CP   Classical Philology
CQ   Classical Quarterly
CR   Classical Review
CW   The Classical Weekly
FGrH   Jacoby,F. Die Fragmente der griechischen Historiker. Berlin - Leiden, 1923-
GGM   Müller,C. Geographici Graeci Minores. Paris, 1855-61
IEJ   Israel Exploration Journal
IG   Inscriptiones Graecae
Inscr. Prien. - Hiller von Gaertringen,F. Die Inscriften von Priene. Berlin, 1906
JBL   Journal of Biblical Literature
JHS   Journal of Hellenic Studies
Milet III. - Wiegand,Th. Ergebnisse der Ausgrabungen und Untersuchungen seit dem Jahre 1899, Bd. I. Heft III
Num. Chron. Numismatic Chronicle
OCD   Oxford Classical Dictionary

OGIS Dittenberger,W. *Orientis Graeci Inscriptiones Selectae.* Leipzig, 1903-5

PCZ Edgar,C.C. *Zenon Papyri.* Cairo, 1925

PEF Palestine Exploration Fund

PEQ Palestine Exploration Quarterly

P Petr. Mahaffy,J.P. & Smyly,J.G. *The Flinders Petrie Papyri.* Dublin, 1891

Proc. Camb. Phil. Soc. - *Proceedings of the Cambridge Philological Society*

P Teb Grenfell,P.B., Hunt,A., Goodspeed,J. *The Tebtunis Papyri.* London, 1907-38

RA *Revue archéologique*

RB *Revue Biblique*

RE Pauly,A., Wissowa,G., Kroll,W. *Real-Encyclopädie der classischen Altertumswissenschaft*

Rev. de Phil. *Revue de Philologie, de littérature et d'histoire anciennes*

REA *Revue des études anciennes*

Riv. de Fil. *Rivista di filologia e d'istruzione classica*

S-B München *Sitzungsberichte der Bayerischen Akademie der Wissenschaften. Phil.-hist. Abteilung*

SEG *Supplementum epigraphicum Graecum*

SEHHW Rostovzeff,M. *Social and Economic History of the Hellenistic World.* Oxford, 1940

Sylloge Dittenberger,W. *Sylloge inscriptionum Graecarum.* Leipzig, 1915-24

ZA *Zeitschrift für Assyriologie und verwandte Gebiete*

ZDPV *Zeitschrift des deutschen Palästinavereins*

Z. Sav. - Stift. - *Zeitschrift der Savigny - Stiftung für Rechtsgeschichte*

All dates are B.C. unless specifically marked A.D.

† in the margin indicates an addendum to be found at the end of the book.

INTRODUCTION

The history of the Seleucid army embraces a period of more than 200 years during which the kings carried on campaigns of different kinds against competitors in the Hellenistic world such as Lysimachus and the Houses of Ptolemy and Antigonus, barbarian invaders like the Galatians, rebels like Hierax, Molon, Achaeus, and Timarchus, subject nations like the Jews and the Persians, and the two rising powers, the Romans in the west and the Parthians in the east, who finally divided the Seleucid domain between them. Some of these conflicts had far-reaching historical implications: the victory over Antigonus destroyed all hope of unifying the Hellenistic world and weakened its ability to meet challenges; the battles at Thermopylae and Magnesia heralded the shift in power in the Mediterranean from east to west; and the abortive attempt to suppress the Jewish religion deeply influenced the evolution of new religious beliefs and standards which left their mark on western civilization for many centuries.

The two outstanding features of the Seleucid army were, on the one hand, its quantitative and qualitative superiority over other Hellenistic armies, and, on the other, its inability to withstand the Roman army. In order to understand the first phenomenon, one must examine the organization of the Seleucid army, trace its sources of manpower, and ascertain the way in which its availability and military standards were maintained. These factors, in conjunction with the tactics and operations of the armies on the battlefield itself, may reveal the defects of the best of the Hellenistic armies when compared with the Roman legions.

The study of the organization and tactics of the Seleucid army first of all provides a lesson in military history and answers a number of questions. How did the Hellenistic armies develop after the meteoric rise of Alexander? Did they carry on his glorious tradition, developing and renewing it, or did they retrogress?

Introduction

What distinguished the Seleucid army from its contemporaries? The answers also provide social, historical, and religious information as we learn how the Seleucid army was used as a military, social, and cultural instrument to impose the rule of the dynasty over the vast regions of the Empire, how it helped to shape Hellenistic society in the east, what caused Roman military success, the flexibility and the efficiency of the maniple system over the phalanx, the rigorous Roman discipline as contrasted with the laxer, more liberal Hellenistic military regulations, or perhaps their defects in command and planning on the battlefield which eventually stopped Antiochus III at the decisive moment and paved the Romans' way to Asia Minor, and finally, behind the rhetorical phrases of Jewish sources, how the performance of the Hasmoneans against the Seleucid armies should be evaluated. Was it, as has been commonly believed, a campaign involving a few zealots who tried by force of religious enthusiasm to stand up to an army far larger and better equipped, but which had degenerated from the military point of view? Or was it a contest between a numerically large, but relatively ill-equipped and inexperienced Jewish force, and one of the best armies of the time, well acquainted with all the secrets of the art of war?

The discussion is divided into two parts: the first, 'Organization', is devoted to an analysis of the army, its numerical strength, sources of manpower, the various contingents, its chain of command, training and discipline. The second, 'The Army in Action', is an attempt to throw light on the disposition of the troops on the battlefield itself, and on the tactical planning and performance. In it I shall discuss in chronological order most of the Seleucid battles that have been recorded in some detail. As the determination of the disposition and tactics is dependent on the discovery of the exact location of the battlefield, on clarification of the enemy's disposition, and sometimes also on identification of the routes taken by the armies to the battlefield or on the quality of the accounts preserved and their sources of information, frequent deviations into such questions cannot be avoided.

Unlike the Ptolemaic army, for whose organization there is abundant papyrological evidence, the Seleucid army is referred to in only a few epigraphical documents, which shed little light, while most of the information has to be drawn from the accounts of the battles themselves and incidental references by ancient historians. With regard to Seleucid tactics we are somewhat more fortunate: about a dozen important literary sources provide considerable detail on battles in addition to half a dozen siege campaigns, as well as some minor military operations, far more than for any other Hellenistic army.

Unfortunately these accounts are unevenly distributed over 150 years, which makes it difficult to follow tactical developments. As against Antiochus III, for whom a relatively large number of battle accounts survive, the intensive military activity of the first Seleucids, especially of the founder of the dynasty, remains almost unreported, while the period between the victory over the Galatians in 273 B.C. and the expeditions against Molon in 220 B.C. is covered only by brief allusions to various military operations. Similarly, Seleucid tactics in the century after Magnesia are illumined only by the battles against Judas Maccabaeus and his brothers, some of which are recorded rather briefly and contribute hardly anything to the understanding of the Seleucid army. Nevertheless, an attempt to sketch general outlines and stages of development in organization as well as in tactics is not unrewarding, although the scantiness of evidence and the length of the period under consideration must constantly be borne in mind.

I could not have undertaken the writing of this monograph on the Seleucid army without the invaluable contributions of scholars who have dealt with particular aspects of the subject. First and foremost there are Bickerman's survey of the military organization in Institutions des Séleucides, many references in Launey's monumental Recherches on the Hellenistic armies, and Tarn's admirable lectures on the tactical development in the Hellenistic period. For more specific questions, Kromayer's analysis of the battles of Thermopylae and Magnesia, Walbank's useful notes on the Seleucid army in his commentary on Polybius, and Pédech's contribution concerning the topography of the battle against Molon and Antiochus III's expedition to the eastern satrapies, as well as Abel's pioneer works on the battlefields of Judaea, Griffith's discussion on the Macedonians and mercenaries in the Seleucid army, and Bengtson's notes on the military commanders, have been of inestimable help. If I have preferred to depart from their views in some cases, it is only because a comprehensive survey of all the questions of organization and tactics over the whole period is likely to produce somewhat different conclusions from discussions concentrated on particular topics.

PART I: ORGANIZATION

1: THE NUMERICAL STRENGTH OF THE SELEUCID ARMIES

Estimates of the numerical strength of armies are of doubtful validity in ancient historical literature and indeed in accounts of modern warfare even as late as the eighteenth century. Commanders-in-chief and official chroniclers have combined to obscure the truth by underestimating the number of their own troops and overestimating that of the enemy's.[1] Greek historians from Thucydides onwards achieved admirable precision and objectivity in estimating the number of troops on their side, which is in striking contrast to the utterly unreliable figures given in oriental literature, but even they are of little value whenever there is reference to the Persian armies, whose size is wildly exaggerated even by the trustworthy and experienced eyewitnesses of Alexander's anabasis. The modest figures quoted for Greek armies during Classical times increase abruptly with Alexander's expedition and become still larger in the armies of the Diadochs, but this is explained by the dimensions of the undertakings, the economic resources then available, and the system of recruitment. Alexander won the day at Gaugamela with 40,000 infantry and 7,000 cavalry (Arr. Anab. 3.12.5), but by the time of the battle of Ipsus a record had been set with approximately 80,000 on either side (Plut. Demetr. 28.3),[2] and, as will be seen later, the tendency towards ever greater numbers of soldiers was more prevalent in the Seleucid armies than among their contemporaries.[3] Nevertheless, since the figures quoted for the Seleucid campaigns are not always derived from first-class sources, they require careful examination.

Where numbers are recorded, we must distinguish between the armies for which constituent units are listed and enumerated in detail, and those for which only the total number of troops has been preserved. The first group, which includes the battles of Raphia, Magnesia, and the festival of Daphne, was reported by Polybius, who presumably based his account, directly or indirectly, on official documents. The total figures for Raphia and Daphne,

62,000 infantry and 6,000 cavalry, 46,000 infantry and 4,500 cavalry, respectively, are beyond dispute, for they tally with the detailed lists of the troops (5.79;30.25, and see p.227 n.107 below on the cavalry at Daphne). Moreover, as Polybius' version of Raphia probably originated in a Ptolemaic source (p.128 below), and the Egyptian side is reported to have had considerable numerical superiority in heavy troops (p.132 below), there is no reason to doubt its reliability.

The battle of Magnesia, which according to Livy (based on Polybius) involved 60,000 Seleucid infantry and 12,000 cavalry (38.37.9),[4] raises some difficulties. H. Delbrück, who describes these figures, as he does the whole account of the battle, as a Phantasie, stressing the biased and pro-Roman character of the sources, has pointed out the great discrepancy in numbers between the huge Seleucid army and the modest Roman force totalling just 30,000 men. In his essay on numbers in history he adopts the view that an army would not venture to join battle with a force markedly superior in manpower, and that all accounts of this sort should be regarded as sheer propaganda or attributed to an understandable desire to enhance the victory.[5] But this view ignores the fact that the same source ascribed to the Romans an overwhelming numerical superiority over Antiochus III at Thermopylae (Livy 36.17.10; App. Syr. 17(71,75), both dependent upon Polybius).

An examination of the list of the various units reported in Livy does, however, at first sight cast some doubt on the reliability of the number given as the total. The cavalry numbers just under 12,000, but the infantry does not exceed 45,200. Kromayer assumes that Livy had ignored 3,000 troops who were guarding the camp, an unknown number, probably about 800-1,000, of light guard attached to the elephants, and above all 10,000 light skirmishers of the front line.[6] The first part of the proposed solution does make sense: Thermopylae, lost mainly because the 'baggage' (aposkeuē) was threatened (see p.162 below), would have taught Antiochus to strengthen the defence of his camp.[7] The light troops attached to the elephants should be estimated rather at around 3,000 - the 54 elephants would each have carried four archers on their backs (Livy 37.40.4) and the standard flank guard of 50 'lights' (see p.82 below) would have followed them. But the omission of the skirmishers is hardly acceptable. Livy himself lists some thousands of light troops, whom he assigns, certainly erroneously, to the extreme flanks, and an analysis of the sources, the battlefield, and the disposition of both armies suggests that these troops were operating as front line skirmishers (see p.166-7 below). Even if this theory is mistaken, and these troops were in fact posted on the flanks, it is hard to believe that Polybius would have ignored the light promachoi had they taken part in the battle and yet listed in detail the light troops of the flanks whose impact on the battle would, in any case, have been slight. It seems preferable to identify the missing 10,000 troops with the argyraspides, the infantry Guard,[8] who are listed as being on the right flank but with no precise figure given (Livy 37.40.7).[9] This contingent usually numbered 10,000, and a study of the disposition of the troops together with tactical considerations makes it quite evident that roughly the same number figured also at Magnesia (see pp.168-9 below).

The second group of campaigns, which consists of the expeditions of Antiochus III and Antiochus Sidetes to the upper satrapies, Thermopylae, and some of the campaigns against the Jews, is the subject of much dispute.[10] In contrast to the figures which are available for the first group of campaigns, the information on these other battles, with the exception of Thermopylae, comes from second-rate sources in which much less trust can be placed. An examination of these campaigns must be based, in the first place, on the availability of troops. In the next chapter, which is devoted to the sources of Seleucid manpower, an attempt is made to trace the provenance of recruits and to estimate their numerical strength. The conclusions, based chiefly on the figures of Raphia, Magnesia, and Daphne, will be a guide in assessing the availability of troops. They suggest that the military settlements could provide 44,000 heavy troops, 3,000 semi-heavy infantry and 8,000-8,500 cavalry, who were reinforced by 10,000-16,000 mercenaries and a highly fluctuating number of allies, vassals, and subjects (see pp.42,51 below). In applying these figures to the various campaigns one must take into account the territorial changes, the political and military circumstances (would it, for instance, have been possible for all the available

troops to be deployed in the battle under consideration?), and the
special character and military requirements of each undertaking,
allowing always for the traditional tendency of the Seleucids to
employ large numbers of soldiers. Attention must be paid also to
the general reliability and special character of the sources,
though this should be only a secondary consideration.

The anabasis of Antiochus III to the east, which lasted six
years and took in Media, Hyrcania, Bactria, and even India, is
recorded in several fragments of Polybius, who, though he describes
the Seleucid army as exceptionally large (10.28.1), unfortunately
makes direct allusion only to the 10,000 infantry and 2,000 cavalry
selected for the forced march in Bactria (10.49.3-4). Justin's
total of 100,000 infantry and 20,000 cavalry (41.5.7) is generally
regarded as completely unreliable,[11] but, while these figures have
obviously been rounded upwards, I am not convinced that they
should be wholly discredited. Antiochus III, unharassed by his
rivals in Egypt and Macedon or by internal disquiet, was able at
this stage to put almost all his resources into the eastern
expedition,[12] as the sheer geographical dimensions of his undertakings suggest. In view of the resistance he was likely to face
in the east, he would naturally recruit exceptionally large
numbers of light troops from his oriental allies and auxiliaries,
whose numbers were almost unlimited, to supplement his regular
army. No less vital was the need of extra manpower to garrison
the recovered territories, as revealed in the high figures
reported for Alexander's Indian expedition.[13] If 60,000 infantry
and 12,000 cavalry took part at Magnesia against a modest Roman
force after a substantial number of some 18,000 troops had been
lost at Thermopylae (see below), there is no reason to suspect
Justin, or rather whoever was the source for Pompeius Trogus, of
excessive exaggeration. We do not know how this enormous number
was maintained and fed, nor how many internal crises it may have
undergone. The anabasis of Antiochus III, unlike that of
Alexander, was not privileged to be perpetuated by enthusiastic
chroniclers, but this is not sufficient argument for underestimating its importance and numerical strength.

Even more obscure is the expedition of Antiochus VII Sidetes
in 129 B.C., planned as a final attempt to recover the eastern

regions from the Parthians. Justin, who stresses the extravagant
and sumptuous character of the expedition, attributes to it a
total of 80,000 soldiers and 200,000 civilian followers (38.10),
and comparable numbers are cited in other sources.[14] The first
figure sounds genuine: while it is true that the settlements in
Asia Minor, which usually provided 8,000 infantry and 500 cavalry,
and the eastern provinces, which provided 14,000 heavy infantry,
3,000 semi-heavy, and 5,000 cavalry (see p.43 below), were no
longer under Seleucid control, the majority of the military
settlers in Media, Persia, and Susiana most likely joined the
Seleucid ranks as soon as Antiochus VII crossed the Tigris. To
compensate for the non-participation of the indigenous contingents
of these regions, the expedition was preceded by an intensive
recruitment drive, and several national groups that had not
previously joined in the Seleucid campaigns, such as the Jews
(who alone could provide some tens of thousands), were forced to
share the burden (Jos. Ant. 13.250-1; cf. I Macc. 10.36, 12.41).
On the other hand, the enormous number of civilian followers
cannot be taken seriously. Bickerman's suggestion that the number
of followers was usually twice or three times that of the soldiers
cannot be accepted:[15] besides Justin's figures, he based his view
on certain funerary stelai of Sidon and Alexandria which show
shield-bearers attached to soldiers. But all these stelai
evidently depict mercenaries, whose 10,000-16,000 troops formed
only a small proportion of the Seleucid army. Moreover, it
appears that shield-bearers were attached only to officers, and
not to rank-and-file mercenaries who appear in other stelai without
attendants.[16] Thus, though there was certainly a substantial
number of civilians, there is no justification for magnifying it.
If Poseidonius of Apamea is to be identified as the original source
of Justin's account (see p.101 below), I would suggest that an
immense number of civilians was cited in order to stress the
frivolous and degenerate atmosphere of the expedition, providing
another link in the chain of episodes serving Poseidonius' purpose
of contrasting the declining East with the rising power of Rome
(see p.99 below). Nevertheless, this conclusion does not discredit
the source as such, and consequently the figure for the soldiers
must be taken into account.

The two Books of the Maccabees furnish a great many figures, of which only those for the battles at Ammaus, Beith-Sour, Beith-Zacharia, and Elasa (165-160 B.C.), since they involved a substantial part of the Seleucid army, concern us here. The religious context and importance of these two books has meant that figures which in any other source would have been rejected at the outset have inspired considerable controversy and arguments.[17] But none of these arguments has taken into account both the availability of the forces and the special character of the sources.

The figures for the Seleucid armies, totalling several tens of thousands, bear no comparison with those for the tiny Jewish force ranging from 800 to 10,000 men.[18] This disproportion alone puts the figures for both armies in considerable doubt. Moreover, careful analysis of the sources indicates that the Hasmonean army, at least after the purification of the temple, numbered well over 20,000 men (see p.185 below). And indeed the distortion of the figures attributed to the Seleucids is not really astonishing: one must bear in mind that, apart from the natural tendency to exaggerate the numbers of the enemy's troops, neither authority used Seleucid official documents or sources in its account of the battles. I Macc., published a generation after the revolt, is partially based on eyewitnesses' reports,[19] but no one would believe an oriental religious zealot to be capable of estimating objectively the size of the enemy's camp. Moreover, being the historian of the Hasmonean House, the author of I Macc. was anxious to glorify the dynasty by attributing high numbers to the enemy and underestimating the Jewish force; II Macc. was written in Cyrene, far from the battlefield, and preserves only a few trustworthy military data. Furthermore, belonging to the Pathetic historiographical school which tended to high-flown style as well as contents aimed at evoking strong feelings of fear, horror, and mercy,[20] its author described the relative strengths of the forces in a way which served to do this. But it is the authors' religious conception of historiography as much as the scantiness or inaccuracy of their sources which is to blame. They both take pains to stress divine influence on the course of events: I Macc. hints with relative moderation at the divine hand behind the scenes, but II Macc., absorbed with epiphanies and miracles, overtly introduces a deus ex machina even when one is hardly necessary.[21] A report of the real numbers, which in some cases might have been in the Jews' favour, would have undermined their didactic purpose.[22]

The Seleucid army in the battle of Ammaus (165 B.C.), totalled, according to I Macc., 40,000 infantry and 7,000 cavalry, apart from Philistine and Edomaean auxiliaries (3.39,41, cf. p.210 n.27); according to II Macc. it totalled 20,000 troops (8.9). The first set of figures is nonsense: even according to I Macc., at the same period at least half of the army followed Antiochus Epiphanes on his expedition to the eastern satrapies (3.37).[23] As the later expedition was much more important than the repression of the revolt in Judaea and as in the same passage I Macc. obviously exaggerates the significance of the Judaean operations, describing the expedition to the east as a preparatory stage to acquire resources for the invasion of Judaea (3.27-37, cf. 6.5-12), it must be assumed that a far smaller number than half of the royal army represented at Daphne could have been considered for Judaea. The total in I Macc. is probably based, as noted by Abel, on a literary association with the numbers of the Aramean troops in Chronicles (I Chron. 19.18).[24] The figure in II Macc., which represents about half the potential soldiers available at that moment, is rather surprising in view of the vast numbers this source mentions in regard to other battles, and of its general untrustworthiness. Despite the temptation to regard the figure as genuine and authentic,[25] it is preferable to assume that it arises from a textual corruption,[26] and was much higher in the original version. But in actual fact, the Seleucid royal troops, together with the Edomaeans and Philistines who did not belong to the royal army, may well have comprised over 20,000 men. At this stage, after two local governors or commanders had been defeated (I Macc. 3.10-26),[27] one would expect Ptolemy, son of Dorymenes, the stratēgos of Coile-Syria and Phoenicia, to have mobilized quite a large force.

Similarly, the figures assigned by the two Books of the Maccabees to the first and second expeditions of Lysias to Judaea must be rejected. For the first expedition, carried out just before the death of Antiochus IV on his eastern venture, I Macc.

reports 60,000 infantry and 5,000 cavalry (4.28), and II Macc. reports 80,000 infantry and 'thousands of cavalry' (11.2, 4). The second expedition, culminating in the battle of Beith-Zacharia, did take place after the king's death but before at least part of the troops returned home (I Macc. 6.55-6). It must be stressed that, in contrast to the impression that may be conveyed by I Macc., a chronological examination indicates the probability that the bulk of the troops crossed back over the Euphrates long before the expedition to Beith-Zacharia, and that the force left in the eastern satrapies comprised the local military settlers and reinforcements to the permanent garrisons in the royal fortresses. I Macc. mentions a large-scale recruitment of mercenaries, bringing the total force there up to 100,000 infantry and 20,000 cavalry (6.30), and II Macc. cites 110,000 infantry but only 5,300 cavalry (13.2). These figures are obviously out of the question, but on the other hand, Josephus in Bellum Judaicum, deriving his brief summary on the Hasmonean Revolt from an unknown but well-informed source, perhaps Nicolaus of Damascus (see p.176 below), gives 50,000 infantry and 5,000 cavalry (1.41). Though these evidently round figures may be a replica of numbers attributed by Polybius in the lost parts of his book to the Seleucid army in one of the great campaigns of Antiochus IV, they are not necessarily entirely out of line. For Lysias, whose prestige as regent and aspirations to the throne were at stake, and who had to prepare himself to face his rivals, certainly recruited many mercenaries (as reported by I Macc. 6.29) and was supported by local people, like the Edomaeans and the Phoenicians,[28] besides much more than half of the standing army.

I Macc. stands on more solid ground in attributing 20,000 infantry and 2,000 cavalry to Bacchides in his second invasion of Judaea, in 160 B.C., which resulted in the death of Judas Maccabaeus at Elasa (9.4). There is, in fact, nothing to object to in these figures: the battle took place in April 160, shortly after the reconquest of Babylonia and the suppression of the revolt of the upper satrapies led by Timarchus, which is dated at the beginning of 160.[29] As the troops of the eastern provinces could not yet be trusted,[30] the available troops were more or less equal in number to those deployed at Daphne. The 20,000 infantry (of

which no more than 10,000 were phalangites) and 2,000 cavalry
represent about half the Seleucid manpower available at the time.
The enthusiastic reception given to Demetrius I in Babylonia (App.
Syr. 47(242-3)) would have enabled him to allocate half his troops
for a concerted drive to settle the situation in Judaea. Moreover,
in view of the estimated numerical order of the Jewish army, the
advanced stage of the revolt, the disastrous defeat of the former
governor, Nicanor, due to the small force at his disposal (see p.268
n.2 below), Bacchides' high rank, and above all, the impending
danger of Roman intervention following the recent Jewish treaty with
Rome, and the extensive and determined character of Bacchides'
undertaking (see p.184 below), the king would hardly have risked a
smaller force.

The author of I Macc. did not exaggerate the number of the
Seleucid army in this case because he gave the extremely low figure
of only 800 men for the Jews (9.4-6), instead of the usual figures
of between 6,000 and 10,000 attributed to Judas Maccabaeus in his
former campaigns, in order to supply an excuse for the death of
Judas Maccabaeus, while, in fact, it seems that the Jewish force
numbered well over 20,000 men. Had he set 100,000 or so Seleucid
soldiers against 800 Jewish zealots, it is doubtful whether such a
contrast would have been swallowed even by those endowed with
oriental imagination (see further pp.185-8 on the Jewish army).

From the enormous numbers involved in the Hasmonean campaigns
we come down to the meagre figures for Thermopylae in 191 B.C.,
among the most decisive battles ever fought by the Seleucids.
Antiochus III's expeditionary force that set sail at the beginning
of the winter is estimated by Livy, based on Polybius, as having
consisted of 10,000 infantry and 500 cavalry (35.43.6).[31] These
modest figures cannot be interpreted as negating the general
impression that the Seleucids had enormous recruiting potential,
for this battle was surrounded by special circumstances: Antiochus
III, for various reasons, crossed hastily to Greece without
waiting for the bulk of his army in the hope that the Greek
federations and perhaps Philip V would join him (App. Syr. 12(47)
etc.).[32] It must also be borne in mind that, if all the troops
had been transported to Greece, defeat would have been tantamount
to suicide. But even on this expedition the Seleucid army was not

necessarily as modest as might appear from the sources.

The figures mentioned above are applied to the Seleucid force that landed at Pteleum (Livy 35.43.5-6); they reappear at the assembly of the forces at Lamia on the eve of the battle (id. 36.15.3), at the battle itself (App. Syr. 17(75)), and are even applied to the losses: 10,000 infantry were killed or captured and 500 escaped (Livy 36.19.11; App. Syr. 20(90)). The number of casualties is obviously false, and the identity between the figure for the forces on landing and the one for those fighting at Thermopylae is in itself rather suspicious: during the winter the Seleucids lost some thousands of troops - 3,000 or 4,000 were captured in Athamania in Thessaly; an unspecified number surrendered, of whom 1,000 were admitted to the Roman army (Livy 36.14.5, 11-12; App. Syr. 17(72)). In addition, there were many other troops that probably did not take part in the battle: Antiochus garrisoned several cities, among them Demetrias and Chalcis, to prevent the Romans from taking the sea route to outflank the dangerous pass (Livy 36.5.1, 33.4-6); sent 1,000 troops to Elis to hold off the Achaeans (id. 36.5.3; Polyb. 20.3.7); and assigned an unknown number to garrison certain cities in Acarnania (Livy 36.12.11).[33]

Livy indicates that on one occasion reinforcements were sent from Asia to Greece (36.15.3-4), and Titus Quinctius Flamininus, addressing the Achaean League, describes the Seleucid force as 'barely equal to two understrength legions' (35.49.10). Accordingly, one might suggest that the reinforcements brought the number of troops that took part in the battle up to the original number of the landing force. But I incline to believe that the reinforcements were fairly small, and that the recurring figure of 10,000 infantry and 500 cavalry is valid only for the battle itself, while the landing force, taking into account the losses sustained before the battle and the garrisons mentioned above, totalled at least 18,000 men: Antiochus landed in Greece at the beginning of the winter 192-191 B.C. (Livy 35.44.5-6; Zon. 9.451A), while the battle took place at the end of April.[34] Between mid-November and mid-March the Aegean is rather dangerous, as Antiochus himself seems to imply (Livy 35.44.5-6).[35] Antiochus would not have trusted a substantial number of troops to a sea crossing in winter, when he was not yet in trouble, and a Roman intervention would also have been ruled out by the rough season. With the approach of spring he sent Polyxenides to Asia to bring the troops but as time dragged on he became increasingly impatient at the convoy's delay (id. 36.15.5; App. Syr. 12(47), 17(74)). Moreover, the incidental reference to reinforcements, in contrast to the exceptionally detailed account of the preparations of both sides for the confrontation further implies that their numbers were not substantial. Flamininus' estimation should not be taken too seriously, as speeches Livy attributed to Roman emissaries and commanders were probably his own fabrication.[36] Finally, Livy himself describes the army assembled at Lamia on the eve of the battle as 'aliquanto pauciores quam umquam antea convenissent' (considerably fewer than ever before had assembled - 36.15.4), obviously referring to previous Seleucid operations in Greece since the landing, although of course it is possible that the comment on the small force is Livy's own contribution.

This conclusion is reinforced by data concerning the vessels used to transport the army to Greece. These comprised 40 decked ships (tecti naves), 60 open (aperti) and 200 cargo ships (Livy 35.43.3). The third category was not used for transporting the troops themselves, but the other two may have been stratiōtides, i.e. war vessels converted temporarily or permanently into troop ships.[37] The suggestion that they were ordinary war-vessels is less likely: expecting to conduct the expedition mainly on land, Antiochus would not have taken the trouble to prepare so many war ships. Moreover, the fast trireme carried only 14 soldiers.[38] Had all the ships been war-vessels and not troop-carriers, Antiochus could have transferred only a small proportion of the 10,000 infantry and 500 cavalry reported by the sources. The possibility that only some of the vessels were troop-carriers must be excluded: the detailed classification made by Livy-Polybius indicates that all the undecked ships belonged to the same category; otherwise a distinction would have been drawn between tacheiai (fast) and hoplitagōgai (troop-carriers), the two types of 'decked' and 'undecked' vessels. The decked vessels were without doubt quinquiremes, and the undecked ones triremes.[39] There is some evidence that the trireme troop ship could carry

about 100 men.⁴⁰ The capacity of the hoplitagōgos quinquireme is
is not known, but taking into account that a quinquireme was about
three times the size of a trireme,⁴¹ they could presumably carry
at least 300 troops, thus bringing the total landing force to a
minimum of 18,000 troops. But whatever the real number of the
landing force was, a Seleucid army of over 18,000 men was
undoubtedly stationed in Greece during the winter of 191 B.C.

There remain to be considered two battles for which no
numerical information at all is recorded. The challenge offered
by Molon in 220 B.C. was finally taken up by all the available
heavy troops, backed up by Cretan, Galatian, and Greek mercenaries
(Polyb. 5.52.4-54.2). At this time Antiochus III ruled only Syria
and Mesopotamia, while the provinces east of the Tigris were under
the control of Molon and Asia Minor was under Achaeus (Polyb.
5.41.1, 42.7, 57.1). The military settlements in Syria and
Mesopotamia were capable of providing 25,000 heavy infantry and
3,500 cavalry (see p. 43 below), from which total the 6,000 rebels
of Cyrrhestica must be deducted (Polyb. 5.57.4). As I have already
mentioned, the number of mercenaries ranged between 10,000 and
16,000. Molon's troops levied from among the settlers of the
eastern satrapies (id. 5.54.8) are to be estimated at about 14,000
heavy infantry, 3,000 semi-heavy, and 5,000 cavalry, in addition
to an unknown number of Cretan and Galatian mercenaries and a
considerable auxiliary force of oriental 'missile troops' (id. 5.
52.5, 53.8).

A chance piece of information from Porphyrios preserved by
Hieronymus provides a clue to the battle of Panion, 200 B.C.:
10,000 Ptolemaic troops fled the battlefield with Scopas into Sidon
(In Dan. 11.15).⁴² Josephus, on Polybius' authority, reports that
the bulk of the Egyptian army was exterminated (Ant. 12.132). One
may assume that most survivors who did not surrender instinctively
fled southward rather than along the rough and mountainous route
to Sidon. The large number of those who found refuge in Sidon
indicates that the total number under the Ptolemies comprised
several tens of thousands. The Seleucid army, as indicated by the
disposition of the troops and the course of the battle (Polyb. 16.
18-19), could not have been inferior. Indirect confirmation of
this conclusion may be found in Daniel 11.13: 'And the king of the

north shall again set forth a multitude, greater than the former'. 'The former' undoubtedly refers to the Seleucid army at Raphia, which comprised 62,000 infantry and 6,000 cavalry. Antiochus' camp at Panion was, accordingly, even larger. Hieronymus adds that Antiochus recruited 'incrediblem ... exercitum' from the upper satrapies (ibid. 13-14). And indeed the main sources of manpower, the military settlements, which were capable of providing around 44,000 heavy infantry and 8,000-8,500 cavalry, were all at Antiochus' disposal, not to mention a greatly fluctuating number of mercenaries, allies, and auxiliaries, especially those of the eastern regions. After the recurrent setbacks to a solution of the problem of Coilē-Syria, one of them just a year earlier, it is not surprising that Antiochus III should mobilize all available troops. But as happened so often in similar circumstances, the confinement of the army to the Palestinian arena cleared the way for the invasion of western Asia Minor by Philip V.[43]

To sum up: it appears that the large numbers of troops recorded for the major campaigns are by and large reliable, except for those given in the two Books of the Maccabees. The figures for Raphia, Magnesia, and Daphne will serve us in the next chapter as milestones in the evaluation of the Seleucid recruitment capability at different periods and in various regions. The conclusions of that analysis will be found to endorse the figures for the eastern expeditions of Antiochus III and VII and the battle of Elasa. Though refuting other figures attributed to the campaigns against Judas Maccabaeus, they support Josephus' figures in Bellum for Beith-Zacharia and indicate that Antiochus III employed very large armies against Molon and at Panion. Even in the 192 B.C. landing in Greece, the 18,000 troops of the spearhead were certainly to have been supplemented by others whom Antiochus III intended to mobilize in Greece, or expected the Aetolians and Macedonians to provide, thus constituting an army which was almost as large as his earlier ones.

2: SOURCES OF MANPOWER

Lesquier in his comprehensive study of the Ptolemaic army established that Ptolemaic sources of manpower consisted of military settlers, mercenaries, and indigenous inhabitants.[1] The Seleucid army, being similarly influenced by the structure of Alexander's army and by Persian military tradition, was based principally on the same components, but their proportion, character, and development were quite different. Consequently, the Seleucid regular army, despite territorial setbacks and heavy losses in its numerous campaigns, maintained itself as a viable force for at least two generations after the final death throes of the Ptolemaic regular army at Panion, and could have survived even longer, had the kingdom not sunk into ceaseless internal strife after the death of Antiochus IV. It will appear from the following pages that most of the differences between the two armies, like the political, economic, and administrative distinctions between the two kingdoms, originated as much from geographical and demographic conditions as from policy.

THE MILITARY SETTLEMENTS

The long-established assumption that military settlers constituted the hard core of Seleucid manpower has not been seriously disputed. The main evidence, apart from analogy with Egypt, seems to be as follows:[2] two phalanx corps, several tens of thousands in all, figure in the great campaigns; one is called alternatively 'phalanx' or 'Macedonians', and the other is an elite corps of argyraspides.[3] It is unlikely that these were mercenaries or indigenous population. Neither hostile Macedonia nor even Greece could provide such a large number, and arming the orientals with heavy weapons would have laid the Seleucids open to the constant danger of native uprisings. In any case, had the phalanx, or part of it, been recruited from among orientals or Greco-Macedonian mercenaries, one would have expected them to be specified as were all the other Seleucid national contingents (Polyb. 5.79; 30.25; Livy 37.40), the Ptolemaic native Egyptian and Libyan phalanx divisions in 218-217 B.C. (Polyb. 5.65.4, 8-9, 82.4-6), and the phalanx of Greek mercenaries at Raphia (id. 5.84.9).[4]

These considerations, along with the description of the argyraspides as 'selected from all regions of the kingdom' (id. 5.79.4)[5] and the numerical stability of both corps, suggest that the phalanx drew its strength from the European population scattered throughout the Empire which had certain military obligations. In addition to these general considerations there are some more precise indications. Many settlements in various regions defined themselves as, or are known to be, Macedonian, and it seems right to assume that they, if any, must have provided the Seleucid army with phalangites.[6] This impression is reinforced by the crises of 142 B.C.: Demetrius II, after establishing the Cretan mercenaries around the court, dismissed 'his ancestors' army each to his own place', which provoked bitter resentment among the population in northern Syria known to be of Macedonian descent (I Macc. 11.38; Jos. Ant. 13.129; Justin 35.2).[7] There are also direct allusions to soldier-settlers: Diodorus recounts that the settlers of Larissa in Seleucis, who originated in Thessalian Larissa, belonged to 'the first agēma of the cavalry' (33.4a). Antiochus III transferred 2,000 Jewish families from Mesopotamia to garrison strategic points and fortresses in Lydia and Phrygia and allotted them land (Jos. Ant. 12.247-53).[8] But the clinching evidence is the treaty between Smyrna and Magnesia of about 244 B.C., which refers to infantry and cavalry having allotments of land in Magnesia and Palai-Magnesia (OGIS 229), and an elegy found in Susa which mentions a Greco-Macedonian garrison holding kleroi in the city under Parthian rule (SEG VII.13), and these were certainly descendants of soldiers settled there by the Seleucids or their Macedonian predecessors.[9]

On the whole, however, Seleucid military settlements, in marked contrast to their counterparts in the south, escaped the notice of ancient historians and document writers, and consequently have been treated in some conflicting ways by modern commentators. In order to determine the numerical contribution of the settlements to Seleucid manpower, we must first try to identify these settlements and the military units the settlers were attached to. Due consideration will be given to the municipal status of the various settlements which may shed light on their political role, to their strategic distribution in the provinces, and to the original nationality of the settlers.

First of all, we must have some criteria for identifying the military settlements. While some scholars have extended the list of settlements by widening the terms of reference, others have been anxious to eliminate established criteria. As always in discussion of this kind, terminology was the first matter to be tackled. Radet and Schulten suggest that the term katoikia, which was applied in second century B.C. Ptolemaic Egypt to military settlements of Greeks and Macedonians to distinguish them from the native cleruchs, was originally the Seleucid term for 'military settlement'.[10] They support their view mainly by the above-mentioned treaty between Magnesia and Smyrna, which refers several times to katoikoi as military settlers. It follows from their assumption that another 45 settlements in Asia Minor, known mainly in the Roman period as katoikiai, were also Seleucid military foundations. But this conjecture has been vigorously attacked by many scholars. Some dispute the interpretation of the katoikoi mentioned in the Smyrnean inscription, and others, though admitting that the Magnesian katoikoi were military settlers, express the view that the term was applied also to some other forms of rural or suburban communities, and consequently a certain katoikia cannot be identified as a military settlement without direct evidence to that effect.

Doubts about the exact status of the katoikoi in Magnesia do not seem justified. Bickerman regards them as soldiers accommodated in barracks or in citizens' homes, and Launey believes they merely 'owned houses' in the settlement,[11] but both Bickerman and Launey ignore the statement that some of the garrison in Palai-Magnesia were formerly katoikoi in nearby Magnesia, each holding one kleros there (ℓℓ. 100, 102).[12] Schalit's view that the katoikoi were civil population, as opposed to the infantry and cavalry garrisoning the city,[13] is even less acceptable. They are repeatedly specified as οἱ ἐμ Μαγνησίαι κάτοικοι οἵ τε κατὰ πόλιν

ἱππεῖς καὶ πεζοί (ℓ. 35 and passim). The pronoun οὕ τε refers to
two components of the preceding noun, which is just the opposite
of what Schalit suggests.[14] And indeed in another reference
instructing the Magnesians to take the oath, they are simply named
as κάτοικοι ἱππέων καὶ πεζῶν (ℓ. 49).[15]

The Smyrnean inscription indicates, then, that at least in
Asia Minor the Seleucid military settlements were known as katoikiai,
and the term is used quite commonly in this sense by modern
historians.[16] Nevertheless, it has been argued, as mentioned
earlier, that not every katoikia was necessarily a military settlement. It has become almost generally accepted that katoikia was a
settlement in an intermediate stage between the polis and the komē,
namely a community having all the traditional municipal
institutions but not enjoying the privileges of a polis.[17] Tarn
interpreted the terms as being sometimes equivalent to the
Ptolemaic politeuma, i.e., quasi-autonomous corporations of non-
Greek nationalities in Greek cities,[18] but this cannot apply to
most of the katiokiai under consideration, which were obviously
self-contained settlements and not just 'quarters' of a city.[19]
The first suggestion, on the other hand, is based on a great
variety of literary and epigraphical allusions to katoikia,
katoikoi and especially the use of the participle of katoikein,
which obviously refer to civilian settlements.

In a discussion of the sources, the participial forms must be
disregarded, as in classical Greek the verb katoikein simply meant
'to inhabit', without reference to the municipal status of the
subject, and there is no evidence to imply that it was understood
in a precise, technical sense in the Hellenistic period. The best
proof of the necessity for discounting the participial form is
provided by Ptolemaic papyrological and epigraphical material
where the terms katoikia and katoikoi are always applied to
military settlements and settlers alone, but the participle is
used loosely for 'inhabitants' and the like.[20] On the other hand,
references from Italy and Greece do suggest the meaning of katoikia
as 'settlement', 'village', etc. (e.g. Polyb. 2.32.4; Plut. Pomp.
47), but obviously the Ptolemaic evidence which does not leave any
doubt about the exact application of the term is more closely
relevant to the Seleucids, because the Ptolemies were dealing with

much the same type of military organization.

Of the literary sources referring to the Seleucid kingdom, Polybius, Diodorus, and Polyaenus apply the word to military settlements only.[21] Strabo, on the other hand, uses it freely to designate settlements in the broad sense (e.g. 14.1.29(643)), but it must be borne in mind that he applies the same loose usage even to Hellenistic Egypt (e.g. 17.1.29(806)). The word appears also in the Septuagint: katoikia - 30 times for mōshav - settlement, residence, domicile; translated also a few times as katoikesia and katoikesis; katoikoi - 6 times for toshavīm (residents, etc.) in 4 of which the best MS have the participle. The loose usage of katoikia was thus the result of the necessity of finding a proper substitute for the Hebrew mōshav (settlement, etc.), but the translators, aware of the need to avoid the form katoikoi for the more general toshavīm, used the participle. The only definite occurrences of katoikoi in Genesis 50.11 and I Macc. 1.31 cannot be taken as decisive evidence for a loose application of the term in the Seleucid Empire as suggested by Bickerman,[22] especially as the translation of Genesis undoubtedly originated in third century B.C. Ptolemaic Egypt.[23]

A conclusion on this point should therefore be based principally on epigraphical evidence relating to the Seleucid realm. The terms katoikia and katoikoi appear, as already mentioned, about forty-five times in inscriptions of Asia Minor, most of which date from the Roman period.[24] Unfortunately the later material does not offer much help. Most of the inscriptions are too short, just naming the katoikia, and even the longer ones do not mention soldiers: settlements formerly military would not, in the Roman period, have retained anything but their old title of katoikiai. As far as the Hellenistic material goes, apart from the Magnesian document, there is no direct evidence that the settlements were military ones, though in one case katoikoi appear in a clearly military context, and all other references pertaining to the Hellenistic period can be interpreted in that way.[25] This being the case, there is every likelihood that the term was used in Seleucid Asia Minor in its restricted 'Ptolemaic' sense. The question remains whether the scores of settlements mentioned in later inscriptions, most of which date from the third century A.D., were originally Seleucid military establishments. The restricted usage of the term in Roman Egypt even in the third century A.D.[26] favours a positive answer.

An analysis of the geographical distribution of the term leads to the same conclusion. It appears only in Phrygia and Lydia, between the Caicus in the north and the Maeander to the south, i.e. in the western part of Asia Minor formerly occupied by the Seleucids and in the neighbourhood of Pergamon.[27] If one assumes that the katoikiai had a military character, their confinement to that area makes sense: there is sufficient evidence for both Macedonian and non-Macedonian military settlements in Phrygia and Lydia.[28] And, on the other hand, nothing seems to suggest similar foundations elsewhere in Asia Minor, not in other Seleucid-ruled territories, or the dynasties or the semi-independent regions or the Ptolemaic areas to the south.[29] With regard to the Ionian cities, Cretan mercenaries whose official classification has not, unfortunately, been preserved were settled around Miletus (Milet III.33-8),[30] and katoikoi are recorded near Priene (see p.216 n.25 below). The latter may well have been originally Seleucid settlers. In any case, the location of Miletus and Priene on the periphery of the Seleucid realm may account for the resemblance in practice as well as in terminology. The matter can be stated another way: if the term katoikia meant 'settlement' in the broad sense, why do we not find even one allusion to a katoikia in the abundant epigraphical material of Bithynia, Caria, Lycia, Pisidia, and Pamphylia?[31] The alternative suggestion, that the administrative terminology in these regions was different from that of Lydia and Phrygia, seems much less acceptable.

To the 45 katoikiai, which according to this conclusion are to be regarded as military settlements, should be added about fifteen settlements, all of which are located in Lydia and Phrygia and defined as Macedonian on coins, inscriptions, and in later lexicographical sources.[32] Although they were technically katoikiai, the soldiers preferred to emphasize their Macedonian descent, and later, in the Roman period, they were in any case granted the municipal status of a polis. It follows that most of the military settlers in that area were not of Macedonian descent. At a later stage we shall examine the implications of this rather surprising deduction.

The occurrence of the term katoikia almost exclusively in Phrygia and Lydia, and the concentration of all the information about Macedonian military settlements in these two districts, suggests that none of the other regions of Asia Minor controlled by the Seleucids was exploited for military settlement. The Ionian coast was occupied by the territories of the autonomous Greek cities, and the wasteland of central Asia Minor would probably not have appealed to Hellenic soldier-settlers.[33] Inner Anatolia was instead allocated to the Galatian tribes, that inexhaustible reservoir of manpower. On the other hand, in Phrygia and Lydia, the most fertile regions of Asia Minor, land could be made available by dispossessing the old feudal owners. Strategic considerations would have contributed no less to the concentration of all available manpower in Asia Minor in these two regions. The settlements were located within close range of possible landing places for the Seleucids' rivals, the Ptolemies and Antigonids on the west, and acted as a barrier between the Greek cities and Galatian incursions from the east.[34] Later, at the time of Pergamon's rise to power, they served to curb its widening influence. As for the defence of the centre of the Empire, the mighty barrier of the Taurus range and the military settlements south of it guaranteed the safety of Cilicia and Syria from the Galatians. This does not mean that lines of communication were abandoned to the mercy of the unreliable Galatians. They were probably guarded by a chain of fortresses manned by mercenaries, and records of two of these survive.[35] The garrisons could certainly not have withstood a mass Galatian onslaught, but that was hardly to be expected in the light of the vulnerability of the Galatians to a pincer movement from the west and the southeast. All in all, despite everything that has been imputed to them, the Galatians proved themselves fairly loyal to the Seleucids.[36]

Much more puzzling is the rare appearance of references in literary sources to katoikiai south of the Taurus, and their complete absence from epigraphical material of these areas. This difficulty, although it cannot refute the conclusion that Asia Minor's katoikiai were military settlements, requires some

explanation and may underline the political-cultural purpose of
the Seleucid establishments. But before turning to this question,
we must identify the trans-Tauric settlements and clarify their
municipal status.

The evidence of name formations is the most widely accepted
criterion for the identification of Seleucid military settlements
across the Taurus. It has been assumed that settlements bearing
names of Macedonian or Greek localities were at least initially
military foundations.[37] At first sight this seems a sound
assumption: as the Macedonian army was organized in local
battalions, one would expect the units that settled in the east
to have called their settlements after their common native homes,
and the same applies to Greek allies or mercenaries. Some
confirmation can be deduced from Diodorus' plain statement that
the settlers of Larissa in Syria originated in Thessaly and served
in the Seleucid cavalry (33.4a).[38] In addition, some cities with
Macedonian names are known to have been inhabited by Macedonians
(see below). Nevertheless, the validity of this theory seems to
be rather doubtful. It has already been pointed out by some that
Anthedon, Pella, Arethusa, and Apollonia (in Palestine) and
Cyrrhus, Megara, and Arethusa (in Syria) were only local Semitic
names slightly altered or translated.[39] How easily a Semitic name
could resemble a Macedonian can be demonstrated from I Macc.,
which transcribes the Hebrew Ḥadasha and Beērā as Αδασα and Βερεα
(7.40, 45, 9.4).[40] Another practice, which has hitherto escaped
notice, is the application to oriental settlements of names of
Macedonian or Greek places that they somewhat resembled in landscape or natural features, possibly by merchants, civilian
immigrants from the Greek world, or even local intelligentsia.
This custom is well reflected in Strabo's account of the renaming
of Orontes, the Apamean peninsula, and the north Syrian coast to,
respectively, Axios, Cheronesus and Pieria, and of the changing of
the name of the oriental inhabitants of the plain of Nisibis to
Mygdones (16.1.23(747), 2.9(751), 2.10(752)). Some oriental
cities may have adopted the same practice: the oasis of Urfa in
northern Mesopotamia is reported to have been renamed after
Macedonian Edessa because of the abundance of its water and the

river which runs through the city (Malalas 418-19).[41] There is certainly nothing in its history to suggest that the population was of Macedonian descent or had a military character.[42] Similarly, we may guess that Mesopotamian Amphipolis,[43] situated where the Euphrates becomes navigable, bore this name because it recalled the mouth of the Strymon. With some imagination the origin of some other Macedonian names may be explained in the same way.

Similar reservations must be applied to Tarn's suggestion that Anatolian names east of the Tigris should be identified as military settlements of Anatolian recruits.[44] Moreover, while the presence of Macedonians is in itself almost certainly an indication of the military character of a place, apoikiai of, for example, Magnesia on the Maeander (OGIS 233) or Ephesus, could well be civilian settlements like the trading stations of the Phoenicians and Babylonians in that area. On the other hand, contrary to the view expressed by some scholars, there is no reason why cities bearing Seleucid dynastic names should not be military settlements,[45] and this applies to local names as well. All in all, the onomastic investigation cannot contribute much to the discussion, and only clear indications of the military role of the settlers or their Macedonian descent can be regarded as reliable evidence.

Examination of the various indications of military settlements in the east shows them scattered in almost every corner of the Empire, from Palestine in the southwest to the Caspian Gates in the northeast. The greatest and best known were concentrated in three of the four satrapies of Seleucis, the Macedonian stronghold in northern Syria.[46]

The imperial military headquarters was established in Pella, later renamed Apamea, which was also the centre of a satrapy bearing the same name. Founded by Macedonians, it was the seat of the royal studs, the elephants, the war office (Stratiōtikon logistērion), and the military training school (Strabo 16.2.10 (752)). On various occasions the Seleucid army is reported to have assembled at Apamea on the eve of a great campaign (Polyb. 5.50.1, 59.1; Livy 37.18.6). Its citizens played a decisive role in the Macedonian revolt against Demetrius II. They were supported by four neighbouring settlements, Larissa, Cassiana,

Megara, and Apollonia, and it may be assumed that at least two of
the four were military foundations; Larissa is referred to as a
katoikia of horsemen (Diod. 33.4a), and Cassiana as a phrourion
(Strabo loc. cit.). As the two terms occur in Strabo and Diodorus,
who are notorious for careless phraseology, they can hardly
indicate anything about municipal status, and in view of the
politico-cultural considerations which seem to have guided the
classification of the settlements (see below), there is no reason
not to regard them as cities. The territory of Apamea to which
these settlements were attached is likely to be the territory of
the satrapy and not necessarily the city, Larissa being 25 km
from Apamea. Strabo adds in the same paragraph that most of the
Macedonians settled in Apamea. Whether this statement is accurate
or not, and whether or not Strabo meant the city alone, it
certainly indicates that the total number of Macedonians in the
satrapy of Apamea was well over the 5,300 of Antioch and the 6,000
of Cyrrhestica (see below).[47]

Antioch, the capital, served also as the administrative
centre of the northwestern satrapy. There are some indications
that it had a military character or, at least, that there was a
military element of considerable size among the population. The
first citizens, numbering 5,300, consisted of Athenians, certainly
soldiers, who had been settled previously by Antigonus in neighbouring Antigoneia, and Macedonians, introduced by Seleucus Nicator
(Malalas 201.12-16).[48] Babylonian Jews, highly regarded for their
military ability, are also recorded among the first settlers (Jos.
Ap. 2.39; Ant. 12.11.9; Bell. 7.43).[49] If the number 5,300 is
reliable, the citizen population probably remained stable, at
least up to 190 B.C.. This figure accords well with that of the
population of Plato's ideal city (Leg. 737E, 740D-E),[50] and
resembles the number of citizens in Cyrrhus and Seleucia-ad-Mare,
which in 218 B.C. still stood at only 6,000 each. The kleroi of
the city numbered only 10,000 even by the time of Julianus (Jul.
Mis. 362C), despite the enormous increase in the overall
population.[51] This suggests that, although the city apparently
developed along civilian lines, the land allocations were reserved
for the descendants of the first settlers, presumably in return
for certain military obligations. One may argue, on the evidence

of the Gurob papyrus (246 B.C.), which refers to soldiers but
fails to list citizens among the various elements in the city
(Holleaux, III 288 ℓℓ. 21-2), that citizenship was granted only
to the soldier-settlers, but 'soldiers' and 'citizens' are
recorded in neighbouring Seleucia, and it is not likely that
there were different arrangements in these two cities founded by
Seleucus I. Moreover, the <u>ochloi</u> listed among the other
Antiocheans may well have been citizens, and the 'soldiers' may
have been mercenaries and guards quartered in the city. In any
case, the author (perhaps a Ptolemaic soldier) was not writing a
legal document, and may not have been acquainted with the social
structure of the city. After the battle of Magnesia, some
Aetolians, Euboeans, and Cretans, probably prominent figures who
could not return to occupied Greece, soldiers who had fled from
the battlefield, and troops evacuated from garrisons in Asia Minor,
were enfranchised (Libanius <u>Or</u>. ℓ. 119).[52] The 3,000 <u>politikoi</u>
cavalry in the parade at Daphne in 166 B.C. (Polyb. 30.25.3) were
not necessarily Antiochean citizens as suggested by some,[53] but
could have been selected from the militia of other cities (cf. I
Macc. 10.71). Military commitments continued to dominate the
city's history during the years of decline: Demetrius II in his
campaign against the Macedonians disarmed the citizens, thus
provoking riots in the city and a general uprising (I Macc. 11.45-7;
Jos. <u>Ant</u>. 13.129-42). Shortly afterwards the Antiocheans were
reinstated in the regular army and suffered heavy casualties in
the disastrous expedition of Antiochus VII to the east: almost
every household is reported to have lost a member (Diod. 34.17).

Seleucia in the Pieria, the second greatest city of the
Antiochean satrapy, which was the first capital of Seleucus I, is
listed by Livy as one of the main concentrations of Macedonians
(38.17.5).[54] The citizenry, perhaps 6,000 men in all (Polyb.
5.61.1, but not all the <u>eleutheroi</u> must be citizens), may have also
admitted non-Macedonians without military obligations. The Gurob
papyrus, if it is to be trusted in this respect, mentions
'citizens' in addition to 'soldiers' (ℓℓ. 23-4), but, as stated
above, much depends on the precision and interpretation of the
two terms in the papyrus.

Cyrrhestica, the northeastern satrapy centred in Cyrrhus,[55] was the least loyal to the Seleucids. The local contingent, 6,000 strong, revolted in 220 B.C. (Polyb. 5.50.7, 57.4), probably in conjunction with Molon and Achaeus (id. 5.57.4).[56] Demetrius Poliorcetes' manoeuvres in northern Syria in 285 B.C. seem to imply that he hoped to find some support among the Cyrrhesteans (see pp.111,114 below). Accordingly, it may be assumed that the revolt in Seleucis at the time of the First Syrian War (OGIS 219 ℓ. 5) originated among these discontented settlers. An epitaph unearthed at Cyrrhus records the Macedonian descent of the population, at least in the capital of the satrapy (IG XII.5.891). The number given for the soldiers recalls that for the citizens of Antioch and Seleucia and suggests that all were concentrated in Cyrrhus. No coins earlier than Alexander Balas were found,[57] but Cyrrhus' status as the centre of the satrapy implies that the community was granted polis rights at once, although they were perhaps withdrawn after 220 B.C., as a further punitive measure, especially as the whole body of citizen-soldiers were in any case ruthlessly massacred. Cyrrhus was reinstated as a polis probably by Balas, who took great pains to secure allies among the Macedonian population (cf. p.70 below).

Another concentration of settlements was situated along the northern Euphrates between its junctions with the Chabor and the Taurus. The best known of them, owing to the thorough excavations carried out, is Doura Europus, described by Isidorus of Charax as a Macedonian foundation (GGM I 248 ℓ. 9). Some light is cast on the administration of the city by parchments of 116 B.C. and 225 A.D., which report Greco-Macedonian settlers owning kleroi in Dura.[58] Despite the impressive remains, the number of the settlers is estimated at less than a hundred families.[59] Other places are known only from brief literary references: Carrhae, Batanae, Anthemus, Inchnae,[60] and Dio mentions Macedonian settlers in Nicephorium and in 'other Mesopotamian cities' (37.40.13). This last statement may refer also to southern Mesopotamia. The active participation of the army in building Seleucia on the Tigris (App. Syr. 58), which served on occasion as the eastern capital, and the role played by that city in Molon's revolt (Polyb. 5.44.3), may just possibly suggest that the citizens were organized along the same lines as at Antioch.

Macedonian settlers in Babylonia are recorded by Livy (38.17.5), but literary and epigraphical sources mention only troops garrisoning the fortress called akrophylakitai.[61] Their status seems to have been identical to that of the soldiers in Palai-Magnesia, i.e. soldiers in active service who were paid with grants of lands (see p.213 n.12 below).

A third group of military settlements were situated in Media around Ecbatana. Tscherikover, followed by Griffith, taking up Diodorus' hint about the settlement of Antigonus' soldiers in Media (19.44.4, 46.1, 15), expressed the view that they founded the four cities in eastern Media bearing Greco-Macedonian names - Laodicia, Apameia, Heraclea, and Europus.[62] The existence of this power base probably encouraged Demetrius Poliorcetes to try to reach Media in 285 B.C. (Plut. Demetr. 46.4). His hopes were not without foundation: the settlers in Media demonstrated their separatist inclinations even two generations later when they allied themselves with Molon; the hard core of Molon's army, the heavy troops (certainly the phalangites of the military settlements), are reported by Polybius to have been sent back to Media after the surrender, together with the 'lights' that formed the national contingents (5.54.8).

There is some evidence for the existence of rural military settlements of Iranian cavalry in western Media. The leases found in Avroman, in Persian Kurdistan (E.H. Minns, JHS 35 (1915) 28-30), originate, as already indicated by some scholars, from a former Seleucid military settlement occupied by soldiers of Iranian descent.[63] As this conjecture has not yet been proven or even expressed cogently, it may be of advantage, in view of its significance, to see what evidence supports it. The prevailing position of the Greek law and language in the documents, despite the Iranian origin of the occupants as appears from the onomastics,[64] suggests that the settlement could not have been founded by the Achaemenides, nor even by the Arsacides, although they called themselves philhellenes. The terminology applied by the documents must, therefore, reflect Macedonian, or rather Seleucid arrangements. That the status of the people involved was that of military settlers emerges from the definition of the allotment as kleros,[65] which in the Hellenistic period had a

definite military designation. But even if one allows for the
possibility that the term may apply to a civilian estate as well,
I can hardly imagine any class of Iranians other than military
settlers who would be granted small allotments in that part of the
world.[66] On top of this, the buyer (or tenant) undertook to abide
by the palaia syngraphē (Minns, 28 ℓ.18 et passim), certainly the
lex coloniae by which the king established the rights and
obligations of the settlers.[67] And indeed, if Egyptians, who were
not a warlike race, were attached to the Ptolemaic army and
granted lots,[68] there is no reason to doubt that the Seleucids
tried to procure the services of the tough and courageous
Iranians, following the lead of Alexander, who introduced them
into his army. The old tradition of horsemanship among the Medes
and their being entrusted with the Seleucid royal stables (Polyb.
5.44.1, 10.27.2) leads me to believe that these settlers provided
manpower for the Seleucid cavalry. In fact that is the only
reason why the Seleucids should conceivably have ventured to take
the risk of maintaining the Median military potential. We know
that the agēma, the crack cavalry Guard regiment, which like the
infantry Guard may have been recruited from among the military
settlers, comprised Medes and 'other races of the same region'
(Livy 37.40.5-6, see p.69 below). In view of the feudal system
that had prevailed under the Achaemenides, the Seleucids would
have had no difficulty in confiscating large estates and assigning
them to Iranian horsemen in order to ensure their service and
loyalty. As far as terminology is concerned, it is worth noting
that Cophanis, the settlement referred to in the Avroman parchment,
is called komē.[69]

The scale of military settlement in Persia proper was
perhaps smaller. Thracian soldiers are reported by Diodorus to
have settled in katoikiai in Persis, the eastern satrapy, as early
as the time of Alexander (19.27.5). Polyaenus is probably
referring to them in two consecutive stratagems (7.39, 40).
According to one, 3,000 Thracian and Macedonian infantry and the
same number of similarly constituted cavalry trapped 3,000 Persian
natives who had revolted against Seleucus, probably the founder
of the dynasty.[70] In the other, 3,000 katoikoi were slaughtered
by Oborzos, identified with Vahuburz, the second dynast (frataraka),

of the independent principality around Persepolis.[71] If Polyaenus is taken literally, that means that 3,000 settlers remained in Seleucid-controlled Persis.[72] The emphasis laid on the Thracian descent of some of these troops, and the appearance of one thousand Thracians, probably settlers, at Raphia in an independent contingent (Polyb. 5.65.10, 79.6, see p.50 below), may indicate that the Thracians retained their national armament and style of warfare like the Thracian and Galatian military settlers in Egypt, and were not absorbed into the phalanx. The Seleucids would have been wise to preserve the traditions of these warlike settlers, in contrast with other nationalities like Greeks, Jews, ?Mysians, etc., whose integration into the phalanx did not constitute any particular loss. As has been stated above with regard to the classification of the Apamean settlements by Diodorus and Strabo, Polynaeus' application of the term katoikoi to the Thracian and Macedonian settlements in Persis can hardly be taken as decisive evidence that they were not granted municipal rights.

Relatively abundant epigraphical information has survived about Seleucia-upon-the-Eulaeus (Susa), the capital of Susiana, the western Persian satrapy. Material of the Seleucid era, as late as Seleucus III, records officers, soldiers, and a person belonging to a cavalry unit (SEG VII.4, 15, 17).[73] Though there is no direct evidence that they were settlers, they may be identified with the soldier-settlers of Greco-Macedonian descent mentioned above, undoubtedly descendants of the Seleucid settlers who garrisoned the local fortress under the Parthians. Referring to themselves as phrouroi, these settlers expressed gratitude in an elegy to the stratiarch for introducing a successful system of irrigation that saved their kleroi (SEG VII.13).[74] If the cavalrymen did not belong to the phrouroi, or were not mercenaries (which is still possible), they may have been citizens of the lower city. The preservation of the epithet phrouroi, if one allows this piece of verse any descriptive value, does not necessarily imply that the Seleucid settlement in Susa was first organized as a village and only later, after being enlarged, turned into a Greek polis, as Tarn argues.[75] The 1,000 Macedonian veterans left by Alexander to garrison the citadel (Curt. 5.2.16) were perhaps the first settlers of Susa. The status of Seleucia-upon-the-Eulaeus as the centre of the satrapy of Susiana (Polyb. 5.46.7, 48.13), its past role as one of the capitals of the Persian kingdom, and its having apparently been named after Seleucus I,[76] suggest that the Greek settlement in Susa was already established as a regular city by the beginning of the Seleucid era. The garrison was indeed integrated in the life of the new city, but its confinement to the citadel, its continual involvement in military duties, and consequently perhaps also its possession of much larger land allotments than the ordinary kleroi, distinguished these soldiers as a special group like the soldiers of Palai-Magnesia, different from other citizens (p.213 n.12 below). But the reservation must be made that some security arrangements, and consequently changes in the status (and designations) of some of the settler-citizens, may have been made by the Arsacides.

A chain of military settlements established by the Ptolemies in the Jordan Valley and the eastern plateau fell into the hands of the Seleucids after Panion in 200 B.C. Syncellus, the most articulate in this respect, has surprisingly escaped notice: among the places occupied by Janaeus in Trans-Jordan he lists Pella, Gadara, Abila, Hippos, Lian (certainly Dion), and Philoteria as Macedonian apoikiai (pp.558-9 ed. Dindorf). As this passage contains valuable information from a reliable source,[77] Syncellus' statement should not be discounted as being influenced by the Greco-Macedonian names of some of the cities (Abila and Gadara are in any case Semitic!) or by their Hellenistic culture. And indeed there is some evidence for the Macedonian descent of certain elements in Dion, Gerasa, and perhaps also Gadara.[78] To these should probably be added some rural settlements in the south, one of which, the cleruchy of Tobiah (PCZ 59003), is well known. The existence of the Ptolemaic stronghold in northern Trans-Jordan explains why Antiochus III started his campaign in Palestine in 219 B.C., as well as in 200 B.C., by occupying Bataneia, Golanitis, and Giladitis (Polyb. 5.70.71; Jos. Ant. 12.136).[79]

West of the Jordan, only Samaria is known to have been settled by Macedonian soldiers. Founded by Alexander, it survived destruction by both Ptolemy I and Demetrius (Euseb. Chron. 199), and Antiochus III twice dispatched special contingents to deal with the area (Polyb. 5.71.11; Jos. Ant. 12.133).[80] Samaria's military character is also well demonstrated by the part it played in the first Seleucid attempt to crush the Jewish rebellion (I Macc. 3.10)[81] and the tough resistance it staged against John Hyrcanus (Jos. Ant. 13.375-8). All in all, the Seleucids did not establish new settlements in Palestine and contented themselves with the existing ones. The campaigns of the third century B.C. taught them that the country could pass from one hand to another, in which case they might lose the settlers to their rivals. Keeping garrisons in citadels whose members, unlike the settlers, had no close connection with the land and could therefore retreat to Syria, seemed to be the best way in the circumstances.

The predominance of Greco-Macedonian names in the onomasticon of Cilicia Pedias has misled some scholars into describing the province as one of the main reservoirs of manpower for the army. But if more substantial evidence is sought, only Aegae - which proclaimed its Macedonian descent on imperial coins[82] - can be regarded as a military settlement, although one would hardly think it the only one.

Thus it appears difficult to detect many more military foundations beyond the settlements enumerated above. Although the list is not exhaustive, it does indicate that the number of military settlements was not large. It should not, however, be concluded on that account that the Seleucid defensive system was thin and ineffective. In any case, the defence of the Empire as a whole depended on the mobility of the royal Guard and the 'strategic reserve' provided by the settlers. On top of this we have already noted that the defensive system of Asia Minor was supplemented by fortresses garrisoned by mercenaries, and the same applies to other parts of the Empire. The dimensions of the garrison system are well illustrated by Demetrius I's celebrated offer to Jonathan to employ 30,000 Jews in garrison duties (I Macc. 10.36).[83] Incidental references to fortresses are few,[84] but we have one detailed account that describes such a defensive operation: the almost complete sealing off of the Judaean mountain after the death of Judas Maccabaeus by a chain of fortresses, an operation which was highly efficient and did not leave many loopholes (I Macc. 9.50-2).[85] This method of defence was probably applied to strategically sensitive regions, communication lines, and places where the population was restless. Thus garrisons were imposed on the Ionian cities before the Roman War (App. Syr. 1(2) etc.). It remains only to speculate why most garrisons were not allocated lands and incorporated into the settlement system. In old cities like Sardis, Babylonia, the Ionian cities, or the Phoenician and Palestinian coastal cities, probably no lands were available, and confiscation would not have served the Seleucid cause. Other places, like the southern coast of Asia Minor and central Anatolia, did not offer enough agricultural prospects. But no less importance must be attached to the soldiers' own wishes: they may have regarded their service as a temporary occupation and wanted to return to their homelands. The Seleucids themselves may have been reluctant to place the defence of some critical points of the Empire in the hands of settlers who would necessarily be less strictly disciplined.

The survey of the military settlements by region having been completed, the next step is to classify them according to their municipal status. They fall into four groups: rural settlements called katoikiai, in Lydia and Phrygia (the settlements in Persis and in Syria referred to as katoikiai were actually poleis); komai - villages of Iranians in western Media; chōrion, phrourion, etc. - fortresses garrisoned by soldiers in active service who were granted larger land allotments in lieu of pay; and finally, the cities concentrated in northern Syria, Mesopotamia, and east Media, were organized as regular Greek poleis. Tarn and Griffith have suggested that these city settlements were originally founded as katoikiai, or, in other words, that some rural military settlements were sometimes granted the status of polis by the Seleucids,[86] but a close examination of the sources would seem to indicate that this was not, in fact, the case. On the one hand, it is clear that the great cities of northern Syria were founded as poleis from the beginning, and on the other hand, there is no evidence to show that a single one of the katoikiai of Asia Minor was recognized as a polis by the Seleucids: all references to Macedonian settlements in Asia Minor as poleis pertain to the period after the treaty of Apamea.[87] The sympoliteia agreement

between Smyrna and Magnesia, which is quoted to illustrate the
transformation of a katoikia into a polis (OGIS 229), is not
strictly relevant here: the great distance between Smyrna and
Magnesia, and the inevitable confinement of the settlers of
Magnesia to their small lots, and of the soldiers in Palai-
Magnesia to their military duties in the chōrion, nullified the
effects of the Smyrnean citizenship granted to them, for it
rendered any practical application impossible, and therefore the
agreement cannot be considered as contravening the clear policy of
the Seleucids to deny municipal rights to the Lydian and Phrygian
settlements (see below). In any case, this may have been an
exceptional conciliatory step taken by Seleucus II, one of the
contenders to the throne in the most difficult period of the
dynasty, in order to secure his rear when crossing the Taurus.
He had nothing to lose and everything to gain by this gesture:
the Magnesians had attacked his favourite city of Smyrna anyway,
and sided with the Ptolemies.[88] As for Magnesia itself, it is
significant that it was not declared a city before 244 B.C.,[89] nor
is there any evidence that its status had changed before the end
of the Seleucid reign in Asia Minor.[90]

The diversity of Seleucid military foundations may be
explained by political considerations arising out of the descent
of the settlers and their political and cultural environment. The
Hellenic elements on either side of the Taurus were differently
organized, on the west in katoikiai and on the east mainly (or
solely) in cities. The latter enjoyed political rights, primarily
because the polis and its institutions were the best means of
consolidating the Seleucid power base in these regions - by
introducing Greek culture to the 'barbaric' east and assimilating
the influential classes in the native population. The settlers
themselves undoubtedly wished to be compensated for their 'exile'
by having their traditional institutions transplanted with them.[91]
Conditions in the west were entirely different: Lydia and
Phrygia had long been within the sphere of Greek influence.
Moreover, to equate the status of the military settlements with
that of the nearby old Ionian cities, which traditionally
insisted on retaining their autonomy and developing a policy of
their own, might have incited the settlements to press for greater

autonomy for themselves and consequently for the abolition of
their military obligation and, what is worse, might have
encouraged the settlers to take up a stand in favour of the
Seleucids' Hellenistic rivals, who were always at hand in this
geopolitically sensitive area. Magnesia-ad-Sipylum probably
sided with the Ptolemies at the time of the Laodicean war, which
is a good illustration of the difficulties encountered in
administering this geographically and politically sensitive zone.
The Iranian settlements in Media on the other hand were not
granted polis rights because they were obviously not able to
contribute to the Hellenization of the area. They do not bear the
name of katoikiai, probably because administrative terms, and even
the principles behind them, developed independently on either side
of the Tigris after the administrative reorganization by
Seleucus Nicator.[92] The fact that the terms katoikia and katoikoi
were applied to Syrian Larissa and the Thracian settlements by
Diodorus and Polyaenus does not indicate that it was prevalent
across the Taurus also. Both sources may have been using
'western' terminology.

We must now turn to the central question of this discussion:
what was the numerical strength of the entire military settlement
and how were the numbers distributed between the various centres?
Estimates range from 15,000 Macedonians, as suggested by Jones,[93]
to the exaggerated totals proposed by some who consider the
Macedonians to have been a very considerable element even in
proportion to the large oriental population,[94] and to these must
be added the non-Macedonian settlers. The list of settlements,
even if complete, could not offer much help. In only a few cases
have we any information on the number of the population or
soldiers, and the enormous gap between the 6,000 Cyrrhestians or
the 5,300 Antiocheian soldier-settlers and a few score men in
Doura Europus renders useless any attempt to calculate the number
of settlers on the basis of the number of settlements and their
municipal status.[95]

In the absence of any direct numerical information we must
adopt the opposite approach and estimate the number of settlers
according to the strength of the units supplied by the settlements.

The validity of this method has been disputed by some scholars, who have expressed the view that the Seleucids did not utilize all the available manpower from the settlements in the great campaigns. They have pointed out the logistical difficulties of mobilizing huge armies, and argued that there was no tactical need to employ a larger phalanx corps (phalangites being the main contribution of the settlements).[96] Bickerman has even gone so far as to suggest that the duty of serving in the army was not individual, but was imposed collectively on a regional basis.[97] But it would seem that the logistic difficulties have been exaggerated and, in any case, are irrelevant with regard to the battles of Raphia, Magnesia, and the procession at Daphne, as these three undertakings, which may serve as a basis for estimating Seleucid manpower, all took place on home or at least on favourable ground. In addition, the Seleucids only occasionally enjoyed numerical superiority over their enemies. At Raphia, for instance, their phalanx was considerably inferior to the combined Macedonian-Egyptian phalanx of the Ptolemies (see pp.132,138 below), and it is difficult to imagine that any additional available force would have been left behind. Moreover, the Seleucids would have preferred soldier-settlers to most of the national contingents, whose effectiveness, loyalty, and integration in the tactical formation were open to doubt. If there were any logistical obstacles, the oriental infantry contingents would have been the first to be dropped, with the exception of some light skirmishers who were essential.

It has been widely accepted that the phalanx was recruited solely from among the military settlers, and it will be argued below that the same source also provided the argyraspides, the infantry Guard, the unspecified cavalry at Raphia, the horse †Guard, and the 'cataphracts' at Magnesia (pp.56,60,69,74 below). The remarkable feature of the figures attributed to the heavy infantry is their relative stability: allowing for territorial changes in the Seleucid realm and the special circumstances surrounding each campaign, there appears to have been basically little fluctuation in the strength of these troops at Raphia, Magnesia, and Daphne, despite the long periods of time between them (27 and 24 years, respectively) and the casualties they

sustained. The explanation lies in the principle of service in
return for land: losses were replaced from the children who grew
to manhood between the campaigns. On inheriting their lands they
were obliged to fill the ranks. The occasional allocation of lots
to newly recruited mercenaries may also have helped to maintain
the number of potential soldiers.

In 217 B.C. at Raphia the number of heavy infantry troops
†stood at 30,000 (Polyb. 5.79.4-5). The Cyrrhesteans, whose
recruitment potential was around 6,000, were not present (id.
5.50.7, 57.5), nor were the military settlers of Asia Minor, which
was at that time occupied by Achaeus.[98] The number of the latter
may be estimated from the force totalling 6,000 troops, apart from
allies, which Achaeus employed against Selge (id. 5.72.3, 73.2).[99]
The identity of Achaeus' troops is revealed by their previous
refusal to march against Antiochus III, 'their natural and original
king' (id. 5.57.6).[100] Although it can be argued that Achaeus left
behind part of the settlers for security reasons, the participation
of 'Mysians' (id. 5.76.7), probably of the Mysian katoikiai who
were in the first front line against Pergamon, indicates that he
did not take proper precautions, perhaps because he and Attalus
were former allies and collaborators (4.48), and indeed Attalus
seems not to have wasted the opportunity and is reported to have
invaded the Mysian katoikiai, among others, evidently with little
trouble (5.77.7). But even if our assumption is wrong, Attalus'
unchallenged activity with the Pergamon force, which is considered
to have been small,[101] indicates that the settlers left behind
were a small force, certainly well below 6,000 in number, and this
does not affect my overall estimate. The potential of heavy
troops stood then at c. 42,000. About the same potential emerges
from Thermopylae and Magnesia: to the 16,000 phalangites
(including probably 2,000 Jews settled several years earlier in
Asia Minor) and the 10,000 argyraspides who took part in the
battle[102] must be added the major portion of the 18,000 troops at
least who were lost in Greece six months earlier,[103] which brings
the number up to about 44,000. The 20,000 phalangites and the
5,000 troops, doubtless of the infantry Guard, who were armed in
Roman style at Daphne (Polyb. 30.25.3), represent the potential
manpower of Syria and Mesopotamia alone: Asia Minor was already

under Roman control, and one would imagine that the settlers on the other side of the Tigris were not mobilized to participate in the festival in view of the current disturbances in their own regions (see p.210 n.23). This last assumption is supported by a substantial decrease in the number of cavalry, which was usually recruited mainly in the eastern provinces (see below), and the absence of national contingents of Indo-Iranian descent.[104] The strength of the heavy infantry from across the Tigris can be deduced by adding the 8,000 recruits of Asia Minor to the 25,000 Syrians and Mesopotamians, and deducting the total from the overall potential of the Empire, which appears to have stood by 192-190 B.C. at 44,000. This gives 11,000 troops from the eastern settlements.

Estimating the number of settlers serving in the cavalry is more difficult. The 500 cavalry led by Achaeus against Selge seem to represent the recruitment potential of Asia Minor. The 6,000 unspecified horses involved at Raphia (5.79.12) are to be attributed to the other centres, but they probably do not represent all the available manpower; Media was still recovering from the effects of Molon's revolt, and some cavalry may have been left behind to garrison the country.[105] Owing to intensive recruitment in the eastern regions, perhaps at the expense of internal security, the number of regular cavalry at Magnesia rose to between 8,000 and 8,500.[106] At Daphne they numbered 4,500 troops,[107] 1,000 of whom belonged to the agēma, the cavalry Guard recruited in Media. In view of the special circumstances mentioned above, the other 3,500 cavalry must be attributed to northern Syria and Mesopotamia alone. This would include the 2,500 cataphracts and Nisaeans, all probably military settlers who adopted heavy armour in the Median style. The high cost of obtaining and maintaining their equipment excludes the possibility of identifying them as mercenaries. When these and the 500 cavalry of Asia Minor are deducted from the 8,000-8,500 total from Magnesia, 4,500-5,000 are left for the eastern provinces.

If we add to these figures about 3,000 Thracian settlers from Persis who retained their traditional armament, the overall recruitment potential of the settlements seems to stand at 44,000 heavy infantry, 3,000 semi-heavy infantry, and 8,000-8,500 cavalry. They were distributed as follows: Asia Minor - 8,000 infantry and 500 cavalry (including the Jewish reinforcement, 2,000 men strong); northern Syria and Mesopotamia - 25,000 infantry and 3,500 cavalry; the eastern provinces (mainly Media) - 11,000 heavy infantry, 3,000 semi-heavy, and 4,500-5,000 cavalry. These figures occasion no surprise as far as Syria-Mesopotamia and Media are concerned, but the presence of relatively few settlers from Asia Minor seems at first sight to contradict the conjecture of the existence of about five dozen military settlements in Phrygia and Lydia. But, as I have already pointed out, the number of soldiers evidently varied considerably from one settlement to another. The overall potential manpower of Asia Minor implies an average of slightly more than one hundred soldiers per settlement, which is about the number of cleruchs in Ptolemaic Kerkeosiris and more than at Doura Europus. The reluctance of the Seleucid kings to grant polis status to the military settlements may account for their relatively small size: the larger they were the more courage they would have had to press for and develop municipal institutions, with all the attendant implications regarding their loyalty. To counter the practical difficulties involved in the dispersion of so few settlers over so many settlements, the katoikiai were concentrated in a relatively small area, recalling the dense concentration of the small Ptolemaic cleruchies.

The distribution of settlers among the regions and the retention of the hard core of the infantry in the centre of northern Syria was motivated by strategic considerations: the guiding principle was to concentrate the bulk of the army in the centre and post smaller forces at the extreme limits of the Empire. In cases of emergency it was difficult to rely on the troops stationed on the remote borders because of the difficulties of mobilization such as Antiochus III experienced on the eve of Thermopylae (App. Syr. 12(47), 17(74) etc.). On the other hand, it might have proved unwise to abandon sensitive border areas and relax control over unreliable populations, as happened before Daphne. The concentration of the largest forces in northern Syria was eminently reasonable, for they could be relatively quickly mobilized to every possible corner of the Empire. Stationing them

in the political centre ensured their loyalty, and at the same
time served as a deterrent to the native population. The troops
settled in Media and Phrygia-Lydia, on the other hand, were
intended to check or delay any invader, as was probably done by
the settlers of Asia Minor in the battle against the Galatians.[108]
The troops also contributed to internal security. The relatively
large concentration of cavalry in Media is an exception to the
general pattern owing to the rich pasture offered by the country
and the traditional association of the Medes with horses. On the
other hand, the small number of troops settled in Asia Minor
derives, apart from the strategic considerations mentioned above,
from the constant danger of their exploitation by a hostile power.
It must be borne in mind that the settlements were founded by the
first kings of the dynasty at a time when Asia Minor, and
especially its western regions, changed hands rather frequently.
The danger may perhaps be illustrated by Nakrasa, which was
presumably founded as a Macedonian settlement, and may already
have fallen into the hands of Pergamon as early as the Laodicean
War, and by the pro-Ptolemaic policy adopted by Magnesia-ad-
Sipylum at the same time. For the same reason the Seleucids were
reluctant to establish military settlements in Palestine.

The ancestry of the settlers varied from region to region,
as emerges from the numerical analysis of the regulars and the
survey of the settlements. The highly controversial question of
the descent of the Seleucid regulars may thus be answered in a way
which satisfies both parties, those who tend to regard them as
genuine Macedonians, and those who interpret the name
'Macedonians', which is occasionally applied to the phalanx, as
being only pseudo-national.[109] The Greco-Macedonian element was
dominant among the settlers in northern Syria and Mesopotamia,
which provided more than half of the phalanx force: 6,000
Cyrrhesteans, about the same number of Antiocheans, an unknown
proportion of the 6,000 citizens of Seleucia-ad-Mare, and at
least an equal number of Apameans, were all of Greco-Macedonian
descent, and brought the number of settlers to not far below the
overall of total regulars and reserve troops recruited in that
area. The balance was made up by men from Mesopotamian settlements who were also described as Macedonians.[110] The settlers

of the Greek cities in eastern Media, who probably served in the
Seleucid phalanx, were of Macedonian descent as well. The
possibility that after two or three generations the epigonoi of the
first settlers in these regions were no longer pure Greco-
Macedonians is not very likely: most of the Macedonians were
concentrated in poleis, and examination of Greco-Macedonian
settlement in Egypt shows that, although mixed marriages were
quite common in rural military settlements, they were rejected by
the soldier-citizens in the poleis, and descendants of such
marriages were not accepted in the citizenry.[111] Assuming a
similarity with the situation in Egypt, and bearing in mind that
citizens' rights, ownership of land, and military service must
have been closely connected in the Seleucid urban military settlements, it can be concluded that the Seleucid soldier-settlers
preserved ethnical purity, or at least that the reservations
toward mixed marriages must have had a restraining effect, so that
the majority of the settlers in the cities remained virtually
Greco-Macedonians. The number of horsemen attributed to Media
implies, on the other hand, that the Iranian element was
predominant in the Seleucid cavalry. The troops of Asia Minor
were the most diversified: in the Lydian and Phrygian katoikiai
Greeks,[112] ?Mysians,[113] Jews,[114] and Persians[115] are definitely
traceable among the settlers, and the Macedonians formed only a
tiny minority, but as the region supplied just a small proportion
of the regulars, this does not tip the balance against the
Macedonians, and, therefore, the Seleucid phalanx is regarded by
ancient authorities as a monolithic corps called 'the phalanx' or
'the Macedonians',[116] with no reference to national divisions like
the Macedonian, Libyan, and Egyptian phalanx noted in the
description of the Ptolemaic army at Raphia (Polyb. 5.65.4, 5, 8
†et passim).

The history of the Seleucid military settlements can thus be
viewed as a success story: despite the casualties they suffered,
the settlements were able to recover in a relatively short time
and maintain their military standards and position as the only
source of recruitment for the regular army. The Ptolemaic
settlement system developed differently. Although I do not share

the view that the native Egyptian element was predominant among
the Ptolemaic phalanx at Raphia (p.138 below), the necessity of
employing these untrustworthy troops at all makes it clear that the
European settlers had deteriorated as an effective military force
before the Fourth Syrian War.

Several theories have been put forward to explain the
different pattern of development. Tarn concentrated on the
inalienability of the Ptolemaic kleros and the absence of automatic
inheritance, as contrasted with the private ownership of land in
the Seleucid settlements.[117] But although liberal arrangements of
this kind may have had the short-term effect of boosting morale
among individuals, in the long run the right of inheritance would
have had a negative effect on the retention of a stable number of
recruits. The introduction of the right of inheritance in the
Egyptian katoikiai before Raphia may have contributed more than
any other factor to the dissolution of the Ptolemaic Macedonian
phalanx.[118] As a matter of fact, the earliest available direct
information on Seleucid agrarian practice pertains to the first
half of the second century B.C.,[119] and the date when private
ownership was introduced is far from certain. At any rate, there
is nothing to indicate that it preceded the reform in Egypt.[120]
Griffith attributed the Seleucid success to the political
institutions and the rights of citizenship granted to their
settlers.[121] This assessment certainly touches on the military
purpose behind the municipal status of some of the Seleucid
settlements; a political consciousness, a sense of identification
with the polis, and the physical training practised in its
institutions combined to keep the citizens up to the military
mark. But this was not the only reason, and, in any case, does
not account for the rural settlements, especially the Medes, who
were the hard core of the cavalry.

The organization of the Guard may well have been the main
factor in the success of the Seleucid system. In the following
chapter I try to prove that the argyraspides, the infantry-
phalanx Guard, was made up of the ablest sons of the settlers who
served in the Guard as long as the land allotted to their family
had someone to look after it. When the father died or was removed
for one reason or another from the reserve force, the Guardsman

returned home and replaced his father. The same system may have
applied to the cavalry Guard. If this suggestion is correct, the
corollary is that almost all the military settlers had served at
one time or another in the Guard, where they received their initial
training, some practical experience and, not least important, a
good deal of indoctrination and a sense of identification with the
crown to see them through the long years of their service in the
reserve. Once a phalangite always a phalangite, especially as the
rather mechanical discipline of phalanx warfare did not require a
particularly long period of retraining before a battle.

It remains only to speculate on why this principle of
organization was developed in the Seleucid kingdom alone and not
in Egypt.[122] In fact, the Seleucids did not have much choice in
view of the enormous dimensions of their Empire. Because of
strategical considerations, about half the military settlers were
scattered in border areas on two frontiers of the Empire. The
immense distances precluded the speedy mobilization of these troops
and compelled the king to have at hand, in addition to the other
half of the settlers, a permanent force of Guardsmen which could
be quickly dispatched to any corner of the kingdom. The remoteness
of some of the settlers from the political and cultural centre of
the Empire would also inevitably have had the effect of weakening
their loyalty and attachment to the dynasty, had they not each
spent a long period near the court or in the royal service.
Conditions in Egypt were rather different: the cleruchs were
settled in a relatively small area, being mainly concentrated in
the Arsinoid <u>nomos</u>, and could theoretically have been called up at
a moment's notice. Moreover, since the country was nearly an
island as far as an invader was concerned, the Ptolemies were
bound to have good warning of an attack, and could expect to have
enough time to assemble and retrain their reserve forces (as
indeed happened before Raphia). In contrast to the loose control
which the Seleucids exercised over their provinces, the
administrative and economic structure of Ptolemaic Egypt did not
allow the settler to forget his obligation to the crown for one
moment. In addition, presumably the Ptolemies' eagerness to fill
their treasury by exploiting any available manpower for tilling
the land prevented them from assigning the sons of the settlers,

the best agricultural labour in the country, to permanent military duties. The grave mistake of the Ptolemies was in not realizing that availability of Macedonian or European manpower did not by itself guarantee a reasonable military standard in phalanx troops.

THE NATIONAL CONTINGENTS

Despite its strength and stability, the phalanx recruited from among the military settlers accounted for only about half the Seleucid manpower at Raphia, Magnesia, and Daphne, and it can be assumed that the same proportion obtained also in other battles except for Thermopylae. The rest of the army included various national elements, so much so that heterogeneity of nationality was recognized as one of the distinguishing features of the Seleucid army (e.g. II Macc. 8.9; Livy 37.40.1).

The various national contingents mentioned in the great campaigns generally included mercenaries, allies, allied-mercenaries, and subjects-vassals, but the status of very few contingents can be established with certainty. The only element defined as mercenaries are the 5,000 Greeks at Raphia (Polyb. 5.79.9), the 2,000 Cappadocians sent by Ariarathes to Magnesia (Livy 37.31.4, 40.10), and the Jews who took part in Antiochus VII's expedition to the eastern provinces under the terms of the 'friendship and alliance' forced on John Hyrcanus (Jos. Ant. 13.250), were allied auxiliaries; a third class comprised auxiliaries from subject or semi-independent nations or tribes like the Cyrtians and Elymaeans at Magnesia (Livy 40.10.4).[123] The sources recount the existence of an intermediate category of allies serving as mercenaries: the Cretans, employed against Molon, certainly mercenaries, are defined as symmachoi (Polyb. 5.53.3), probably as a result of certain treaties signed with Cretan cities which granted an option to recruit.[124] The same applies to the Pisidian symmachoi mentioned on the stelai of Sidon, who may have served the Ptolemies as well as the Seleucids.[125] Mountainous, inaccessible Pisidia separated the realms of the two Empires, and both the Seleucids and Ptolemies were anxious to bind its independent warlike people to their cause. Demetrius I's offer to Jonathan to employ 30,000 Jewish mercenaries in garrisons recorded by I Macc. reflects a similar state of affairs (10.38). Certain military settlers who preserved their national armament and style of warfare may have constituted national contingents and not been absorbed into the phalanx.

Apart from the instances mentioned above, no classification of the national contingents is recorded. But some criteria may be drawn up for identification purposes. The position of every nation with regard to the Seleucid Empire is the first consideration, though even this is not always clear cut, as the Galatian tribes, for instance, although part of the Seleucid realm, should be regarded rather as mercenaries (so Livy 37.17.7). Secondly, some significance should be accorded to the attachment of several units to one contingent or to the same commander; mercenary units may not have been quartered with subjects or allies whose standard of discipline, warfare, and motivation were quite different. On the other hand, contingents from neighbouring nations or from nations bearing similar arms may have been combined because they understood each other better and could more conveniently operate together.

The list of national contingents at Raphia preserved by Polybius (5.79) is the most detailed, and includes the names of the commanders. The mercenaries consisted, in the first place, of the 5,000 Greeks, and the 1,500 Cretans and 1,000 Neo-Cretans, the last two probably under treaty (79.9,10), and also the 5,000 Dahae, Carmanian, and Cilician 'lights' (79.3). The Dahae, a war-like Scythian tribe from north of Hyrcania, and the Cilicians, certainly the highly regarded 'lights' of independent Cilicia Trachis,[126] were not under Seleucid control, and there was nothing to compel them to serve as allies. The Carmanians were part of the Seleucid realm, and their appearance in this group seems to be a scribal error, as they are mentioned once again in a different group of 5,000 troops, all from the upper satrapies (79.7). The imperfect state of preservation of the text is evident in some other cases in this list.[127]

Zabdiel's 10,000 Arabs, probably tribes of the Syrian desert under a local sheikh, are to be identified as allies.[128] Their control of the main commercial route from south Arabia and India to the Mediterranean ports, then occupied by Antiochus, may have driven them to make overtures to the Seleucids. Some of the contingents described below as 'subjects' should also be perhaps regarded rather as allies.

The 'subjects' included 5,000 Medes, Cissians (Elymaeans), Cadusians, and Carmanians, although the Cadusians came from the vassal state of Atropatene,[129] and the Carmanians, whose status is not clear,[130] may have been allies. The same applies to the 1,000 Cardaces, who are probably to be identified as Kurds, occasionally called Kardouchoi, from Media or Atropatene.[131] The participation of 500 Lydian akontists sounds strange: Lydia was the stronghold of the rebel Achaeus, who had had an understanding with the Egyptians. Besides, akontistai implies an uncivilized and mountainous people, which the Lydians of Asia Minor in the third century B.C. were not. Even much earlier, Herodotus' 'catalogue' of auxiliaries taking part in Xerxes' invasion of Greece, which is the latest reference to Lydians as a fighting force, describes them as 'most like the armour of the Greeks' (7.74.7).[132] Their grouping with the Cardaces under one commander indicates that these Lydoi originated in the eastern provinces. And indeed some biblical and Assyrian sources suggest that certain tribes bearing a similar name (Lūd in Hebrew, Lubdu in Assyrian) inhabited certain parts of western Media and Atropatene.[133]

The Persians, who formed a unit 2,000 strong with the Agrianians, may have been allies from the semi-independent Persian principality around Persepolis or auxiliaries from Seleucid Persis.[134] The name 'Agrianians' may be pseudo-national and applied to Persians armed in the Agrianian style.[135] The Persians-Agrianians and the 1,000 Thracians shared a common commander, which suggests that the Thracians were recruited from the same area, and should therefore be identified with the Thracian military settlers in Persis (Polyaenus 7.40). If this is true, the Agrianians may also have been settlers of Thracian-Agrianian descent rather than Persians. The alternative of regarding the 'Thracians' and the 'Agrianians' as mercenaries from Thrace and the 'Persians' as a pseudo-national contingent of mercenaries[136] is less likely. The absence of Thracian mercenaries at Raphia could be easily explained by the political condition in Thrace and Asia Minor, but it is hard to imagine that the skilled and celebrated Persian archers, who were actually part of the Empire, were not in the Seleucid front line.[137]

To sum up: the national contingents at Raphia consisted of 12,500 mercenaries, 10,000 allies, 9,500 subjects, and 1,000-2,000 military settlers. The Galatians, who usually played an important role in the Seleucid armies, were not represented, probably because the intensive military activity of Pergamon and Achaeus (e.g. Polyb. 5.77.2) kept them fully occupied.

The classification of the national contingents at Magnesia appears clearer (Livy 37.40; App. Syr. 32). The mercenary force consisted of the 1,200 Dahaean cavalry and 3,000 Trallians, and the 'mercenaries under treaty' were 1,500 Cretans, 1,000 Neo-Cretans, and probably the 4,000 Galatians who included some Europeans (Livy 37.18.7; App. Syr. 6). On top of the 2,000 allied auxiliaries sent by Ariarathes, we must regard as allies the 2,500 Mysians who may have been aiming at the elimination of their expansionist neighbours of Pergamon. The 'subjects' included 8,000 Cyrtians and Elymaeans,[138] 4,500 Pisidians, Pamphylians, Lycians, Carians, and Cilicians, and probably also Livy's 2,700 auxiliares mixti omnium generum, presumably levied from among some of the oriental nationals mentioned at Raphia such as Persians, Carmanians, etc. They are described by Appian as xenoi, and consequently by some commentators as Greek mercenaries, but circumstances in Greece, and especially in Aetolia, did not facilitate recruitment during the interval between Thermopylae and Magnesia.[139] In any case, had they been Greeks, Polybius would not have failed to identify them, as he did in other battles. Livy's description of the various contingents proves here also, as already generally accepted, to be the more reliable. The Thracian settlers are not mentioned, but it may be assumed that they comprised the hard core of the probably 3,000-strong camp guard (see p.8 above). Their semi-heavy armament, as well as their loyalty as settlers and warlike tradition qualified them, more than any other national contingent, for this highly responsible and crucial task, the importance of which had been so fatally demonstrated by the recent disaster at Thermopylae. It is interesting to note that Thracian troops served as camp guards on the Roman side also (Livy 37.39.12).[140] All in all the mercenaries totalled 10,700, the allies 4,500, the subjects 15,200, and troops from military settlements around 3,000.

The national contingents at Daphne comprised only mercenaries numbering 16,000 (Polyb. 30.25). These included 5,000 Mysians, the same number of Galatians, 3,000 Cilician 'lights', who, from the evidence of their armament, must have been recruited in independent upper Cilicia, and the 3,000 Thracians, who cannot be identified with the military settlers in Persis, whose presence in the rebellious eastern regions was at this time more important.[141]

The striking absentees from the three great performances of the Seleucid army are the people of Mesopotamia and Syria. Phoenicians indeed were presumably the backbone of the Seleucid navy, but in general, it seems evident that the Seleucids were †reluctant to employ Syrians and Babylonians (apart from the Jews, who were a special case) in their land forces.[142] The current explanation, based on some ancient comments originating in Roman circles, that the Syrians and Mesopotamians were effeminate and 'soft',[143] certainly has no substance. Roman propaganda should not obscure the long military traditions of these people. Considerations of Seleucid internal politics are more acceptable reasons: arming the indigenous peoples at the nerve-centre of the Empire and developing their military potential was too risky an undertaking and also partially superfluous in view of the heavy concentration of the regular army in northern Syria. On the periphery, on the other hand, where the Macedonian element was rather sparse, local contingents may well have proved indispensable against outside aggression and could always be dispatched to other fronts as auxiliaries. A revolt of armed natives in the remoter provinces could always have been put down by resolute action from the centre, but an uprising in Syria would have undermined the very existence of the kingdom.

Fluctuation in the proportions of the various categories was due to the special needs of the moment. At Magnesia, when all the national contingents were available, and Antiochus in any case had a substantial numerical superiority over the Romans, the number of mercenaries decreased considerably in comparison with Raphia. The severance of Asia Minor from the kingdom and the declining security of the eastern provinces, which were the main source of subject and allied contingents, was responsible for the record number of mercenaries at Daphne who were preparing themselves for the eastern expedition. In any case, Griffith's conclusion that mercenaries played only a minor part in the Seleucid army, in comparison with their predominance in the Ptolemaic forces,[144] seems to be well corroborated. The number of mercenaries on garrison duties cannot be estimated, but presumably most of them were assigned to the battlefields, and at any rate they did not exceed those of the Ptolemies in number.

This major difference in the composition of the two armies is explainable by the Seleucid success in keeping up the standards of the military settlers, and by the enormous territory with a warlike indigenous population they controlled, which decreased their dependence on mercenaries. The Seleucid system ensured the constant availability of troops (though not speedy mobilization, as was proved on the eve of Thermopylae), and eased the economic burden. But it must be stressed that these benefits were outweighed by the military and tactical disadvantages. The reliance on 'light' national contingents instead of mercenaries, and their deployment opposite superior heavy or semi-heavy troops, was a decisive factor in the defeat at Raphia and impeded Antiochus III at Magnesia. Thus the Seleucids fell victim in the great campaigns to the efficiency of their recruitment system. But all in all it should be borne in mind that great campaigns, however decisive, were rare occurrences, and the army could not have been geared to these occasions alone. The 'light' national contingents, which were only marginally effective in great battles, may have been perfectly effective in military operations in the various localities of the huge Empire. Nevertheless, the Seleucids were aware of the need to keep Syrian and Babylonian nationals out of their armies in order to safeguard the centre of the kingdom, while the Ptolemies admitted the Egyptian machimoi to their phalanx and suffered an extended internal upheaval that brought about the loss of most of Egypt's overseas Empire.[145]

3: THE REGULAR ARMY

We have seen how heterogeneous the national contingents of the Seleucid army were. It was also diversified in the units of the regular army. Most of the names of these units were inherited from Alexander's period, but they did not always have the same meaning and significance. The frequent use of different terms to designate the same contingents, which is the main stumbling-block to any attempt at classifying Alexander's troops, occurs also in accounts of the Seleucid army. The difficulties are aggravated in the case of the latter by the scarcity of sources compared with the relatively abundant information about Alexander's army. In the following pages an attempt is made to distinguish the various units of the regular army, and to follow their development.

HEAVY INFANTRY

The largest corps of the Seleucid army was, as in the armies of other Hellenistic kingdoms, the phalanx, which is found in the centre of the battlefield in all the great battles. Apart from 'phalanx' and 'the Macedonians', it is also called occasionally 'the heavy troops' (τὰ βαρέα τῶν ὅπλων), pezetairoi, and sarisophoroi, the last three names certainly being unofficial.[1]

References to the Seleucid army do not contribute very much to the extremely complicated question of the equipment of the phalangites. Their sarissa was certainly the long variety, 21 feet in length, attributed to the Antigonids, and not the shorter type of Alexander's time.[2] Neither the Seleucids nor the Ptolemies could afford to lag behind their western rivals. From this the further implication may be drawn that the conventional shield used by the Seleucid phalanx was of the smaller variety, 45 cm in diameter, which had the effect of leaving both hands free to handle the pike.[3]

With regard to the cuirass, Griffith has argued with probability that the soldiers of Philip and Alexander's phalanx

were not equipped with any sort of breastplate, and he has tried
to apply the same conclusion to Philip V's phalangites, and on this
basis to all the Hellenistic armies.[4] The last statement is based
mainly on the military code of Amphipolis, which imposes fines for
failure to carry various items of armour and weaponry, but
mentions breastplates only with reference to officers.[5] This may
be correct as far as the Antigonid army is concerned: the
military tradition of the armies of Philip and Alexander is likely
to have been stronger there than in other Hellenistic monarchies,
and the rarity of 'missile troops' in the European arena made this
extra weight of armour unnecessary – and besides, the financial
resources of the Antigonids were rather limited. But these
considerations can hardly apply to the other Hellenistic armies.
The well-known increase in weight of the phalanx equipment during
the third century B.C.; the need to find an answer to the Cretan
and Persian archers and the other Thracian and oriental 'missile
troops' that were to be found in almost all the armies of the
east, especially as protection against them had been weakened by
the decrease in the size of the shield; the abundance of resources
to finance the supply and maintenance of breastplates; all these
factors tilt the balance against Griffith's assumption. But these
are still only general considerations. The only direct evidence
for phalanx troops' using breastplates comes from Philopoemen's
Achaean army (Plut. Philop. 9).[6] The statements of later
tacticians (Arr. Tact. 3; Onas. 24) cannot be accepted
unquestioningly owing to the dubious and compilatory character of
their manuals.

The same conclusion applies to the Seleucid phalangites, and
perhaps with more reason, since in their campaigns east of the
Tigris they had to face mainly light 'snipers'. But even in this
case there is no direct evidence. The Seleucid phalanx at Beith-
Zacharia is indeed described by I Macc. as 'equipped with coats of
mail' (τεθωρακισμένους ἐν ἁλυσιδωτοῖς- 6.35), but the source,
perhaps an eye witness, was evidently carried away by the sight of
the one contingent armed in Roman style, which is recorded as being
similarly equipped at Daphne (Polyb. 30.25.3).[7] The generalization
may also be attributable to the positioning of the 'Roman' infantry
in the advance 'elephant divisions', which were first to enter the

defile (see p.181 below). It is not likely that the author was
just succumbing to the temptation to use the well-known biblical
phrase occurring in the description of the combat between David and
Goliath (I Sam. 17.5, cf. I Macc. 3.10-12), because he does not
elsewhere, with regard to battles and occurrences about which he
certainly was sufficiently well informed, ever employ biblical
phrases that do not faithfully reflect the actual events. The
emphatic statement that the 'Roman' contingent at Daphne was
equipped with coats of mail may indicate at the most that if other
phalanx units possessed breastplates at all, they were of a somewhat different style.

The phalanx of Antiochus Epiphanes was composed of chrysaspides
and chalkaspides, in addition to the argyraspides (Polyb. 30.25.5:
I Macc. 6.39),[8] the infantry Guard attached to it, all of whom
figure in the armies of the Successors. Only the leukaspides
mentioned as part of Philip V's phalanx[9] are absent. Although the
adornment of shields and other items of armament has precedents
even among Epaminondas' Thebans and the troops of Eumenes of Cardia,
and served to impress and frighten the enemy,[10] its absence from
the many accounts of Antiochus III's campaigns may mean that only
Antiochus Epiphanes, in line with his general striving for luxury
and splendour, introduced some of these ornamented shields.[11]
Nevertheless, the practice of polishing shields before battle, for
the purpose of frightening the enemy as well as of properly
maintaining the armour, was probably as common in the Seleucid as
in other Hellenistic armies even earlier.[12]

With regard to the source of recruitment of the phalangites
and their descent, I have already pointed out in the discussion
devoted to the military settlements the unanimity of opinion which
exists in relating the phalanx to these settlements alone, and I
have suggested that they were mainly, though not entirely, of
Greco-Macedonian origin. The connection between the phalangites
and the Seleucid settlements has been decisively established by
Griffith, in his study of the mercenaries in the Hellenistic
world, by a chain of convincing reasoning which more or less
eliminates the possibility that the phalanx could have consisted
of mercenaries or oriental auxiliaries. As a last point with
regard to the phalanx, I would like to draw attention to a piece

of direct textual evidence on the participation of military settlers in the phalanx, provided by the frequently quoted treaty between Smyrna and Magnesia (OGIS 229). The third part of the inscription (ℓℓ.89-109) lists several privileges granted to the various elements occupying Palai-Magnesia, the fortress of Magnesia, in order to secure their loyalty to Seleucus II after the recent revolt. One of the units garrisoning the old citadel under an officer called Timōn is defined as 'those detached from the phalanx for the guarding of the fortress' (ℓ.103). This unit cannot be identified with the original garrison settled there one generation earlier because the latter is listed in the preceding group (ℓℓ.100-2); neither can it have consisted of mercenaries from any source for the following reasons: firstly, mercenaries employed by Smyrna and Persians (the latter probably a detachment of the hypaithroi, the Seleucid mercenaries encamping in Magnesia) are specified as a separate group (ℓ.104-5); secondly, pay was not guaranteed to the phalangites as it was to the mercenaries mentioned above (ℓ.107); last, but not least, the ateleia granted to the phalangites is referred to as 'the same ateleia which already applied to the others' (ℓ.104), i.e. similar to the exemption granted to the old garrison (ℓ.102), which according to the context is certainly to be identified with the exemption from tithes mentioned in an adjacent line (ℓ.100 - adekateutoi).[13] As nothing seems to indicate that lands were allocated to the phalangites at the beginning of the short period of time within which the events alluded to in this document took place, they cannot have been a special category of mercenaries. It should be noted that the ateleia is not shared by the Smyrnean and Persian mercenaries (ℓℓ.104-8). Thus the only alternative is to assume that this unit was a detachment of the Magnesian katoikoi, the military settlers, designated in this context only by their military affiliation. Support for this identification seems to be provided by the firm statement 'and they must be in the fortress' (ℓ.104), applied to the phalangites alone. This must be interpreted as a warning to the soldier-settlers not to abandon the fortress despite the possible inconvenience and hardship caused by their separation from their allotments, or perhaps as a reservation to the effect that the concessions would apply only so long as Timōn's soldiers stayed in the fortress. It is true that they received the compensation of exemption from tithes, a thing not granted to the other settlers who remained in Magnesia, but it was not enough: on top of the exemption from taxes the old garrison of Palai-Magnesia, formerly katoikoi in Magnesia, were compensated by Antiochus I for being transferred to the old citadel by the gift of two additional kleroi (ll.100-1).[14] Shortage of land probably prevented Seleucus II from displaying similar generosity, whence the anxiety indicated with regard to Timōn's detachment. As no one would have been enthusiastic about moving to the fortress under these conditions, the detachment may have been selected by lot.[15]

Besides the phalanx, the Seleucid regular infantry included other units, hypaspists, argyraspides, and peltasts. That they belonged to the regular army is evident from the absence of any national identification. Their nature and development in the armies of Alexander and the Antigonids had long been disputed, but Spendel, Tarn, and Walbank have decisively established that they were synonymous with the infantry of the Guard though the different names are used at different periods and in different places.[16] The hypaspists had already emerged in Philip's reign as a small unit, the 'agēma of the hypaspists', or 'royal hypaspists', replacing the old royal Guard of the sōmatophylakes. They were reinforced on the eve of Alexander's expedition by new units called 'royal hypaspists' or just 'hypaspists', although the original agēma retained its position as the 'royal hypaspists' par excellence. The hypaspists changed their name in India to argyraspides (Arr. Anab. 7.11.3),[17] and retained their new name in the armies of the Diadochs up to the battle of Ipsus. In third and second-century B.C. Macedon and Egypt, the infantry Guard reemerges as hypaspists,[18] but such an authority as Polybius is consistent in referring to the Antigonid hypaspists as 'peltasts', and is also inclined to apply the same term to the Ptolemaic infantry Guard,[19] although in the last case he is probably not reflecting official terminology. Likewise the term agēma was reserved to designate the crack battalion of the Guard in the Antigonid as well as in the Ptolemaic army.[20]

What armour and weapons were used by Alexander's infantry Guard is rather obscure. On one hand the infantry Guard seems to have played the same tactical role as the phalanx, but on the other hand their high mobility on certain occasions may imply that they carried lighter equipment. Consequently, although basically they are regarded as phalangites, their equipment is described by some scholars as lighter than that of the ordinary phalanx.[21]

The Seleucid infantry Guard retained the traditional name argyraspides ('silver shields'). Their tactical role was demonstrated at Raphia and Magnesia, where they fought beside the phalanx against the Ptolemaic phalanx and Roman legions (Polyb. 5.79.4, 82.2, 85.10; Livy 37.40.7), and at Daphne, where they were reported as being in the ranks of the phalanx (Polyb. 30.25.5). Polybius defines them as being armed 'in the Macedonian manner' (5.79.4, 82.2), which refers obviously to the equipment of the phalangites. His accounts of the decisive battle against Molon and the crossing of the Elburz, which distinguish the main units, do not mention the argyraspides as a separate category, evidently reckoning them among the phalangites (5.53; 10.29). Their silver shields, their position near the king at Magnesia, and especially Livy's definition of them as regia cohors (37.40.7), makes it quite evident that they are to be identified as infantry Guard.[22]

Polybius' description of the argyraspides at Raphia as 'chosen from the whole kingdom' (5.79.4), when considered in light of the internal struggle at the court of Demetrius II, can be used to help ascertain their recruiting system. Demetrius had dismissed the Macedonians 'every one to his own place' (11.38). As it was peace time and Josephus, who seems to have used trustworthy Hellenistic sources in his narrative of the internal crises of the Seleucid kingdom, implies that they had been kept permanently together in the centre of the kingdom by earlier kings (Ant. 13.129-30),[23] these Macedonians are obviously to be identified with the Guard. It has already been suggested that the 'Macedonians' were sent back to the military settlements, and it needs no stretch of the imagination to identify the argyraspides, the Guard selected from 'the whole kingdom', with the Macedonian Guard sent back to the military settlements. The argyraspides were, then, military settlers selected to serve as Guards in the centre of the Empire and not oriental recruits, as usually thought.[24]

What were the criteria of selection, and how was it possible for settlers to be attracted into the royal service far from their land allotments, and yet maintain their connection with the settlements, a connection demonstrated by the 'Macedonians' sent home by Demetrius II? The problem can at first sight be resolved by suggesting that recruits to the Guard were given high salaries and that they retained their allotments in the distant settlements, which provided them with another source of income, or that they were perhaps even allocated enlarged allotments (cf. the phalangites on garrison duty at Palai-Magnesia - OGIS 229 ℓ.101). But the description of the Roman contingent mentioned in the parade at Daphne (Polyb. 30.25.3) provides another clue and indicates that the Guardsmen were too young to have been former reservists who were recruited for Guard duties: The training of the 'Roman' contingent in the new style and their classification as picked troops suggests that this contingent could not have consisted of ordinary settlers called up in time of emergency, but was a permanent Guard. Analysis of the numerical strength of the argyraspides reinforces the impression that the Roman-style contingent originally belonged to the infantry Guard. At Raphia the argyraspides formed a corps of 10,000 (id. 5.79.4);[25] their number at Magnesia is unfortunately not recorded, but comparison of the total figure of the troops with the detailed numbers of the various contingents, as well as the actual space probably occupied by them on the battlefield, suggests that their number was the same as at Raphia (see p.9 above, and p.168 below); at Daphne there were only 5,000 argyraspides (id. 30.25.5), but as the numerical level of royal corps tends to remain basically stable (see also below on the 10,000 peltasts-argyraspides in the expedition to Bactria), the 5,000 'Romans' seem the obvious solution in bringing the number up to 10,000. The 'Roman' detachment of the Guard is described as 'men in the prime of life'. And indeed the troops of the Guard 'chosen from the whole kingdom' would be likely to consist of young soldiers at the peak of their physical condition. This description recalls the celebrated decision of the assembly of Thera, which was eager to colonize Cyrene (SEG IX.3): each household was committed to send one of its adult sons (τοὺς ἡβῶτας - 'in their prime') to settle in Cyrene. A similar arrangement seems to have existed between the Seleucid monarchs and the military settlers. The argyraspides were, therefore, the offspring of the military settlers, and as such would not yet have inherited their fathers' allotments, and could be kept in military quarters far from their homes. The constant numerical strength of the corps suggests either that service was not an individual responsibility, but was imposed collectively on regions or settlements, or that soldiers served a limited term so as to allow for the admission of new recruits, or that perhaps incompetent soldiers, troublemakers, and those who inherited lands on their father's death were continually being replaced by young and promising recruits so as to maintain the total number at 10,000 and, after retiring to their settlements, the discharged Guardsmen were transferred to the reserve units of the phalangites. In view of the evident success of the Seleucid recruitment system, as proved by its durability, the first possibility is not credible. A collective levy would not have worked among farmers who needed their ablest sons as a labour force. As has already been suggested in the discussion on the military settlements, the service of the would-be settlers in the Guard was mainly responsible for keeping up their military standard as phalangites in the reserve ranks, and, consequently, for the relative success of the Seleucid military organization.

The system may perhaps be illustrated by Diodorus' anecdote about Diophantus' hermaphrodite daughter (32.10.2-9). His only son died young, and when the girl, called Herais, turned into a man renamed Diophantus, the young lad enrolled in the cavalry and is reported to have followed Alexander Balas in his flight to Abae. The permanent character of his service in the cavalry during peacetime and the fact that his unit was attached to the king indicate that Diophantus junior belonged to the Guard. His father, a Macedonian living in Abae on the edge of the Syrian desert, could well have been a military settler; the Greek name of the place is not sufficient evidence,[26] but Macedonians living in that area - and Diophantus was certainly not the only Macedonian at Abae - are likely to have been settled by the authorities for military purposes. Alexander Balas' attempt to find refuge among them in his flight from the Ptolemaic army and Demetrius' Cretan mercenaries supports this possibility. Diophantus was then called up to the Guard in his father's lifetime like other male heirs of military settlers.

The recruitment system of the argyraspides may not have originated with the Seleucids but rather continued an established Macedonian practice. Theopompus states that the pezetairoi who, according to him, served as footguard, consisted of troops selected from all regions of Macedon for their strength and physique (FGrH 115 f.348),[27] and Anaximenes, who describes them as prothymotatoi, attributes the foundation of the corps to the time of an Alexander (ibid., 72 f.4(7)), probably the second (369-368 B.C.).[28] Despite the difficulty of describing as 'Guard' the pezetairoi, who are known from Alexander's anabasis to have been territorial units, this information carries considerable weight in view of Theopompus' stay at Philip II's court, and seems to me to suggest that pezetairoi (as well as sōmatophylakes) preceded hypaspists for the infantry Guard.[29] And just as Philip's and Alexander's hetairoi designated the royal cavalry Guard before the great expedition, the term pezetairoi is likely to have been its counterpart among the infantry, and as hetairoi was later used in a broader sense for all the Macedonian cavalry, so pezetairoi came to cover the entire Macedonian infantry. We do not know the nature of the legal obligation to serve in the ancient Macedonian footguard or how the recruitment system worked,[30] but since the regional divisions formed the backbone of the Macedonian army, it is not impossible that the Seleucid system differed little from it.

The peltasts are mentioned on three occasions: in the battle against the Galatians in 273 B.C., in Antiochus III's forced march against Euthydemus in Bactria in 208, and in Appian's version of Thermopylae in 191. Polybius' allusion to the peltasts in the Bactrian expedition is the most interesting. Here they consisted of 10,000 troops (10.49.3), although no contingent of peltasts of this size can be detected in any of the great campaigns and not even in the references to the main units crossing the Elburz in the same Bactrian expedition (10.29-31).

Their absence on the last occasion suggests that they were counted in with the phalanx. The selection of the 'peltasts' for the special Bactrian undertaking, the participation of the cavalry Guard in the same march (10.49.7), and the numerical strength of these 'peltasts', suggest that they should be identified with the argyraspides. Polybius is thus applying Antigonid terminology to the Seleucid Guard in the same way as he does to the Ptolemaic infantry agēma. The participation of the peltasts in the forced march does not refute the suggestion that they are to be identified with the heavily-armed argyraspides. On the contrary: it is to be expected that the young and well-trained argyraspides should have been selected for any unconventional and demanding adventure in the same way as some phalanx and Guard units in Alexander and Philip V's armies.[31]

The same conclusion applies to the 'peltasts' of Thermopylae. Kromayer rightly suggested, by comparing Appian and Livy's versions, that Appian's 'peltasts' (18(83)) were defined by Polybius as 'Macedonians' or 'armed in Macedonian style'.[32] But he is wrong in assuming that they were the traditional peltasts. 'Macedonian style' in Polybius, and in Hellenistic historiography and military manuals in general, always means phalanx warfare. As the Seleucid phalanx at Thermopylae is referred to separately, by the process of elimination the 'peltasts' were therefore argyraspides; hence their position in front of the rampart as defensive spearhead (Livy 36.18.5; App. Syr. 18(93)).

Lucian's rhetorical account of Antiochus I's battle against the Galatians (Zeuxis 8-11) cannot of course be read as support for my conclusion, but the application of the word 'peltasts' there may perhaps be interpreted to have our suggested meaning. Analysis of the historical and chronological background indicates that of the regular army in addition to the naturally mixed military settlers of Lydia and Phrygia, only the royal Guard, part of which was encamped at Sardis, was available for the Galatian front.[33] The Guard is perhaps referred to by Lucian himself when reporting that 'the Macedonians' hailed Antiochus as kallinikos at the end of the battle (11). The Seleucid troops are described as 'mostly peltasts and lights (psilikon) and the lights (gymnētes) made up one half of the army' (10). Lucian is obviously trying to stress, by the use of the word 'peltasts', the light arming in the Seleucid camp, but if he took this term from his source and did not invent it himself, which is of course a possibility, it may have meant the infantry Guard, though, admittedly, the peltasts could also have comprised semi-heavy troops of mercenaries or militia from the neighbouring Greek cities.

Of all the units known in the forces of Alexander and the Successors, the major absentee from the Seleucid army is the agēma, or in its full name 'the agēma of the hypaspists', the royal infantry Guard, or rather the crack battalion of the infantry Guard. Its absence from the rather detailed account of the Seleucid disposition and battle order in the major campaigns, coupled with relatively frequent allusions to the cavalry agēma, suggests that the omission is not accidental. It appears that they retained only the second half of their full name and were renamed 'hypaspists'. In my view, therefore, the Seleucid hypaspists were not synonymous with the argyraspides, as suggested by some,[34] but formed a crack force within the corps of the infantry Guardsmen. The hypaspists are first mentioned at Cyrrhestica. The bravest among them accompanied the king in his courageous and surprising outflanking manoeuvre recorded by Polyaenus (4.9.3). Dionysius, the commander of the hypaspists, is described by Polybius as one of the three ablest officers in the army besieging Sardis in 214 B.C. (7.16.2). At Panion the hypaspists, defined by Polybius as 'the best unit', were posted around the king, together with the Companions (id. 16.18.7, 19.7), the cavalry royal Guard, one of the two 1,000-horse strong crack battalions of the cavalry. The last reference suggests that they were not a large force of the same order as the argyraspides, and, along with the preceding reference, refutes the alternative of regarding them merely as a personal Guard.[35] Due consideration ought to be given also to the Thermopylae fragment of Antisthenes. Although he inaccurately describes the 500 who accompanied Antiochus III on his flight as hypaspists (FGrH 257.f.36) when they were actually drawn from the cavalry (App. Syr. 20(91)),[36] presumably from the Companions, the cavalry royal Guard, he may be interpreted as implying that this term applied to the counterparts of the Companions in the infantry.

In the three detailed descriptions of the Seleucid army the

hypaspists probably formed an integral part of the large corps of the infantry Guard, the argyraspides, and are therefore not counted separately, although Polybius, in listing the troops at Raphia, seems to have considered them as separate from the argyraspides, but forming part of the general footguard (Polyb. 5.79.4).[37] Consequently their numerical strength is not recorded. Alexander's infantry agēma numbered 1,000 troops.[38] On administrative grounds, the Seleucid hypaspists may be considered to have consisted of double this figure: the footguard, totalling 10,000, would have allowed two stratēgiai, the largest tactical units, to the ordinary argyraspides, thus leaving 2 chiliarchies to the hypaspists. It is worth noting that the cavalry Guard also numbered 2,000, divided into two independent units of 1,000 troops each. The 2,000 storm troops at Sardis (Polyb. 7.16.6, 18.3) may, therefore, be identified with the hypaspists.

The controversy over the equipment of Alexander's hypaspists applies also to the Seleucid argyraspides, as well as to their contemporary Antigonid hypaspists-peltasts.[39] The pelte borrowed by Seleucus I in Cyrrhestica (Polyaenus 4.9.3), probably from one of the hypaspists, and the name 'peltasts' occasionally attached to them, constitute the only direct evidence we have about their armament, but this shield was not necessarily smaller than the hoplon of the phalangites. The standard 45 cm Macedonian shield of the Hellenistic phalangite could and was occasionally called 'peltē'.[40] On the other hand, the positioning of the argyraspides at Raphia opposite the highly regarded Ptolemaic 'Macedonian' phalanx and not opposite the disparaged natives' phalanx, added to the fact that they put up a relatively tough resistance in contrast to the rapid collapse of the Seleucid phalanx facing the Egyptians (Polyb. 5.82.2, 85.8-10), makes it inconceivable that they were inferior to the ordinary phalanx in length of pikes or dimension and weight of shields. The heavy equipment would not have impeded them in a forced march such as the Bactrian expedition: the six kg sarissa[41] and the even lighter shield were much less of a burden than the equipment of the Roman legionary, which is considered, even at the lowest estimate, to have been not less than 20 kg,[42] and there is no reason to suspect that these young and vigorous troops were not trained in route marches like

Philip's army and the Roman legions (cf. p. 95 below).

As to breastplates, there seems no reason to suggest that the argyraspides did not possess heavy, defensive armour. On forced marches these heavy items of equipment could perhaps have been left behind in the camp so as not to slow down the pace. The argyraspides were selected for undertakings requiring rapid movement because of their greater military expertise and better physical condition, and not because of any difference in type of armament. But even if it is argued that the argyraspides would not have been separated from such an essential part of their equipment when going into action, their physical condition and superior training would have enabled them to advance much faster than any other unit, even with the additional burden of breastplates. On the other hand, the general considerations supporting the suggested introduction of breastplates in the Seleucid phalanx apply even more forcibly to the Guard; it would have been much easier to supply, maintain, and store the rather expensive armour in the permanent royal barracks of the far smaller Guard than to distribute it among the remote settlers.

Next to nothing is known about the tactical units of the Seleucid phalanx and their subdivisions. It is generally assumed, on the evidence of some scattered references, that the Antigonid and Ptolemaic phalanx was divided into stratēgiai of 4,000 each, the stratēgiai into four chiliarchies of 1,000 each, the chiliarchy into four speirai of 256, the speira into four tetrarchies of sixty four, and the tetrarchy into four 16-man dekades or sēmaiai in Egypt, and lochoi in Antigonid Macedon.[43] All these subdivisions are obviously based on the file of 16 men (see Polyb. 18.30.1),[44] because it was mainly within the file that proper coordination was needed. The stratēgia itself is never mentioned as a tactical unit in the Seleucid army, but some of the Seleucid stratēgoi, usually regarded as governors of provinces or officers of independent contingents, may well have been commanders of stratēgiai.[45] Smaller subunits are mentioned twice: the secretaries of the Magnesian tagmata were in charge of the register of all the soldiers (OGIS 229 ℓ.46), and the peltasts-argyraspides formed sēmaiai when Antiochus III engaged the

Bactrians (Polyb. 10.49.7). Tagma refers to subdivisions in
general and does not designate a particular unit,[46] while the use
of sēmaia may indicate that in the Seleucid army it replaced the
old Macedonian dekas, the smallest subdivision of Alexander's
phalanx.[47]

CAVALRY

The 'regulars' of the Seleucid cavalry included, like the infantry,
royal Guard, Guard, and ordinary troops. In contrast to the scanty
information available about the ordinary troops, there are
relatively many allusions to the Guard. The various contingents,
numbering about 1,000 horse each, are named hetairoi, ilē basilikē,
agēma, and, Polybius seems to indicate, also philoi and epilekloi.
Since the Seleucid cavalry, even more than the infantry, was
influenced by the nomenclature and structure of Alexander's army,
we must first of all outline the development of Alexander's
cavalry Guard.

Alexander's cavalry underwent several reforms and
reorganizations which have prompted heated discussion as they were
reported in rather vague terms.[48] For our purpose it is sufficient
to point out certain stages of development which are beyond
question: Alexander inherited from Philip the royal Guard,
probably 300 horse strong, called 'royal ala' (ilē basilikē), with
or without the attributive 'of the Companions' (hetairoi). By the
time Alexander crossed to Asia, the force had grown to eight
squadrons, each called 'royal', forming together the celebrated
'cavalry of the Companions'. The original royal squadron retained
its position as the royal squadron par excellence, but after
Bactria it was called by a new name, the 'agēma', with the
attributives 'of the cavalry', 'of the Companions', or 'of the
Companion cavalry'. By a later modification, the date, form, and
significance of which are much disputed, the eight squadrons,
supplemented by oriental cavalry, were reorganized into
hipparchiai. On leaving India, Alexander sent the oriental troops
home and amalgamated the survivors of the original Macedonian
squadrons, including the agēma, into one chiliarchy.[49] Gradually,
some Persian nobles came to be attached to the agēma. The mutiny
at Opis, begun as a protest against Persian influence, was

crumbled under the threat of a reform which was, inter alia, to
replace the Macedonian horse Guard with Persian troops, called
for the first time by the traditional names of 'the cavalry of the
Companions' and 'the royal agēma'.

The original Companions and agēma were dissolved sometime
after Alexander's death. But they reappeared in the armies of the
first Successors, though without the royal attributive. As
Macedonian horsemen became scarce, the name agēma was occasionally
attached to the crack oriental cavalry, at least in Eumenes'
army,[50] while 'Companions' was reserved for Macedonian troops.[51]
After Gaza (312 B.C.),[52] the cavalry agēma disappeared from the
accounts of Ptolemaic and Antigonid armies, as did the Seleucid
infantry agēma.

The last stage in the development of Alexander's cavalry had
the greatest impact on the Seleucid Guard. The basic nomenclature
was retained though with some changes: one regiment was called
agēma and another 'the royal ala of the Companions'. Like
Alexander's chiliarchy, each of them totalled 1,000 troops, and,
like the agēma of Eumenes, that of the Seleucids was composed of
oriental troops. The great difference was the expansion of the
agēma to 1,000 horse, and, consequently, its complete separation
from the Companions.

The separation of the two regiments is obvious from the
mention of them at Magnesia and Daphne as different units, each
1,000 strong (Livy 37.40.6,11; App. Syr. 32(163-4); Polyb.
30.25.8). On the other hand, there is no doubt that the ilē
basilikē, and the hetairoi, or hippos hetairikē, are identical.[53]
The two names appear in various campaigns but never occur
concurrently as different units on the same battlefield (Polyb.
5.53.4, 84.1, 85.12; 16.18.7; 30.25.7; Polyaenus 4.9.6). That
they are in fact identical is decisively proved by the account of
Magnesia: Livy (37.40.11) posts the regia ala in the same
position on the battlefield as Appian's hippos hetairikē (Syr.
32(164)), which indicates that 'the royal ala of the Companions'
(ἴλη βασιλικὴ τῶν ἑταίρων) was its full name in Polybius, the sole
source for the versions of Livy and Appian (see p.163 below).

In contrast to their different roles in Alexander's army,
the Seleucid agēma and Companions were both attached to the king

at different times: at Raphia and Panion the Companions
surrounded the king (Polyb. 5.85.12; 16.18.7), while at Magnesia
he fought amidst the agēma (Livy 37.40.6, 41.1; App. Syr. 33(170),
34(177)). Consequently, the 2,000 picked cavalry accompanying
the king on the forced march to Bactria, described as 'the
cavalry who were accustomed to fight around him' (Polyb. 10.49.7,
13), probably comprised both the agēma and Companions,[54] and the
same applies to the 2,000 forward horse around the king at Raphia
(Polyb. 5.82.9, 84.1, 85.12).[55] It is difficult to know whether
there was any difference in equipment: Appian describes the
Companions at Magnesia as 'lightly equipped' (Syr. 32(164)), but
Livy's version makes it clear that Polybius was merely comparing
them with the cataphracts positioned on their right (37.40.11).
On the other hand, there was a difference in the provenance and
nationality of recruits and consequently in the standard of the
two regiments. According to Livy the agēma included 'Medi ...
eiusdem regionis mixti multarum gentium', while the Companions
were recruited from 'Syri plerique ... Phrygibus et Lydis immixti'
(37.40.6,11).[56] The wording of the second half of the reference
to the agēma indicates that the Medes were indigenous, and indeed
one would expect the agēma to have been drawn from this source,
for the Medes were regarded as the best cavalry men in the east,
while the 'Syrians, Phrygians and Lydians', of whatever nationality
they may actually have been, were of much lesser repute. It may
be rewarding to proceed one step further and define both units
more precisely. Livy's geographical and ethnological indications
suggest, what can a priori be assumed, that like the infantry
Guard, the agēma and Companions drew their recruits from the
military settlements. We may recall that military settlers of
Iranian descent are recorded in western Media, and that of the
various regions of Asia Minor, only Phrygia and Lydia appear on
the map of the Seleucid military foundations (see pp.25,32
above). Syria, which provided the bulk of the settlers forming
the infantry, also heads the list of suppliers of recruits to the
Companions. The 'Syrians, Phrygians and Lydians' were, then,
composed mainly of Macedonians and Greeks, the dominant element
in the western settlements.[57] Diodorus' piquant episode about
the hermaphrodite girl of Macedonian descent who enrolled in the

cavalry Guard of Alexander Balas (32.10.2-9, see p.61 above) seems
to support this deduction. And indeed indigenous Syrian, Phrygian,
and Lydian horsemen, with no reputation for, or tradition of,
cavalry warfare, are very unlikely to have formed a crack force
and served as the king's Guard. The suggested origin of the
recruits for the agēma explains that unit's disappearance from the
royal battle-order against Molon (Polyb. 5.53.1-4), who was in
control of the eastern part of the Empire, and was supported by
the local troops.

Diodorus' statement that the inhabitants of Syrian Larissa
belonged to the 'first agēma of the cavalry' (33.4a) does not
necessarily contradict these conclusions. The historical context
is the revolt of Tryphon in 142 B.C. After the Parthian
occupation of Media, which took place in 148-147 B.C. at the
latest, and perhaps as early as the time of Timarchus' revolt in
162-161 B.C.,[58] epigonoi of Thessalian settlers replaced the
Medes who were now no longer available.[59] One may assume that
consequently the veteran Companions were now also granted the much
envied title of agēma, and that both contingents were called
'agēma of the Companions', possibly accounting for the description
of the Larisseans as 'first agēma'. This step may well have been
in line with Alexander Balas' policy of securing allies by means
of the ceremonious bestowal of honorary titles (e.g. I Macc.
10.60,65, cf. p.31 above).

The recruitment system of the cavalry Guard may probably have
resembled that of the argyraspides. Based on the young sons of
the settlers in Media, Syria, and Asia Minor, it guaranteed the
constant availability of crack troops on the one hand, and on the
other, prepared trained and experienced reservists for the years
to come. After being cut off from Media, and having increasing
need for troops for his internal struggle, it is possible that
Alexander Balas complemented the agēma with older settlers who
were called up only in time of emergency, as may be indicated by
the statement that the Larisseans served in the agēma. It was
undoubtedly relatively easy to call them to duty at short notice
because they resided in the centre of the dismembered kingdom.
But Diodorus may be referring only to the Guardsmen who were
sent home by Demetrius II when he was trying to base his Cretan

mercenaries (I Macc. 11.38, see p.59 above). The last alternative illumines the material reasons that inspired the uprising of the Larisseans against Cretan despotism in Antioch (Strabo 16.2.10 (752)).

What is the explanation for the separate development of the agēma and the Companions? The unit with the more prestigious title of the agēma was probably the first in the field. The nucleus of the corps was formed by the 300 horse or 200 horsemen who followed Seleucus in 312 B.C. to Babylonia (Diod. 19.90.1; App. Syr. 54).[60] Their number corresponds to the usual complement of the agēma in the armies of the Successors.[61] One may presume that the cavalry appointed by Ptolemy to recover Babylonia for his ally was Macedonian, but Diodorus has Seleucus addressing his rather disheartened philoi as Alexandran veterans without referring to the accomplishments of the horsemen (19.90.3), which would have been highly encouraging had the agēma indeed been Macedonian. Be this as it may, the impending campaigns east of the Tigris would quite quickly have led to the expansion of the agēma to the level of a chiliarchy through the addition of orientals, presumably of Median descent; for the numbers of Macedonian horsemen were declining, some Macedonian settlers were reluctant to join Seleucus' ranks (Diod. 19.91.1),[62] and there was the further consideration of the very high standard of horsemanship in that part of the world. Furthermore, even if the original Guardsmen were Macedonian, they would by this time have been promoted to prominent positions in the royal army and administration, so that the agēma would have become, in any case, purely oriental. And indeed Diodorus indicates that a considerable number of oriental cavalry joined Seleucus shortly after 312 B.C. (19.91.5, 92.1,2,5). As the adjective 'royal' was not attached to the later agēma, this contingent may perhaps have assumed its final form before 306 B.C., when the Diadochs adopted royal titles. Similarly 'royal' was omitted from the denomination of the cavalry agēma of other Successors before 306. The reason that, unlike the later infantry agēma of the Ptolemies and Antigonids, they were not termed 'royal' after 306 either, derives from Seleucid internal policy and is better deferred until we have traced the development of the Companions.

After Ipsus in 301 B.C., when Greek and Macedonian troops became available and the system of military settlements was established, the Guard was reorganized: part of Seleucus' former cavalry, comprising the agēma and oriental mercenaries, probably was settled in Media and organized as a reserve force, committed to supplying young recruits to the cavalry crack force. At the same time the Companions, recruited among Macedonian and Greek settlers, were introduced for the first time. It is noteworthy that they adopted the original name of Alexander's Macedonian agēma 'ile basilikē' and not merely 'Companions', although their numerical strength exceeded the size of an ilē. This adherence to the old Macedonian tradition suggests that the omission of the royal title and the attribute 'of the Companions' from the agēma was not accidental. After the occupation of the upper satrapies some time before Seleucus assumed the crown (Diod. 20.53.3-4), the Macedonians settled there by Alexander became the hard core of his army. The strength of the Macedonian element was reinforced through the establishment of the military settlements shortly after Ipsus. The best way to secure the loyalty of the Macedonians in face of the frequent challenge from the rival Macedonian monarchies was for Seleucus to establish himself as the true Macedonian Successor by creating in the east a new Macedon, with similar civil as well as military institutions, not to mention an adherence to Greek culture and language. In these circumstances he could not have ignored the drama of Opis. To call the Median agēma 'royal' or 'of the Companions' would have offended the Macedonians and discredited them as the most influential element in the Court. On the other hand, it was too late to rob the Medes of their original name. In fact, it was hardly necessary; the root of the word agēma means 'lead', 'leading', etc., and the word itself originally meant simply 'the leading contingent' or 'picked troops'.[63] Even if it had always been applied only to royal bodyguards, which seems rather doubtful,[64] the term must have lost something of its traditional appeal, especially the implied influential position in the Court, when it was deprived of its royal attribute and its officers probably of their royal robes and emblems, and was generally understood to mean once more merely 'picked troops'. If this is so, renaming the infantry Guard hypaspists instead of the traditional agēma (see p.64 above) was a way of dissociating the royal status and prestige of this Macedonian infantry crack force from the oriental cavalry agēma.

In addition to the agēma and the Companions, Polybius mentions two other cavalry contingents, philoi and epilektoi, each 1,000-troops strong, which took part in the parade at Daphne (30.25.8). The first does not seem to have been an ordinary military contingent, but a collection for ceremonial purposes of all the nobility bearing the title philoi, i.e. state officials, courtiers, high-ranking military officers, vassal dynasts, and other people who enjoyed the king's favour.[65] Their number is not known but since incidental references in papyrological sources record the names of about 100 philoi at the Ptolemaic court, which, in imitation of its neighbours, adopted this title for the nobility only in the second century B.C.,[66] their total number in the Seleucid kingdom could have approached the 1,000 mark. They were not the only civilian participants in the 'military' part of the procession: the 140 gladiators and the chariots drawn by six horses or four elephants (25.5,11) certainly did not have any military connection.

With regard to the epilektoi ('selected'), it may be noted that 1,000 'selected' horse are mentioned by I Macc. in Gorgias' attempt to surprise Judas Maccabaeus at his camp at Mispā (4.1). But as that book applies the term epilektoi freely to the whole of the Seleucid infantry at Beith-Sour (4.28; cf. 12.41) and to the whole of the cavalry at Beith-Zacharia (6.35), and as such a contingent is not mentioned elsewhere, I prefer to assume that Polybius' text, preserved by Athenaeus, is corrupt, as is evident with regard to another passage in the same paragraph, and that the word epilektoi is an adjective modifying the agēma described in the same sentence as 'the strongest ... unit of the cavalry'.[67] And indeed the agēma is described as 'selected' at Magnesia and in accounts of other Hellenistic battles (e.g. App. Syr. 32(163); Livy 37.40.6; Diod. 18.30.5). But one should not conclude that every anonymous contingent called epilektoi is to be equated with the agēma: the term is used loosely to define various crack units like the argyraspides at Raphia (Polyb. 5.85.9-10, 91.4) and sometimes a selection of soldiers from several units (e.g. id. 2.65.3; Diod. 19.28.3, 29.2). It is possible that on other occasions Gorgias' picked cavalry may perhaps have been identified with the agēma despite the unreliable terminology of I Macc., but at this time these Median horsemen were likely to have been chosen to accompany the king on his eastern expedition (see 3.37).

Like the phalanx of the military settlers, Seleucid regular cavalry from among the reservists in the military settlements can be identified in the sources by the absence of any national identification. Just 2,000 of the 6,000 cavalry at Raphia are to be identified as Guardsmen (see p.69 above), and the others, being anonymous, could only have been regulars, and not mercenaries or allies. The same applies to 6,000 cataphracts who are mentioned at Magnesia without any further identification (Livy 37.40.5,11), while the nationality of other cavalry contingents is clearly stated. Besides the cataphracts at Daphne, Polybius enumerates also Nisaeans (30.25.6). As the name designates a style of warfare and equipment typical of horses of Median breed and not nationality,[68] they must be regarded, like the cataphracts, as regulars.

For the study of the equipment and the subdivisions of the Seleucid regular and Guard cavalry, information must be sought for the most part in sources outside those concerned with the Seleucid kingdom. The 'regular' horseman from Alexander on wore a coat of mail and carried a xyston,[69] to which the Diadochs added the shield.[70] Antiochus' right wing in his battle against Molon included xystophoroi cavalry (Polyb. 5.53.2), and Flamininus in his address to the Achaeans described the Seleucid cavalry as 'lonchophoroi and xystophoroi' (Plut. Flam. 17.5). From the battle of Panion onwards, Seleucid regular cavalry seem to have been heavily armoured (Polyb. 16.17.6, 30.25.6; Livy 37.40.6,11). Tarn rightly suggests that Antiochus transformed his regular cavalry into cataphracts after becoming acquainted with this type of horseman in the course of his invasion of Parthia in 210-206 B.C.[71] The positioning of the Companions in the centre at Panion (Polyb. 16.18.7) and of the agēma opposite a Roman legion at

Magnesia (see p.168 below) suggests that by then the Guard
contingents may have been turned into heavy units and armoured as
well. And indeed the Companions at Magnesia are defined as 'with
lighter armour for themselves and their horses, but otherwise with
equipment not unlike the rest (i.e. the cataphracts)' (Livy
37.40.11), which certainly means that they were heavier than the
ordinary Hellenistic xystophoroi horsemen. The length of their
spears and weight and size of armour is anyone's guess, but it
is rather doubtful that Seleucid cataphracts were equipped with a
long pike like the infantry sarissa, and that man and horse were
fully armoured like the Parthian cataphracts of the first century
B.C.[72]

According to the tacticians, whose data are supported by
papyrological material and by the known subdivision of
Philopoemen's cavalry, the chiliarchy, the largest tactical unit
of the cavalry, was divided into two hipparchiai of 512 men each,
and the hipparchia into eight ilai called also oulamoi by Polybius
(10.21.3; 18.19.9),[73] of 64 horse each.[74] All these units
figured in the Seleucid cavalry. The agēma and the Companions
were composed of 1,000 each. Detachments of 500 cavalry took part
at Thermopylae (Livy 35.42.6; App. Syr. 17(75), 20(90)), Magnesia
(Livy 37.40.13),[75] and Beith-Zacharia (I Macc. 6.35), in addition
to the 1,500 cataphracts at Daphne (Polyb. 30.25.9). The oulamoi
are reported in Antiochus III's march in Bactria as basic tactical
units of the cavalry (Polyb. 10.49.7).

ELEPHANTS AND CHARIOTS

The Hellenistic period is remarkable for the extravagance of its
military devices, on both land and sea. Artillery and siege
machines, which at this period attained unprecedented sizes, do
not concern us, however, as field battles are our interest here.
Thermopylae was the only occasion on which the Seleucids brought
artillery into operation in a field battle, but unfortunately the
types of the 'machines', their number and effect are not recorded,
and have to be deduced from accounts of other armies and battles.
The main themes of this chapter are therefore (a) the elephant,
the most extravagant military device of the period, used by the
Seleucids in almost all the great campaigns, and (b) the scythed

chariot, which already had a long and glorious record in oriental armies, but served its last years in the Seleucid army.

The first appearance of elephants in the Seleucid army was the most impressive and successful. Strabo recounts that on the eve of Ipsus (302 B.C.) Seleucus I received 500 elephants from the Indian king, Chandragupta, in exchange for bringing the war between them to an end (15.2.9(724); 16.2.10(752); Plut. Alex. 52).[76] According to Diodorus, Seleucus arrived in Cappadocia during the winter before Ipsus with 480 elephants (20.113.4), while Plutarch records that 400 elephants took part in the battle itself (Demetr. 28.3). It seems likely that 20 elephants had to be abandoned on the way to Cappadocia because of the difficult route and the speed of the march,[77] and 80 more were unfit for the battle in the summer, either because of the exhausting effects of the march, or because of the severe Cappadocian winter.[78] As there is no inconsistency between the figures, they may all derive from Hieronymus of Cardia, the main source for the first Successors.

Tarn, in a special article devoted to this subject,[79] disputes the reliability of these high figures, mainly because they substantially exceed all the recorded numbers of war elephants in the Hellenistic armies. In his view, Strabo's report of 500 elephants originated from Megasthenes, Seleucus' ambassador at the Indian court, who, relying on oral information from Indian sources, recorded a stereotyped figure used frequently in the Indian literature to express vast numbers. Tarn presumes that Seleucus received only 150 elephants, similar to the maximum number in the possession of Antiochus III, who was trying, in Tarn's opinion, to imitate, in this as in other things, the founder of the dynasty. To the battle itself Tarn assigns just 130 elephants.

Tarn's theory, though at first sight quite attractive, breaks down on several counts. Comparison with later allusions to elephants does not discredit the figures attributed to Seleucus I. Still remembering the effect of Porus' elephants, he may have been particularly anxious to acquire a large herd for himself. As far as the Indian king is concerned, he may not have considered the gift of 500 elephants too great a price to pay for the restoration of peace and the recovery of certain territories which

had been lost to Alexander, especially since a loss of even this
magnitude would not have jeopardized his overwhelming superiority
in this style of warfare (see e.g. Diod. 17.93.2; Plut. Alex. 62.2,
despite the evidently exaggerated figures). The number of
elephants declined in later generations because numerical
superiority ceased to be so important: the African elephant of
the Ptolemies was in any case no match for the Seleucid Indian
elephant,[80] and technical devices developed during the period
would easily have counteracted the advantages of a superior number
of elephants.[81] Moreover, the main value of elephants was as a
'screen' against cavalry, but after 301 B.C. the Seleucids themselves controlled by far the biggest and best reservoir of cavalry.
The enormous expense involved in obtaining elephants, especially
after the 244 B.C. secession of Bactria, which had been the link
with India where the elephants came from, and the difficulties of
maintaining a herd in the unsuitable conditions of Syria, were
not encouraging factors. The course of the battle of Ipsus also
argues against Tarn: as Antigonus had 75 elephants (Plut. Demetr.
28.3), one may assume that at least an equal number of Seleucid
elephants were drawn up to combat them, thus leaving 55, according
to Tarn's suggested total, for the decisive manoeuvre of blocking
the way for the cavalry of Demetrius to return to the battlefield
(ibid. 29.3). But the topographical conditions called for the
allocation of a substantially larger herd of the order of some
hundred elephants for this purpose (see p.108 below). Lastly,
Tarn's explanations of the origin of Diodorus' and Plutarch's figures do not make sense: he credits Duris, Plutarch's main source,
with a degree of elaborate arithmetical calculation and historical
association which could hardly be expected of any Hellenistic
historian, save perhaps Polybius, and certainly not of a Pathetic
writer like Duris. As for Diodorus, since Hieronymus of Cardia
was his main, if not his sole, source for the twentieth book (see
p.247 n.6 below), how could he have ignored the figures of
Hieronymus, especially since Hieronymus, as an eyewitness of Ipsus
(Lucian, Macr. 11), would have possessed first hand information?

After the battle of Ipsus and the foundation of the Seleucid
centre in northern Syria, the elephants were stabled at Apamea,
the military centre of the Empire, which eventually became their

permanent base (Strabo 16.2.10(752)). Elephants certainly figure on Apamean coins more frequently than on those of any other city.[82] Elephants took part in the last battle against Demetrius Poliorcetes, in 285 B.C. According to Polyaenus, Seleucus surprised the Antigonid force by outflanking them, using a side route, and taking with him eight elephants (4.9.3). As this force could have been only a small detachment, the number of elephants used would not indicate the size of the whole Seleucid elephant force at that moment. Plutarch's account of the battle does not refer to elephants at all (Demetr. 49.2), but his version is obviously a general and vague one. Nevertheless, it is possible that most of the elephants of Ipsus were no longer alive in 285 B.C. (see below), and therefore that only a few elephants took part in the campaign against Demetrius.

Two pieces of information have emerged from the mist surrounding the First Syrian War (275-273 B.C.) in the time of Antiochus I: an astronomical tablet in cuneiform records the despatch from Babylonia to Syria of 20 elephants that the governor of Bactria had sent to the king (B.M. 92688.$\ell\ell$.12-13);[83] and in Lucian's version of the battle against the Galatians credit for the victory of Antiochus is given to his 16 elephants (Zeuxis 11). There seems little doubt that these elephants were among the 20 transported from Bactria, as Tarn suggests,[84] but his assumption that the discrepancy in the number was due to the long and exhausting march is less convincing: the 20 elephants set out in good shape for battle from Babylonia and not from Bactria, and a loss of 20% is unlikely in the short distance to Asia Minor. The discrepancy should rather be attributed to losses sustained in the campaign against the rebels in Seleucis which, in my opinion, took place shortly before the 'elephant victory' in 273 B.C.[85] The actual number of elephants sent from Bactria to Babylonia is anybody's guess.

The summoning of such small reinforcements suggests that very few, if any, of the hundreds of elephants at Ipsus were still alive. Tarn, assuming that they were killed during the revolt at Seleucis,[86] bases his dating of the sequence of events on this assumption. But there is no reason to believe that the elephants survived so long: an elephant is ready for battle at the age of

12, and reaches the peak of its physical strength at 20-25. The normal life expectancy of elephants is up to 60 years, but is considerably reduced in captivity and ranges from 20 to 30 years.[87] As India was independent, the Seleucids could only hope for small reinforcements from time to time by way of occupied Bactria, which was not itself an elephant-breeding country. As to the possibility of a new generation of elephants, bred at Apamea, there is some reason to suppose that the elephants of Ipsus were all bulls. The bull-elephant is taller, heavier, and stronger, and, what is most important, has a long tusk, while the cow has a small tusk or none at all. These advantages are decisive in a battle between elephants (see e.g. Polyb. 5.84),[88] and indeed only bulls are represented on Seleucid monuments, terracottas, and coins. Although allowance should be made for the possibility that the bulls alone were depicted just because of their impressive appearance and did not in fact comprise the whole herd, on the other hand, the Indian kings are likely to have tried to preserve their monopoly over the supply of elephants by offering only bulls. I would not deny the possibility that Seleucus had some Indian cow-elephants, as Antigonus and Pyrrhos apparently had,[89] but they are not likely to have been acquired in the deal with Chandragupta and were too few to produce a new herd, especially as elephants rarely breed in captivity[90] and the climate in Apamea would not have been favourable. In conclusion, then, it would seem that Seleucus I ran short of elephants as early as the first decade of the third century B.C., and occasionally replenished the stock with reinforcements like those which took part in the 'elephant victory'. The necessity of bringing further reinforcements from Bactria probably arose out of the preceding Egyptian invasion, when the relatively few Seleucid elephants may all have been captured. This may account for the possible appearance of Indian elephants in the procession of Philadelphos and on a gold stater of his.[91]

From the long and obscure period between the First Syrian War and the accession of Antiochus III we have no documents alluding to elephants, but the scarcity of the sources prevents us from drawing any conclusions. Nevertheless, the tiny number, ten in all, drawn up against Molon (Polyb. 5.53.4), suggests that the herd was reduced to the minimum, and this was certainly a result of the successful Bactrian rebellion in the forties. However, Antiochus III took great pains to replenish the stock of elephants. In 217 B.C. at Raphia he was already able to deploy 102 elephants (id. 5.79.13). In his expedition to the eastern satrapies in 210-206 B.C., he was able, through a political deal with local dynasts, to bring the number up to 150 (id. 11.34.10-2). This great number played a decisive role at Panion, where the battle took place in two separate arenas. In one arena Antiochus' elephants had to confront the entire Ptolemaic elephant force, which could not have been small in view of the special efforts made by the Ptolemies to establish 'elephant stations' in east Africa,[92] and in the other to act as a second line defence (id. 16.18-19, see p.155 below). At Thermopylae and Magnesia, 18 years after the great herd had been procured, their number was substantially reduced: the six elephants (Livy 35.43.6) were admittedly only part of the detachment hastily transported to Greece, but at Magnesia, where Antiochus mustered all his available forces, he was able to produce only 54 elephants (id. 37.40.2,6,14), most of which were probably newly acquired.

In a provision similar to that forced on the Carthaginians after Zama, the treaty of Apamea signed after the Seleucid defeat at Magnesia stipulated the surrender of all elephants to the Romans and prohibited their use in subsequent military engagements (id. 38.38; App. Syr. 38-9; Polyb. 15.18.3). The Romans insisted on this clause because they were well aware of what elephants were capable of, rather than impressed by their performance at Magnesia. But just as they disregarded the provision restricting recruitment north of the Taurus, so later Seleucids, especially Antiochus Epiphanes, defied the restriction concerning elephants.

Antiochus IV took with him on his Egyptian expedition an undetermined number of elephants (I Macc. 1.17). The 36 or 42 elephants paraded in the procession at Daphne probably represent the total complement at his disposal, at least half of which accompanied him on the eastern expedition (Polyb. 30.25.11; I Macc. 3.34). Some of the rest were mobilized shortly after the king's death for the fighting in Judaea, and, by breaking the Jewish ranks, decided the battle of Beith-Zacharia. Their number varies

according to the sources, I Macc. giving 32 (6.30), II Macc. 22
(13.2), and Josephus, in the Bellum Iudaicum, 80 (1.41). In view
of the rather modest numbers of elephants cited in the two Books
of the Maccabees, in comparison with the highly exaggerated
numbers of Seleucid infantry and cavalry they attribute to the
same battle, it is surprising that Josephus, whose figures in
Bellum for Beith-Zacharia sound quite reasonable, and who used a
well-informed source (see pp.14,176), fails to quote an
acceptable number of elephants. I would suggest this was the
result of the corruption to $\Pi(80)$ of a source which read $H(8)$,[93]
a number which accords with the Seleucid disposition along with
the condition of the terrain and the tactical requirements (see
p.181 below), and, since it is about one quarter of the Seleucid
elephant force at Daphne, could reasonably be considered for the
undertaking in Judaea.

Lysias' second expedition to Judaea in 162 B.C. was the last
appearance of the Seleucid elephants. Soon afterwards Gnaius
Octavius, the Roman emissary, slaughtered the entire herd at
Apamea (App. Syr. 46(239-40); Polyb. 31.2.9-11). The stock was
not renewed because of Roman involvement in the internal crisis in
Syria, or possibly also as a result of the enormous transportation
difficulties imposed by the Parthian expansion westwards. The
sporadic allusions to elephants which occur thenceforward are
insignificant: II Macc. is certainly unreliable in attributing
elephants to Nicanor in the second round of his campaign against
Judas Maccabaeus (15.20). This battle occurred in March 161 B.C.,
not long after the slaughter of the elephants at Apamea (see p.268
n.2 below), and the version in II Macc. as a whole is rather
fantastic in comparison with the realistic narrative of I Macc.
which does not mention elephants at all (7.39-47). Later,
Ptolemy VI's horse is said to have been alarmed at the sound of an
elephant in the battle against Alexander Balas (Jos. Ant. 13.117),[94]
which indicates that elephants were not actually seen on the
battlefield. Tryphon used elephants possibly to storm the
fortifications of Antioch (I Macc. 11.56),[95] but for this purpose
a few elephants would have sufficed. The appearance of elephants
on the coins of the last Seleucids should be disregarded: the
elephant became a common emblem on Seleucid coinage, and even

figures on the coins of Seleucus II,[96] although the circumstances of his accession and events in the upper satrapies during his reign make it very unlikely that he possessed a herd of elephants.

Like the tanks of World War II,[97] the elephants were surrounded by light troops defending their vulnerable flanks. Appian, in his version of Thermopylae, indicates that there were a standard number of soldiers in the elephant Guard (18(83) - 'the unit (stiphos) that always accompanied them').[98] Its strength at Gaza suggests that the number stood around fifty (Diod. 19.82.3). This impression is supported by the composition of Seleucus I's army at Ipsus. Considering the small number of heavy troops at his disposal,[99] the necessity of leaving a heavy force in Babylonia to protect his power base from a repetition of the Antigonid surprise attack of 312 B.C. (Diod. 19.100.5-7; Plut. Demetr. 7.2),[100] and, moreover, the expected superior phalanx strength of his allies, especially Lysimachus, the 20,000 strong infantry of Seleucus may have included only light Asiatic troops and could thus allocate 50 fighters to each of the 400 elephants. 2,500 Cretan archers and neo-Cretans were attached to 60 elephants in the Seleucid right wing at Raphia (Polyb. 79.10, 82.8-10), which works out to about 40 men per elephant. The remaining 42 elephants on the left (79.13, 82.8,13) seem to have been left without flank guard (82.13), like the elephants of the enemy in the opposing wing (82.5-7), because Antiochus III, as well as Ptolemy IV (see 65.7), was short of manpower suitable for this purpose, and fewer than 40 troops per elephant was probably regarded as completely useless. An undefined number of bowmen and slingers are reported by Polybius to have been posted in the spaces between the elephants at Panion (16.18.7). At Magnesia a number of elephants are said to have alternated with the battalions of the phalanx in the line, but these, as well as the other elephants deployed on the flanks (Livy 37.40.3-4,6,14), seem to have been guarded by light troops. The huge discrepancy between the total number of troops and the detailed list of the various contingents allows for the addition of about 3,000 troops, 50 to each of the 54 elephants, over and above some other unlisted contingents whose participation in the battle seems more than likely (see p. 8 above). The disposition at Beith-Zacharia was presumably different: every elephant was surrounded by a massive guard of 1,000 heavy infantry and 500 cavalry (I Macc. 6.35). The vivid description of Eleazar's heroic onslaught on the leading elephant shows him breaking through the lines of the phalanx in order to reach the elephant itself (ibid. 45-6). The narrow field and the considerable number of Jewish light troops in this battle were the reason for this tactical change (see p.181 below).

The use of scythed chariots in the Seleucid army has a shorter history. The Seleucids, unlike the other Hellenistic kingdoms, could not resist the temptation to use this traditional oriental weapon, despite its repeated failures.[101] Only the disaster inflicted on the whole force at Magnesia by the retreat of the chariots persuaded the Seleucids to withdraw them for good.

As early as Ipsus, Seleucus had at his disposal 120 chariots (Diod. 20.113.4; Plut. Demetr. 28.3), and one can assume that they were left over from the Persian 'inheritance'. The sources are elliptical and fragmentary, and the performance of the chariots on the battlefield is not recorded; but despite the broad, flat terrain of the battle area, I incline to think that they were recognized as useless and did not figure in the battle. On another occasion, Seleucus launched a chariot attack without success in one of the preliminary skirmishes with Demetrius in Cilicia (Plut. Demetr. 48.2). The scythed chariots are not heard of again in the royal army until Magnesia. Molon drew up chariots, probably in insignificant numbers, against Antiochus III, but their effect was 'neutralized' by the elephants in the opposing royal army (Polyb. 5.53.10). At Magnesia, an unspecified number of chariots were deployed in front of the left flank. Their responsibility for the collapse of this flank and, consequently, of the whole line (Livy 37.41.6-42, esp. 42.1), brought to a close the unhappy story of scythed chariots in the Seleucid army.

Some references of rather doubtful reliability in Jewish sources attribute scythed chariots to Antiochus IV's army. Chariots are mentioned by I Macc. in a brief reference to Antiochus' Egyptian expedition (1.17),[102] but the sandy terrain of Egypt's western frontier did not favour armaments of this kind. Although II Macc. lists chariots in his version of Lysias' second expedition (13.2), their omission from the more reliable I Macc. and Josephus' *Bellum* make the participation of chariots most unlikely. The mountainous route chosen by Lysias, the scarcity in the Judaean plateau of flat, even plains of sufficient length to allow them to gather speed, and the light character of the Jewish armament, all confirm this impression.[103] The 140 chariots paraded at Daphne did not have any military significance and were probably kept only for ceremonial occasions: scythes are not mentioned despite the detailed description of all the participants, and a number of the chariots were drawn by six horses, others by four, and one even by 4 elephants (Polyb. 30.25.11). One may recall the chariots of Ptolemy II Philadelphus in his celebrated procession, which were drawn by curious animals and driven by children disguised as warriors (Athen. 5.200f).[104]

4: THE COMMAND - KING, STRATĒGOI AND OTHER OFFICERS

As might be expected in the case of an army for which relatively little documentary evidence survives, it is possible to reconstruct the Seleucid military hierarchy only in its upper ranks, going no lower than the commanders of the independent contingents. Nothing apart from their ranks (which presumably were equivalent to those used in other Hellenistic armies) is known about officers of lower grades; no data are available on their identity, descent, nationality, and system of promotion. This is in contrast to the relatively abundant information on the Ptolemaic army supplied by Ptolemaic documents. Nevertheless, the little we do know about the cadre of the high-ranking commanders may contribute to our understanding of the reasons for the superiority of the Seleucid military organization over the Ptolemaic system.

The supreme command in the main campaigns was usually held by the king himself: Seleucus I at Ipsus, Cyrrhestica, and Curupedion; Antiochus I against the Galatians; Antiochus III against Molon, in the Fourth Syrian War (Seleucia, Porphyrion, Rabatamana, Raphia), against Achaeus (Sardis), in the expedition to the upper satrapies, in the Fifth Syrian War (Gaza, Panion), and in the Roman war (Thermopylae and Magnesia); Antiochus IV in his expeditions to Egypt and to the east; Demetrius I against Alexander Balas and Antiochus VII Sidetes in his campaign against the Parthians.[1] In exceptional cases, when the terrain prevented him from fighting among his cavalry Guard, we find the king content to direct operations from behind the front line, or on its periphery, as at Porphyrion, Seleucia, Rabatamana, Sardis, and the Elburz. Occasionally he supervised one of the flanks, usually the traditionally more prestigious right,[2] as in the battle against Molon, at Raphia, Thermopylae, and Magnesia, but more often took personal command of the storm troops, mainly cavalry, as at Cyrrhestica, Raphia, Bactria, and Magnesia. Although by actively

Organization

participating in the battle the kings were unable to keep an eye
on the tactical developments and often virtually lost control over
their various contingents (a fact which led to the disasters of
Raphia and Magnesia), their direct involvement in the actual
fighting certainly boosted the morale of the troops and reinforced
the settler-soldiers' sense of identification with the crown. In
contrast to the notorious effeminate reputation of some of the
Ptolemaic monarchs[3] who only rarely led their troops personally,
the personal example set by the Seleucid kings was of inestimable
value, although of course the Seleucids were only following the
lead of all Greek and nearly all Macedonian commanders in acting
in this way.

The king was occasionally replaced as the supreme commander
of the army or of expeditionary forces by various other
functionaries: the viceroy and regent, Lysias, in the two
expeditions to Judaea; the crown prince, Seleucus, in the siege of
Pergamon, 191 B.C.; Achaeus, Seleucus II's uncle, and his son
Andromachus against Antiochus Hierax; provincial governors like
Bacchides in Judaea; and even professional soldiers like Xenoitas
the Achaean, Xenon, and Theodotos Hemiolios in the campaign against
Molon.[4]

The question of the terminology of the supreme command has
been discussed by several scholars. Otto and Bengtson have
suggested that the 'chief secretary of the forces' (ἀρχιγραμτεὺς
τῶν δυναμέων) was the chief of staff,[5] but, from the evidence
provided by this post in Alexander's and the Ptolemaic army, he
seems rather to have been a general administrator, probably the
officer in charge of finance, concerned above all with pay, etc.[6]
And indeed if the situation had been otherwise, the appointment of
Tychon, the former 'chief secretary', as the satrap of 'the
province of the Red Sea' (Polyb. 5.54.12), would have been a
considerable demotion. Even more decisive is the evidence
provided by a recently discovered inscription implying that the
governor of Coilē-Syria at the time of Antiochus VII's great
expedition to the east was formerly the 'chief secretary of the
forces'.[7] This seems to indicate that once the army was on its
way, the secretary's duties as the officer in charge of finance
and personnel were finished. Significantly enough, this chief

secretary was no higher at the court hierarchy than 'the first friends', which further argues against Otto-Bengtson's suggestion.

Bengtson went on to suggest that Seleucid commanders who were in independent charge of expeditions were officially called στρατηγοὶ τοῦ βασιλέως to distinguish them from the ordinary stratēgoi.[8] But this phrase is mentioned only in connection with the revolt of Molon and the Cyrrhesteans by Polybius (5.42.5, 45.2, 50.8), who obviously uses it first as a literary variant for the names of the king's two generals sent against Molon, Xenon, and Theodotus (42.5, 43.7), and who writes 'one of the king's generals' later because he does not know which general dealt with the Cyrrhesteans, or perhaps also in order to designate the loyal commanders as opposed to the rebels. In the same way stratēgos autokratōr, applied to Xenoitas (id. 5.45.6), does not represent official terminology in the sense of denoting a special category of stratēgos. The title occurs nowhere else in a Seleucid context, and in this context it means quite clearly that the two generals Xenon and Theodotus, already in the field, were to be subordinate to Xenoitas on his arrival.[9] In a probably authentic, official document inserted into II Macc., Antiochus IV calls himself 'king and stratēgos' in a letter sent to the Jews while on his eastern expedition (9.19),[10] and we may assume that the supreme commander was known simply as 'stratēgos', although the same rank designated other officials also (see below).

The names of the commanders of the separate contingents are listed in Polybius' account of Raphia, but occur only incidentally in the scattered references to other campaigns. Apart from local sheikhs and dynasts, like Zabdiel the Arab and Aspasianus the Mede at Raphia (Polyb. 5.79.7,8,11) and John Hyrcanus in Antiochus VII's expedition (Jos. Ant. 13.251), who commanded their own national contingents, the cadre of the Seleucid high command included, in addition to members of the royal family who were usually in charge of the flanks,[11] generals of various nationalities, mainly Greeks, and high ranking Macedonians. The first may in theory have been Greeks who had settled in Asia and preserved their Greek nationality in the same way as the Greek cleruchs in Egypt, but the defection of a number of them from the Egyptian army during the Fourth

Syrian War suggests that at least some were experienced
professional officers from the Greek world who served various
masters. The former Ptolemaic officers, who immediately took up
senior positions in the Seleucid army, were Theodotus and
Nicolaus the Aetolians, Lagoras the Cretan, Hippolochus the
Thessalian, and Ptolemy, son of Menestheus.[12] Other prominent
figures among the mercenaries were Xenoitas the Achaean, who led
the second campaign against Molon, Menedamus of Alabanda and
Lysimachus the Galatian at Raphia, Nicomedes of Cos and the
nauarch Polyxenides of Rhodes in the anabasis of Antiochus III.[13]
While the Ptolemaic high command seems to have been almost
entirely dependent on such mercenary generals (e.g. Polyb. 5.63-
64.5),[14] a substantial number of Seleucid commanders may be
assumed to have been Macedonians drawn from the small circle of
the top Macedonian nobility in the court (e.g. *ibid*. 82.8,13),
and at least some of them may have been promoted on merit from
among the rank and file of the sons of the Macedonian military
settlers serving in the Guard. Some commanders are definitely
known to have been Macedonians: Lysias and his descendants who
served the Seleucids for some generations, Byttacus at Raphia,
Zeuxis against Molon and at Magnesia, Menippus in Antiochus III's
expedition to Greece, Andronicus at Ephesus in 190 B.C., and
Tryphon, a military settler from Seleucis, who served under
Alexander Balas and Demetrius II before acceding himself to the
throne.[15] Polybius' failure to specify the nationality of
several other commanders, which is not his common practice when
referring to mercenaries, may suggest that they were 'locals',
i.e. Macedonians who were brought up in the Seleucid Empire, such
as Xenon against Molon, Diocles at Porphyrion, Nicarchus and
Theodotus Hemiolios at Porphyrion, Philadelphia, and Raphia,
Hermogenes and Diognetus at Seleucia, Ardys against Molon, at
Seleucia and near Sardis in 197 B.C.,[16] Themison and Eurylochus
at Raphia, Diogenes in the Elburz range, Mendis and Philip 'the
elephantarch' at Magnesia.[17] The absence of an organization
similar to the Seleucid <u>argyraspides</u> in the Ptolemaic army
prevented the emergence of an 'internal' cadre of experienced
military men, and led to absolute Ptolemaic dependence on
unreliable high-ranking officers who hired out their swords to

the highest bidder.

There is some reason to believe that the service of mercenary commanders in the Seleucid army was not the normal state of affairs, and that the relatively large number of these commanders recorded by the sources is simply due to the fact that the coverage of the first period of Antiochus III's reign is better preserved. The number of mercenary officers may have been increased by the time of the Fourth Syrian War because of the influx of Ptolemaic deserters who were well acquainted with the Palestinean arena and their former host army. Further reasons for the increase were that confidence in the military settlers had been considerably shaken by their participation in Molon's revolt and the concurrent rebellion in Cyrrhestica, and that, at the beginning of the Fourth Syrian War at least, when the unpopular Hermeias was dominant at the Court, the Macedonian nobility was opposed to him and could not therefore be trusted in military undertakings.[18] The Macedonians seem to have resumed their former position in the campaigns of the first decade of the second century B.C., and to have retained it through the stormy days of Antiochus Epiphanes. Macedonian resentment of Demetrius II was perhaps due to the introduction of mercenaries to commanding positions no less than to his dissolution of the Macedonian Guard.

As in the similar structure of Alexander's army, the commanders of the independent contingents seem to have been subordinated directly to the king or to the supreme commander. Although there were no official titles to distinguish among the senior commanders, there was undoubtedly a certain hierarchy among them which determined their appointment to the various contingents. Bickerman and Bengtson's conclusion that there was no cursus honorum among the Seleucid senior officers, and that they were selected at random by the kings,[19] is impractical and unprecedented. The evidence produced by Bickerman to illustrate the circulation of commanders from highly important contingents to smaller and secondary units and vice versa does not stand up to critical examination: though it is true that Hippolochus the Thessalian had only 400 cavalry with him when he defected, his sharing the command of 5,000 infantry a short time later is not necessarily a very sudden promotion: we cannot tell if the 400

cavalry represented the total force under his command in the
Ptolemaic army, or whether his contribution to the command of the
troops was not in fact the command of the same number of cavalry,
this information being omitted from Polybius' rather compressed
text (5.70.11, 71.11, 79.9). In any case, 400 horse is the
tactical equivalent of 5,000 infantry. Theodotus the Aetolian,
the former Ptolemaic <u>stratēgos</u> of Coilē-Syria, was certainly not
being demoted when he was entrusted at Raphia with the command of
10,000 <u>argyraspides</u> (<u>id</u>. 5.40.1, 79.4), the cream of the Seleucid
army. Lagoras the Cretan, who led the picked troops, among them
Theodotus himself and other senior officers, in the courageous
assault on Sardis (<u>id</u>. 7.16.2), was not replacing Theodotus, as
Bickerman thinks. The stratagem had been devised by Lagoras
(<u>ibid</u>. 15.2ff), and the task was therefore entrusted to him.
Polyxenides the Rhodian, Antiochus III's experienced admiral, had
only 2,000 Cretans in his command in the Elburz (<u>id</u>. 10.29.6),
but in view of the crucial role as 'bait' (see p.144 below), a
senior officer of his rank would certainly have been needed to
conduct them on their dangerous adventure. Antipater, Antiochus
III's nephew, was in command of the right wing at Raphia, which
numbered 4,000 horse (<u>id</u>. 5.79.12), while Polybius in his
questions on Zeno's version of Panion mentions 'the Tarantines
with Antipater' (16.18.7), a contingent which usually numbered
only a few hundred, but at Magnesia he was reinstated in the
command of the much larger flank (Livy 37.41.1). His position at
Panion need not be interpreted as a setback in his career: it
may well be that Antipater was in charge of the <u>promachoi</u> that
comprised the Tarantines, the light infantry, and the elephants
deployed between them. The Tarantines were designated as 'those
with Antipater', either because he was personally fighting amongst
them, or because he was the permanent commander of that unit even
in peace time (see below on the standing army in peacetime). The
transfer from command of 4,000 cavalry to about 100 elephants and
their light guard is by no means a demotion. On the contrary,
Antipater was clearly promoted during the seventeen years between
Raphia and Panion. Similarly in modern armies a 'mobile-infantry'
regimental commander has at his disposal many more soldiers than
a commander of a tank regiment, though both are of similar

standing. The importance of the elephant command is well
illustrated by the case of Philip 'the elephantarch', who
actually commanded the phalanx at Magnesia (Livy ibid.; App. Syr.
33(170)), probably because the elephants were scattered in the
centre and the flanks. It may look at first sight as if Nicanor
'the elephantarch', who was appointed provincial governor in
Judaea in 163-162 B.C. (II Macc. 14.12),[20] was actually demoted,
but it must be borne in mind that all the Seleucid elephants had
been slaughtered some months earlier by the Romans, and that the
Seleucids had become obsessed with the Jewish problem and may
have tried to find a radical solution by appointing an experienced
and high-ranking soldier as a governor.

It appears, then, that although there was a certain hierarchy
among the senior officers, and commanders were not promoted or
demoted overnight, there was a considerable shifting of personnel
between command of the various contingents and other military
duties. In addition to the examples mentioned above, the most
outstanding is the case of Nicarchus, who served on the same
expedition alternately as combat commander of the light troops that
occupied the Beirut Pass, and as 'camp commander' of the heavy
infantry that were later left behind (Polyb. 5.68.9,11). The
principle behind these appointments can be detected by a comparison
with the practice of 'emergency appointment' common in modern
armies based mainly on reserve forces. In peacetime the Seleucid
senior officers were employed in staff duties, command of the
Guard, and the standing army, and as provincial civil and military
governors charged with the supervision of local reserve forces,
Guard units, and mercenaries in garrisons. In wartime, when the
size of the army was doubled and trebled by the addition of military
settlers, mercenaries and auxiliaries, the commanders were assigned
much larger contingents, but as has already been stated, the
hierarchy was more or less observed, and a commander's emergency
appointment was roughly equivalent to his ordinary rank.

The data on the senior commanders do not offer much help in
determining their official ranks. Only three terms occur more than
once in the sources: stratēgos, hegemōn, and hipparchos.
Bickerman expressed the view that stratēgos designated every
officer in command of a tactically independent unit (probably a

Organization

'contingent'), while hegemōn and hipparchos designate every other infantry or cavalry officer in the military hierarchy as in Alexander's army.[21] But we can perhaps be somewhat more precise and distinguish, at least tentatively, three variations on the three terms: the 'general' military usage applied to senior commanders and junior officers, the more specific military usage designating the official ranks of certain officers, and in the terminology of the provincial administration - the officials in charge of local forces and garrisons.

The first application of the term is common especially in dedications, ceremonial language, speeches, etc. The king addresses the army, or the army introduces itself, as 'the stratēgoi, hipparchoi, hegemones and soldiers', namely: senior commanders, officers (cavalry and infantry), and rank and file soldiers. The same phrase is commonly applied also in other Hellenistic armies.[22] The Seleucid army, or certain of its units, is presented in this way in a dedication of the military settlers at Thyateira (only hegemones and soldiers), in a letter of Antiochus III to the army concerning the immunity of the local sanctuary at Amyzon, and in the Gurob papyrus, which recounts the reception of the Egyptian invaders in Seleucia and Antioch.[23] Since Thyateira like other military settlements in Asia Minor could not have provided more than a few dozen soldiers (p.43 above), the term hegemōn seems to have been applied even to the lowest ranks of command down to the commander of the file.

The second more specific usage applied the term stratēgos to the commander of a stratēgia, hegemōn to the chiliarchos, and hipparchos to the commander of a hipparchia. Among stratēgoi indicated by Bengtson as commanders of stratēgia, only Tryphon was in the position to have served as a commander of a stratēgia under Demetrius II (Jos. Ant. 13.131). The term hegemōn was applied in the Antigonid and perhaps also in the Ptolemaic army to the chiliarchos, the commander of a 1,000-men strong infantry battalion.[24] The only probable usage of the term in this sense in the Seleucid army refers to Amaktion, the hegemōn of the basilikē ilē at Ancyra known to be 1,000-horse strong (Polyaenus 4.9.6). Being in charge of an independent unit, he would have been called stratēgos had the 'general' terminology been applied. For similar

reasons it seems that the term hipparchos, applied according to
Antisthenes to Bouplagos, Antiochus III's cavalry commander at
Thermopylae (FGrH 257.f.36 p.1174) actually meant that he
commanded a hipparchia, which numbered usually 512 horse, perhaps
the 500 Seleucid cavalry which took part in the battle of
Thermopylae (Livy 36.15.4).

In the provincial administration stratēgos, at least in the
time of Antiochus III, designated the satrap, and perhaps even
governors of lower rank like the hyparchos and meridarchēs who
were in charge of the local reserve troops and the garrisons.[25]
The word hegemōn was perhaps applied in this context to commanders
of citadels and garrisons as in Ptolemaic Egypt (e.g. PCZ 59004)
and possibly also in Antigonid Macedon.[26] The Susa dedication by
'Leon, the hegemones under him, and the troops', dating from the
time of Seleucus III (SEG VII.4), can be construed as follows:
Leon was probably the satrap of Susiana, residing at Susa,[27] and
the hegemones under him may well have been the commanders of the
various citadels in the province, and not necessarily the junior
officers in the citadel of Susa as usually presumed. The same may
perhaps apply to the hegemones listed with the satraps in the
Gurob papyrus (Holleaux III.288 ℓℓ.20-1), although admittedly in
both cases these officers may have been called hegemones not in
their capacity as commanders of citadels, but as low-ranking
officers.

5: TRAINING AND DISCIPLINE

A high standard of training and discipline was a prerequisite for the tactical success of the military organization just described, but we can glean information about it from only a few scattered sources, which refer only to certain aspects. They can scarcely be said to paint a vivid picture, so that one has to be content with a general impression, keeping in mind that some references may apply only to a certain campaign and commander and may not be indicative of general practice.

In contrast to the Roman and, to a lesser degree, the Classical Greek armies about whose weapons and tactical training comprehensive accounts survive,[1] Seleucid training practice, as well as that of other Hellenistic armies, is entirely obscure. Passing over various references to the pre-military functions of the gymnasiums,[2] which ought not to be overestimated, all the information we have is that weapon and warfare instructors served in the military training school at Apamea (Strabo 16.2.10(752)). In view of the presumable organization of the Guard, it may be concluded that new recruits to the Guard, i.e. the sons of the military settlers, received their initial training there, which means in effect that all military settlers were trained at Apamea at one time or another. I do not imagine that there was a similar military school in the eastern part of the Empire, despite the administrative division of the Seleucid realm into two separate parts and despite the enormous distances recruits from Media had to cover on the way to Apamea. The basic motive for the organization of the Guard seems to have been to produce a relationship of dependence and identification between the dynasty and the potential soldiers, which would not have been effectively achieved in an alternative military centre somewhere in Media. The refusal of Achaeus' soldiers to march against their legitimate king, and the affection alleged to be demonstrated by Molon's soldiers toward the king of

Antioch (Polyb. 5.54.1-2, 57.6), however exaggerated and irrelevant to the actual outcome of the battle (p.121), suggest that they passed some time of their military service in close contact with the Court.

The principles of basic training probably did not differ from those practised in the armies of Philip and Alexander. One aspect of the training in Philip's time is illumined by Polyaenus, who refers to frequent route marches in panoply, including rations and other gear, for a distance of 300 stadia (4.2.10).[3] This practice, which is not found in the training programme of the Classical armies but became so prominent in the Roman army, introduced an entirely new conception of what distances an army could cover in a forced march,[4] and was probably adopted by the Seleucids also. Unfortunately, all the relevant information we have is Polybius' brief account of the forced march in Bactria (10.49.4), but the impression is reinforced by the five days' march of the huge Ptolemaic army under the scorching sun of the Sinai desert from Pelusium to Raphia (id. 5.80.1-3), which works out at 36 km a day.

Two pieces of information do at first sight point to considerable negligence in the conduct and operation of winter quarters. On the eve of Raphia, Antiochus III, expecting the negotiations with the Ptolemaic emissaries to be successful, 'dismissed the forces (δυνάμεις) to their winter quarters and henceforward neglected to exercise the ochloi' (Polyb. 5.66.6). But in fact the term ochloi, if it is not used here for stylistic variety (would not stratiōtes have been better for this purpose?), could refer to the military settlers (cf. id. 5.43.5) of northern Syria, the hard core of the reserve troops, whom one would expect to have stayed in their nearby homes as long as the promising negotiations proceeded, but the Guard, the settlers of the eastern provinces, and the mercenaries, who were living in winter quarters, were not necessarily left idle. Better known is the notorious conduct of Antiochus III in Euboea in winter 192-191 B.C. (id. 20.8; Livy 36.11: Diod. 29.2; Athen. 10.739 e-f). Much was said by ancient authors about the old man who was carried away by his passion for the young girl, Euboea, and let his army deteriorate in a life of luxury and degeneration which eventually brought about the calamity of Thermopylae. But it was proved long ago, mainly on chronological grounds, that these traditions reflect anti-Seleucid propaganda and have no historical foundations.[5] On the other hand, Appian's comment on the caution displayed by the legions in approaching the phalanx at Magnesia 'fearing the experience ... of the trained men' (Syr. 35(182)) is obviously his own and not Polybius', and consequently must not be taken to imply a high standard of training: as has already been indicated, Appian consistently presents the Seleucid phalanx and infantry Guard as the true successors of Alexander's celebrated contingents (cf. p.237 n.56 below).

To turn from training to discipline, there can be no doubt that the Hellenistic practice could not match the celebrated rigorous standards of the Romans, as Polybius seems to indicate here and there (e.g. 6.42; 10.16-17.1). Then as now, stern discipline by itself does not guarantee a high standard of military performance and may in fact suppress any positive initiative on the part of the individual, whereas liberal methods basing their appeal on enthusiasm and ideals[6] may produce better results provided they do not deteriorate into anarchy. But this general rule does not apply to every military formation, and the Seleucid settlers, who were motivated by their long established loyalty to the dynasty and by their attachment to the settlements, fought in the phalanx, a formation in which blind obedience was all important, while other troops - mercenaries, allies, vassals, and subjects - arrayed in formations that required them to exercise initiative, lacked any real motivation to do so. The best examples of the lack of discipline among the phalangites is their collapse at Thermopylae when they saw that Cato had occupied the camp in their rear (Livy 36.19.3; App. Syr. 19(86-7)), and the precipitate flight of the military settlers at Raphia in panic at the prospect of being outflanked by the cavalry (Polyb. 5.85.10). But it must be stressed that despite some other reference to occurrences of this kind (see below), the liberal approach to discipline in the Seleucid armies did not acquire the dimensions of complete anarchy.

Discipline means, basically, compliance with instructions, and its effects can be traced in standard of maintenance (weapon, armour, supplies, etc.), alertness, vigilance (especially at night), resistance in battle, etc. The fragments of Macedonian military codes of the time of Philip V discovered at Amphipolis and Chalcis refer to just three aspects of discipline: the first code imposes fines for failing to wear certain items of armour and for negligence on sentry duty, and the second deals with the proper maintenance of stores by officials of fairly high rank.[7] The first code, which refers to rank and file soldiers, makes no reference to the corporal punishment which was so common in the Roman punitive system. One has only to consider the severe Roman 'fustuarium' for soldiers who fell asleep on watch or did not properly perform the ephodos mentioned also in the code of Amphipolis[8] to appreciate the liberal and lenient attitude of Hellenistic military law. Moreover, it has been suggested that even these mild measures were introduced by Philip V only after Cynoscephalae, in an attempt to tighten discipline after the Roman model.[9] The above-mentioned reference to the ephodos and the regulations about plunder, which seem to have been quite an innovation in the Greek world (Polyb. 10.16,17.1ff.), support this possibility. But despite the Roman influence Philip V could not depart too far from custom with regard to the punishment itself. There is a general probability that these value standards of conduct and punishment are not likely to have differed greatly between Antioch or Doura and Amphipolis or Pella.

The standard of discipline of the Seleucid army as deduced from some casual references seems to have been more or less in line with the Antigonid code. There are just two fragments, one from the beginning and one from the waning years of the Seleucid kingdom, that indicate a possible practice of wearing arms at all times: Seleucus I, with the intention of surprising Demetrius' army at early dawn, ordered his troops to be fully armed at supper and to sleep in military formation (Polyaenus 4.9.1). It is indeed arguable that these measures were taken in the face of special circumstances, but, being much more difficult to perform at night, they would hardly have succeeded unless they were already part of day-time discipline. Two hundred years later, Heracleon of Beroea, who was in the service of Antiochus Grypus (125-96 B.C.), trained his soldiers to dine in silence sitting on the ground in groups of 1,000, eating simple, coarse food, served by <u>doryphoroi</u> (Athen. 12.54(540)). We shall refer later to other aspects of this second fragment, with regard to the standard of alertness, for although this is not mentioned, soldiers who were served by <u>doryphoroi</u> and kept in their original chiliarchy formation certainly had their equipment at their side. No light is thrown on the Seleucid code during the long period between the founder of the dynasty and Antiochus Gryphus. It cannot be the case that this rigorous standard, if it was ever adopted as permanent practice, was retained during the years of deterioration and turmoil which followed the death of Antiochus Epiphanes. It may, in any case, have been practised only by the Guard, who were easier to control. Likewise the code of Amphipolis refers only to the Guard.[10]

A casual reading of two episodes in the reign of Antiochus III conveys the impression that the royal army suffered from a poor standard of alertness. When Molon withdrew from his camp by night, Xenoitas ordered the troops to be ready for the pursuit next morning, but instead of obeying his order they looted the abandoned camp and got drunk, so that Molon was easily able to surprise the sleeping camp at dawn (Polyb. 5.45-6). But although Molon's stratagem obviously worked, and the Seleucids may not have had strict rules about plunder, the description of the unfortunate commander trying in vain to awaken the drunken soldiers and finally dashing madly into the ranks of the enemy is probably exaggerated. Molon may well have anticipated Xenoitas' readiness to pursue by only a very short time. We must bear in mind that this account, as well as the whole tradition of Molon's revolt, was derived, as has been commonly recognized, from an 'anti-Hermeian' source (see esp. 42.6, 50),[11] and it could be suggested that the 'colouring' of this episode is actually directed against Hermeias on whose advice and at whose instigation Xenoitas had been sent to subdue the revolt, in the face of contrary advice from his rivals and in spite of the king's wish to lead his own troops against Molon. The hostile character of the source is also detectable in the comments on Xenoitas' personality (45.5-6, 46.6, 47.3), and the whole account of this incident may be designed to illustrate his inability to control and lead the troops. The second episode occurred during the siege of Pergamon, conducted by

Seleucus, son of Antiochus III, on the eve of Magnesia. The besiegers, apart from a small guard, were passing their time in enjoying themselves, although encamped in face of the enemy. Some had fallen asleep, and a substantial number of the horses had been pastured unharnessed. Taking advantage of this situation, Diophanes the Achaean made a surprise attack and succeeded in driving off the besiegers (Livy 37.20; App. Syr. 26(125-6)). But, in any case, this episode must not be taken as indicative of the standard and attitude of the army as a whole: the detachment sent to Pergamon consisted mainly of the notoriously undisciplined Galatians[12] in addition to 600 'mixed' cavalry (Livy 37.18.7 in comparison to 20.7), perhaps orientals (cf. id. 37.40.11 and see p. 51 above).

This holiday atmosphere indeed prevailed also in the grotesque appearance of the Apameans in their conflict with neighbouring Larissa in about 142 B.C., described in a fragment by Poseidonius of Apamea. Their daggers and lances were covered with rust and dirt, they wore hats with brims, carried horns full of wine and plenty of food, and were even accompanied by flutes and pipes (Athen. 4.176b). But since it was only shortly afterwards that the Apamean citizens, probably epigonoi of military settlers, played a major role in overthrowing the despotic regime of the Cretan mercenaries (Strabo 16.2.10(752)), and the city was the military centre of the Empire, it is extremely unlikely that their discipline and military standard had degenerated to such an extent. Poseidonius, who as a Stoic despised greed and luxury,[13] deliberately depicts his compatriots in grotesque terms as a part of a general historical method stressing the decline of the degenerate Hellenistic world compared with the rise of vigorous Rome.[14] The element of satire is evident from the description of the weapons, which stands in marked contrast to the tendency of the Hellenistic armies to overindulge in burnishing and polishing their arms and armour.[15] Generally speaking, Poseidonius often departs from the truth when criticizing persons as well as facts, and his accounts are replete with gross exaggerations.[16] Nevertheless the kernel of truth in this curious account may perhaps lie in an attempt of the Apameans to demonstrate their contempt and superiority over their neighbours.

For information about the night watch we have primarily Polyaenus' 'stratagem' referring to the eve of the battle at Cyrrhos. The capture of the Aetolian defectors by the Seleucid prophylakē, and the immediate state of alert of the camp (4.9.2), indicates that like any other well-conducted army the Seleucids took precautions to prevent night raids, and the same may be implied by the cavalry's patrolling the Seleucid camp at Ammaus in Judaea at dawn (I Macc. 4.7).

Another subject closely connected with discipline is the conditions of service. Roman commanders like Scipio and Corbulo tried to make conditions as rough as possible in order to toughen the soldiers for future action and possible hardships. Their policy was to have the soldiers eat meals off coarse pottery, sleep on the bare ground, wear light clothing even in severe weather, and they banned all traders from the near vicinity as well. Although Scipio and Corbulo took an extreme line, they reflected the prevailing tendency in the Roman army, for instance in denying the soldiers the right to legitimate marriage, a measure aimed at facilitating the mobility of the troops.[17] But life in Hellenistic armies was conducted quite differently: even Alexander's army was followed by women, children, and merchants,[18] and it is unlikely that the troops maintained the strict and tough conditions so well pictured in the celebrated episode in Polyaenus, where Philip II demoted Dokimos the Tarentine for bathing in hot water (4.2.1).[19]

The Seleucid army, like the armies of the first Successors, reached quite a low standard.[20] The camp was accompanied by hordes of civilians, merchants, wives, concubines, children, craftsmen, cooks, bakers, butlers, shield-bearers, etc. (Polyaenus 8.61; Athen. 13.593e; I Macc. 3.41; Justin 38.10). Their reported number in Antiochus VII's expedition to the east (Justin 38.10) is certainly wildly exaggerated (cf. p. 11 above), but several thousands should not be regarded as an overestimation. Gold and silver tableware was used on this same expedition, as it was probably also at Raphia and Ammaus.[21] All this, coupled with the enormous numbers of cooks and bakers and Justin's comment that the army looked as if it was on the way to a banquet, inclines one to think that Poseidonius' anecdote about the splendid feasts held by

Antiochus VII Sidetes refers to this expedition and not to peacetime (Athen. 12.540b-c).[22] It seems worth remarking that the prevailing tone of Justin's account suggests that it originated, however indirectly, from Poseidonius.[23] If this is the case, one must regard it with a certain scepticism, and make allowance for some exaggeration due to Poseidonius' antipathy to luxury and greed and his historical approach. Heracleon of Beroea, according to the fragment mentioned above, made an attempt to restore some military style, at least as far as dining routine was concerned, and it may be imagined that the same applied to other aspects of service conditions. But this spark of self-restraint and good sense was too late to have any effect on the destiny of the kingdom.

The treasures stored in the camp, and the civilians who followed (the aposkeuē),[24] not only had a bad influence on the soldiers, but became a tactical handicap: strong detachments had to be assigned to their defence, and occupation of the camp by the enemy brought about an immediate collapse in the morale of the troops, as occurred so often in the Hellenistic period and probably happened to the Seleucids at Thermopylae.[25]

We see then that the Seleucid recruiting system, which served them so well in providing a continuous supply of trained manpower, turned out to be an impediment to the maintenance of a modest style of military life: it is indeed not surprising that it proved impossible to maintain conditions of Spartan simplicity for tens of thousands of men, of whom some were settlers enjoying unprecedented economic prosperity, some were auxiliary contingents controlled only nominally by the Seleucids, and some independent allies and mercenaries who were the object of sharp competition between the various monarchies. The general atmosphere must have had an effect on the Guard contingents, too.

Generally speaking, the standard of most aspects of training and discipline in the Seleucid army was, thus, more or less up to the military mark as may be deduced from references to route marches, alertness, night vigilance, etc., despite some episodes which might seem to indicate the contrary. But the absence of a severe punishment system and tough service conditions, which could in itself raise the morale of troops and contribute to the performance of highly motivated soldiers whose task required the exercise of original initiative, sometimes brought about total disaster in the case of the settlers and the attached troops, who were put in the chains of an inflexible formation and lacked any motivation, respectively. The phalanx twice failed to resist the enemy in desperate circumstances, in contrast to the Roman legions who were deterred by the inhuman decimation, and the 'baggage' attracted, at least once, the soldiers' attention from their military duties.

PART II: THE ARMY IN ACTION

6: SELEUCUS I AT IPSUS (301 B.C.)

Seleucus I's intensive military activity after the occupation of Babylonia in 312 B.C., which laid the foundations of the Empire, is recorded only once, and this is in the account of his part in the battle of Ipsus (301 B.C.), which decided the dispute over Alexander's domain between Antigonus and his son Demetrius, who were in favour of unification, and the former generals Lysimachus, Cassander, Seleucus, and Ptolemy, who preferred to see the Empire divided among themselves. Although Seleucus' troops, who actually won the day, comprised only one part of the Allied army, which was mainly based on Lysimachus' infantry and a detachment sent by Cassander, the course of the battle, unique as it was, is reminiscent in its general outline of the tactics of the later Seleucids.

In fact only part of the battle can be reconstructed. The main source, Plutarch in his biography of Demetrius (28-30), focuses his interest, as may be expected, on Demetrius' activity and the tragic fate of Antigonus, paying scant attention to the military manoeuvres.[1] His dramatic treatment of the event and its tragic features indicate that he relied here, as in other biographies, on Duris of Samos, whose emotional and sensational style must be approached with caution.[2] But even if Plutarch had based his account of Ipsus on Hieronymus of Cardia, an eyewitness and experienced soldier whose report was certainly excellent,[3] Plutarch's own lack of understanding of military affairs, his frequent distortion of reliable military authorities,[4] and <u>his tendency to impose his own conception of his hero's character on the facts</u>,[5] must be borne in mind when evaluating his interpretation. Diodorus' version, presumably paraphrasing Hieronymus of Cardia,[6] was lost. The 20th book of Diodorus, which records the events preceding the battle, has been preserved, but of the 21st book, which opened with the narrative of the battle, only a few fragments, abbreviated and paraphrased in Byzantine anthologies

The army in action

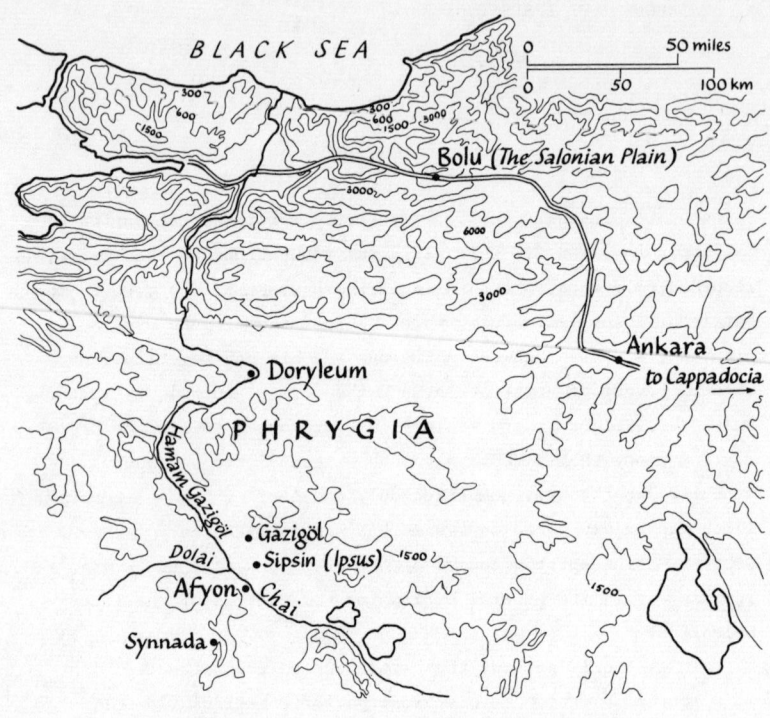

1 The campaign of 301 B.C.

(1-4b), have survived.[7]

The battlefield, the identification of which was disputed for many years, has been conclusively located by Honnigman in the wide plain near the Turkish village of Sipsin (10 km north of Afyon, see Map 1), which has preserved the ancient name.[8] The plain (Dolai Chai) probably served as winter quarters for Antigonus' troops and was not far from Synnada, where he kept his treasure.[9] The route from the Salonian plain (Bolu), Lysimachus' winter quarters and later the assembling place of the Allies (Diod. 20.109.6),[10] to Ipsus followed the riverbeds that cut through western Anatolia. Antigonus did not try to intercept the enemy en route, being presumably aware of Seleucus' superiority in 'lights' and elephants, and preferring to utilize a stratagem to decide the issue on the open field.

Antigonus' force numbered 70,000 infantry, 10,000 cavalry, and 75 elephants (Plut. Demetr. 38.3), while 64,000 infantry, 15,000 cavalry, 400 elephants, and 120 chariots comprised the Allied army (ibid. 28.3), to which Seleucus contributed 20,000 light infantry, most of the cavalry, and all the elephants and chariots (Diod. 20.113).[11]

Only general outlines of the battle order can be sketched. As customary in the battles of the Successors, the infantry in the centre was protected by cavalry on the flanks. Demetrius commanded the largest and strongest division of the cavalry on one flank as a counterpart to Antiochus, the son of Seleucus, on the opposite Allied flank (Plut. Demetr. 29.3).[12] Antigonus could not therefore have been in command on the other flank, but seems to have headed the central phalanx, perhaps on horseback surrounded by the Guard.[13] The elephants are recorded in both sources: according to Plutarch they blocked Demetrius' way back to the battlefield (ibid. 29.3), and an excerpt of Diodorus mentions a bitter struggle between the elephants of Lysimachus and those of Antigonus (21.1-2). Antigonus had only enough elephants for the front lines of the flanks, and must have intended to impede the bulk of the Allies' elephants in the centre by ground-level obstacles, as was done to his son successfully at Gaza (Diod. 19.83.2). The battle between the elephants seems to have occurred on the other flank, and the attribution of the Allies' elephants to Lysimachus suggests that he was in command of this flank. As Antigonus had 73 elephants, presumably at least an equal number of Seleucid elephants were drawn up to confront them, leaving about 300 elephants for the decisive manoeuvre. I very much doubt if the Allies maintained a reserve force of elephants behind the centre under Seleucus' command as Tarn suggests:[14] a second defence line might have betrayed their tactical plan of drawing Demetrius out of the battlefield (see below). Seleucus' force that harassed Antigonus' centre (Plut. *Demetr*. 29.3,5; Diod. 21.4b),[15] probably comprising mounted archers and akontists, may have been originally posted in front of the Allied centre among the elephants and light infantry, as in the case of the Tarentines at Panion (Polyb. 16.18.7). The elephants and their light defenders were therefore under Seleucus' personal command, quite a natural situation in view of their prominent role in the battle and the difficulty of coordination between the troops.[16] Nothing is said about the chariots, and despite the flat arena I incline to think that they were rather superfluous and did not participate in the battle.

The course of the battle is described in two stages: at the beginning Demetrius' cavalry routed Antiochus' flank, presumably circumventing the elephants in front of it and attacking it from the side (cf. Polyb. 5.84.8), and pursued Antiochus' horsemen for a long distance. Meanwhile, the Allies' elephants (certainly those that were kept out of action in the centre) blocked Demetrius' way back to the battlefield (Plut. *Demetr*. 29.3). As the Allies came from the north, it is clear that the pursuit took place along the valley of Hammam Gaziğol. Its width, between 1,000 and 2,000 metres, the low, gently sloping hills (not over fifty m high on either side) and the trails along the lateral gullies meant that a substantial number of elephants was required to effectively block Demetrius' route back. In order not to lose sight of the battlefield, they would have had to be posted at the entrance to the valley of Ipsus near the village of Gaziğöl. But this would have been easy to circumvent by side routes leading into the plain of Ipsus, especially to the east, and certainly would have required not fewer than 300 elephants to stop Demetrius' cavalry. In the second stage of the battle, with Antigonus' phalanx exposed on one flank, Seleucus' mounted archers came into action and without

actually charging it harassed the phalanx from a distance as the
Romans later did to Antiochus III's phalanx at Magnesia. Meanwhile the battle on the other flank seems to have been continuing
without advantage to either side, as Diodorus' fragment about the
elephants implies. The consistent harassment from the rear,
coupled perhaps with frontal attack by the Allied phalanx, broke
the lines of Antigonus' centre, so that his soldiers defected or
fled, and he himself, almost isolated, was killed.

The basic tactics of both sides are a matter of speculation.[17]
Plutarch's comment on Demetrius' pursuit of Antiochus' cavalry
(29.3) may perhaps be taken to imply that Demetrius was too rash;[18]
but in view of what has been said above about the nature of
Plutarch's source and of his own interpretative method, this
implication, expressed in rather vague terms, should not
necessarily be given too much credence, especially as it is well in
line with the usual description of Demetrius as a daring and rash
figure. If Polybius could explain Antiochus III's pursuits at
Raphia and Magnesia as sheer rashness disregarding tactical
considerations (see below), one should not expect too much of
Plutarch. It may indeed be that Antiochus' retreating cavalry had
not been sufficiently disrupted to allow Demetrius to come
confidently back to the battlefield, and allowance has to be made
for the natural difficulty of breaking off a cavalry pursuit, but
the evident tactical inferiority of Antigonus on the battlefield
leads me to think that Demetrius was trying to carry out the
stratagem, so successfully applied on occasion by his father, of
capturing the enemy's 'baggage' (aposkeue - Diod. 18.20.6, 40.8,
19.42.2).[19] In any case, the Allies would have expected this
manoeuvre and could have taken proper precautions by strengthening
and fortifying the camp.[20] Moreover, Lysimachus seems in the past
to have employed severe punitive measures to discourage the troops
from caring too much for their personal belongings.[21] The
prospect of capturing Antigonus' treasure at Synnada would also
have contributed to the troops' determination and their disregard
for their own 'baggage'. The Allies were arranged on the battlefield in a way that made the most of their overwhelming superiority
in elephants and cavalry, but perhaps it is better to follow Tarn
and suggest that Antiochus laid a trap for Demetrius by having a

sham retreat in order to cut off Demetrius' cavalry and expose the
Antigonid flank to Seleucus' light cavalry.[22] I incline to this
view especially since the above mentioned topographical difficulties
of effectively blocking Demetrius' route back and the awkwardness
of moving the mass of elephants in time to take up proper positions
called for careful preparation and planning, which could not have
been improvised on the spot in the heat of the battle. If this
was the case, we may further reckon that the Allies presumed that
their elephants in the centre would be kept out of action by
ground obstacles, and posted them there only to camouflage their
real intentions of moving them in time to block Demetrius' route.
To keep the elephants in reserve would have given away their plan.
The absence of any reference in Plutarch to these suggestions
does not in the least discredit their probability.

7: AGAINST DEMETRIUS AT CYRRHESTICA (285 B.C.)

In the following years Demetrius did not abandon his desire to
unify the Hellenistic world, which had been smashed to pieces at
Ipsus. The second battle of Seleucus I for which we have a
relatively detailed record, the battle of Cyrrhestica in 285 B.C.,
brought this hope and Demetrius' career to an end.

After losing Macedon, which had been his base of power, to
Lysimachus and Pyrrhus in 287 B.C. (Plut. Demetr. 44),[1] Demetrius
escaped to Asia Minor with a small army of mercenaries, determined
to recover his father's Asian Empire. At first he tried to stir
the Ionian cities to rebellion, but the appearance of Agathocles,
son of Lysimachus, compelled him to turn eastwards. His plan was
now to reach Media, then under Seleucus' control, and with the help
of the soldiers settled there by his father reconquer the east.
But the troubles and hardship he met on his flight from Agathocles
and the soldiers' refusal to set off on the long expedition to
Media forced him to try to come to terms with Seleucus and ask him
for a small territory on the northern slopes of the Taurus. After
being turned back, and after some preliminary skirmishes in
Cilicia, Demetrius played his last card. He invaded Syria and
arrived at Cyrrhestica with his small mercenary force (ibid. 46-8;
Polyaenus 4.7.12). Contrary to the accepted assumption - that
this was the desperate action of a wounded beast - Demetrius may
well have been taking a calculated risk, counting on the
disloyalty of the Macedonian settlers of Cyrrhestica, who are
known to have revolted during the First Syrian War as Molon and
perhaps Achaeus tried to do 65 years later (cf. p.31), and hoping
with their support to undermine the Seleucid Empire at its very
roots. However, Seleucus dispatched his troops to that
untrustworthy satrapy on the first day of the invasion and so
probably prevented a general uprising.

Plutarch's biography of Demetrius, the main source for the
battle (48.4-49), is supplemented by a stratagem of Polyaenus

(4.9.3). The considerable knowledge demonstrated by both authorities in discussing Demetrius' plans and considerations, his movements, and the internal crisis in his camp, suggest that they drew directly or indirectly on Hieronymus of Cardia who may have accompanied his patron, Demetrius, on his last adventure. Nevertheless, Plutarch's account is, as usual, rather elliptic, and displays more interest in his hero's psychology than in the military developments. The vagueness and omissions of significant military data are clearly demonstrated by a comparison of his version of Seleucus' appearance before Demetrius' soldiers with the much more militarily convincing description in Polyaenus.

Location of the battlefield may help in determining the manoeuvres of both sides and the course of the battle. Plutarch relates that Demetrius' 'crossing the Amanus devastated the lower country as far as Cyrrhestica' (ἄχρι τῆς Κυρρηστικῆς - 48.4), while Seleucus encamped nearby, and the battle took place on that spot (49.1 and see Map 2). The expression ἄχρι τῆς Κυρρηστικῆς raises some difficulty: as it stands, it means that Demetrius' invasion extended only up to the territory of Cyrrhestica, but as the Amanus range undoubtedly bounded the satrapy on the west,[2] the 'lower country' beyond the Amanus, reported to have been invaded by Demetrius, was within it. Moreover, the topographical indications of the sources suggest that the battle took place in the hilly country 20-40 km east of the slopes of the Amanus. I would suggest that Hieronymus, Plutarch's source, had in mind Cyrrhus, the centre of the satrapy, which had the greatest concentration of Macedonians, and which was perhaps founded by Antigonus.[3] In the time of Hieronymus the recently established satrapy of Cyrrhestica was less well known than Cyrrhus, its capital, which gave the satrapy its name, and he may have written ἄχρι τῆς Κυρρηστικῆς (sc. χώρας), meaning just as far as the city-territory of Cyrrhus, or ἄχρι τῆς Κυρρηστῶν χώρας, referring to the settlers in the city.[4] Cyrrhus was 35 km east of the Amanus passes, so that Demetrius could have arrived there in one day's march as may be implied by Plutarch (48.4-49.1), and could have reached the Amanus by nightfall in his flight (49.1-2) after the

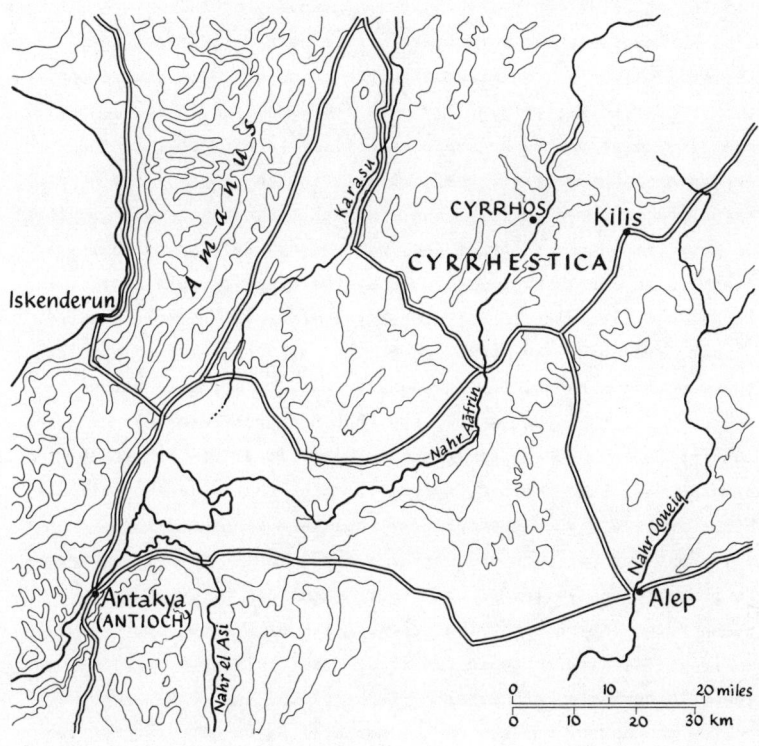

2 The Amanus and Cyrrhestica

battle, which probably took place at dawn.[5]

The battle would seem therefore to have taken place near Cyrrhus, which is identified with the ruins of Awāris, near Sheikh Cyrus, between Merseyi and Zeylunek (see Map 3).[6] A more specific location can be supported by some indications in the accounts of the battle: the participation and role of the elephants reported by Polyaenus imply that the battle was launched on level ground, and one of the two parties was exposed on its flank to an outflanking manoeuvre by the enemy through an unobserved flat side route, probably a river tributary. But it cannot have been very wide: Demetrius' army numbered only a few thousand,[7] and the bitter and equally matched struggle which emerges from the sources suggests that Seleucus' army was not much stronger. But as Demetrius' manoeuvres at Cilicia would have put him on the alert, I tend to think that Seleucus failed to bring forward a much greater army, not because of the speed of the invasion, but owing to the narrow arena. These limitations seem to indicate the valley of the river Afrin west of Cyrrhus, or Sabun-Suyu, one of its tributaries, north of Cyrrhus, each 500-750 m wide. The side route in the first case could have been one of the tributaries on either side of the plain, and in the second, one of the narrow valleys to the north of Sabun-Suyu (access from the south being blocked by the massive of Yhhoroz-Dâgh). But in either case, taking into account that Demetrius escaped to the Amanus mountains and Seleucus appears to have blocked the passes beforehand (Polyaenus 4.9.5), it seems evident that Seleucus approached the enemy by a detour from the southeast, which suggests that he was determined to force Demetrius into a pitched battle by blocking his way, either in order to prevent the Cyrrhestians from gradually joining his ranks, or to cut off his way to Media, his former destination.

The two armies were divided into two flanks consisting probably of infantry alone because of the narrowness of the arena. One of Demetrius' flanks was pressed hard by the opposite flank, but, receiving reinforcements, succeeded in withstanding the enemy, while the other flank, commanded personally by Demetrius himself, seems to have forced the enemy's opposing flank into a partial withdrawal. In this situation, with the outcome very

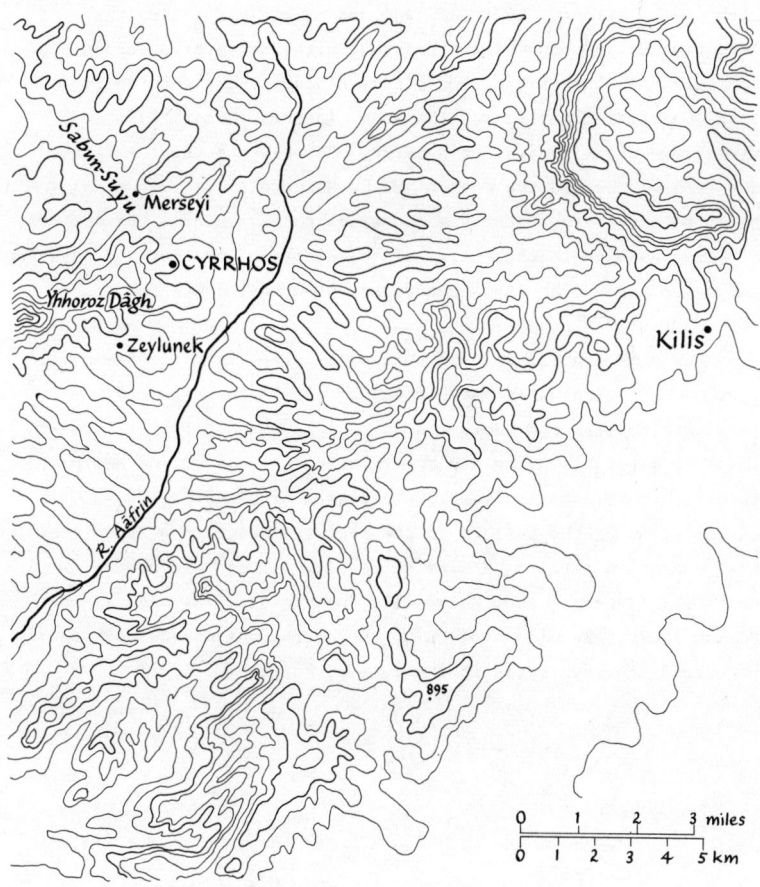

3 Cyrrhos

much in the balance, Seleucus, who was probably watching the developments from an observation post with the reserve forces, took eight elephants and some of the hypaspists, the infantry royal Guard, and outflanked the enemy (perhaps Demetrius' victorious flank) by way of a narrow unobserved pass. He is said not to have charged the enemy, but by using all his rhetorical power to have persuaded the mercenaries to surrender. The threat of being exposed to the charge of the elephants on their vulnerable and unprotected flank may have contributed no less to the mercenaries' decision.

The main significance of this battle lies in the evidence it provides of Seleucus' strategic and tactical courage: his readiness to risk confrontation on an unfavourable battlefield that prevented his using his superiority in manpower and equipment in order to forestall disastrous political results; his exploitation of the terrain to the best advantage in a manoeuvre that was quite rare in battles of regular armies (excluding guerrilla forces);[8] and, above all, the personal example he set to the later Seleucids by leading the courageous manoeuvre himself and standing unprotected in the face of the enemy.

8: THE VICTORY OVER MOLON (220 B.C.)

After a gap of more than 50 years for which there is little documentation, information about Seleucid activity in the battlefield becomes available again with Polybius' account of the decisive battle against Molon (5.48.17-54), which opens a series of battle accounts covering Antiochus III's reign.

Molon, the satrap of Media, revolted in 222 B.C. shortly after Antiochus III's accession, crowned himself king, and took possession of all the eastern satrapies.[1] Antiochus, who at first concentrated his efforts on the southern frontier, contented himself with sending relatively small expeditions under second-rank generals to prevent Molon from occupying Babylonia (Polyb. 5.41-2, 5, 43.5-45.7, 46.6-48.16). But when the various expeditions had all been defeated, and Molon had taken control of much of Mesopotamia, Antiochus himself was compelled to assemble all the royal troops and lead them in a decisive confrontation with the rebel.

At the beginning of the campaign Molon was in winter quarters near Seleucia-upon-the-Tigris (48.15-16, 52.6). Antiochus marched swiftly across Mesopotamia and arrived at Apollonia,[2] identified as Baradan Tepe, close to the junction of the Diala and the Narin Tchai (see Map 4).[3] Molon was informed too late about Antiochus' drive,[4] and, decamping in haste, set out for the hilly region of Apollonitis on his way to Media.

Some of the strategy of both sides is outlined by Polybius. Antiochus was eager to block Molon's way back to Media, which passed through Apollonitis, and was anxious to control this fertile region, which would give him a firm logistic base if Molon tried to play for time (51.8-11). Molon, on the other hand, while naturally wishing to return to his Median stronghold, meanwhile put all his energy into reaching Apollonitis, presumably the north-eastern section near Chanikin, where he would be able to rely on his Cyrtian slingers (52.5). He may have had a considerable

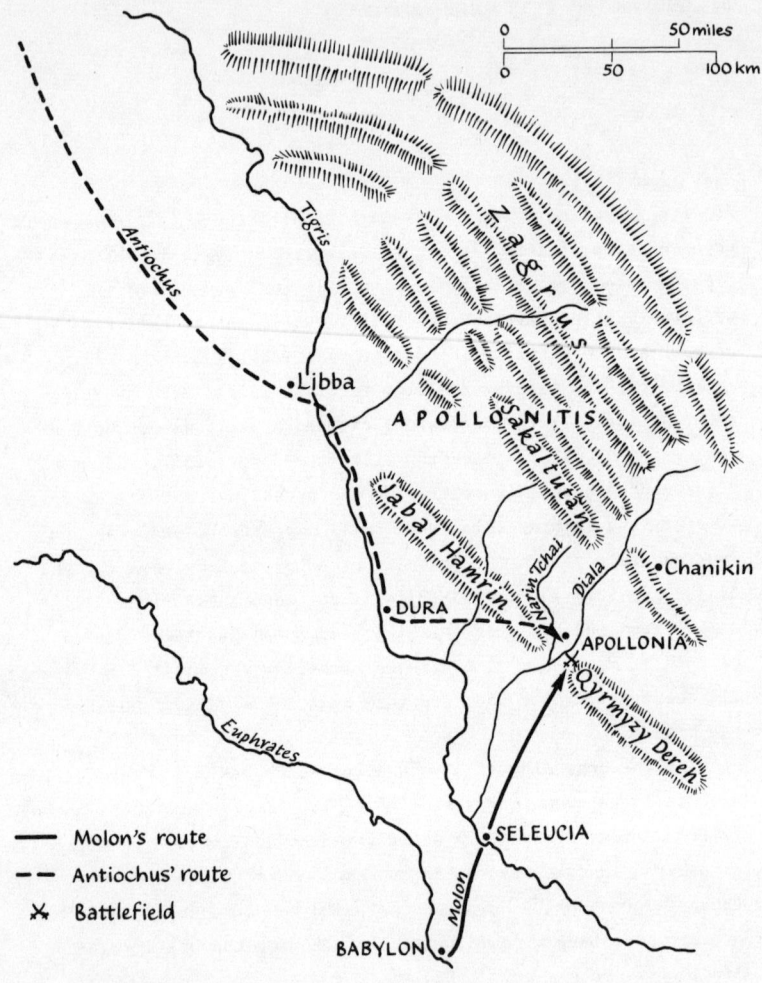

4 Antiochus' expedition against Molon

number of oriental 'missile troops' in his camp: Antiochus III employed 8,000 Cyrtians and Elymaeans at Magnesia (Livy 37.40.9,14).

Shortly after Antiochus left Apollonia, his light vanguard met Molon's van on certain mountain passes (52.7). The range has been identified by Pédech with Qyrmyzy Dereh, the continuation of Jabal Hamrin (Oriekon), the first range in a series rising gradually eastwards toward the Zagrus mountains, and the main pass referred to is probably the Kurdaruz pass.[5] These identifications suggest that while he was staying at Apollonia, Antiochus, who was in friendly relations with the local population (5.51.8-9), received the news that Molon was approaching, and he therefore crossed the Diala and sent advance troops to the southwest to block the pass. Both sides withdrew for the night and camped at a distance of 40 stadia from each other (52.8-9). As they could not have pitched camp on the rough slopes themselves, their camps must have been located on either side of the 7-8 km (40 stadia) wide range.[6]

The battlefield itself seems to me to have extended over the ridge line, which is a plateau 500 m wide and 4 km in length (see Map 5). The height of the ridge line is 140-180 m, with a slight rise to the northeast,[7] an arena that somewhat recalls the battlefield of Cynoscephalae (Polyb. 18.18.6-7).[8] For Molon this arena was the lesser of two evils since it partially restricted the superior royal phalanx (see below), while Antiochus had to be content with the somewhat less than perfect arena if he wished to prevent the enemy from evading a battle.

The battle order of the two sides is described schematically and without any numerical details. Antiochus' centre was occupied by the phalanx (53.3). The right flank, which he himself led, consisted of, from right to left, xystophoroi cavalry (53.2), Cretans, presumably archers, Galatians, and Greek mercenaries (53.2), possibly heavy.[9] The left flank comprised only the Companion cavalry (53.4), which usually numbered 1,000 horse. The 'front' (presumably of the centre) was covered by 10 elephants, undoubtedly for the purpose of countering the chariots on the opposite side. Polybius also mentions cavalry and infantry reserve troops divided between the two flanks (53.5).[10]

Molon had, in the centre, phalanx and Galatians (53.8-9)

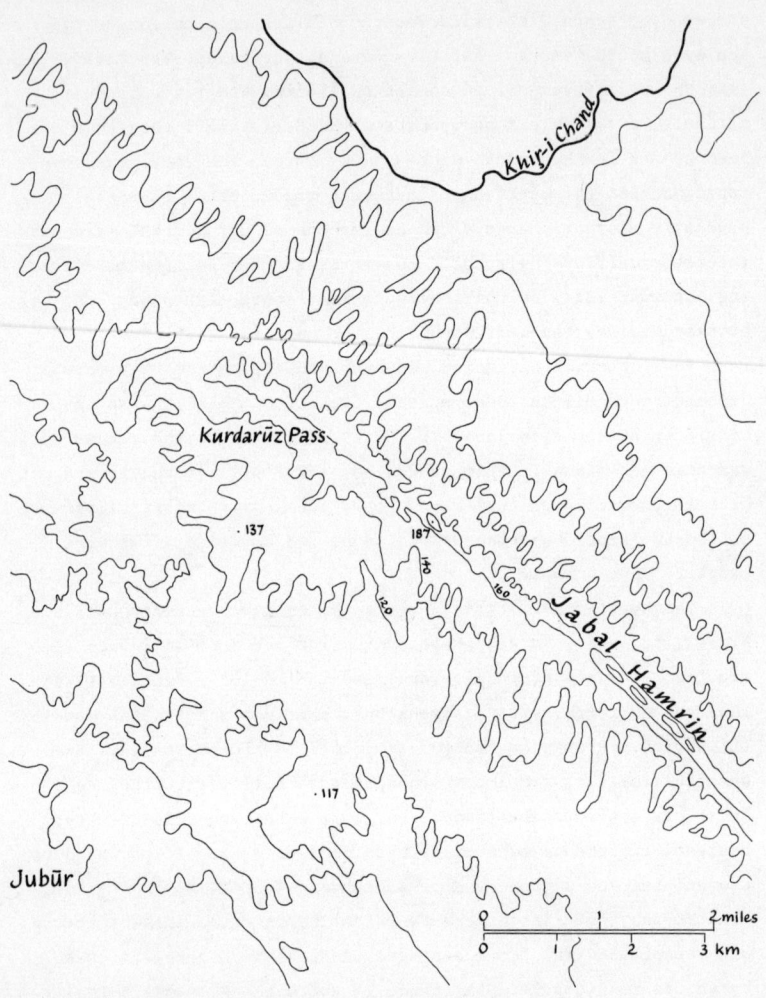

5 The battlefield against Molon

preceded by scythed chariots designed to cut down the opposing
phalanx; on the flanks were the cavalry, and beyond the cavalry
(ἐκτὸς τῶν ἱππέων παρ' ἑκάτερα), the light infantry (archers,
slingers, etc.). This unique disposition of the 'lights'[11] was
perhaps due to the condition of the terrain. They may have been
posted beyond the plateau on the rough ground where the Seleucid
cavalry could not charge, for the purpose of using cross-fire to
check the outflanking manoeuvres of the enemies' strong cavalry
(cf. Onasan. 18). Molon himself commanded the right, and his
brother Naolaus the left, opposite the king (53.11).

In my earlier discussion of the numerical strength of the
Seleucid forces I came to the conclusion that Antiochus had a
considerable numerical superiority in heavy infantry, while Molon
was somewhat stronger in cavalry, and outnumbered the king in
oriental 'missile troops' (p. 18 above). The relative strength
of the two sides has some bearing on a correct understanding of
military developments.

Polybius' version of the course of the battle is rather
brief: Molon's left wing charged the enemy, but the troops on the
right surrendered as soon as they saw the king. The infantry in
the centre, finding itself exposed in its flank, soon followed
suit. The pressure on Molon's wing, which was surrounded, was
thus increased, and Molon lost heart and committed suicide (54.1-4).

This interpretation obviously attributes the result to the
personal appearance of Antiochus and his effect on Molon's troops,
who are said to have felt more attachment to the legitimate king
than to the rebel satrap. Such an explanation should be treated
with suspicion from the outset because Polybius' narrative was
based, as is widely acknowledged, on sources hostile to Hermeias
(p.245 n.11), who was opposed to Antiochus' own participation in
the battle, in contrast to the opinion expressed by Epigenes, his
main rival at the court, that Antiochus' personal appearance in
the battlefield would tilt the balance in his favour by inducing
the rebels to surrender (5.41.7-9: cf. 47.4-48.9). This advice,
though it was also perhaps intended to flatter the king (cf.
Plut. Eum. 7), does make sense, as the phalangites, the Greco-
Macedonian military settlers, were probably in some way attached
to the dynasty by their previous service in the ranks of the

Guard. But, in fact, the wing alleged to have surrendered
comprised cavalry, certainly Median cavalry reservists (p.32
above) - who, although they too had been allotted land by the
Seleucids, would have naturally preferred the local satrap -
oriental auxiliary cavalry, and light oriental infantry, who would
not have had any special feelings for the legitimate Seleucid king.
Further doubts are raised by the omission of the figures for the
two sides: Schmitt noted cogently that Polybius' source refrained
from quoting numbers for the forces in order to avoid the obvious
impression that numerical superiority, and not Antiochus' personal
appearance, secured his victory.[12]

It therefore seems to me that the battle order, Antiochus'
instructions, and the terrain may provide a better clue to the
military developments than the biased version which inspired
Polybius' account. Antiochus is reported to have divided the
infantry and cavalry reserve (epitagmata) between the two wings
(53.5). Their designation as 'reserve' means that they were
posted somewhere behind the two wings and not on the extreme flanks
of the battle line. They were instructed to 'encircle the enemy
when the battle was joined' (ibid.). If this manoeuvre was
actually carried out in the battle - and there is no reason to
think otherwise - it may have been a decisive factor. But if the
purpose was to take the enemy from the rear as soon as possible,
the encircling forces would have been ordinary troops rather than
epitagmata. The task of reserve troops in the Hellenistic armies
was mainly defensive: to stage a second-line barrier and to
reinforce the front-line troops in advanced stages of a battle.
The topography of the battlefield suggests that the reserve troops
were actually posted out of range of the rebels' observation, at a
short distance from the battlefield on the northeastern slopes of
the range. Their sudden appearance from behind the flanks may
have caught the enemy unprepared and unable to change its battle
order accordingly, and may also perhaps have given rise to
apprehension regarding the possibility of further reinforcement
of the king's army (see e.g. Onasan. 22.2). The terrain being
ideally suited to it, one would hardly imagine that Antiochus did
not apply this stratagem, which was well known in antiquity,
especially as he, in any case, used the reserve in an offensive

role. This unexpected manoeuvre, in addition to the obvious superiority of Antiochus' centre, would have convinced the opposing flank that there was no point in resisting, and the phalanx, being exposed in the flank, would have surrendered as well. Although apart from Antiochus' reported instructions the active involvement of the reserve troops in the battle itself is not referred to, it is my belief that their encircling manoeuvre actually decided the battle; but even if this theory is wrong, and Polybius' explanation that Antiochus' appearance won the day is correct, Antiochus certainly could not have relied on such an effect and his tactical plan, at least, would have been along these lines. All in all, Antiochus must have been eager to bring about the surrender of the rebels without too much bloodshed, so that he could secure trained and competent manpower for the tremendous undertakings he planned for the future.

9: THE STORMING OF THE PORPHYRION PASS (218 B.C.)

After the suppression of Molon's revolt, Antiochus III diverted his attention to the Ptolemaic frontier in his bid to occupy Coilē-Syria. Polybius devotes to these efforts a considerable part of the Asian section in the fifth book. After two abortive attempts to break through the Ptolemaic forts guarding the Marsyas Valley, the central route from Syria to Palestine, which passes between the Lebanon and Anti-Lebanon (45.1-46.5, 61.3-62.6), he chose the more difficult, coastal route. The narrow pass and the steep cliffs that extend in several places almost to the water-line could be easily defended by the Ptolemies. But Antiochus was able to count on Tyre and Acre in the Ptolemies' rear, which had earlier come over to his side after the defection of Theodotus the Aetolian, the Ptolemaic mercenary-officer.

The main Ptolemaic defence was concentrated near Porphyrion, identified with the ruins in the triangle between Khan Nebi Younes and the villages Barja and Jiye, near Ras Nebi Younes, 25 km south of Beirut,[1] and the battle is said to have taken place in the nearby narrow pass (see Map 6). Abel located the battle in Ras El Sadiyatt, 4-5 km to the north of Porphyrion,[2] but Ras Nebi Younes, which is nearer Porphyrion, seems to be more suitable: Ras El Sadiyatt is 500 m to the south of the river Damouras (Damour), mentioned as the place where Antiochus camped before the battle (68.5), and, had the battle taken place nearby, it would naturally have been called after the river (cf. the fords of the river Lycus mentioned in the report of the same expedition, 68.9). If this were to be the battlefield, one would expect the Ptolemaic defensive deployment to have been based primarily on the Damouras, which is a considerable obstacle, as was proved in the Second World War. But there is no reference to a struggle on the banks of the Damouras, and Antiochus crossed it with a considerable force without interference on his reconnaisance mission (68.9-11), which was in itself necessary only if we assume that the Ptolemies

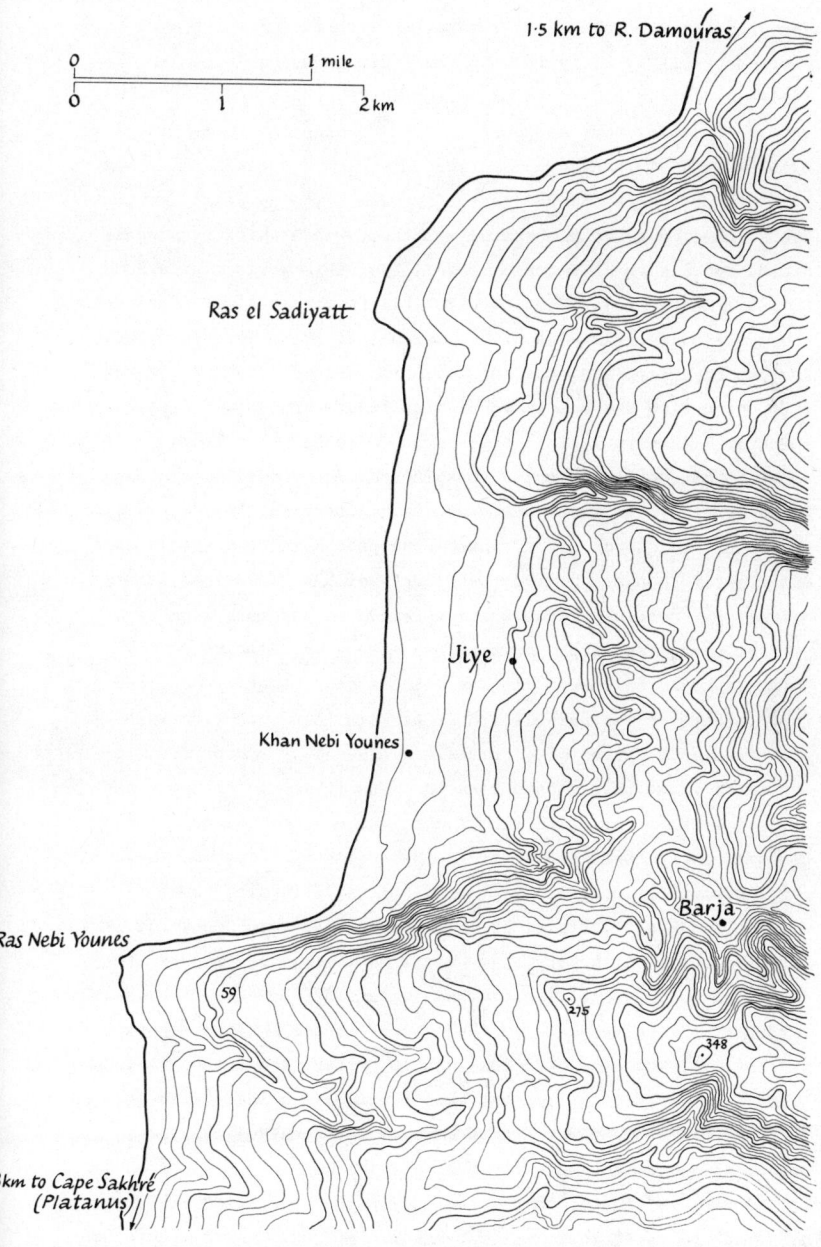

6 The battlefield of Porphyrion

were concentrated near Nebi Younes, observation of which was
blocked by Ras El Sadiyatt. On the other hand, we hear that the
Ptolemies laid elephant traps there (69.2), which would certainly
have been superfluous had they decided to stop the enemy near Ras
El Sadiyatt. Furthermore, the second Ptolemaic defence line was
posted in Platanus (El Rmaileh - Cap Sakhré),[3] the pass next to
Nebi Younes, 5 km to the south, and there was a third pass near
Sidon, the Ptolemaic stronghold (69.11). This would indicate a
triple line of defence on the three cliffs within sight of each
other. Finally, Ras El Sadiyatt appears to the observer on the
spot to be an integral part of the Lebanon range and not single
ridge bisecting the pass, as Polybius indicates - a description
which applies very well to the Ras Nebi Younes. The latter cliff
seems to have been preferred, despite the natural defence of Ras
El Sadiyatt by the river Damouras, mainly because an army
posted on its slopes could control the pass more comfortably and
effectively than on the moderate slopes of Ras El Sadiyatt (see
below), and possibly because its narrow pass was much longer.

Polybius describes the line of defence in relative detail
which seems to be based on an eyewitness account by his source.
The entrance to the pass, which is no more than 50 m wide, was
protected by a system of obstructions as well as troops (69.2).
The steep ridge that runs across the pass (69.1) is probably the
hill Trig. Point 59. Its almost vertical northern slope,
dominating the 'bottleneck' of the pass from 40-50 m, was
certainly occupied by archers and slingers, while its gentle
western slope was occupied by light troops who were ready for
hand-to-hand fighting to defend their position, and prepared to
descend into the pass if Antiochus' vanguard succeeded in breaking
through. The third post, on the 'slopes of the Lebanon Mountain'
(69.3-4, 9), may have been designed to prevent the defenders from
being bypassed from above, and must therefore be identified with
Trig. Points 275 and 348, which more or less control all the
mountainous tracks around the pass.

Antiochus' force, comprising only light troops (68.11), was
divided into three independent contingents. One, under Theodotus
the Aetolian, had to mount the slopes of the Lebanon, dislodge the
Ptolemaic guard, and carry on to attack, with the advantage of

height, the post overlooking the pass (Trig. Point 63). The second contingent under Menedamus had to try to climb up this last post, undoubtedly from the east, while the third contingent, under Diocles, tried to break through the pass itself (69.3-5). In view of their topographical disadvantage, the role of the last two contingents could not, in fact, have been more than to divert the Ptolemies' attention from Theodotus' decisive manoeuvre. Antiochus, contrary to his habit, observed the battle from behind the line (69.7), perhaps because he could not fight among the cavalry as he was accustomed to. At the same time both navies approached each other along the seaboard (69.6).

The attack began at the same time on all fronts (69.9). As could have been predicted, the Ptolemaic force at first held their own in the pass and on the ridge. The day was won by Theodotus, who overcame the guard on the slopes of the Lebanon, and then turned on the forces on the ridge so as to allow the Seleucid troops in the pass to break through (69.9-10).

The battle of Porphyrion demonstrates considerable tactical flexibility, manoeuvring ability, and courage in conditions of terrain much more difficult than those which faced the Romans later at Thermopylae. This impression is strengthened by an analysis of the crossing of the Elburz range by Antiochus III about eight years later.

10: THE BATTLE OF RAPHIA (217 B.C.)

The breakthrough at the Porphyrion Pass opened the way for the invasion of Coilē-Syria by the Seleucid troops. After systematically winning control over the various regions, Antiochus retired to winter quarters at Acre (Polyb. 5.71.12). The Ptolemaic army, which had deteriorated through being idle for about a generation, was reassembled in 219 B.C. and subjected to intensive training (ibid. 63-5). When the preparations were completed, in June 217 B.C. (Gauthier-Sottas, pp.34. ℓℓ.10-11), Ptolemy IV made a forced march of five days to southern Palestine and encamped 50 stadia to the southwest of Raphia. Antiochus, hearing of the enemies' advance, left Acre and proceeded with speed along the coastline via Gaza to Raphia (ibid. 80.3-4). The Ptolemaic victory in the battle settled the dispute over Coilē-Syria for another 17 years.

The sources for Polybius' detailed account of the battle (5.79-85) are uncertain. While Momigliano considers them to be pro-Ptolemaic and suggests Zeno of Rhodes as Polybius' direct source, Otto and others, who lay much stress on the recurrence of comments on Ptolemy's love of luxury and indifference to external affairs (5.87.3,7; cf. 34, 42.4, 62.7, 107; 14.12.2-3 et passim), prefer to regard Polybius' sources as pro-Seleucid.[1] But it is doubtful whether Seleucid sources would have so described the king who in so decisive a manner defeated Antiochus III, given the appellation 'the Great' a few years later. On the other hand, the indications of a 'Ptolemaic' source are much more impressive: Ptolemy's secret military preparation are recorded in detail (5.65-8); Ptolemy's personal appearance in the ranks of the phalanx is credited with inspiring his troops and lowering the morale of the enemy (85.8). Above all, the people of Coilē-Syria, the bone of contention between the two kingdoms, are said to be traditionally inclined to favour the Ptolemies (86.9-10), while it stands to reason that, owing to the Ptolemaic economic policy,

they would have sided with the Seleucids. Indeed there are some
indications to suggest this,[2] and, in any case, a Seleucid source
would not have supported the Ptolemaic claim over Coile-Syria by
such an admission. The casual remarks on Ptolemy's character may
rather be attributed to the use of a source dependent on the
'hawks' in the Alexandrian court who were angered by Ptolemy's
indifference to his foreign domain.[3] This source was perhaps
Ptolemy of Megalopolis,[4] Polybius' compatriot who served in the
Egyptian court and wrote a scandalous history of Ptolemy IV that
was known to Polybius.[5] The identification of Polybius' source
will be useful in evaluating the reliability of his comment about
†Antiochus' manoeuvres and tactical planning.

Polybius places the battlefield on the road from Pelusium to
Raphia, 50 *stadia* (9.25 km) from Raphia (80.3). According to the
description of the Seleucid march, battle, and retreat, which
indicate the use of the main road from Gaza to Raphia, he could
not have meant maritime Raphia but rather the old city, which was
situated beyond the sea dunes. It has recently been decisively
established at Al-Shaykh Sulaymān Rafakh (Trig. Point 42; long.
07850/lat. 07915), a wooded mound on the edge of the dunes west
of modern Rafiaḥ (see Map 7).[6] Polybius states that Ptolemy
planned to reach that spot (80.3). The fantastic speed of the
five-day march (*ibid.*) of 75,000 troops (79.2), with all their
baggage, under the scorching June sun of the Sinai desert (80.1-2),
along the 180 km route from Pelusium to the battlefield, which
works out at 36 km a day,[7] reaffirms Polybius' statement and
suggests that he was eager to avoid unfavourable terrain and to
dictate the site of the battle himself. Ptolemy's calculations
must have been based on the assessment of the availability of the
troops. He had at his disposal over 60,000 phalangites and 6,000
semi-heavy troops (see below), while Antiochus' recruitment
potential of heavy troops, which usually stood at about 42,000-
44,000, was reduced by the revolts in Asia Minor and Cyrrhestica
to no more than 30,000 men (see p.41 above). Large-scale
recruitment of Greek mercenaries to fill the gap was obviously
out of the question. Ptolemy could therefore have counted on an
overwhelming numerical superiority in phalanx, but in view of
Seleucid control of the upper satrapies he must have expected to

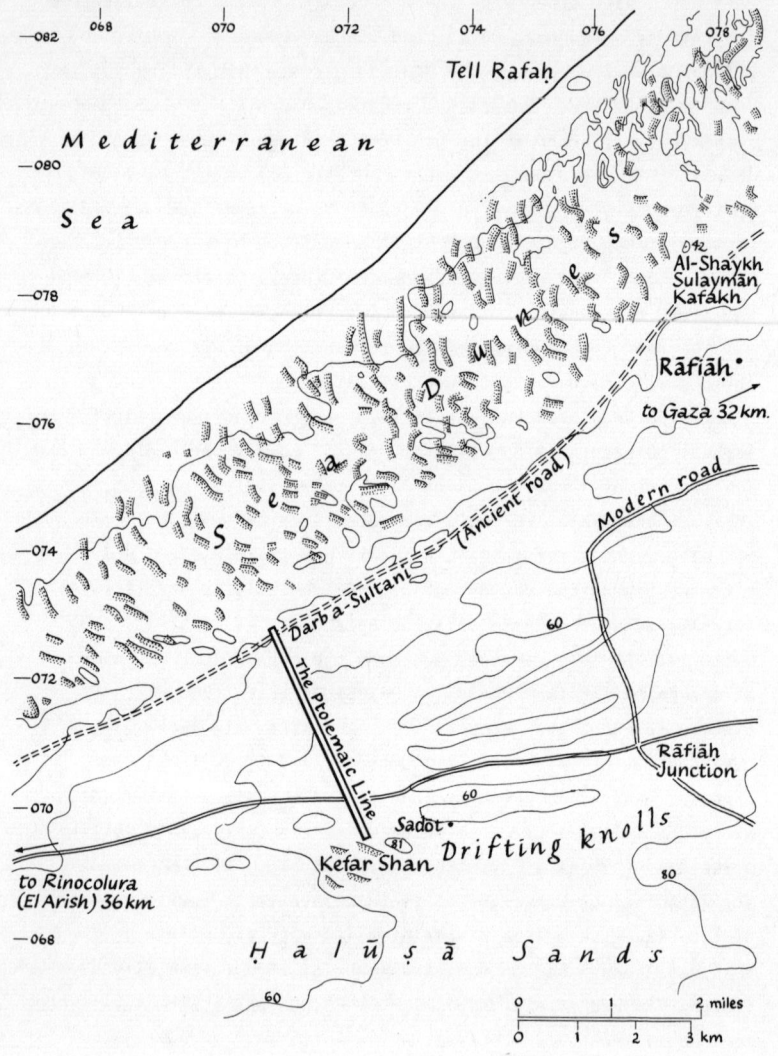

7 The battlefield of Raphia

be heavily outnumbered in cavalry and light infantry and inferior in quality of elephants at his disposal (see p.240 n.80). Examination of the route from the Egyptian frontier at Rinocolura (El Arish) northwards throws light on his considerations. Shortly after leaving Rinocolura, the route enters a 10 km long pass 200-300 m wide (the Jiradi Pass), blocked by impassable sea dunes on the northwest and desert sands on the southeast. Such an arena would have favoured the Seleucid elephants if they were posted in the front supported by lights on the flanks, and would have trapped the heavy Ptolemaic column, rendering it useless. The pass between the sand dunes broadens to well over 10 km at the exit from the Jiradi, but it seems that this alternative arena did not satisfy Ptolemy either. He chose to encamp near the so called 'Rāfiāh Junction', where the Ḥaluṣa Sands extend a 'finger' consisting of disconnected knolls of drifting sand to the west which here and there limit the width of the pass to 3.4-5 km. The nature of the terrain and its impassibility at the time have recently been somewhat obscured by levelling and land preparation projects for the village of Sadot in the Rāfiāh area. North of the junction the pass widens out again to the southeast.

A distance of 9.25 km from Raphia brings us to the point where the present width of the pass stands at 3.4 km, confined between the large knoll of Kefar Shan to the south and the sea dunes to the north. The surface to the northeast is fairly suitable for infantry and cavalry warfare. According to geomorphic calculations based on the possible advance of the sea dunes during the last 2,200 years, it seems that the pass was about 5.6 km wide in 217 B.C.[8] An arena 5.6 km wide would have enabled Ptolemy to occupy the whole width of the pass with his troops deployed according to the usual standard, without dangerously thinning his battle array and so jeopardizing its ability to withstand a frontal attack.[9] The dunes on either side would have provided the wings with protection against the Seleucid cavalry, which was expected to be far superior in numbers and quality. The Seleucids would have been forced in that case to deploy only part of their cavalry on the wings, and concentrate their 'lights', whose efficacy in frontal battle was quite limited, in the front line against the phalanx. The alternatives which faced Antiochus, either to deepen his cavalry line beyond eight lines, or to post cavalry units instead of some of his infantry against the Ptolemaic phalanx, were impractical, as there was no tactical advantage to deepening the cavalry (see Polyb. 12.18.3), and conventional cavalry could not operate against the long pikes of phalangites.[10] On the other hand, in a wider arena Antiochus could have been expected to extend his superior cavalry beyond the Ptolemaic line in order to facilitate a quick outflanking manoeuvre supported by the light skirmishers. Indeed, in such an arena, by thinning his centre to the depth of only 16 lines, Ptolemy could have forced the enemy to deploy light troops to engage a considerable number of Ptolemaic phalangites, but the danger of exposing his vulnerable flanks seems to have outweighed this advantage.

In fact, one decisive assumption proved false: Ptolemy did have overwhelming numerical superiority in heavy and semi-heavy troops - 61,000 phalangites (5.65)[11] and 6,000 Thracian and Galatians as against Antiochus' 35,000 phalangites (5.79)[12] - but in cavalry the two sides were almost equal - 6,000 Seleucid cavalry against 5,000 Ptolemaic horse. The only forecast that was verified was the Seleucid advantage in light troops: 21,000 'lights' were arrayed in the Seleucid battle line, while Ptolemy had only 3,000 Cretans at his disposal. The Seleucid cavalry was below its normal strength, probably because there was still some unrest in the eastern provinces and horsemen were the most efficient force to patrol these vast regions. It may well be that not all the military settlers in Media and the oriental national contingents could be trusted after Molon's revolt. Ptolemy could not have predicted these developments, and, in any case, had to plan his movements on the assumption that Antiochus would try to compensate for any loss of manpower by additional mercenary forces of cavalry (Thracians, Galatians, etc.). If Antiochus actually did not try to reinforce his troops, it is mainly because Ptolemy was successful in concealing his recruitment and training drive.

Antiochus, for his part, seems to have been in a hurry on his way to the south (80.3-4), presumably because he was anxious to prevent the reoccupation of Gaza, the traditional Ptolemaic stronghold which in the event of a Ptolemaic defeat was capable of standing a long siege (cf. Polyb. 16.22a), offering a sanctuary to

Ptolemy's troops and facilities for evacuation by sea. Antiochus' prompt reaction later proved also to be a tactical necessity: being unaware of the shift in the balance of power he first encamped 10 *stadia* (1.8 km) from the Ptolemaic camp (80.4), presumably intending to launch battle on the wider part of the pass (6.2-6.7 km), where a gap in the sands on the south could offer his cavalry some freedom of manoeuvre. Informed of the surprising increase in the size of the Ptolemaic phalanx and the equality in cavalry, however, he made haste to change position and advanced 5 *stadia* forward (80.6-7), preferring the narrowest possible arena. The grim alternative of having to confront part of the Ptolemaic phalanx with light troops was much more dangerous than the possibility of facing a deep phalanx array in the centre. The unconventional depth of the phalanx was designed mainly to replenish the front lines in a long and exhausting combat, and Antiochus doubtless hoped that his experienced phalangites would not let the battle reach this stage.

As appears from the statement that the right wing cavalry of both sides overtook the elephants in their front lines and charged the enemy's cavalry coming from the front and behind (84.8, 85.1), the Ptolemaic army was not in fact protected by the dunes. In view of the equality of both sides in cavalry, this was indeed hardly necessary. On the other hand, in order to allow the numerical superiority of his phalanx to have its full effect, Ptolemy had to deepen his centre beyond the conventional sixteen lines, probably to as much as thirty-two (see below), which reduced the width of the front. Moreover, the advantage of the Seleucid Indian elephants over the Ptolemaic African elephants in front of the cavalry required a certain space to be left between the extremities of the line and the dunes in order to allow the cavalry more room for manoeuvre to avoid the elephant charge and to attack the enemy's cavalry.[13] I would imagine that, had Ptolemy had to face a superior Seleucid army and defend his flanks by the dunes, he would have put the Seleucid Indian elephants out of action with technical devices as was done so successfully by Ptolemy Lagos at Gaza.

The order of battle of the two armies was dictated partly by the military tradition of the Seleucids, partly by their relative

strength or weakness in this arm or that. After camping near
Raphia for five days, the two sides had probably learned from
defectors, spies, and captives about each other's forces, and,
being arrayed face to face, were able to plan their disposition
accordingly (see Map 8 at end). Generally speaking, the
Seleucid phalangites were posted in the centre, the cavalry in
the wings, and the other infantry on the flanks between the
phalanx and cavalry. The right flank was as usual the strongest,
and the cavalry of the right wing, led by Antiochus himself
(82.8, 84.8), was twice as strong as the left-wing horse (79.12,
82.5,8). Half of this force was deployed in a block to the right
and in advance of the battle line (82.9 - ἐν ἐπικαμπίῳ).[14]
Antiochus himself was in command of these 2,000 advance cavalry,
which was composed of the 1,000 Companions (84.1, 85.12), and
probably the 1,000 men strong agēma (cf. p.69 above). As a
result of the numerical superiority of the enemy in phalanx and
semi-heavy troops, Antiochus was forced to oppose light troops to
some of these contingents. In addition to cavalry the left flank
comprised only 'lights' (82.11-2), and the right was divided
between 5,000 Greek mercenaries, equipped as phalangites, and
5,000 'lights' of the eastern provinces (82.10).[15] In these
circumstances one would expect Antiochus to have protected the
light troops by posting elephants in front of them, but he was
prevented from doing so by the disposition of the Ptolemaic
elephants in front of the cavalry of the two wings and part of
†the infantry of the right flank (82.7, 84.9). Significantly
enough, Ptolemy did not cover his Libyan phalanx, which was
opposing the Seleucid oriental lights, but only the agēma and
'peltasts' who could be matched by the Greek heavy mercenaries.
Being confined to the line, the 'lights', excluding the Cretans,
who were probably posted between the right-wing elephants (82.8,
10) to counter Ptolemy's Cretans (82.4,7),[16] were deprived of
their traditional role as skirmishers in front of the troops.
The centre comprised two contingents: its right was occupied by
10,000 argyraspides (79.4, 82.8,10),[17] the crack force of the
infantry, in line with the traditional practice of posting the
best troops on this side; and its left by 20,000 'phalanx'
troops (79.5, 82.12), i.e. the military settlers serving in the

reserve.

The Ptolemaic disposition seems to have been well adapted to face the Seleucid battle order. The cavalry left wing was stronger than the right one, and Ptolemy himself, surrounded by the Guard, occupied the position opposite the Seleucid king (82.7, 84.1, 85.7). The infantry on the right were all phalangites (excluding the Cretans who served as a guard to the elephants), while the weaker Seleucid left was confronted by the semi-heavy Thracians and Galatians, in addition to the Greek mercenary phalangites (82.5-6). In the centre, where 45,000 Ptolemaic phalangites (65.4,9, 82.4,6) were pitted against 30,000 Seleucid phalangites (82.2-3, 85.9-10), the Ptolemaic troops were arrayed in greater depth. As the usual depth of phalangites (and of the Seleucid phalanx) was 16 lines (Polyb. 18.30.1 and see p.66 above), the Ptolemaic phalangites must have been deployed to the depth of, at least, 24 lines. In view of the necessity of narrowing the front line in order to leave the cavalry enough room to manoeuvre (see above), the Ptolemaic phalanx may well have been deepened even to 32 lines, like the Seleucid phalanx at Magnesia (Livy 37.40.2; App. Syr. 32(162), and cf. Arr. Tact. 5.6). The Seleucid troops had to adapt themselves, and were, consequently drawn up in 24 lines. The location of the newly recruited and inexperienced native Egyptian phalanx[18] merits attention: it was posted on the right (82.5-6), i.e. opposite the Seleucid phalanx, which consisted of reserve men from the Seleucid settlements, and not opposite the much more competent contingent of the argyraspides, the Guard infantry, which were to be tackled by the Ptolemaic 'phalanx' comprising European military settlers. Its location to the right of the centre was also designed to avoid the psychological effect on these inexperienced troops of a possible collapse of the left flank, since failure of the Ptolemaic right was much less likely.

The battle started with the onslaught of the Seleucid elephants on the right. The inferior Ptolemaic elephants were driven back, and pressed their own cavalry Guard behind, which was flanked at the same time by the opposing cavalry, commanded personally by Antiochus, who routed the Ptolemaic cavalry on the left and began a headlong pursuit (84.8-10, 85.11-12). Ptolemy

himself succeeded in slipping away and joining the ranks of the
phalangites in the centre (85.7-8). The reverse happened on the
other flank where the right-wing Ptolemaic cavalry got the upper
hand in almost the same way (85.1-4). Only incidental information
has been recorded on the fate of the other contingents on the
flanks. On the right the Seleucid Greek mercenaries routed the
Ptolemaic 'peltasts' (84.9), and on the other side the Ptolemaic
Greek mercenaries defeated the Arabs and the light oriental
infantry (85.2,4). Polybius speaks in general terms about
Seleucid victory on the right and defeat on the left (85.5). He
goes on to say that the phalangites in the centre of both armies
remained exposed on both flanks (85.6), but one should not pay
too much attention to this bare statement. Having quickly
defeated the opposing flank (85.4), the Ptolemaic right-flank
cavalry and infantry had no reason to launch a headlong pursuit,
especially after witnessing the defeat of their left flank. At
any rate, in contrast to the detailed description of the route
followed by the Seleucid right-wing cavalry, such a pursuit is
not mentioned. As for the infantry on the Ptolemaic right, their
heavy equipment, and consequent slow mobility in comparison with
the opposing Seleucid 'lights', excludes the possibility that
they, too, were tempted to hasten in pursuit. The same can be
said about some of the victorious infantry of the Seleucid right
who were too heavy to carry out an effective pursuit. The clash
of the phalanxes could perhaps have begun, the two sides being
exposed, but the Ptolemaic cavalry and infantry on the right
would certainly have come back in time to support their troops.
In any case, the developments in the centre would be otherwise
unintelligible. The Seleucid phalanx, i.e. the military
settlers, gave way almost at once (85.10; see 79.5 on Nicarchus),
while the <u>argyraspides</u> resisted for a time. As the greater depth
of the Ptolemaic phalanx would not have had any effect until
after a long and exhausting struggle, the hasty retreat of the
Seleucid phalangite-settlers can be explained only if there had
been a real threat of their being outflanked by the Ptolemaic
cavalry right wing. As the 'phalanx' confronted the inexperienced
Egyptian <u>machimoi</u>, and the <u>argyraspides</u> faced the Ptolemaic
European phalanx, which should have been stronger than the

natives both physically and because they had tradition of phalanx warfare, the difference in the behaviour of the two contingents of the Seleucid centre cannot be explained solely by the higher military standard of the Seleucid royal Guard. The argyraspides were not broken by the first shock because their right flank was not exposed to the Ptolemaic cavalry, and was perhaps protected by some of the victorious Seleucid infantry contingents of the right flank. The 'phalanx', on the other hand, was abandoned to the mercy of the Ptolemaic right flank. After the flight of their comrades on the left, the danger to the argyraspides became more imminent and they had to admit defeat.

Thus the battle was won by Ptolemy because Antiochus and his cavalry were absent from the battlefield. Polybius attributes Antiochus' long pursuit to his inexperience and his belief that the other wing was also successful (85.11). The second part of Polybius' explanation goes to show that whoever supplied this statement did not know the truth, and was as puzzled as ourselves at Antiochus' irresponsible action. In view of the weakness of his left and the numerical inferiority of the centre, Antiochus could not have expected a similar success in these parts of his line, and ought to have been aware of the necessity of his presence and the presence of his right wing on the battlefield. Antiochus' alleged 'inexperience' must also be viewed with some scepticism: by the time of Raphia he had already proved himself in the decisive battle against Molon, in the brilliant storming of the Porphyrion fortifications, and in several siege campaigns in the occupied territories in Palestine. The possibility of Antiochus' carrying on the pursuit in order to prevent the enemy from reforming and returning to the battlefield is not likely either: even according to the Ptolemaic source underlying Polybius, what we are concerned with was a rout of cavalry that had previously been thrown into utter confusion by the onslaught of the elephants (84.7-8). The appearance of elephants almost invariably caused horses to panic, and in the narrow battlefield hemmed in by dunes on both sides, could in any case be counted on to block their way back to their deserted flank, as was the case when the elephants of Seleucus confronted Demetrius Poliorcetes at Ipsus (see p.108 above).

The only explanation I can imagine for Antiochus' fatal miscalculation is that he was trying to kill Ptolemy and decide the outcome of the battle that way. Ptolemy, however, succeeded in slipping away and efforts to trace him may account for the long duration of the pursuit. Polybius says that Antiochus intended to fight Ptolemy personally (82.8), and Theodotus' abortive attempt to kill the Egyptian king in his tent (81)[19] may also point in this direction. A plan like this would account for the panic said to have been sown among the Seleucid phalangites by the unexpected return of Ptolemy to the battlefield (85.8). In view of the generally derogatory attitudes of Polybius' source to Ptolemy IV, this reference cannot be taken as flattery, although admittedly the panic might be attributed to the natural apprehension of the phalangites for the fate of Antiochus III in the cavalry confrontation. Antiochus may have applied these tactics not only because he was following Alexander's style, but principally because the composition of his army was deficient. It may also be that he was trying to determine the battle without too much bloodshed in order to spare his soldiers and perhaps gain potential manpower from the enemy for his future expeditions to Asia Minor and the lost eastern provinces. That Polybius gives a different explanation does not, in the least, discredit the suggested interpretation: the Ptolemaic courtier who was Polybius' direct or indirect source may have been unacquainted with Antiochus' plan of battle, as is indeed suggested by his dubious explanation of Antiochus' pursuit.

In the course of this discussion I have taken for granted the figures recorded by Polybius for the Ptolemaic phalanx in the centre, and tried to understand the tactical considerations and the developments in the field accordingly. But as these figures have been disputed by some, it is worth re-examining them in the light of the suggested reconstruction of the battle.

In the list of contingents assembled and trained before Raphia, Polybius enumerates 25,000 'phalanx' troops and 20,000 Egyptians equipped in the Macedonian style each under a different commander (65.4,9). These two contingents are mentioned again in the account of the battle and are said to have comprised the

The battle of Raphia

Ptolemaic centre (82.2, 85.9 and see 65.3,9 on Andromachus and Sosibius). Polybius' total for the Ptolemaic infantry, standing at 70,000 men (79.2), takes into account 45,000 phalangites in the centre.

Mahaffy and Griffith have presumed that the Ptolemaic phalanx included only 25,000 troops.[20] But while Mahaffy thinks that only a minority of these were Egyptians, Griffith suggests that 20,000 out of the 25,000 were Egyptian machimoi. This difference of opinion derives from different explanations for the origin of Polybius' figures: Mahaffy regards the figure of 20,000 attributed to the Egyptian phalanx as an interpolation designed to make the number of the troops in the various contingents fit the total of 70,000 given by Polybius. In his view, the figure 70,000 itself is a paleographic corruption for 50,000. Griffith thinks that Polybius was mistaken in taking the figure 25,000 found in his source as referring only to the separate contingent of the European settlers, and believes it represents the total Ptolemaic phalanx.

Mahaffy and Griffith's main argument for discrediting Polybius' total of 45,000 phalangites for the centre is that such an overwhelming numerical superiority over the Seleucid centre would have had an obvious influence on Ptolemaic tactics. One would have expected Ptolemy to charge first in the centre, but instead the phalanx was left behind inactive until the issue was decided on the flanks. Cary has even gone so far as to suggest that the Ptolemaic phalanx, had it comprised 45,000 troops, could have broken the Seleucid line in the first clash. Griffith supports his own interpretation by noting the motivation behind the Egyptians' revolt shortly after Raphia, arguing that had the Egyptians totalled less than half of the Ptolemaic centre, they would not have taken the credit for the victory (107.1-3). These arguments seem at first sight to be reinforced by Polybius' statements that Ptolemy was delighted at his unexpected success (87.3), and that both kings had put the greatest reliance on their phalanx (83.2), which may suggest that Ptolemy was generally inferior in manpower, and that the phalangites were approximately equal in strength.

But, in fact, Ptolemy could not have counted on his numerical superiority in the centre. The proportion of three to two between the two sides would not have guaranteed a Ptolemaic success, especially as the Egyptian phalanx was an innovation as yet untried on the battlefield, and the training of the European settlers had been neglected for many years, while the Seleucid army was engaged in constant military undertakings, not to mention the high standard of the Guard. The depth of the phalanx would be of advantage only at a later stage of the struggle, when both phalanxes were exhausted, but Ptolemy could not have been confident of the ability of his troops to reach this stage. All these considerations also explain why, despite his numerical superiority, Ptolemy was surprised by his success, and why Antiochus relied on his phalanx, although one must allow for the possibility that these two remarks may well be Polybius' own comment, and he certainly, even in Griffith's view, regarded the Ptolemaic phalanx as being superior in numbers. Moreover, as the pace of cavalry warfare was by far the faster, if the Ptolemaic phalanx had already been involved in actual fighting in the first stage of the battle, it would inevitably have been exposed by a Seleucid victory on the flank to a circumventing manoeuvre. By remaining at distance from the enemy's line, it would have had the time, space and courage to adopt its defensive formation to face the additional challenge,[21] and this would have been facilitated by its numerical superiority over the enemy's phalanx.

As to the role of the Egyptian machimoi in the Ptolemaic success, it was noted by Permans that Polybius' phrase 'being confident in themselves as a result of their victory at Raphia' does not necessarily imply that they attributed the victory to themselves, but that this underestimated and low grade of warriors was encouraged by its relative success.[22] But, as a matter of fact, they did have some reason to believe that they had actually decided the fate of the battle: the collapse of the Seleucid phalanx which confronted them, although due to its exposure to the cavalry on the flank rather than to the performance of the Egyptian phalangites in its front, brought about the total defeat of the Seleucid army shortly afterwards when the argyraspides, the cream of the infantry, gave way.

Turning to Griffith's estimate of the European manpower, it is difficult to believe that the Ptolemaic military settlements were unable to provide more than 5,000 soldiers of European descent for the phalanx. We do not have concrete data for the numerical strength of European military settlement in Egypt, but the figures for Ptolemaic armies at the end of the fourth century B.C. are several tens of thousands in addition to deserters and captives from the various enemies.[23] Although the epigonoi undoubtedly turned into farmers rather than part-time soldiers and neglected their military duties, one would have expected Ptolemy to have preferred to train them before Raphia rather than the Egyptian machimoi, who were also only recently recruited and trained. More trust could be placed in the European settlers, and their military and physical potential was much higher thanks to their better standard of nutrition[24] and heredity, which must not be underestimated. Nonetheless, I do not dispute Griffith's significant conclusion that the Ptolemaic military settlements failed to accomplish the purpose behind their foundation, that of ensuring the constant provision of competent phalanx troops for the Egyptian army; but the evidence for this is not the alleged small number at Raphia, but that the 25,000 European settlers were fit for nothing when called to the flag in 219 B.C., and that it took about two years to turn them into a combat contingent, while Ptolemy in the meantime lost ground in his foreign domains.

11: THE CROSSING OF THE ELBURZ RANGE (210 B.C.)

After his defeat at Raphia, Antiochus III concentrated on recovering Asia Minor. Having succeeded in capturing Achaeus and bringing the rebellion to an end in 214 B.C., he turned to the pursuit of his great dream: the reestablishment of the territorial dimensions of the Empire in the time of Seleucus I by means of a forceful anabasis to the east.[1] Only a few fragments of Polybius refer to this great expedition and include some account of military operations (10.28-31, 48-9). The most interesting is the detailed description, based probably on eyewitness' accounts,[2] of the crossing of the Elburz range on the way from Hecatompylus to Hyrcania, which demonstrates the march order and tactics of Antiochus III in difficult mountain passes (28-31).

Antiochus' route has been identified as the central pass of the Elburz range leading from Shahrud through the Chalchanlyan Pass to the Chasman - Sawer valley, and from there through the Quzluq Pass to Astrabad (Gorgan, see Map 9).[3] The main part of the route follows a riverbed which enters a narrow and precipitous gorge with cliffs soaring some 800-1200 m above the defile about 6 km from the Chalchanlyan Pass (30.2), a circumstance which led Antiochus to fear an ambush either by local tribes or Arsaces' troops. His anxiety was increased by Arsaces' reluctance to join battle, even near Hecatompylus, which was ideal for cavalry warfare, in which the Parthians obviously had a considerable advantage.[4] And indeed the 'barbarians', probably the local Tapurians,[5] occupied the cliffs on either side of the gorge, near the Chalchanlyan Pass, blocking the road itself by barricades of rocks and trees to stop the advancing column and trap the army in cross fire (30.2-3). Since Antiochus took the risk of concentrating all his troops in one pass (unlike Alexander, who divided his army between three passes in the same range (Diod. 17.75; Arr. Anab. 3.23)), we must assume that he had definite information about the general location of the ambush,[6] obtained

The crossing of the Elburz range 143

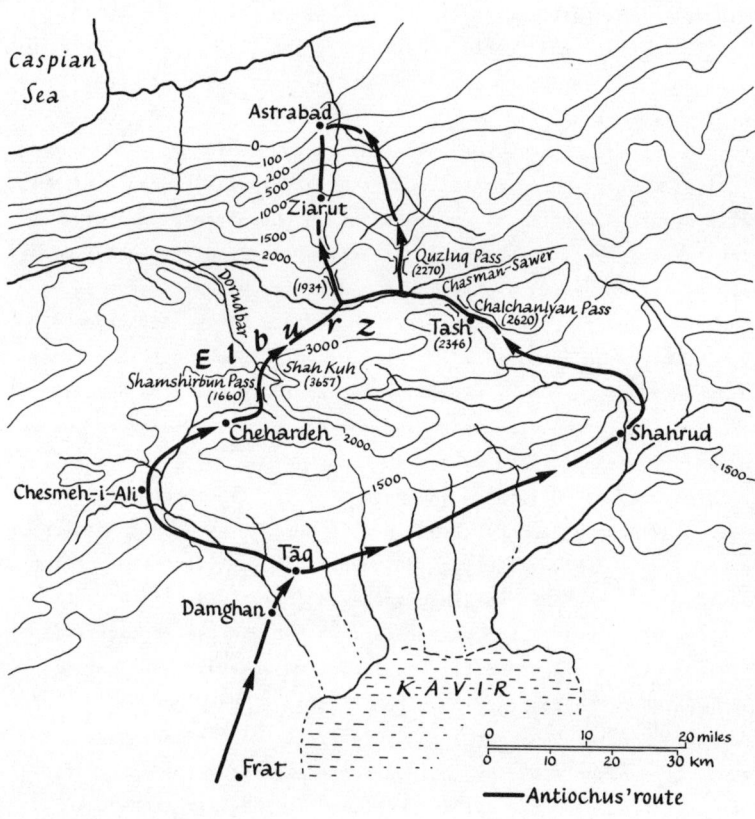

9 The Elburz

probably from the Greek settlers east of the Parthian-occupied Caspian Gates,[7] who doubtless supported the Seleucids and certainly also supplied guides to lead some of the units along the mountain trails (see below).

On entering the gorge Antiochus arranged his troops in the following way: the 'lights', comprising 'missile troops' (archers, slingers, and akontists) from mountainous countries, were divided into small groups to be led separately by their officers by different routes (29.4), probably hidden tracks on the summit of the ranges overlooking the gorge, so as to have the advantage of height over the enemy (30.7,9, cf. Onasan. 8), who were certainly positioned on the lower slopes nearer to the pass. The Seleucid main column in the pass was headed by Cretan shield bearers[8] whose movements are described as ἐφεδρευόντων καὶ παρ' αὐτὴν τὴν χαράδραν παραπορευομένων <ἐν> τάξει καὶ βάδην (30.9). The expression ἐφεδρευόντων may be understood in this context as either 'acting as a covering force' or 'acting in support'.[9] The first explanation would mean to support the 'mountaineers' by sniping at the overhanging positions of the barbarians.[10] But a dense concentration of 2000 archers in the defile would not have served this purpose, but would on the contrary have constituted an easy and open target. However, even the other interpretation - 'acting in support' - taken with the obvious connection to the advance of the Seleucid troops on the cliffs mentioned in the same sentence, indicates that the latter were supported by the Cretans in the defile. But what is the actual meaning of this 'support'? The exposure of the Cretans in front of the column and their seemingly confident march (τάξει καὶ βάδην) suggest that they were actually a reconnaissance or rather a 'soft' vanguard acting as bait in order to help the 'mountaineers' to quickly locate the hiding places of the barbarians by drawing their fire, and so prevent them from inflicting heavy losses on the phalanx and the rear, the hard core of the Seleucid army.[11] The risk and daring involved in their task is underlined by the appointment of Polyxenides, the Rhodian-Seleucid admiral (see p.243 n.13 below) to head the contingent.

The Cretans were followed by thorakitai and thyreaphoroi under Nicomedes of Cos and Nicolaus the Aetolian.[12] They were probably

divided in fact into two units, as the oblong shield certainly
rendered additional body armour rather unnecessary; the naming of
two stratēgoi may further indicate that they were entrusted with
different tasks. I would speculate that the thōrakitai, whose
breastplates offered protection against the barrage of missiles,
leaving their hands free, were to climb up the cliffs and fight
hand to hand with the enemy in case Antiochus' 'lights', who had
occupied the summits, failed to dislodge the 'barbarians' from
their commanding positions, while the thyreaphoroi followed them
to face the enemy in pitched battle if they came down into the
gorge. The van was followed by a group of 'engineers' whose job
it was to level and clear the road for the phalanx and the
'baggage' (29.4, 30.7-9), which was advancing slowly in the rear
(30.5).

Antiochus' strategy was thus to be carried out in three
stages: the Cretans were to absorb the first enemy salvo and thus
uncover their hiding places; a counter-salvo by Antiochus'
'snipers' from above would 'soften up' the enemy's positions, so
to allow the light 'mountaineers', reinforced if necessary by the
thōrakitai climbing up the cliffs, to bear down upon the
barbarians. In an emergency the Cretans and the thyreaphoroi
would hinder any attempt by the enemy to force their way down the
road and engage the vulnerable heavy contingents.

The march proceeded as planned: the 'lights' occupied the
summits, the Cretans in the gorge probably attracted enemy fire
and exposed them to the mercy of Antiochus' light mountaineers,
who, after sniping from above, overran their positions (30.7-9).

The outstanding feature of Antiochus' plan was the use of the
Cretans as bait, a device quite common in modern warfare and
usually performed by crack forces in unarmoured vehicles
(especially jeeps), but, so far as I know, unique in Classical
and Hellenistic battles.[13] The combined manoeuvre of the 'missile
troops' and the thōrakitai is also interesting. One has only to
compare it with Hannibal's unhappy experiences in crossing the
Alps (Polyb. 3.49.5-56.4) to appreciate fully Antiochus' military
skill and ingenuity.

12: THE BATTLE OF PANION (200 B.C.)

Seleucid ambitions to occupy Coilē-Syria, which received a setback at Raphia, revived after the death of Ptolemy IV Philopator in 204 B.C. Under Ptolemy's infant son, the Egyptian court soon sank into an atmosphere of intrigue which facilitated the Seleucid invasion southwards in 202 B.C. (Polyb. 15.20; Hieron. In Dan. 11.13-14).[1] Antiochus III failed to occupy Gaza, the last Ptolemaic stronghold in southern Palestine, during 201 B.C. (Polyb. 16.22a),[2] and in winter of 201-200 B.C. he retired to Syria after setting up garrisons in key positions (see Map 10).[3] The Ptolemies, however, did not give up: supported by new recruits from Greece (Polyb. 15.25.16; Livy 31.43.5-7),[4] Scopas, the Aetolian officer serving as chief of staff in the Ptolemaic army, reoccupied Coilē-Syria in the winter of 200 B.C. (Jos. Ant. 12.131, 135; Hieron. loc.cit.).[5] Antiochus' counterattack probably took place the following summer.[6] The Egyptian army tried in vain to halt the enemy near the northern frontier, at Panion, and was defeated and scattered. Scopas himself, with 10,000 survivors, took refuge in Sidon (Hieron. op.cit. 15-16, based on Porphyrios),[7] probably in the hope of being evacuated by sea, but the Egyptian navy seems to have been delayed, and Scopas had to surrender to Antiochus' besieging force. Thus the long struggle in Coilē-Syria was decided ultimately in favour of the Seleucids.

Unfortunately, the only extant account of the battle is an indirect report which has survived in the sixteenth book of Polybius (par. 18-19). Berating Zeno of Rhodes for what he calls his preference for rhetorical phraseology over historical accuracy, Polybius tries to illustrate his argument by criticizing the version presented by Zeno of the battle of Panion. Consequently, we have at our disposal only those details which Polybius found to be unlikely, which makes it extremely difficult to evaluate his arguments and, of course, to reconstruct the course of the battle.

The battle of Panion   147

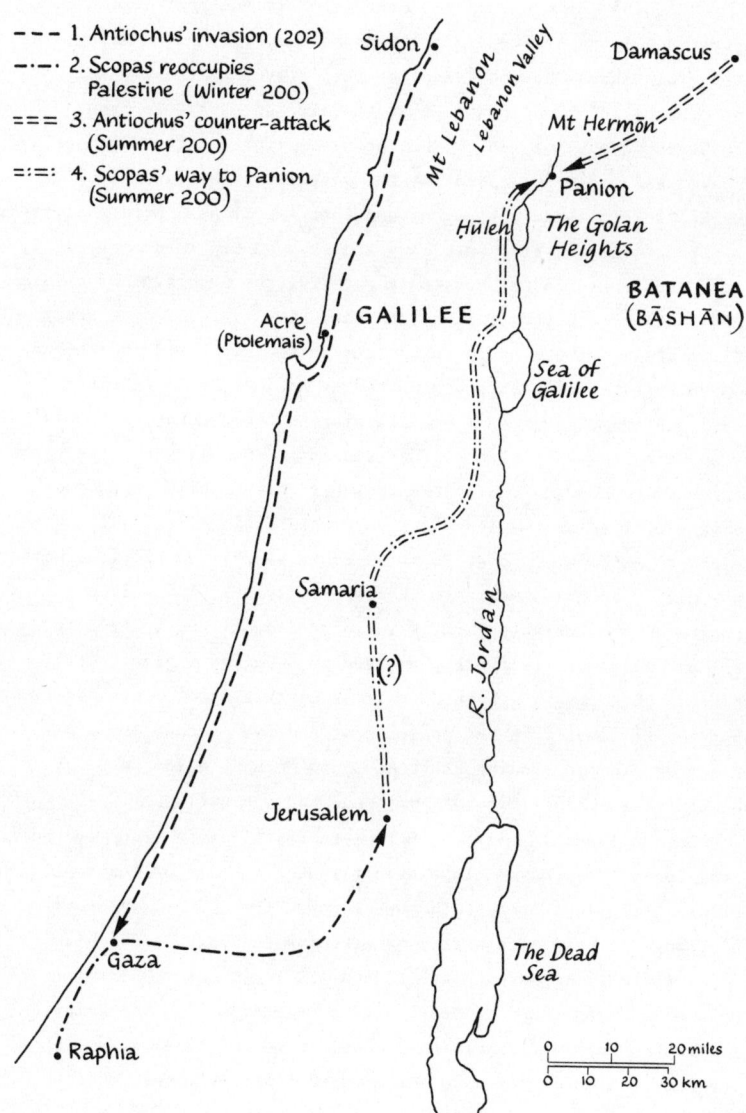

10 The Fifth Syrian War

Polybius' main points of contention are the positioning and operation of the Seleucid elephants and the Ptolemaic cavalry, the timing of Scopas' retreat, and the part played by the two sons of Antiochus III.[8] Zeno states that the elephants were in front of the Seleucid phalanx (18.7), but he also refers to the clash of two 'phalanxes' (18.9-10), ignoring the elephants. He also says that the Seleucid phalanx retreated, and that the elephants in their rear frightened the charging Aetolians and stopped their advance (19.1, 4). With regard to the Ptolemaic cavalry, the Aetolian horses are said to have been terrified by the elephants (19.4,6), but other statements attribute tough resistance to the right-wing horse and report that the left wing was routed by Antiochus' cataphracts (18.8, 19.4-6). Even more embarrassing is the account of Scopas' escape from the battlefield. He is said in one place to have retreated as soon as the centre was surrounded, while in another he is glorified as the last to abandon the field (19.10-11). With regard to Antiochus' sons, Polybius expresses his conviction that only one of them took part in the battle (19.8-9) while Zeno reports on the active participation of Antiochus the Younger as well as the Elder. Although he gives no detailed explanation,[9] it seems that what may have given rise to this opinion was the apparent similarity in the position of the two brothers on a hill or a mountain overlooking the enemy, and perhaps also the youthfulness at this time of Antiochus the Younger.

We shall consider later whether the battle site required the participation of the contingents attributed to both of the sons, but it should be stated at the outset that the age of Antiochus the Younger cannot necessarily be taken as support for Polybius' view. Although we have no exact details, it is not impossible that he was then about 15 years old.[10] Alexander led the campaign against the Thracian rebels at the age of 16 (Plut. Alex. 9.1);[11] Antiochus V Eupator, as a boy of 9 or 12 (App. Syr. 66: Euseb. Chron. I,p.254; I Macc. 6.28ff.), took part in the Seleucid expedition to Judaea; and Demetrius II, at 14, took an active part in the campaign that led to the dethronement of Alexander Balas (Justin 35.2.2). It may well be that even if Antiochus the Younger did not actually lead his contingent like Alexander, he at least played a token role, as his son did later in Judaea. In a period in which kings and princes played such important roles that men like Antigonus, Lysimachus, and Seleucus I took an active part and commanded their troops when in their eighties, 'command' by Antiochus IV at Panion does not appear too strange.

In his commentary on Polybius Walbank suspects Polybius himself of being responsible for the confusion over the battle: 'One cannot evaluate Polybius' criticism of Zeno's account in Panium simply on the basis of what Polybius says: he may have read Zeno carelessly' (II.523). But Polybius should surely be credited with being aware of the danger of carelessness at the very time when he is condemning the incompetence of the popular Rhodian historian. As will be shown below, Zeno's failure to refer to a certain topographical feature of the battlefield, and maybe also a few small inaccuracies in his terminology, rendered his account incomprehensible to Polybius and to anyone else who was not familiar with the battlefield. In fairness to Zeno, however, it must be stressed that the difficulty of describing the battle is aggravated by the tricky topography of the battle site and the resultant unconventional disposition of the troops.

Identification of the route taken by Antiochus to the battlefield may shed light on the strategy of the two sides. The location of the battlefield near Panion does not offer many alternatives: Panion, which has been identified beyond question with the village of Bānyās,[12] lies on the edge of one branch of the road from Damascus,[13] the eastern of the three main routes leading from Syria to northern Palestine, and Antiochus must therefore have tried to enter Palestine by this route.[14] It may be that like the Phoenician Passes near Sidon on the western road, the fortresses of Gerrha and Brochoi on the central road which controlled the pass into the Lebanon Valley and had proved to be so difficult to break through during the Fourth Syrian War, were now reoccupied by the Ptolemies (Polyb. 5.46.3-5, 61.7; Hieron. *In Dan.* 11.15-16). As the Damascus-Panion route was shortest, although the most difficult of the branches descending from Damascus to the western bank of the Jordan, it is evident that Antiochus was eager to reach flat ground as soon as possible. On the other hand, the Ptolemaic inferiority in phalanx[15] and elephants (see p.240 n.80 below) must have compelled Scopas to try to intercept the Seleucid army on the way down from the Golan Heights in order to block the entrance to the flat valley of the 'Via Maris' leading to Egypt, with the intention of forcing a battle in hilly ground on the east which would have favoured his Aetolian mercenaries and obstructed the Seleucid elephants and phalanx. But as appears from the location of the battle and its course he was too late; Antiochus had already encamped on the level ground west of Panion before Scopas arrived (18.6), and the decisive part of the battle had to be fought on this terrain.

The exact site of the battlefield should be sought in the immediate vicinity of Panion. The locality gained some importance only in the Roman period (known by that time as Caesarea Philippi), and therefore a battle bearing the name of Panion could not have taken place too far away. Panion itself is situated at the junction of the Golan Heights on the southeast with the slopes of Mt Hermon on the north (see Map 11 at end). A crescent-shaped plain juts out from Panion to the west to form a 1.5 km wide 'platform' that descends sharply to the Ḥuleh Valley. This platform, now named 'Bānyās Plateau', is dominated on its northern side by Tel Ḥamrā, a foothill of Mt Ḥermon. The El-Bānyās River, which emerges from a cave, flows along the edge of the platform on the east and on the south and being fairly shallow for 1.5 km it does not constitute any obstacle, but, as it approaches the slopes of the Golan Heights near Taḥūnet ūm Ra'ai, its banks become precipitous and it cannot be crossed. It continues like this for 2 km, until the river turns sharply westward into the Ḥuleh Valley. On the other side of the river, south of Bānyās Plateau, soars Tel-'Azzāziyāt. This hill, the lowest terrace of the Golan Heights, is dominated by Tel-Fakhr in the east and is separated from it by a rough and uneven plateau. The course the river takes imposes an impassable barrier between the Bānyās Plateau and the hilly area on its south and southeast.

Polybius' topographical references suggest that the left part of the battlefield was flat (18.4,6), separated from the Seleucid camp by the river (18.6), and dominated on the left side by a hill or a mountain,[16] while the other part, at least on the Ptolemaic side, was on the lowest slopes of a mountain (ὑπωρεία - 18.4). The only ground in the vicinity of Panion that fits these requirements

is the area on both sides of the canyon of Nahr El-Bānyās: the
'level ground' is to be identified with Bānyās Plateau; the
river with Nahr El-Bānyās; the commanding hill with Tel-Ḥamrā; and
the lowest slopes of the mountain with Tel-'Azzāziyāt.[17] As the
main part of the Seleucid army crossed the river, arrayed itself in
the flat ground, and utilized its right flank to occupy the hill
which dominated the plain, it can be concluded that the Seleucids
were posted in the east and the Ptolemies in the west, as is
indeed evident from the identification of the route taken by
Antiochus and the strategy of Scopas. I shall try now to analyse
in more detail the various topographical indications and locate
them in the battlefield:

(1) The main part of the Seleucid army, including the
elephants and phalanx, left the camp, which was probably located in
Panion itself, crossed the river, and took up positions on the
'level ground' (18.6). Antiochus must have crossed the river in
the 'bottleneck' of Bānyās Plateau between Panion and Taḥūnet ūm
Ra'ai, where the water is shallow and traversable. The Seleucid
force was posted then along the length of Bānyās Plateau facing
the enemy from east to west.

(2) The Ptolemaic left was posted on the 'level ground' -
Bānyās Plateau - and its right, consisting mainly of Aetolian
infantry and some cavalry, on the lowest slopes of a mountain
(ὑπώρεια - 18.4).[18] As the Ptolemaic right was posted in the
south, the designation ὑπώρεια does fit Tel-'Azzāziyāt and the
neighbouring hills, which form the lowest terrace of the Golan
Heights.[19]

(3) Antiochus the Younger, commanding the heavy cavalry
which was part of the main corps, occupied a 'mountain' on the
right, which dominated the left wing of that part of the
Ptolemaic army posted in the flat ground (18.8). Tel-Ḥamrā, which
is undoubtedly the hill referred to, can easily be occupied by a
force coming from Panion, and its moderate slopes to the south did
not pose particular difficulties for the Seleucid heavy cavalry in
descending toward Scopas' left flank on Bānyās Plateau.

(4) A contingent under Antiochus the Elder was sent by the
king in the early morning, before he crossed the river, to occupy
mountainous positions overlooking the enemy (18.5, 19.8).[20] As

the northern hill (Tel-Ḥamrā) was occupied by Antiochus the
Younger, the only possible identification for this hill area is
with Tel-Fakhr, overlooking Tel-'Azzāziyāt from the east. This
suggestion receives some support from the absence of any
reference to the troops of Antiochus the Elder's crossing the
river, aside from the obvious necessity of posting a substantial
force diagonally on Tel-Fakhr to contain the Aetolians on Tel-
'Azzāziyāt, who could have attacked the Seleucid rear camp at
Panion and the troops on the plain from the rear.

But the statement that Antiochus the Elder occupied
positions 'which commanded the enemy' (ὑπερκειμένους τῶν πολεμίων
τόπους) poses a considerable difficulty in itself: as the
Ptolemaic camp was situated across the river, i.e. on Bānyās
Plateau or, what is more probable, to its west (18.6) in the Ḥuleh
Valley, and could not be dominated by troops posted on Tel-Fakhr,
we must assume that Scopas occupied Tel-'Azzāziyāt before
Antiochus began his manoeuvres. But if he was so quick, why did he
fail to occupy the nearby position of Tel-Ḥamrā, which proved to be
so fateful in the course of the battle (18.8)? The only alternative
explanation to the puzzling description of the position of
Antiochus the Elder is, therefore, that Zeno was not being precise
in his language, and the 'mountainous positions' commanded a part
of the Ptolemaic enemy only at a later stage, when Scopas sent his
troops to Tel-'Azzāziyāt. Zeno, basing his account on Ptolemaic
sources, describes the Ptolemaic battle order first (18.4), in
disregard of the actual sequence of events, and this may account
for his careless wording. It may well be that, turning later to
the Seleucid disposition, he tried, as an historian who took so
much pain with style, to avoid verbosity, and instead of saying
'mountainous positions which commanded the lowest terrace of the
mountain' phrased it negligently as 'positions which commanded the
places of the enemy'.

Piecing together these conclusions it seems clear that the
battle took place in two different arenas separated by the
precipitous banks of Nahr El-Bānyās, Bānyās Plateau in the north,
and the rough plateau between Tel-'Azzāziyāt and Tel-Fakhr in the
south, each force having a centre and two wings on each of the
battlefields. The two arenas together offered a battlefield 3 km

wide and, assuming that the Seleucid phalanx was deployed 32 lines deep (cf. Livy 37.40.2), and that a considerable part of the cavalry was heavy (p.74 above), so that each horse occupied 3 feet of space leaving no gaps between the *ilai* (see p.168 below), this accords with the conclusion that the battle was on a scale similar to that of Raphia and Magnesia (p.19 above). It should be noted that the separation of the forces and the resultant difficulties of controlling them simultaneously do not conflict with my suggestion and are well in line with the tactics of the period: in a battle line extending over 3-4 km such as occasionally occurred in the Hellenistic period, it was, in any case, impossible for the commander-in-chief to control the extreme wings.[21] At any rate, it should be noted that Bānyās Plateau is visible from the southern arena and vice versa.

The condition of the terrain and the special character of the double arena would have dictated the tactics and the disposition of the troops. Antiochus was anxious to make sure of a position on Tel-Ḥamrā and Tel-Fakhr, hence his manoeuvres in the early morning. He took the offensive in the northern flat arena, which was advantageous to his elephants and phalanx, and offered him a commanding position over Scopas' left wing (from Tel-Ḥamrā), and he took the defensive in the hilly southern arena, which favoured the Aetolians.[22] A Seleucid victory in the south could not affect the developments in the north, since the Ptolemies in Bānyās Plateau were protected by the river on their right, but the failure of the Seleucid defence in the south could have brought the total collapse of the main corps in the north: Scopas' only chance was to break the Seleucid line around Tel-Fakhr and reach the enemy camp at Panion. I would suggest that his tactics were based mainly on capturing the Seleucid *aposkeuē*,[23] although he may have aimed also at taking the Seleucids on Bānyās Plateau from the rear while in the north he had to be content with holding the front. The early occupation of Tel-Ḥamrā forced him to set the bulk of the Aetolian cavalry, regarded at that time as the best among the Greeks (Polyb. 18.22.5), to defending the vulnerable left wing facing this hill (18.6, 19.4), while the remaining cavalry together with the Aetolian infantry was sent to Tel-'Azzāziyāt (19.1,4).

The elephants standing 'in the front of the phalanx' would then have been positioned in the northern flat arena where they could easily charge the enemy, while on the rough terrain in the south they could have been used only as a second-line defence behind the infantry (18.7, 19.1-3).[24] Consequently, the cavalry mentioned by Zeno as being terrified by the sight of the elephants must have been the unit posted in the south which, supported by the Aetolian infantry, probably succeeded in breaking the Seleucid infantry line and then had to tackle the elephants. Antiochus had enough elephants in 200 B.C. to apply these tactics; in his Indian expedition, 206 B.C., he brought the number of elephants up to 150 (Polyb. 11.34.10-12). As the Aetolians who were routed by Antiochus the Younger occupied the left (north) of the northern arena, the cavalry 'on the right' that maintained its position (19.4-5) must have been on the right of that arena.

It seems then, that the identification of the battlefield provides a solution to most of the arguments raised by Polybius. But, as a matter of fact, the absurdity of the contradictions alone suggest the existence of two different arenas. The relative abundance of topographical details indicates that Zeno's authority was an eyewitness. Even if Zeno was extremely negligent,[25] he certainly did not invent the contradictory details. A distortion of his reliable and authentic information in the way it is recorded in Polybius is out of question, and any set of identifications that fails to tackle the difficulties must be ruled out.

Turning back to Polybius' criticism, it seems clear that Zeno is guilty of not describing the special topographical background of the battle, although this is, in fact, something that Polybius does only occasionally himself. Judging Zeno's account by Polybius' standards, his main fault was in failing to make clear that the river separated the battlefield into two arenas, and that the battle was fought simultaneously in both. Polybius does not usually ignore such details, and one would imagine that, had he found it in Zeno's account, he would have dropped most of his arguments. It may also be that Polybius was further misled by a misuse of terminology. The term <u>keras</u> could have been applied to both arenas as well as to the wings of each (see e.g. 18.4). Even if Zeno had been more precise, and had used meros to define the troops in each arena and keras for the wing (e.g. 18.5), it is possible that Polybius, not understanding the topographical background, could have interpreted these two terms as synonyms (cf. I Macc. 9.15 and p.275 n.34 below). And indeed even an occasional use of undefined 'left' or 'right' could well have caused a good deal of confusion (see e.g. 18.6,8; 19.5).[26]

To bring the fragments of the picture together it will help to summarize the disposition of the forces and the course of the battle. The northern arena, under Antiochus III himself, was protected on the right by the heavy cavalry, the cataphracts, under the nominal command of Antiochus the Younger, posted on Tel-Ḥamrā (18.6,8). The elephants were drawn up in front of the centre, the intervals between them being filled, as was customary, by archers and slingers, in addition to the Tarentines (18.7), whose duty as light cavalry was probably to protect the elephants on their vulnerable flanks, and perhaps also to pursue the enemy in case the centre collapsed before the issue in the wings had been decided. The centre is described by Polybius as consisting of phalanx (18.6-7), but it included other contingents also, since Antiochus III, accompanied by the Companions and the hypaspists, was said to have been posted 'behind the elephants' (18.7-8,19.7). The identity of the cavalry on the right is not known (19.5). The Egyptian disposition is more obscure: the only fact that can be stated with confidence is that the left flank, under Ptolemy, son of Aeropos, was occupied by Aetolian cavalry (18.8). It may be suggested that Scopas deployed elephants in front of the centre to protect it from the superior Seleucid phalanx. The absence of a clear indication in Polybius' references and even the possibility that Zeno himself did not mention them do not necessarily prove that they did not take part in the battle: the superiority of the Seleucid Indian elephant over the Ptolemaic African elephant rendered their fight a mere formality.

The southern arena, commanded by Antiochus the Elder, was occupied by phalanx and some cavalry backed by a 'wall' of elephants as a second defence line (18.5, 9, 19.1, 4). They were posted diagonally on the northwestern slopes of Tel-Fakhr blocking the approach to Panion. The Aetolians on Tel-'Azzāziyāt, although they are described as forming a 'phalanx' (18.4, 9, 19.1), seem to have consisted mainly of medium-heavy infantry: Zeno, or perhaps Polybius, is obviously simplifying the names and disposition of the †troops. The infantry was supported by Aetolian cavalry (18.4, 19.4).

The battle was actually decided by the success of the Seleucid right wing in the northern arena. Taking advantage of their commanding position and heavy armour, the 'cataphracts' swept away the Aetolian cavalry and came back to take the Ptolemaic phalanx from the rear (18.8, 19.10). This manoeuvre, coupled with the charge of the elephants, which had meanwhile presumably dispersed the Ptolemaic skirmishers or elephant corps, put pressure on the Ptolemaic infantry in the centre (19.11), and probably caused the cavalry on the right, which had so far stood firm (19.5), to give way. It follows that the Seleucid centre did not come into contact with the Ptolemaic line, hence the absence of any reference to Antiochus' part in the actual fighting. At the same time the struggle in the south had reached deadlock: the Aetolians had scattered the Seleucid phalanx, but were cut off by the living wall of the elephants (19.1,4) until the issue was decided in the north.

One enigma in Zeno's account has yet to be solved. Even if Polybius' criticism concerning the escape of Scopas has substance, there must be some explanation for this confusion. Scopas is reported to have lost heart and, in Polybius' words, ποιεῖσθαι τὴν ἀποχώρησιν when his centre was surrounded (19.10). But, in fact, he may just have 'retreated' from the northern arena without actually leaving the battlefield. Scopas, realising that his presence in the north would be of no help, made haste to the south (certainly on horseback) in a desperate attempt to break the deadlock and turn the scales. Later, as the situation in the north was deteriorating and the struggle in the south remained undecided, Scopas took the decision to retreat. The favourable position of the troops in that arena facilitated an organized withdrawal so that Scopas could afford to be among the last to abandon the field, leaving behind the phalanx in the north, which was torn to pieces by the Seleucid pincer movement. The retreat of the considerable number of 10,000 soldiers with Scopas to Sidon may perhaps be explained by the suggestion that they comprised the

Aetolians posted in the southern arena: the rough and hostile route to Sidon necessitated a perfectly organized and controlled retreat, which was impossible for the surrounded troops in the northern arena. The latter were probably those said by Josephus, certainly on the authority of Polybius, to have been exterminated at Panion (Ant. 12.132). On this point Zeno certainly did not fall victim to the topographical obscurities, but must be blamed for careless reporting of his sources, or rather for the omission of some vital details about Scopas' movements.

To sum up: although Zeno's account is not the best or most accurate one could wish to find, it generally lives up to the average standard of ancient historiography. On the other hand, Polybius' ruthless attack did not arise from 'careless reading', as Walbank suggests, but was occasioned by the obscurities of a unique topographical situation. Polybius himself was perhaps not completely confident of the accuracy of his criticism. Otherwise his letter would have drawn Zeno's attention to the absurdity of his account, as it did with regard to Zeno's topographical errors in regard to Nabis' attempt on Messene (16.20.5-7).[27] Is it too bold a conjecture that Polybius, who was so satisfied with Zeno's admission of his ignorance with regard to the topography of the area of Megalopolis (16.20.7),[28] Polybius' native city, sensed that perhaps some answers to his questions about Panion were to be found in the topography of the place which neither he nor Zeno were acquainted with?[29]

13: THE DEFENCE OF THERMOPYLAE (191 B.C.)

With the settlement of the eastern problem and the occupation of Coilē-Syria, Antiochus III was now free to turn his attention to the Aegean world. His operations in the area soon brought him in conflict with Rome. Diplomatic negotiations failed to achieve an agreement, and Antiochus, disheartened by the toughening of the Roman policy, yielded to the promises and enticements of the Aetolians, incited by the overthrow of the pro-Roman faction at Demetrias, to 'liberate' Greece and thereby possibly improve his bargaining position.[1] Antiochus had at his disposal in Asia Minor only about 18,000 troops (see p.18 above), but he crossed the Aegean hastily at the beginning of the winter hoping to receive support, especially from the Aetolians and Philip V. In the first months of his stay in Greece he engaged in an exhaustive diplomatic and military campaign to make sure of allies for the expected confrontation with the Romans. But the Roman invasion came too soon: 20,000 infantry, 2,000 cavalry, and 15 elephants crossed to Greece from Brundisium in the early spring (Livy 36.14.1; App. Syr. 15(65)). Antiochus was caught unprepared: the bulk of the army, especially the cavalry, was stranded in Asia; part of his landing force was scattered over Greece in garrisons, and a number of them surrendered to the Romans. Worse, the expected local help did not materialize: Philip V sided with Rome and the Aetolian auxiliary numbered only 4,000 infantry. At this stage Antiochus had 10,000 infantry, 500 cavalry, and six elephants of his own (Livy 36.15.3). In these circumstances he had to rule out a confrontation on the open field. A Roman detachment had occupied the Tempe Pass some time before (Livy 36.10.11), and so the only alternative was to make an attempt at the old battlefield at the pass of Thermopylae (see Map 12).

Antiochus' strategy was to bar the Roman advance by blocking the pass itself and preventing any possibility of detour either by sea or land, aiming in this way to gain time until the expected

The defence of Thermopylae

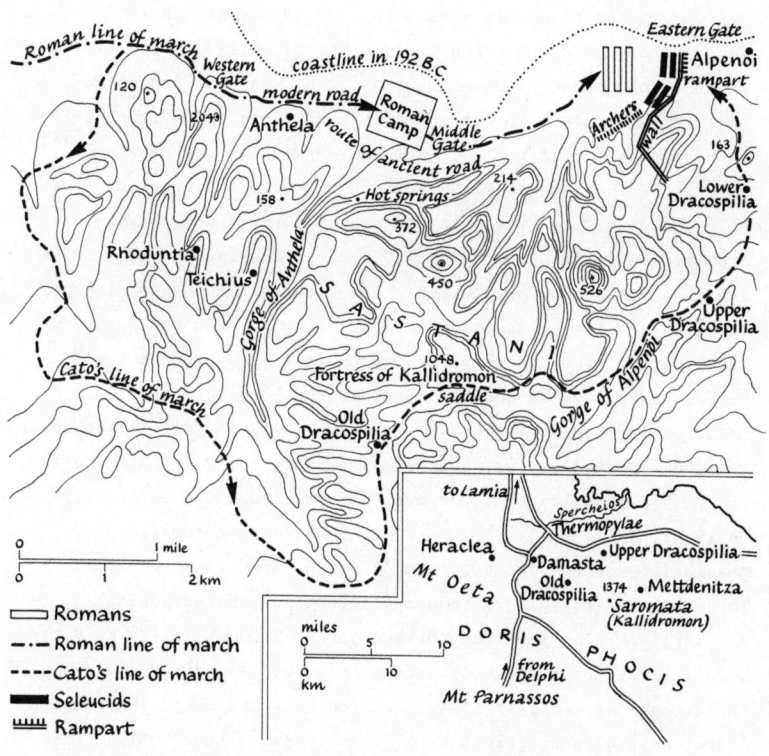

12 The battlefield of Thermopylae according to Kromayer's
    reconstruction (<u>Schlachtfelder Atlas, Röm. Abt.</u> Sh.8)

arrival of the troops from Asia that would enable him to launch a decisive attack on the open field (App. Syr. 17(75)). Taking into account topographical advantage, his line was designed to be able to turn immediately to the offensive and destroy the Roman forces in case they should try to break the defence in the pass. The defence of the 'gates' was spread over several fronts: the pass in the middle, the trails in the mountain range dominating the pass from the south, and a rough circle enclosing the area. The sea side was blocked by the navy and garrisons at Chalcis, Cape Konaion, and Demetrias (Livy 36.5.1, 33.4-6),[2] and the land route on the other side, passing through the Aesopos gorge to the Dorian plain, was barred by the 2,000 Aetolians garrisoning Heraclea and Hypata (Livy 36.17.10; App. Syr. 18(79)).[3] The range overlooking the pass was guarded by another 2,000 Aetolians drawn up on three summits, Callidromus, Teichius, and Rhoduntia (Livy 36.16.11, 17.1, 2, 18.8), which presumably prevented any possibility of the Seleucid army's being taken from the rear.[4] This force seems to have been sufficient for the purpose: Justinian is also reported to have posted 2,000 soldiers to guard the trails through the Callidromus (Procop. De Aedific. 4.2.7-10).[5] The defence of the pass itself was concentrated round the eastern 'gate' near Alpenoi (Livy 36.16.1; App. Syr. 17-18(76-8).[6] This access was preferred to the central and western gates because there were fewer trails bypassing it by way of Callidromus, so that the range could more easily be blocked. Furthermore, as the slopes of the hills overlooking the eastern gate were less steep than those above the other two entries, Antiochus was able to station 'snipers' there.[7]

The eastern gate was blocked by low earthworks with a ditch in front, both extending to the sea (Livy 36.16.3, 18.8; App. Syr. 18(78)).[8] The width of the pass at its narrowest point is estimated to have been 90 m.[9] The rampart gave way to a stone wall the remains of which can still be seen, which climbed 1,800 m up the hill in the south until it reached an impassable cliff.[10] A pair of ravines in front of the stone wall protected it on the north.[11] The wall was designed to prevent the Romans from outflanking the Seleucid force if they succeeded in dislodging its light troops posted on the hill in front of the wall.

According to Appian, Antiochus placed mēchanai, i.e. artillery machines of various types, on the wall (probably the stone wall, and not the rampart) so that they could provide 'cover' for the front of the rampart (App. Syr. 18(78)).[12] Special towers were probably built on the wall to house the 'machines',[13] and these, in addition to their fine defensive position, constituted additional protection against capture. Nothing is said about the operation of the artillery in the course of the battle, but then the role of the snipers on the hill is also passed over in silence. The battle of Thermopylae thus seems to be the only case on record in which the Seleucids used artillery in a field battle. But, in fact, the defensive character of the engagement and the condition of the terrain make this battle similar to siege warfare in which the Hellenistic armies used artillery in the defence as well.[14] Philip V used artillery in similar circumstances at the River Aous (Livy 37.18.5).[15] The stationing and assembling of the machines well in advance in a safe place, and the 'static' nature of the battle, which meant that the lines between the two armies were clearly drawn, avoided the difficulties that usually hindered the use of artillery in pitched battles.[16]

The phalanx was posted behind the rampart, and the 'lights' and the 'peltasts' in front of it; the latter unit is to be identified with the argyraspides, the crack force of the infantry (see p.63 above). The left flank was defended by archers, slingers, and dart throwers posted on the hills on the south outside the wall, who in view of their location could not have comprised more than a few hundred, and the right wing near the sea was protected by the elephants, followed by the cavalry commanded by Antiochus himself (Livy 36.18.3, 5,19.4; App. Syr. 18-19; Plut. Cat.Mai. 14.1).

This battle order was designed to provide for two possibilities: in one case, the artillery, the 'snipers' on the hills, and the lights and argyraspides in front of the rampart, after breaking the enemy's onslaught, were to turn immediately to the offensive and pursue the enemy, with the support of the cavalry behind the elephants; in the second, if the Romans succeeded in dispersing the skirmishers and 'peltasts', they would end up in front of the rampart facing the phalanx with no possibility of outflanking it, for the two wings would be protected by the elephants on the sea side and by the wall on the hillside. The front lines of the phalanx were stationed on the rampart so that the ditch and the soldiers' long sarissae would aggravate the difficulties of approaching the Seleucid centre (App. Syr. 19(84); Livy 36.18.3).

This dense line of defence proved to be effective: although the attempt to break the Roman line failed, and the Seleucid skirmishers and 'peltasts' gave way and retreated behind the rampart, the impenetrable line of the phalanx's pikes succeeded in bringing the battle to a deadlock. The Roman breakthrough occurred on Callidromus where the position was stormed by Cato. It may be suggested that, being in a position far from the main trails, the watch was somewhat negligent, as Appian indicates (18(81)),[17] and was taken by surprise. The appearance of Cato in the Seleucid rear decided the battle. Appian comments that Cato's detachment seemed large to the Seleucids, whom the reputation of the Romans and rumours about their style of warfare threw into panic (19(86)).[18] This may partly account for the Seleucid reaction, but Cato himself, when he took with him a relatively small detachment, could not have relied in advance on the effect of the 'Roman reputation'. Despite its rigidity, the phalanx could be split to face an attack from the rear, and the argyraspides and 'lights' who had retreated behind the phalanx lines could surely have withstood Cato's men. Cato must have been planning to capture the Seleucid camp and the aposkeuē, and this threat, coupled with the impression that he had with him a considerable force, demoralized Antiochus' army. Appian in fact states that Antiochus' troops, fearing for the safety of the camp, hastened to its defence (18(87)), no doubt in a desperate attempt to save the 'baggage' accumulated in Greece in the course of several months.[19]

14: THE BATTLE OF MAGNESIA (190 B.C.)

The abortive invasion of Greece, which revealed Antiochus as an open and declared enemy of Rome, made necessary military intervention to back up Roman demands for the evacuation of Thrace and the Ionian cities. Antiochus at first tried to fortify the Hellespont against the expected crossing by Roman expedition, but, after losing control over the Aegean in the naval battle of Myonnesus (off Teos), he realized that the naval supremacy of the Romans would enable them to bypass his land fortifications in the Dardanelles, and he abandoned them. After the failure of further negotiations, both sides were determined to seek a solution by arms. Antiochus mobilized his army from Sardis along the Hermos Valley to Magnesia-ad-Sipylum against the Romans, who were advancing from the Pergamon area to Thyateira in the Hyrcanian Plain, and thence along the Phrygios southwards.[1] Magnesia, which in 281 B.C. had been the site of the battle of Curupedion, which was decisive in opening the way to the west for the Seleucids,[2] was now to see the beginnings of Roman expansion in the east and Seleucid decline.

The main sources for the battle are the parallel versions of Livy 37.37-44 and Appian Syr. 30-6, based solely on Polybius,[3] who himself made extensive use of Rhodian, Achaean and Pergamene sources, probably in addition to reports from eyewitnesses.[4] Apart from occasional references, we have at our disposal three shorter versions of later epitomators: Florus, based on Roman annalists (1.24.16-18), is worthless; Justin, epitomizing Pompeius Trogus, who follows the Polybian tradition in the main, preserves at least one vital detail omitted by the two main sources (36.8.1-8); Zonaras' narrative (9.20 A-C) shows the influence of both the Polybian and annalistic traditions drawn on by Dio Cassius, his source,[5] but apart from some trivial details does not contribute much.

The precise identification of the battlefield, the location

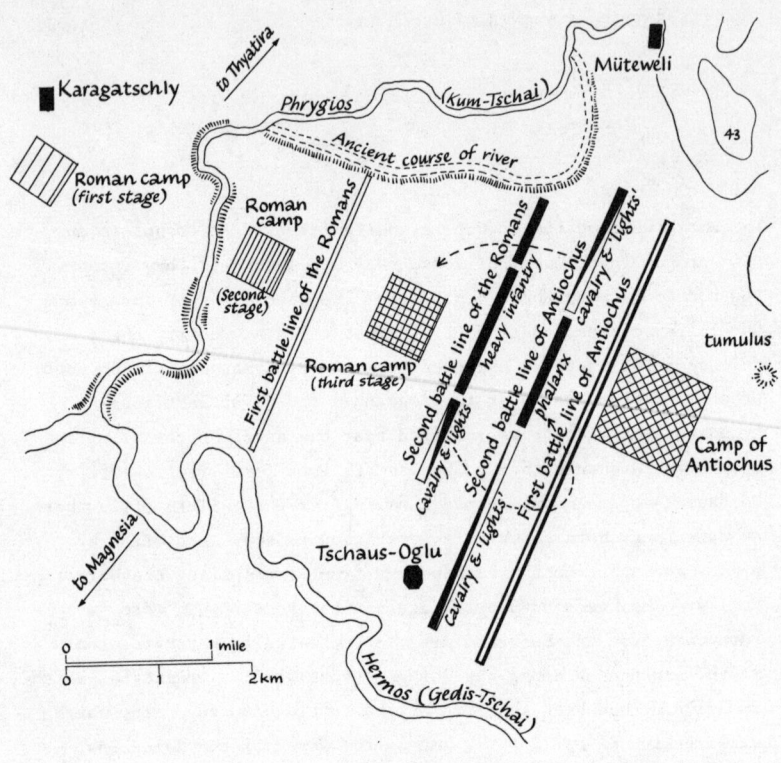

13 The battlefield of Magnesia according to Kromayer's reconstruction (<u>Schlachtfelder Atlas, Röm. Abt</u>. Sh.9, M.8)

of the two camps, and the movements of both sides on the eve of the battle were decisively established by Kromayer (see Map 13), to whom we owe also the first comprehensive analysis of the battle. According to various indications in Livy, Kromayer set the battlefield on the level ground between the Phrygios (Kum) and Hermos (Gedis) rivers northeast of Magnesia (Manisa), close to the main road from Smyrna to Sardis. The arena, bounded on three sides by the rivers, the Hermos to the south and the Phrygios to the west and north, is shaped like a horseshoe with the open end to the east.[6]

The Romans, who came from the northwest, crossed the Phrygios and awaited Antiochus in the narrow part of the 'horseshoe' on the west in order to diminish the effect of Antiochus' great numerical superiority and gain protection against attack on their flanks by Antiochus' superior cavalry from the rivers (see below), but, when their challenge was refused, they could not afford to play for time because of the approaching winter, and advanced (Livy 37.37.5, 39.5), making some concession to the enemy by approaching the point where the Phrygios makes a 90° turn northwards and the width of the horseshoe between the Hermos and the Phrygios was 4.7 km (see Map 13 - 'second battleline of the Romans'). Although the Roman force could put one of its flanks against the river (ibid. 11), the new challenge seemed more acceptable to Antiochus. He would of course have preferred to force a battle on the open field further to the east, but being aware of the implications to the morale of his troops, who in view of their numerical superiority might have lost heart on witnessing his evasive manoeuvres, and perhaps being informed of the Romans' intentions of storming his camp (possibly at night) if he persisted in refusing battle (id. 37.39.4, 6), he ultimately decided to accept the challenge.

Of the two battle lines, the Roman's is easier to reconstruct and can help in clarifying some obscurities in Antiochus' array (see Map 14 at end). The force, 30,000 strong (id. 37.39.7-10; App. Syr. 31(157-9)), was drawn up as follows: 4 turmae, numbering probably 120 cavalry,[7] were posted on the extreme left, next to the Phrygios (Livy 37.39.11). A long line of two Roman legions covered on their flanks by two Latin alae, occupied the Roman centre (id. 37.39.8; App. Syr. 31(157)).[8] The right wing comprised

3,000 Pergamene and Achaean peltasts, and on their flank were 3,000 cavalry of whom 800 were Pergamene and the rest Roman (Livy 37.39.9), who probably belonged to the legions.[9] Some 500 Trallians and 500 Cretans were deployed next to them, or rather in advance of the right.[10] The _velites_ of the legions, numbering probably about 6,000, can be assumed to have been posted in front of the legions in their traditional role as skirmishers.[11]

Without counting the intervals between the various contingents, the Roman line probably extended over 3,000 m: the 4 _turmae_ on the left did not occupy much space; the centre, allowing 450 m to each legion and _ala_,[12] can be estimated to have occupied over 1,800 m. The 3,000 cavalry on the right would have occupied 675 m,[13] and the 3,000 peltasts, standing in a closer formation (see p.252 n.9 below), probably took up half that, so that, all in all, the right wing occupied about 1,000 m.

The main stumbling block in the reconstruction of the Seleucid line is the position of the light infantry. According to Livy and Appian's lists the Seleucid line comprised 16,000 phalangites in the centre; to their right were Galatian infantry, cataphracts, the cavalry _agēma_, _argyraspides_, and Dahae horse; on the left were Galatians, Cappadocians, infantry of mixed nationalities, cataphract cavalry, and the Companion cavalry (Livy 37.40.1-8; App. _Syr._ 32(161 -5)). Livy adds a considerable number of light infantry on the extreme flanks - 10,000 to the right and 15,000 to the left (37.40. 8-9, 13-14) - while Appian combines them in a single list after describing the basic line mentioned above (32(166-7)). Livy's list is usually regarded as more accurate,[14] but on this point I prefer to follow Appian and suggest that the separate mention of the light infantry indicates that they served as front-line skirmishers.[15] Livy's failure to list the skirmishers supports this assumption, especially in view of the various references to the participation of Antiochus' light _promachoi_ in the battle (Livy 37.42.4; App. _Syr._ 33(169,170), 35(178)), and the obvious necessity of such a force to confront the Roman _velites_. Moreover, if Livy's battle order is to be accepted, it follows that the light infantry on the right had to face a Latin _ala_. The suggestion that Antiochus would at the same time have deepened the phalanx to the extraordinary depth of 32 lines, and yet abandoned

the light infantry to the mercy of the Latin _ala_, is highly
unacceptable. On the left he would have had 15,000 light troops
extending beyond the Roman line; it might have been sound tactics
to deploy cavalry in this way, but to post archers, etc., a few
kilometres away from the battle line does not make sense. The
description of the light contingents placed by Livy on the
extreme left as '_alia multitudo, par ei, quae in dextro cornu erat_'
(40.13), which recalls Appian's _plēthos_ (32(166)), suggests that
Polybius considered these troops a separate group. If one does not
attribute this classification to the heterogeneity of their light
equipment, it indicates that Polybius posted them separately from
the flanks in the front. Livy, who lacked proper understanding in
military affairs, may have been misled by vague or ambiguous terms
used by Polybius and perhaps carried away by patriotic feelings as
he so often was;[16] by attributing an extraordinary length to the
Seleucid line he made the Roman victory seem all the more glorious.

Having disposed of this obstacle we may turn to the analysis
of the Seleucid disposition. Antiochus' army totalled 60,000
infantry and 12,000 cavalry. The phalanx at the centre was
divided into 10 divisions (_merē_), each made up of 32 lines in
depth and 50 men abreast, and each flanked on each side by 2
elephants and their light guard (Livy 37.40.1-4).[17] As a
phalangite required 3 feet in breadth (Polyb. 18.29.2), each _meros_
took up 150 feet (45 m), and all the divisions together about 450
m, while the total of the spaces between the _merē_, assuming each
elephant to have been accompanied by 50 'lights' (see p.8 above),
may be estimated at about 200 m. Thus the phalanx line equalled a
legion and a half. It may well be that the 3,000 Galatians on
either side of the phalanx, though adhering to their traditional
style, supplemented the phalanx facing the legion and the Latin
ala on the Roman right. This view receives a measure of support
from the curious mistake of Appian's which, when rectified,
suggests that 22 elephants were assigned to all the divisions
(32(162))[18] This implies that there were elephants in the spaces
between the outside divisions and the Galatians, who could then
be considered an intrinsic part of Antiochus' centre.

Antiochus' right flank therefore faced the Roman legion and
Latin _ala_ on the Roman left and their 4 _turmae_. It consisted of

3,000 cataphract cavalry, 1,000 cavalry agēma, an unspecified
number of argyraspides, and 1,200 Dahae horse (Livy 37.40.5-8).[19]
There were presumably no special intervals between the ilai of
heavy, armoured cavalry (in contrast to ordinary cavalry, Polyb.
12.18.3-4) in view of their vulnerability in the flanks, their
inability to turn and face enemy troops on their sides, and the
necessity of deploying them in a close, compact line, similar to
that of the phalangites in order to best exploit their offensive
advantages. The 4,000 cataphracts and agēma each occupied,
therefore, a space no more than 3 feet wide (on the heavy equipment
of the agēma in the second century B.C., see p. 74 above) in the
usual 8-line formation and thus covered an area 450 m wide,
matching the left Roman legion. This leaves the argyraspides - the
infantry Guard equipped and operating in the style of the phalanx -
to face the Latin ala on the extreme left. The Dahae should be
left out of consideration because light cavalry could not have
charged the Latin ala, and, had the argyraspides been only a small
contingent, Antiochus would have thinned his phalanx in the centre
rather than risk his flank in such an unequal fight. As
Antiochus' right was not confined by the river, the Dahae would
have been posted for part of their length opposite the turmae, but
would mainly have extended beyond the Roman line as a mobile
reserve force and as a defence for the flank of the argyraspides.

In the discussion of the argyraspides reference was made to
some sources suggesting that the standard strength of this
contingent stood at 10,000 troops (pp.60,62 above). The space
of 450 m suggested for the Latin ala on the opposite side
corresponds to a phalanx disposition of 24 lines deep. The
relative thinness of this line in comparison with the 32 lines of
the centre may be attributed to the higher military standard of
the Guard and the obvious necessity of posting a strong contingent
to face the whole opposing legion. Without being too dogmatic,
even allowing for a thinner line of argyraspides, or the rather
remote possibility that some Dahae confronted the ala, it must be
admitted that the number of about 10,000 argyraspides is highly
probable. In discussing the numerical strength of the Seleucid
armies I have already suggested that the omission of these 10,000
argyraspides may account for the substantial discrepancy between

the total number of troops and the figures attributed by Livy to each of the various contingents (p.9 above). It must be added that the absence of any figure for the argyraspides and of any reference to their role in the battle does not prove that they were only a small unit. Polybius similarly fails to give the number of the chariots despite the crucial part they played in the course of the battle, and his battle accounts are by no means comprehensive: e.g. in the description of Raphia, developments involving contingents not much smaller than the suggested 10,000 argyraspides are passed over in silence (see p.136 below).

The cavalry, the 3,000 peltasts of Eumenes, and the light infantry of the Roman right wing were confronted, from left to right, by 2,000 Cappadocians equipped in the Galatian style, and 2,700 auxiliares mixti omnium generum, probably light oriental infantry (see p.51 above), covering together a front equivalent to that occupied by the peltasts alone. The cavalry on the extreme flank, consisting of 3,000 cataphracts and 1,000 regia ala (the Companions, Livy 37.40.10-13), had to face 3,000 Roman horse. As the Roman cavalry formation required twice as much space as the Seleucid heavy cavalry, it certainly overlapped the Seleucid line by a few hundred metres, but the 2,500 Galatian cavalry and the possibly 500 Tarentines (see p.239 n.75 below; Livy 37.40.13), who were undoubtedly posted on the left of the Companions and cataphracts in advance of them (cf. Polyb. 5.82.9), provided protection for the flank of the Seleucid heavy cavalry. An unspecified number of chariots were deployed in front of Antiochus' cavalry on the left. Elephants were posted in the reserve behind the argyraspides on the right and the cavalry on the left as a second line barrier to prevent outflanking, similar to their disposition in one of the battle arenas at Panion (id. 37.40.6,14). Light infantry of various nationalities operating as skirmishers were deployed in front of the battle line on the right of the chariots.

The description of the course of the battle, despite some considerable gaps, is rather clear in general but imposes one difficult question: whom did Antiochus charge on the right flank? Appian recounts that commanding 'the right wing cavalry' (33(170) - probably the agēma, the cavalry Guard, and the cataphracts, but not the Dahae, who were posted too far away), Antiochus broke through 'the line of the Roman phalanx' (34(177), 36(184)). Livy, who attributes to Antiochus the command of the whole right wing (37.41.1), states that he used the cataphracts and 'auxiliaries', according to their location, probably the agēma (see p.237 n.56 below), to charge the turmae near the river both by a frontal attack and an outflanking movement, routing the tiny Roman cavalry force and part of the adjacent infantry (42.7-8). This version is little short of amazing: there was no need of 3,000 cataphracts and 1,000 Guardsmen on top of the 1,200 Dahae to break 120 horse; moreover, had the cataphracts abandoned their position and attacked the turmae in a diagonal movement, they would have opened a dangerous gap in the flank of their own phalanx. Justin's version is the most interesting: to the disgrace of the Romans, Antiochus is said to have charged the Roman legion posted opposite his right flank and routed it (36.8.6). In view of the disposition of both armies, Justin seems to be more reliable:[20] the agēma and cataphracts confronted the left Roman legion, and a head-on charge sounds reasonable since the cataphracts were well enough equipped to overcome the legion from the front. As the total collapse of a Roman legion was quite rare and is described by Justin as a disgrace, it is hardly possible that he or Pompeius Trogus, his source, was confusing part of the extreme Latin ala with the adjacent Roman legion. On the other hand, Livy's desire to write off this calamity is quite understandable and could have inspired his absurd account. It may be that Polybius, not making a clear distinction between the legions and the alae in the course of his narrative (cf. Livy 37.39.8),[21] and perhaps making some mention of the onslaught of the Dahae cavalry on the turmae, confused Livy into believing in the authenticity of his reconstruction.

The general outline of the battle seems to be as follows. Antiochus' army charged simultaneously on both wings. On the right, the cataphracts and the agēma broke the lines of the left Roman legion, routing it as far as the nearby camp. The legion, reorganized by the tribune Marcus Aemilius Lepidus, harassed the pursuing cavalry and prevented it from either occupying the Roman camp or turning back to outflank the right Roman legion (Livy 37.43.1-5; App. Syr. 36(185)).[22] Zeuxis' independent attempt,

doubtless in exploitation of Lepidus' preoccupation with
Antiochus' cavalry, to use some of his promachoi to penetrate the
Roman camp, defended by 2,000 Macedonians and Thracians, was not
successful, either (Livy 37.39.12-13, 43.4; App. Syr. 33(170);
Zon. p.309).

On the left flank the attack was begun by the chariots. As
soon as they moved forward they were attacked by a barrage of
arrows and missiles directed at the horses by the Cretans and
Trallians. The crippled horses turned back to their own line and
threw the cataphracts into utter confusion. The narrow space
between the two opposing lines, which did not allow the chariots
to develop enough speed, was a further factor in their failure.[23]
This was the signal awaited by the Roman cavalry, which immediately
charged the cataphracts. The Seleucid heavy cavalry, which had
already suffered considerable losses from their own chariots,
could not withstand the highly mobile opponent and retreated,
bringing about the total collapse of the other cavalry on the left
wing (Livy 37.41.9-42.3; App. Syr. 33-4(173-6)).[24] The Roman
cavalry was now free to outflank the semi-heavy troops protecting
the phalanx's flank, supported probably by Eumenes' peltasts from
the front.

Meanwhile, the Roman skirmishers in the centre overpowered
the Seleucid promachoi who retreated between the lines of the
phalanx (Livy 37.42.4; App. Syr. 35(178)). The massive heavy
troops and elephants, now exposed to the outflanking of the
victorious Roman cavalry on the left and to frontal attack by the
right legion and ala, reformed in a square formation.[25] The Roman
legionaries could not get close to this massive defensive
formation and tried to break it by a barrage of missiles. The
phalanx stood up well until the elephants, driven wild by the
constant 'sniping', ran amok, broke the ranks, and put the
phalanx to disorderly flight (App. Syr. 35(180-2)). Antiochus,
withdrawing from the unsuccessful pursuit, had to admit defeat,
and escaped to Sardis.[26]

The suggested disposition and the course of the battle reveal
Antiochus' basic tactics: in view of the position of the cavalry
next to the centre, and not in the flank, it seems that he planned
to break one legion by means of a frontal onslaught by the heavy

cavalry, thus dividing the rest of the legions into two groups exposed to cavalry outflanking on both sides, but for one reason or another he was prevented from pursuing the original plan and tried instead to storm the Roman camp, assuming that this would have a decisive effect on the morale of the enemy, perhaps especially the auxiliaries, some of whom were mercenaries.[27] As a preparatory stage to the cavalry outflanking on the left, he tried to use chariots against the opposing Roman cavalry. The success of the outflanking manoeuvres would have prepared the way for the frontal charge of the phalanx and argyraspides on the legions.[28] All in all, the employment of chariots, the frontal attack on the legion by the cavalry, and the attempt to attack the Roman camp indicate that Antiochus was trying to use something new to disconcert the enemy (cf. Livy 37.41.6), whom he may have reckoned to have been expecting the conventional Hellenistic tactics.

Antiochus' deviation from the general pattern of Hellenistic warfare seems to have derived from the lessons of some recent performances of the Roman army: the disaster brought about by Hannibal's elephants at Zama (Polyb. 15.12) taught him to employ elephants principally in defence (but he was amazingly shortsighted not to have applied the same conclusion to his chariots!); his own experience at Thermopylae, Philip V's decisive defeat at Cynoscephalae, and the acquaintance of Hannibal, his mentor, with the Roman army, must have made him aware of the tremendous flexibility and mobility of the Romans when confronting the phalanx. His tactics failed, because he relied too much on outmoded chariots without taking the necessary precautions to 'neutralize' the enemy's archers, and expended too much energy on attempting to destroy the Roman camp instead of conducting outflanking manoeuvres from the open gap created on the legion flank.[29] Generally speaking, 'old fashioned' phalanx warfare (i.e. disposition which concentrated the cavalry on the flanks of the phalanx and spread the phalanx to cover the complete line of the legions by thinning its depth) might have produced much better results on the plain of Magnesia. This comment is echoed in the criticism made by Antiochus' courtiers after the battle (App. Syr. 32(165); 37(191)).[30] Polybius, in his general assessment of the phalanx's capability, expressed the view that on a flat battlefield, without

The battle of Magnesia

any ground obstacles, the odds were in favour of the Macedonian phalanx (18.31.3). Antiochus' mistake was in forgetting that the Hermos valley, ideal for phalanx warfare, was quite different from the hills of Cynoscephalae. In fact, one might almost say that the fate of Magnesia-ad-Sipylum in 190 B.C. was actually decided not far from Magnesia Graeciae seven years earlier.

15: THE MARCH TO BEITH-ZACHARIA (162 B.C.)

After the relative abundance of information about the battles of Antiochus III, references to expeditions and military operations of his Successors are vague and given in general terms. Only the campaigns against the Jews are described in any detail but, unfortunately, only in Jewish sources, most of which do not match up to the historiographical standard of those discussed so far. Of all the campaigns against the Jews, the most detailed and interesting from the tactical point of view is the second expedition of Lysias to Judaea and the battle of Beith-Zacharia in 162 B.C.

Judas Maccabaeus had in the past frustrated four Seleucid attempts to invade Judaea (I Macc. 3.10-26, 38-4.35), and when Lysias abandoned his first expedition Judas reoccupied Jerusalem, purified the temple, and evacuated the Jews who lived in the neighbourhood of the Hellenized cities (ibid. 4.34-5.68). Although a part of the army was still stationed in the eastern satrapies (ibid. 6,7.55-6), Lysias decided to try once more to subdue the revolt, perhaps in order to establish his position on the domestic front. Antiochus V Eupator, aged 9 or 12 (App. Syr. 66; Euseb. I p.254), also took part in the expedition (I Macc. 6.28ff.).

As he had already done on the previous expedition (I Macc. 4.29), Lysias avoided the dangerous passes to the Judaean plateau on the north and northwest, which were surrounded by a hostile Jewish population, and took a southwestern route, which passed through the territory of the Edomeans who supported the Seleucids against the Jews.[1] Entering Jewish territory along the Edomean-controlled plateau of Mt Hebron, he first had to capture the fortress of Beith-Sour (Bēt Ṣour, now H'et-Ṭabeiqa), about 1 km off the main road to Jerusalem,[2] which he was apparently anxious to occupy in order to prevent the Jews from cutting off his retreat in case of defeat. After a heavy siege the Seleucids succeeded in occupying the fortress (II Macc. 13.19-22; Jos. Bell.

1.41; Ant. 12.367-76),[3] and the road to Jerusalem, 27 km to the north, seems now to have been open to the troops.

Judas Maccabaeus positioned his army at Beith-Zacharia (Bēt Zekharyā), identified with the village Bēt Zakariya, 9 km to the north of Beith-Sour beside the road to Jerusalem,[4] in a desperate attempt to stop the Seleucid force from reaching the holy city and perhaps reestablishing the pagan cult in the temple. To defend the city against a siege was out of question: it was the year following the Sabbatical year and the Jews were consequently short of supplies, and the Akra, the citadel of Jerusalem, was still occupied by the besieged garrison and Hellenized Jews (I Macc. 6.18-27,54).

The main source for the expedition and the battle is I Macc. 6.28-47. I am not sure that the author was an eyewitness, as some commentators suggest.[5] Two of the details that might convey this impression are in themselves unreliable: he stresses that the Seleucid shields glimmered in the sun and were reflected by the mountains (6.39), but as the march set off early in the morning (6.33), and should have arrived near Beith-Zacharia not later than two hours after dawn, the sun would obviously have been behind the Seleucid troops. The description of Eleazar's celebrated assault on the elephant (6.43-6) is likewise unacceptable: Eleazar might perhaps have been crushed by the elephant, but the elephant could not have been killed. On the contrary, an elephant stabbed in the belly would go wild and become even more dangerous (although he might die a few days later).[6] These points are not any more conclusive proof that the author did not witness the battle than the inflated numbers are, but they certainly provide no support for believing that he did. On the other hand, the references to the transformation of the Seleucid battle order and to the battle being fought in a defile (6.35, 38-40) could be attributed to the use of reliable first-hand oral or written information. All in all, whether or not the writer was an eyewitness, his account is evidently incomplete, and being eager to excuse the Jewish defeat he concentrates on those details which may impress the reader.

II Macc., which describes in detail the Seleucid expedition and the siege of Beith-Sour on the eve of the battle, devotes only half a verse to the battle itself and, as usual in this source, turns the defeat into a victory (13.22b). Josephus' account in Bellum Judaicum (1.41-6), on the other hand, provides some valuable details. The passage is part of an epitomized account of the persecutions and revolt, which is sometimes utterly distorted and may be based on the author's memory or on another source which followed a similar pattern, perhaps Nicolaus of Damascus.[7] In contrast to the rest of the chapter, however, it includes some information which is either absent or contradictory in I Macc., but always makes sense. The figure quoted for the Seleucid army is relatively moderate and more or less in line with the availability of troops (see p.14 above); the sequence of events is more acceptable (see p.265 n.3 below), and, above all, the statement that appears only in the Bellum (1.45) - that Judas fled to Gofnitis, the mountainous toparchy northwest of Jerusalem - seems basically reliable (see p.268 n.23 below); the battlefield is described as a mountain pass (41), a conclusion that can be deduced from a careful reading of I Macc. (6.40) but is not expressly said; Josephus refers to the participation of Jewish phalangites (45), who are nowhere mentioned in the two Books of the Maccabees, but analysis of the course of some battles after the purification of the Temple proves that they were not absent from the rebels' ranks (see p.182 below). These additional or different details cannot be explained as merely free inventions by Josephus or his source, based on I Macc.; their accuracy suggests that Bellum's version on Beith-Zacharia was not based on the author's memory or that of his source but derived directly or indirectly from a well-informed source. I would venture to say that the piquancy of the elephant story led Josephus or his source to draw on a detailed written account here instead of relying on his memory.[8] In his report on Judas Maccabaeus' campaigns in the later Antiquitates, Josephus, it is widely agreed, merely paraphrased I Macc.[9] However, his account of Beith-Zacharia, although basically adhering to the I Macc. version, contributes some additional details. These may theoretically be attributed to his personal acquaintance with the area and understanding of Hellenistic warfare,[10] but, in fact, he is even more likely, when trying to understand the somewhat vague narrative of I Macc., to have recalled, perhaps subconsciously, some of the prominent features of the battle recorded in the source he had used 20 years earlier.

In discussing the numerical strength of the Seleucid armies and elephants, I expressed the view that Josephus' estimate in Bellum Judaicum of 50,000 infantry and 5,000 cavalry, although rounded upwards, is not far from the truth, and includes a considerable number of local auxiliaries (p.14 above), and that his seemingly exaggerated figure of eighty elephants is a corruption of eight (p.81 above). As is suggested by the analysis of the operations after the purification of the temple, at this stage Judas Maccabaeus must have had well over 20,000 men who could be called up at short notice (see p.186, below), some of whom were phalangites and horsemen (see p.194, below). As the battle was preceded by the long siege on Beith-Sour, Judas †would have had enough time to rally all his forces. Nevertheless, the Seleucid expeditionary force had a considerable numerical superiority over the Jewish army as is attested even by the Hellenistic source that inspired Josephus in Bellum (1.45).

The various suggested locations of the battlefield[11] all fail to consider at least one of three basic requirements indicated by the sources: that the battle took place (a) on the route from Beith-Sour to Beith-Zacharia (or rather to Jerusalem - I Macc. 6.33), (b) near Beith-Zacharia (ibid. 31-2), and (c) in a defile or a narrow pass (ibid. 40; Jos. Ant. 12.370; Bell. 1.41 - στενός).[12] The Roman milestones and the PEF maps suggest that of the two routes which lead from Beith-Sour to Jerusalem, only one passed by Beith-Zacharia (see Map 15).[13] The second, about 1-3 km to the east, and in some parts identical with the modern main road, †must obviously be excluded. The western route passes in turn through wide plains, narrow defiles, mountainous saddles and narrow ridge lines. About 5 km to the south of Beith-Zacharia the route crosses a plain 1.5 km wide and 2.5 km long (popularly known as 'Valley of Blessing'), and then divides into two branches - one climbing a ridge (Russian Hill), and the other entering a defile (Wadi Shehēt), 60-150 m wide and 1 km in length, which climbs up the saddle between Balloutat el Yerza (Tree Hill) and Yellow Hill, where it rejoins the other branch to approach Beith-Zacharia. The only possible identification of the defile is

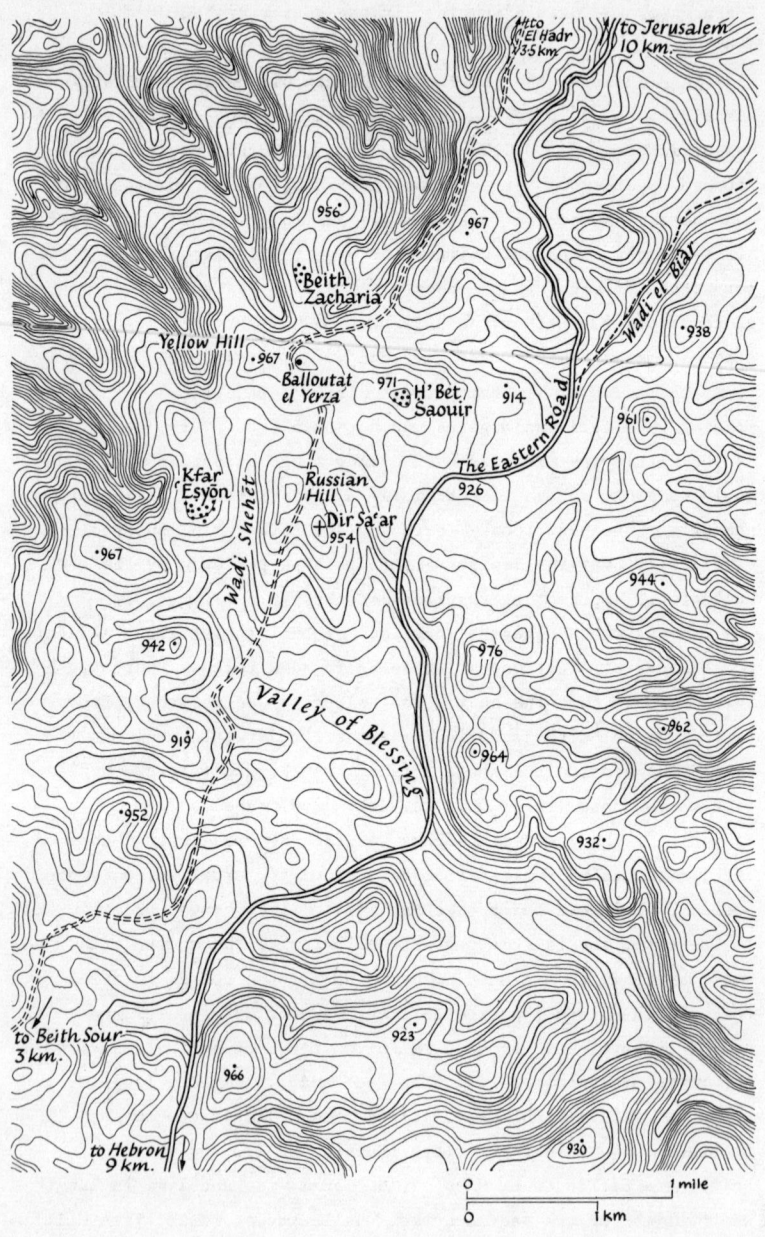

15 The battlefield of Beith-Zacharia

therefore with Wadi Sheḥēt. This defile was chosen because it was the last defence line on the road from Beith-Sour to Jerusalem capable of containing, to a great extent, the operations of the Seleucid forces, which were at that time exceptionally large. The road to the north of Beith-Zacharia passed a ridge line which, though no wider than about 100 m, effectively controls all sides, and then 4 km north of Beith-Zacharia, near El-Hadr (east of Beith-Lehem), entered a relatively broad plateau (approximately 1.5 km) stretching to Jerusalem.

The account in I Macc. does not reveal whether Lysias did not have the Jewish positions in sight, so that Judas actually set a trap for him, or whether the Jews staged a conventional frontal battle.[14] The absence of any reference to an ambush is not decisive: only with regard to one battle does I Macc. clearly state that Judas Maccabaeus surprised the enemy (3.23), though in reality there is little doubt that some other confrontations were decided in the same way.[15] If I Macc. is obscure here as in accounts of other battles, it may be because, as has already been mentioned, he was trying to indicate the divine hand's governing the course of events. An ambush from a superior position would not have served his religious-historiographic purpose. The main factor influencing the Jewish tactics must have been the amount of cover Judas could have expected to have from the plantation on the hills above the defile. Had the slopes been wooded, which is a possibility in view of the impressive remains of later afforestation on the saddle,[16] or had they been planted with olives, etc., the area would have been ideal for setting an ambush and Judas would hardly have missed this opportunity: he could have been quite confident that Lysias would not take the eastern route to Jerusalem since that way he would have had to march five km in the gorge of Wadi-el-Biâr, which was much more dangerous than the relatively short defiles on the west. But had the hills been bare or planted with low vegetation, Judas would have made a stand in the open, taking advantage of his superior topographical position and the limitations the arena imposed on the deployment and manoeuvring of the Seleucid heavy troops.

As appears from the sources, the Seleucid marching order was transformed in the neighbourhood of Beith-Zacharia from a frontal

battle line to a long column protected by troops who climbed up the
hills on either side of the defile (I Macc. 6.34-8,40; Jos. Ant.
12.371). The wide line was probably adopted in the broad plain to
the south of the defile, and if the battle did in fact start with
an ambush, it may be assumed that the Seleucids were marching in
accordance with Xenophon's recommendation to constantly transform
the marching-order from a frontal line to a long column and vice
versa according to the variation of the terrain, when location of
the enemy is uncertain (Xen. Eq.Mag. 4.1-3; cf. Arr. Anab. 1.13.1-
2). If Judas waited for the enemy in the open, the deployment of
the Seleucid army in a battle line across the Valley of Blessing
could be understood as a challenge to the Jews, but since Lysias
would not have been deluded by the remote prospect of Judas'
abandoning his advantageous position, the frontal array looks like
a show designed to impress and terrify the Jews, like Antiochus
III's 'demonstration of force' on his way to the siege of Larissa
in 191 B.C. (Livy 36.10.4). The impression conveyed by a column
formation would not have been as striking as the splendour of the
front line, in which all the elephants and the shiny shields,
coats of mail, and weapons could be seen simultaneously. Generally
speaking, efforts to impress and terrify the Jews occupy a rather
prominent place in the plan for this expedition, and even if the
description in I Macc. somewhat exaggerates, it certainly reflects
the shock inflicted on the Jews by the appearance of the Seleucid
army.[17]

The Seleucid disposition in the first stage (along the wide
valley) is described by I Macc. as follows: the centre, protected
by cavalry, probably 'lights', on the flanks (6.38), comprised
several divisions, each disposed round an elephant and each
numbering 1,000 infantry and 500 cavalry (6.35). The infantry,
which is twice named 'phalanx' (35,38,45),[18] probably included
also a detachment of the Guard armed in the Roman style (35 and
see p.60 above). The cavalry attached to the elephants, which was
called epilektoi, could have included the agēma and the Companions
but must have comprised mainly regular heavy infantry (on the
flexible usage of epilektoi in I Macc. and the composition of the
Seleucid regular cavalry see p.73 above). The phalangites and
the 'Roman' infantry were probably posted on the flanks of the

phalangites. As to the figures attributed to each division, despite the incredibility of the total number of the troops attributed by I Macc. to the Seleucids, I do not see any reason to suspect these data, which accord well with the tactical division of the Seleucid infantry and cavalry into subunits, make sense from the tactical point of view, and partially recall the disposition of Antiochus III's centre at Magnesia. A division of 1,000 phalangites and 500 heavy cavalry would have occupied just under 120-150 m.[19] As no plain on the way to Jerusalem was over 1.5 km wide, a battle line formed by elephant divisions (taking into account also the light cavalry on the wings) could not have comprised more than 8 divisions, and this fits in with the suggested number of the Seleucid elephants. I would hardly imagine that elephants that took part in the expedition were left behind the front line.

The Seleucid disposition in the second stage, when entering the defile, is described somewhat obscurely in I Macc., which states only that part of the force was deployed 'over the high mountains' and the rest 'over the low ground' (6.40). Josephus in *Antiquitates* explains (or adds from memory based on his source for *Bellum*) that the 'elephant divisions' were drawn up in a column before entering the defile (12.371), while the rest of the army (probably the light cavalry posted in the initial formation in the extreme wings), preceded by the 'lights', climbed up the hills. This suggests that the main idea behind the 'elephant divisions' was to form a flexible and 'self-contained' unit (apart from the skirmishers), which could modify its formation according to the width of the defiles and confront the enemy independently in the defile in a 'mini-formation' of the conventional Hellenistic battle line. This division could be 'compressed' into a width of 80-100 m in the narrowest parts of the defiles by deepening its phalanx to 32 lines. As has already been suggested, the description of the phalanx as 'equipped with coats of mail' (6.35) is due to the replacement of phalangites by infantry troops of the Roman Guard in the advance divisions (p.[55] above). As these troops were certainly more adaptable in rough terrain than were the traditional phalangites, their selection for the advance divisions is comprehensible. One has but to pay tribute to the ingenuity of this solution in bringing into effect the advantages of the Hellenistic traditional formation even in this unfavourable terrain.

Light Seleucid troops in the front of the line are not mentioned in I Macc. and Josephus, but later, in his account of the battle in Antiquitates, Josephus calls the troops in front of the elephants prodromoi (12.372), i.e. mounted skirmishers (cf. e.g. Diod. 17.17.4; Arr. Anab. 1.12.7; Arist. Ath. 49.1). Furthermore, in Bellum he recounts that Eleazar's attack preceded the clash of the 'phalanxes' (1.42), while according to I Macc. 600 Seleucid troops fell before Eleazar reached the enemy (6.42). Though combining two unrelated sources may be somewhat illegitimate, to send the phalanx (or the Roman unit) into a defile without a van of light skirmishers would, in any case, have been tantamount to suicide had the enemy suddenly blocked the route. I Macc. ignored the skirmishers either because his eyewitness source was not as impressed by their appearance as he was by that of the heavy troops, elephants, and cavalry, or because the author himself did not regard them as proper material for his historiographical purposes.

The scanty references to the part played by the lights in the defile and on the hills makes it difficult to reconstruct the Seleucid tactics with certainty. If the location of the Jews was not known, it seems to me likely that the principle of combined manoeuvres to locate the enemy's concentrations around a defile, demonstrated by Antiochus III in the Elburz range, would have become textbook practice for the Seleucid armies and therefore have guided Lysias' tactics at Beith-Zacharia.[20] But the primary manoeuvres in the defile itself to help in locating the enemy may have been performed by much smaller units than in the Elburz and were followed shortly by the phalanx's advance. Whether or not it was an ambush, the innovation of Beith-Zacharia lay in the active role assigned to the heavy troops and their flexible composition and deployment, in contrast to their grouping together in the rear in the Elburz to keep them well away from any confrontation (Polyb. 10.29). On the one hand, the rather low hills on the flanks promised a much easier task of dislodging the hidden troops than did the threatening steep slopes of the Elburz, so

that the danger of exposing the phalanx to an attack on its flanks
was considerably reduced, and, on the other, the prospect of a
frontal onslaught, which did not exist in the Elburz, necessitated
the positioning of the phalangites next to the prodromoi in the
defile. Had the Jews succeeded in dispersing the Seleucid
skirmishers, they would have had to face the 'Roman' troops or the
impenetrable phalanx, while the cavalry, offering protection in
the flanks, could easily have turned about to break and rout the
enemy. One must also take into account that Antiochus III could
not afford to lose the indispensable phalangites in a skirmish of
secondary importance in the Elburz, but Lysias' expedition was to
reach its culmination in this very battle. Another important
consideration that decided the deployment of the contingents must
also have been the demoralizing effect of the 'elephant divisions'
with their unique composition and colourful shields on the Jewish
warriors, most of whom were Palestinians isolated from the coast
and the arterial road to Egypt, who would not have been acquainted
with elephant warfare.[21]

The account of the battle suggests that the Seleucids
succeeded in putting the forces on either side of the defile out of
action. The Jews' only success was in the centre, where they
defeated the Seleucid prodromoi and approached the front 'elephant
division'. Despite Eleazar's heroic sacrifice, aimed probably at
setting an example to his comrades,[22] the Jews were unable to
withstand Seleucid pressure and fled to the inaccessible mountainous
region of 'Āfrayiim (Apherema) - Gōfnā, 25 km northwest of Jerusalem,
where the revolt had possibly first gathered momentum.[23]

16: BACCHIDES AGAINST JUDAS MACCABAEUS AT ELASA (160 B.C.)

The Jewish rebellion, which sustained a bad setback from the heavy blow received at Beith-Zacharia, soon recovered its momentum, taking advantage of the internal crisis in the Empire and the struggle for succession at Antioch. Once established on the throne, Demetrius experimented with a new policy by granting Judaea the status of an eparchy, and appointing Nicanor, a high-ranking officer who formerly served as elephantarch, as the stratēgos of the new eparchy (II Macc. 14.12).[1] But Judas Maccabaeus, encouraged by the confinement of the bulk of the Seleucid army in the eastern provinces in the expedition against the rebel Timarchos, defeated Nicanor twice in the battlefield.[2] Nicanor himself was killed in the battle of Adasa and his body was displayed to the public in Jerusalem and mutilated (I Macc. 7.31-50; II Macc. 14.15-25, 15). The Hasmoneans resumed power all over Judaea after the victory. There was certainly nothing new in this development, but the Jewish treaty with Rome, which made imminent the danger of Roman intervention (I Macc. 8.17-32, esp. 31-2),[3] forced Demetrius to react promptly and vigorously.[4] After subduing the revolt in Babylonia (see p.210 n.29 above), he sent to Judaea Bacchides, who in his absence was in charge of the western regions of the Empire,[5] in a determined effort to put down the Jewish revolt once and for all. As will be shown below, Bacchides' determination to achieve this purpose is well demonstrated by every step: the choice of the route, battlefield, and tactics and, even after the battle, by the construction of the chain of fortresses to seal off almost hermetically the Judaean mountains after the battle of Elasa (ibid. 9.50-2),[6] and by the ruthless pursuit of the survivors in the desert (ibid. 32-49, 58-68).

Bacchides' army is estimated by I Macc. at 20,000 infantry and 2,000 cavalry (9.4), while Judas Maccabaeus is reported to have had 3,000 troops, of which only 800 remained after they sighted the enemy (9.4-6). As pointed out above (p.14) the figures attributed to Bacchides are quite acceptable and actually could not have been smaller, and included at most 10,000 phalangites. The figures attributed to the Jewish force, on the other hand, must be flatly rejected. According to the battle account (which makes sense from the military point of view) the Jews staged a tough resistance and only a brilliant stratagem of Bacchides decided the issue (9.10-17, esp. 13, and see below), but 800 men could not stand indefinitely against 20,000 infantry and 2,000 cavalry, not even for a short while, and at any rate, such a small force would not have ventured to undertake a pitched battle against Bacchides' army.

The sources are consistent in reporting small forces of between 3,000 to 10,000 troops (I Macc. 4.6, 29, 7.40: II Macc. 8.1, 16), and there is no doubt that for the first stages of the revolt these figures are accurate, but careful examination of the sources reveals that the real strength of the Jewish force after the purification of the temple was well over 20,000, and some thousands more must be taken into account in later stages. The four years which elapsed between the beginning of the revolt and the purification of the temple certainly brought in thousands of volunteers, following the pattern of national liberation movements: starting with a small nucleus of rebels, they turn into a mass movement in the wake of the first successes. The purification of the temple contributed more than any other thing to raising morale †and attracting a larger number of the rebels.

The main source of information for a realistic estimation of the strength of the Jewish force is the report about the simultaneous operations carried on by the rebels after the purification of the temple. We are grateful to the late Prof. Avi-Yonah who was the first to draw attention to the figures ascribed to these operations and expressed the view that the Jewish force stood at 15,000 men.[7] But he is still too cautious: I Macc., in describing the rescue missions after the purification of the temple, notes casually that 3,000 men followed Simon to Galilee, 8,000 followed Judas Maccabaeus to Gilead (Galaaditis, 5.20), and at the same time 2,000 Jews were killed in the battle against Gorgias (5.55-60). As these figures do not serve any ulterior

purpose,[8] there is no reason to suspect their reliability. While it is true that inaccurate figures occur in ancient sources even when no special purpose can be detected, as a rule they are provided when sufficient true information is unavailable. I Macc., which is well informed on the generation of the revolt, would hardly be expected to invent these figures at random. Without being too dogmatic, it can be said that the casualty rate in battles of the period (given the fire-power, weapons, and tactics then employed) could have been at most 20 per cent (excluding the exceptional circumstances of an army's being cut off in a hostile country) and was usually no more than 10 per cent.[9] The battle against Gorgias took place according to II Macc. in the plain near Marisa (12.35),[10] near hilly country populated by Jews, and from which a short, flat, and convenient escape route led to Odollam ('Adullām), the Jewish rear headquarters (12.38). In these circumstances one cannot assume a high percentage of casualties, certainly not inflicted by the army of Gorgias, which was rather small even according to II Macc. (12.32). The figure of 2,000 casualties does seem rounded off, perhaps upwards, but 20 per cent of casualties is the highest percentage one can expect, and the average is far less, so that the number of Jews who took part at Marisa could not have been less than 10,000. This conclusion brings the total of the three expeditions up to at least 20,000 Jewish combatants. The number was certainly augmented by the refugees and homeless people transferred to Judaea (I Macc. 5.23, 44, 53) and it may be accepted that people who did not take part in these salvation missions joined
† the ranks during later Seleucid expeditions in defence of their own territory. As there was no significant change in demographic conditions and internal politics in Judaea at the time of Jonathan, there is no reason to think that the recruitment potential of Judas Maccabaeus at this stage was far lower than that of Jonathan, which in 152 stood at well over 30,000 soldiers (I Macc. 10.36)[11] and by the time of Jonathan's death in 143 was as high as 40,000 men (I Macc. 12.41).[12] Although only a few thousands of those were the standing army, the logistical and economic problems involved in the maintenance of this multitude of soldiers mobilized in time of emergency are certainly puzzling and the system used to call them up is anyone's guess. Nevertheless these difficulties are not sufficient to refute my suggestion as to the total number. With modern

examples in mind, there is a natural tendency to exaggerate
the logistic difficulties of ancient armies, but the Jews were
used to primitive living conditions, were fighting on home
ground and easily got supplies from the local population.
Parallels from the Classical and Hellenistic periods cite peace
time military diets showing levels of consumption which in
modern terms would make them starvation diets.[13] All the more so
in time of war.

This assessment of the Jewish recruitment potential also
applies to the circumstances that surrounded the battle of Elasa.
The great national revival after the death of Nicanor, and the
holiday established to commemorate the event would have
strengthened the Jewish army or at least not weakened it. The
possibility that Judas was taken by surprise and therefore did not
manage to rally all the available manpower is not very likely.
Though the invasion of Judaea was carried out rather quickly,
Bacchides seems to have stayed in the Bēt-Ēl area for some time in
order to establish his control over the routes in the region, and
also probably in order to draw Judas Maccabaeus to do battle in
terrain favourable to the Seleucid heavy troops (see below). This
span of time would have afforded enough 'breathing space' to
mobilize the Jewish army from the limited area of Judaea, which
was no larger than a day's walk from Jerusalem in each direction.
But even if we assume that Bacchides succeeded in 'purging' the
routes so quickly that Judas could not organize his troops, a
pitched battle with a small force in Elasa still does not make
sense. If the purpose was to avoid the reoccupation of Jerusalem
(a step which was not the target of the Seleucid commander, but
which the Jews might have had reason to fear), the best way was to
dig in in the city and harass the besieging forces from outside
with the troops who had not managed to reach the city. Having in
mind that a siege of Jerusalem always imposed considerable
logistical difficulties to the besieger, and that the city had
the benefit of natural defences, this way would have been much
more efficient and would have done more for the salvation of the
Jews in the rural areas north of Jerusalem than confronting the
'heavy' enemy with a small force in a flat area, a plan doomed to
failure at the outset.

The figure of 800 Jewish combatants must be understood in the
context of the historiographical-religious character and didactic
purpose of I Macc. As has already been stated, the exaggerated
figures attributed to the Seleucid armies in I Macc. are designed
to imply a divine hand behind the scenes that rescues the loyal
believers despite their numerical inferiority (p.12 above); hence
the underestimation of the Jewish manpower. In the case of Elasa
the figures are even lower than the average 6,000 Jewish troops,
because the author took pains to alibi the Jewish defeat and
glorify the hero, Judas Maccabaeus, in his last adventure. The
author, who wrote at least 25-30 years after the battle, did not
have to be aware of possible criticism as did other historians of
the Hellenistic period: the Jews did not have a tradition of
historiographical criticism; only a few of the Jews who took part
in the battle were still alive and, in light of the limited
circulation of books, the likelihood of their seeing it was rather
slight. If by chance the account was read by a participant in the
battle the latter would probably not have disclosed the truth and
so diminished the Hasmonean glory and his own.[14]

Identification of the route chosen by Bacchides to the battlefield
can contribute to the identification of the battlefield itself,
clarify some manoeuvres, and illumine Bacchides' strategy. In
I Macc. the expedition is described as follows: καὶ ἐπορεύθησαν
ὁδὸν τὴν εἰς Γαλγαλα καὶ παρενέβαλον ἐπὶ Μαισαλωθ τὴν ἐν
'Αρβήλοις καὶ προκατελάβοντο αὐτὴν καὶ ἀπώλεσαν ψυχὰς ἀνθρώπων
πολλάς (9.2). Josephus in Antiquitates, which is, as has already
been said, only a paraphrase of I Macc. (p.176 above), locates Arbēl
in Galilee (12.421), and indeed such a comment is to be expected in
view of his personal acquaintance as the commander of Galilee with
the later Galilean stronghold (Jos. Bell. 1.305; id. Vit. 118, 311).
But Bacchides' expedition was directed against Judaea and a siege of
this isolated cliff in the far north would have been, to say the
least, somewhat superfluous, especially as I Macc. records the
evacuation of all the Jews in Galilee to Judaea after the purification of the temple in 164 B.C. (5.23). Even if I Macc. is not
correct in this statement, as some scholars argue without any
positive evidence,[15] the Jews were obviously on the defensive and

Bacchides would not have wasted time (and 22,000 troops) in uprooting the remaining Jews in the area. Besides, the identifications suggested for Maisalōth and Galgala by some of those who accept Josephus' interpretation do not make sense.[16] The same arguments apply against the suggestion to identify the place with the Gileadite Arbēl.[17] Other suggestions, which rightly try to identify all the topographical references in Samaria and Judaea, fail to provide a satisfactory geographical context for the term 'Gilgāl Road', which is the clue to any further identifications.[18]

It seems likely that Gilgāl Road is the route ascending the ridge line from the Jordan Valley, not far to the north of Jericho, to the Judaean plateau near Ramūn and Bā'al-Hasōr (see Map 16).[19] The route was named after the known Gilgāl at its starting point near Jericho,[20] and another place bearing a similar name where it arrives at the plateau, near the village Ramūn: Bēt ha-Gilgāl is mentioned in Neh. 12.29 beside 'the fields of Gev'a and 'Azmavet' (today Jab'a and Hizma). According to the geographical progression of the verse from north to south, Bēt ha-Gilgāl seems to be north of Jab'a, and indeed near the village of Ramūn there is a wide Roman cemetery called Jaljil by the Arabs and a Sheikh's tomb called Sheikh-Jiljil.[21] The place merits thorough archaeological examination, but it is worth noting that almost all the sites called Jiljal, Jaljilia, etc. by the Arabs are situated in a topographical context making it possible to identify them with one of the places named Gilgāl in the Hebrew sources. It therefore stands to reason that even if this Jiljal is not identical with Bēt ha-Gilgāl, it does, however, preserve the old Hebrew name Gilgāl. The name Arbēl, which is not found in the Judaean Mountains,[22] may be a corruption of the Hebrew phrase Har Bēt-El (the mountain of Bēt-El), which was combined into one word and slightly shortened in the Hebrew version to perhaps Harbēēl (cf. the omission of the tav of Bēt in I Macc. 7.19 et passim, perhaps influenced by the Aramaic) and so transcribed with the Greek plural ending.[23] One must bear in mind that the translator of I Macc. obviously did not understand the topographical references, as may be deduced from the transliteration of the Hebrew word mesillōt (Maisaloth in the Greek) as a geographical name and the understanding of the word as a singular (αὐτήν) and not plural (see below). Har Bēt-El is mentioned twice in the Bible and refers to the mountainous

The army in action

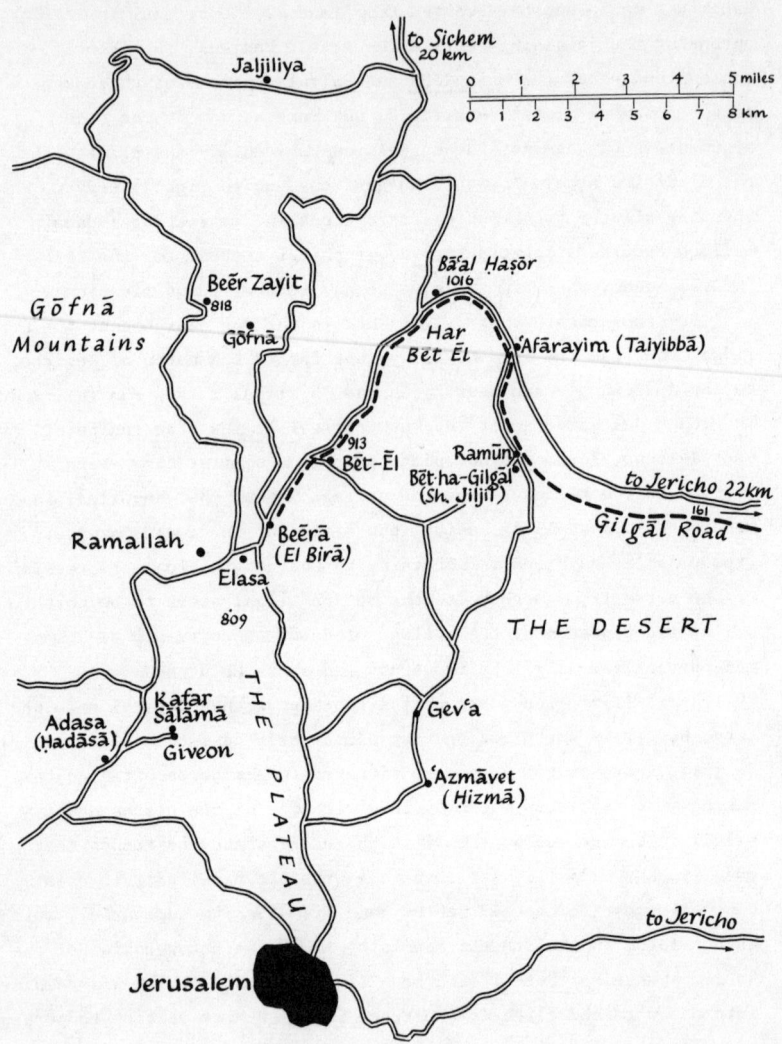

16 Bacchides' expedition to Judaea

massif of Bēt Ēl-Ḥaṣōr (Joshua 16.1; I Sam. 13.2),[24] the highest in the Judaean plateau, which is linked to the Jordan Valley by the Gilgāl Road. The word <u>Maisalōth</u> is, as already accepted by some, a transliteration of the Hebrew <u>mesillōt</u> (routes, tracks, etc.).[25] Significantly enough this word, which is fairly uncommon in the Bible, occurs three times to describe routes in the Bēt-Ēl area (Jud. 20.31, 45, 21.19). This combination of biblical names and terms to describe geographical places is characteristic of the author of I Macc., who is absorbed with biblical associations, and one can only admire his precision in describing Bacchides' route as 'on Gilgāl Road .. on the routes of Bēt-Ēl Mountain'.

To sum up: Bacchides marched through the Jordan Valley north of Jericho and penetrated the Judaean mountains via the route to Ramūn. Reaching the Bēt-Ēl mountain he camped in the area that controls all the routes, probably near Bā'al-Ḥaṣōr. We shall see below that Bacchides retreated to Bā'al-Ḥaṣōr, which may indicate that he was on the way to his nearby headquarters. If my suggestion is correct, the choice of this route indicates a courageous but well-calculated strategy arising from Seleucid experience in former attempts: the topographical problem they always had to face was how to climb up the Judaean plateau by the difficult ascents without being trapped by an ambush, or forced to do battle in an unfavourable terrain. Bacchides took the Jews by surprise using the most difficult but least observed and most unexpected route: the Jordan Valley, as well as the semi-desert to the east of Ramūn, was only sparsely populated by Jews and therefore Bacchides' movements were unobserved, and, in any case, Judas could not have been alerted in time to lay an ambush since the Seleucid troops were able to climb the 21 km long ascent in less than a day's march. In addition, Judas may have been unaware of a possible invasion from this direction, regarding it as unfavourable logistically and topographically (an ascent of 1,000 m in an aerial distance of 21 km).

After reaching the plateau Bacchides had a virtually clear road to Jerusalem, but he does not seem to have been in any hurry and tried, first of all, to establish his control over the various routes in the region and terrorize the rural population (I Macc. 9.2).[26] Analysis of his tactics in the battle itself and the

operations after the battle makes clear that Bacchides' main aim in
the expedition was not the occupation of territories or mere
military victory, but the liquidation of the rebellion by the
personal extermination of Judas Maccabaeus and his close adherents.
And indeed, at this stage, after eight years of intensive military
activity, the authorities were well acquainted with Judas'
prominent position and Nicanor had earlier been ordered to kill
him (II Macc. 14.13) and tried to capture him by a trick (I Macc.
7.28-30; II Macc. 14.18-25). Bacchides' strategy would, therefore,
have been to force the battle on the plateau between Mt Bēt-Ēl and
Jerusalem where his qualitative superiority, especially in heavy
troops, would have provided him with freedom of manoeuvre to
capture the Jewish leader. Bacchides challenged Judas on his
operations in Mt Bēt-Ēl. The occupation of all the routes
excluded the possibility of sudden Jewish attacks on the Seleucid
camps, and the massacre in the area to the north of Jerusalem
forced Judas to accept the challenge. Bacchides obviously tried
to arouse Judas' compassion, and, had the latter declined battle,
he might well have been in danger of losing public support to the
moderate 'Hellenists' of Alcimos' party who preferred religious
freedom under Seleucid rule to carrying on the struggle for
national sovereignty (I Macc. 7.5-7, 23-5). This was the only
occasion in which a Seleucid general succeeded in dictating the
battlefield to Judas Maccabaeus. However, Judas Maccabaeus showed
more readiness this time to accept the challenge because he had
gained confidence as a result of victories against Nicanor on flat
ground.[27]

Bacchides is reported to have encamped before the battle at
Beera (or Berethem, according to the Old Latin) identified by Abel
with El-Birā near Ramallah,[28] while Judas was at Elasa (I Macc.
9.3-11), identified with Hirbet El-Ashi on the southern outskirts
of Ramallah to the southwest of El-Birā.[29] Since 1 km separated
the two camps, the battle must have been located on the 2 km wide
plateau of El Birā-Ramallah. The arena is not in fact absolutely
flat; it does not, however, significantly differ from other
battlefields in which phalangites are reported to have operated
quite efficiently. In the battle itself Bacchides' flank is said
to have retreated ἕως 'Αζώτου ὄρους (ibid. 15). The present

reading is certainly unacceptable, as the only Azōtos (Ashdod) in
Palestine was the well-known Hellenized city on the southern coast.
Abel suggested the reading Ἀζώρου ὄρους, which refers to Bā'al-
Ḥaṣōr, 9 km northeast of the battlefield.[30] The difficulty in
this emendation is that it does not follow the general
syntactical practice of the translator of I Macc. in rendering
Hebrew geographical names.[31] Others, among them Abel himself in
his later commentary to I Macc., assume that the corruption
occurred in the Hebrew original by a slight change from ashdōt
hā-Hār (the mountain slopes) to Ashdōd hā-Hār (the mountain
Ashdōd - Azōtos).[32] In view of the location of the two camps,
Bacchides' possible route of retreat could be only in the direction
of the eastern slopes of the Judaean mountains, somewhat to the
southeast of Bā'al-Ḥaṣōr in the Taiyibbā-Ramūn area. And, indeed,
the biblical expression ashdōt, when referring to western
Palestine, probably means the eastern slopes of the Judaean
mountains (Joshua 10.40, 12.8). At any rate, as only 3 km separate
the foot of Bā'al-Ḥaṣōr from the eastern slopes of the Judaean
mountains, whichever of these emendations is right, the general
direction of the retreat was toward Bā'al-Ḥaṣōr, covering at least
9 km.[33]

The Seleucid battle line was rather conventional: the phalanx was
divided into two divisions (merē, I Macc. 9.12a); since it
numbered less than 10,000, these were perhaps two stratēgiai of
4,000 men each; the wings were occupied by the cavalry and the
front by the light skirmishers (promachoi, ibid. 11b). Bacchides
himself led the stronger right wing (ibid. 12a), which was
traditionally the position of the cream of the cavalry. After the
skirmish of the promachoi, the phalanx advanced in two divisions
(ibid. 12), but nothing is said about the movements of the
cavalry, which implies that they remained behind. Judas
Maccabaeus, observing Bacchides' location, charged with his
strongest force and pursued the fleeing wing as far as Bā'al-Ḥaṣōr
(ibid. 14-15).[34] The other wing, certainly the cavalry on the
left, came to the help of their comrades and closed on Judas from
behind (ibid. 16). The routed cavalry turning to confront him,
Judas was caught between two fires, and after tough resistance

finally fell in the battle (ibid. 17).

Before discussing the Seleucid tactics, let us first of all try to establish the composition of the Jewish army. The two Books of the Maccabees, the main sources on the revolt, do not classify the Jewish troops, and describe them merely as andres (men, e.g. I Macc. 4.6, 29, 5.20, 7.40, 9.5). Only once is a reference made to a cavalry unit, and even this after the establishment of the independence in 140 B.C., in the account of Simon's battle in the Valley of Ayalon (I Macc. 16.7). There is no doubt that the Jewish armament was quite inferior at the beginning of the revolt, and I Macc. indicates a severe shortage in arms (3.12, 4.6, 6.6, 13), but all allusions to such a deficiency refer to the period before the purification of the temple and do not recur later. On the other hand, a slip of the pen in the description of the battle at Marisa, Josephus' version in Bellum on Beith-Zacharia, the topography of the battlefields of Adasa and Kefar-Salama, and analysis of the course of the battle of Elasa and the battle of Jonathan against Apollonius, suggest that in the second stage of the revolt, after the purification of the temple, the Jews employed phalangites as well as cavalry. The silence of the sources is well in line with their religious-didactic purpose. Had the authors mentioned the use of up-to-date arms and armour by the Jews, in addition to the real numbers of both sides, this would have detracted the importance of the successes and stressed the gravity of the defeats, and, at any rate, the reader would not have felt the hidden divine hand behind the scenes hinted at by I Macc. or the necessity of open and direct divine intervention stressed by II Macc.

In the description of the battle against Gorgias in Marisa, II Macc. mentions in passing a Jewish horseman named Dositheus (12.35). As this was neither a decisive nor a vital battle, and was, contrary to instructions, fought outside Judaea while Judas Maccabaeus himself and Simon were occupied in the north (I Macc. 5.55, 57, 61), it is hardly credible that cavalry was not involved in the major battles after the purification of the temple. The information survived in II Macc. only because the author (or the epitomator) was too enthusiastic about the bravery of Dositheus to delete the story. This conclusion is supported by analysis of the

course of the battle at Elasa: the long pursuit after Bacchides'
wing indicates that quite a few of the Jewish troops were mounted:
Judas Maccabaeus' wing might perhaps have dispersed Bacchides'
wing by an infantry attack but could not have pursued the select
cavalry, certainly not to a distance of 9-12 km. The participation
of the second Seleucid wing, which caught up with the Jewish
detachment near Ba‘al-Hasōr, further indicates that the pursuit was
performed at cavalry and not infantry pace.[35]

No 'slip of the pen' referring to Jewish phalangites is
extant in the Books of the Maccabees, but examination of some
battles makes the participation of heavy troops in the Jewish side
more than likely. Judas Maccabaeus defeated the enemy in a frontal
attack on the flat battlefields of Adasa and Kefar-Salama (I Macc.
7.31-2, 39-49 and see p.273 n.27 below). Although we do not have
reliable information on the composition of Nicanor's army, and the
perfect disposition attributed to him by II Macc. at Adasa (15.
20-1) is but pure invention, it is hardly conceivable that Nicanor,
being considerably inferior in manpower due to the confinement of
the Seleucid army to Babylonia (see p.184 above), risked battle
on such terrain without heavy troops, the trump card of the
Seleucid army. In these two battles Judas Maccabaeus did not have
to defend the holy city because it was in any case occupied by the
enemy (I Macc. 7.32-9), and if he displayed readiness to engage
the enemy in a battle arena that was ideal for the Seleucid heavy
force, it can be only because he had equivalent forces at his
disposal. A similar conclusion is to be drawn from the
description of the battle at Elasa. The clash between the two
sides went on, after the withdrawal of the Seleucid skirmishers,
in the words of I Macc., 'from morning to evening' (9.13), a
biblical phrase (cf. II Sam. 13.13, etc.) which should not be
taken literally but undoubtedly reflects a bitter struggle.
Except in I Macc. 10.80, where there is no reason to doubt its
reliability (see below), the phrase does not figure in the Books
of the Maccabees, not even to 'soften' Jewish defeats. The
activity of the wings makes it clear that the issue was not
decided easily: had the infantry in the centre, which was
certainly the main part of the Jewish force, been defeated at the
first clash, there would have been no point in Judas Maccabaeus'

attacking the enemy's right-wing cavalry. On a battlefield like
Elasa light infantry had no chance of standing against phalangites,
not even for a short while. Light troops could, of course, have
manoeuvred against phalanx in 'hit-and-run' tactics and drawn the
enemy into nearby difficult terrain, but the description makes it
evident that the assault of the Seleucid phalanx took place only
after the withdrawal of their promachoi, whose duty was usually to
confront the enemy's 'lights'. It may be argued that the Seleucid
heavy troops 'played for time' and did not crush the Jewish force
in the first clash as a part of their plan to draw Judas Maccabaeus
into the trap (see below), but in this case one would expect the
promachoi to carry on and not leave the phalanx unprotected by
'lights'. Even if the Seleucid promachoi, who numbered at least
10,000 men, were unable to stand up to the Jewish 'lights' and
therefore withdrew, it must be borne in mind that usually
hesitation on the part of phalangites in advancing independently
against light infantry and snipers might easily end disastrously.
The fact that the battle in the centre lasted as long as it did
makes it, therefore, inconceivable that only light troops were
used against the Seleucid phalanx at Elasa. Thirteen years later,
in the battle near Azōtos in the coastal plain, Jonathan defended
himself against mounted archers who surprised him from the rear as
he faced the enemy's phalanx in the front. Jonathan's troops
stood fast on the defence until the enemy's archers exhausted
their ammunition and then Simon, his brother, assaulted and
defeated the enemy's phalanx (I Macc. 10.77-82, esp. 80-2).
Success against the enemy's phalanx in a flat and wide-open battle
arena indicates, as has been said above, that the Jews employed
heavy troops and, in any case, the Seleucid phalanx could have
exploited the opportunity presented by the stationary position of
Jonathan's troops and destroyed them had they been 'lights'.
Moreover, the passive stationary formation set against the sniping
of the archers itself suggests that the Jewish force could not
have been 'light' and indicates what the Jewish armament must have
been; such a formation necessitated long pikes and shields and
recalls a Hellensistic defence formation typical of phalanx troops
which had to face similar situations, namely the synaspismos, i.e.
'joining shields', in which the phalangites created a quadrate

formation in which every side is a front and the lines dispose a
'turtle' of shields to defend themselves from sniping.[36] Josephus
in <u>Antiquitates</u> interprets Jonathan's formation in this way (13.95
-6). I Macc., on the other hand, is content with a general
description of the events and does not classify the Jewish force
as phalanx, a term which is applied only to the enemy (10.82) in a
similar way as in the descriptions of Beith-Zacharia and Elasa.
The battle near Azōtos admittedly happened long after Judas
Maccabaeus had died and the Jewish army had had the time and
opportunity to develop,[37] but it is significant that even this
episode is silent about the composition of the Jewish army.
Turning to information of non-Jewish origin, it should be noted
that Josephus, in his version on Beith-Zacharia in <u>Bellum</u>, which
contains, as has been stated above, valuable details (p.176 above),
refers to the clash of the phalanxes of the two sides (1.42). The
narrative is indeed based on a Hellenistic source and even
Polybius applies the term 'phalanx' rather flexibly and not in the
precise technical meaning it had in the Hellenistic period (see
1.33.6; 3.73.7, 115.12 and cf. p.156 above), but the term could
not, in any case, apply to light infantry. It should be added
that combination of the sources indicates that there was a
confrontation of the skirmishers of both sides before the clash of
the 'phalanxes' (see p.182 above), so that the term 'phalanx' in
this context cannot refer to the army as a whole.

On reaching this conclusion one cannot avoid the question of
where the Jewish horses and phalangites came from. Judaea was not
a horse-breeding country, and the Jews in Palestine had no
tradition of cavalry and phalanx warfare. One possible
explanation is that weapons and horses were procured from booty,
and I Macc. perhaps indicates this possibility (6.6), but the
horsemen and part of the phalangites must have come from outside
Judaea. Dositheus, the cavalryman mentioned above, is described
as 'one of the <u>Toubiēnoi</u>',[38] presumably from the former Ptolemaic
cleruchy in trans-Jordan led by the influential family of Tobiah,
which also included horsemen.[39] The elder sons of Joseph, son of
Tobiah, identified themselves with the Seleucid cause, but
Hyrcanus, the youngest son, sided with the Ptolemies, assembled a
great force and established an independent principality in trans-

Jordan. He is reported to have committed suicide at the beginning
of Antiochus IV's reign (Jos. Ant. 12.228-36), but resentment of
the Seleucid occupation in that area did not die down, as is
clearly indicated by the flight of Iason, the former high priest,
to Ammonitis (II Macc. 3.11).[40] Apart from this reference, we
find no indication of the participation of Jews from outside
Judaea, but in view of the didactic purpose of the sources they
could hardly be expected to elaborate on this. The references to
Dositheus might therefore be taken as a 'slip of the pen', which
points to a possible solution: at least some of the phalangites
and cavalrymen were Jews from abroad.[41] Jews from Egypt who
served in regular as well as in exclusively Jewish units in the
Ptolemaic army[42] and maintained close contact with the religious
centre in Jerusalem may have been deeply enough moved by the
religious persecutions to offer their help. The Ptolemaic
authorities may have encouraged such initiative, especially as
they would not have feared Seleucid retaliatory measures in view
of the Roman 'umbrella' which had recently proved itself so
powerful in the 'days of Eleusis'. The same applies to the Jewish
military settlers in Phrygia and Lydia, then under Pergamene
supervision. I would not even exclude the participation of some
Jewish volunteers from the military settlements in the Seleucid
realm. If Judas and Jonathan, his brother, were so politically
minded as to establish diplomatic relations with Rome and Sparta,
would they have failed to mobilize their compatriots with military
training from all over the Jewish diaspora? The mobilization of
Jews in the diaspora did not take place overnight. It gained
momentum and was consolidated only four years after the outset of
the revolt by the purification of the temple, which produced
considerable elation in the diaspora. Palestinian Jews were also
incorporated into the phalanx: it did not require very much time
to train such troops as was proved by the Ptolemies before 217 B.C.

The Seleucid tactics, as emerges from the disposition and
manoeuvres of their forces, were quite different from the basic
tactics of the period. The phalanx, and not the cavalry, attacked
first. Such a move was regarded as superfluous and as a waste of
manpower, since success in the centre did not secure victory
because the infantry was still open to cavalry attack in the wings.

In a conventional battle the phalangite formations in the centre engaged only when the cavalry confrontation remained undecided. The only explanation I can imagine for these rather curious tactics is that Bacchides was determined to kill or capture Judas Maccabaeus and his staff. Had the cavalry in Bacchides' wing attacked Judas' wing first, they would certainly have got the upper hand and the Jewish wing would have collapsed, but Judas and his men might easily have escaped through the open way southwards as they had done after the defeat at Beith-Zacharia. By refraining from attacking on the wing, Bacchides did not leave Judas Maccabaeus much choice: Judas, as the leader, could not afford to stand idle because in this case his centre would have 'broken' under the pressure of the experienced Seleucid phalanx and he would have had to retreat without actually taking part in the battle. Two possibilities were left: the first, to attack the exposed flanks of the advancing Seleucid phalanx, was rejected because it would have exposed Judas Maccabaeus' wing to an outflanking manoeuvre by Bacchides' cavalry. The second, to assault Bacchides' wing, seemed to offer the best chance in light of the assumption which had proved itself in the battle against Nicanor, that the death of the commander brings about the collapse of his army (I Macc. 7.43; cf. 3.11). Bacchides, who had already been in Judaea (I Macc. 7.8-20) and was, therefore, acquainted with Judas Maccabaeus' methods and limitations, probably expected him to choose this alternative. According to I Macc. Judas Maccabaeus assembled his select troops, charged Bacchides' wing, defeated, and pursued it. I very much doubt if Judas' cavalry, whatever its origins, could actually have defeated Bacchides' right wing of experienced horsemen, who probably belonged to the Guard. Moreover, in retreating, Bacchides' cavalry would have been dispersed and unable to turn against the pursuers along the rough and uneven plateau on the way to Bā‘al-Ḥasōr unless such a manoeuvre was done deliberately and carefully planned beforehand. If one considers the suggested aim of Bacchides, to liquidate the rebellion by killing the leaders, it occurs to me that Bacchides actually staged a trap by pretending to retreat in order to catch Judas between two fires. As has already been indicated, had Bacchides confronted him vigorously, when his flank was attacked, he would have got the upper hand, but his prey could still have escaped. The over-enthusiastic Jewish historian cannot be expected to have been acquainted with Bacchides' plan and the real character of his 'retreat', inasmuch as Polybius' source did not know the real purpose of Antiochus III in pursuing the Ptolemaic left wing at Raphia, but, even if he had known them, he would not have included the information in his report and so detracted from his hero's 'success' in his last hour. Judas Maccabaeus, on his part, carried on the pursuit and actually abandoned his infantry on the battlefield, because Bacchides himself was not killed, and his cavalry was not broken. In this situation Judas had to fear the reorganization of the routed cavalry and its return to the battlefield, and hoped perhaps that his threatening advance toward what was possibly the Seleucid rear camp (and the aposkeuē) near Bāʿal-Ḥaṣōr would demoralize the Seleucid troops in the field (cf. the battle of Ammaus - I Macc. 4.20-1).

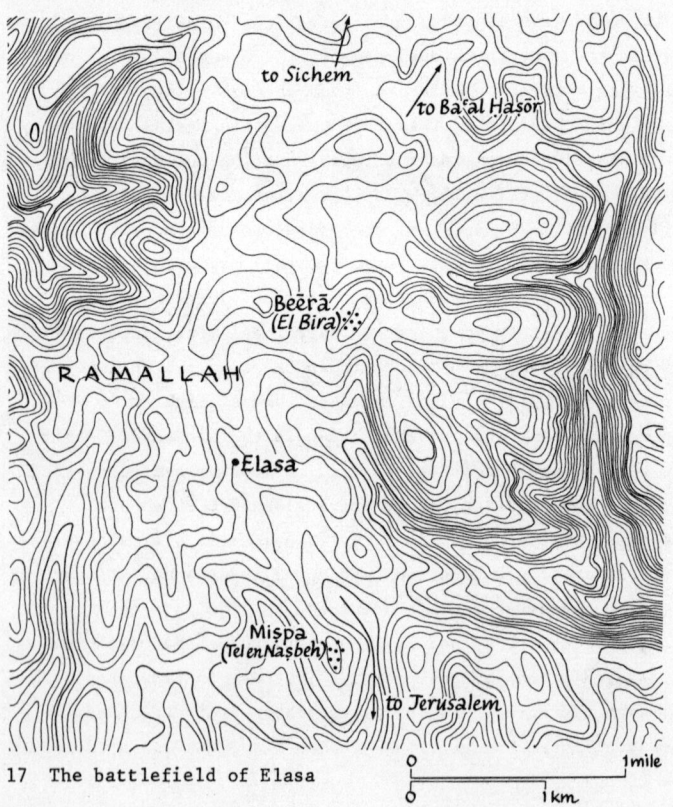

17 The battlefield of Elasa

CONCLUSION

Antigonus, Ptolemy, and Seleucus, the first Hellenistic rulers in the east, were faced with an unprecedented politico-military dilemma when they turned their attention to the administration of their realms. The territories at their disposal were together more or less equal in size to the enormous dimensions of the Persian realm, but the Macedonian generals, unlike the deposed oriental kings, were an alien element in the area. They therefore had no local power base which would permit them to mobilize the indigenous population in defence of their territorial achievements, nor any outside the area, since Macedon itself was occupied by their rivals.

It has long been established that a solution to this problem was found in the settling of soldiers, mostly European by descent, on allotments of land in the newly occupied territories in return for certain military obligations. The ingenious concept of military settlements achieved two advantages: on the one hand it established islands of Greco-Macedonian population among the oriental natives, thus spreading the influence of Greek culture among the upper classes of the subjugated nations, and, on the other, it provided a reservoir of trained and loyal manpower that served mainly in the phalanx and was always ready for any call to duty.

In Ptolemaic Egypt this system did not last long, and certainly by the last quarter of the third century B.C. the Ptolemies, being short of trained manpower, had become more and more dependent on the services of European mercenaries and of untrained Egyptian recruits, a situation which considerably jeopardized the armies' state of readiness and even inspired local revolts among the population, who, for the first time, realized their bargaining power and the weak base of the Macedonian regime. On the other hand, the Seleucid military settlements, a number of which were founded by Antigonus, went on to provide trained and competent manpower for the phalanx and the cavalry throughout the

third century and more than half of the second, too, although the
Seleucid Empire was much larger and the settlers were dispersed to
distant corners of the realm for reasons of regional security.
This dispersal did not make the task any easier, and could well have
destroyed the attachment of the soldier-settlers to the remote
throne in Antioch and led to a deterioration in the military
standard of these reservists, who were first and foremost farmers.

As I have tried to suggest, the key to the Seleucid success
may be found in their practice of filling the ranks of the Guardsmen, the argyraspides of the infantry, and the 'Companions' and the
agēma of the cavalry, with sons of the military settlers. After
their initial training in the military centre at Apamea, the young
men were ready for immediate mobilization to any corner of the
Empire. A Guardsman continued to serve in the royal contingent
until, for one reason or another, his father was withdrawn from the
reserve. Returning to his allotment and replacing his father in
the reserve, he applied the military skills acquired in his regular
service and, though hundreds of kilometres from Antioch, he was in
no doubt as to who the legitimate king of the Empire was and where
his own loyalty and obligations lay. The organization of the Guard
also made possible a constant infusion of new blood into the ranks
of the command through the promotion of able Guardsmen to
prominent positions in the army. In the Ptolemaic army, on the
contrary, an almost absolute dependence on mercenary generals from
the Greek world is discernible.

Despite the socio-cultural motivation behind the foundation of
tne military settlements, their chief importance lay in military
and security considerations, and therefore the military settlements
of heavy horsemen in Media consisted mainly of Iranians, famed for
their tradition of cavalry warfare, and not of Greco-Macedonian
soldiers. It was in the interests of security that, despite the
role of the polis as an agent of the Seleucid imperial policy,
municipal rights were denied to the settlers north of the Taurus
although a substantial number of them were of Hellenic descent.

Thus, the military settlements provided mainly the phalangites
and the heavy cavalry, other units being supplied by the local
population in the Empire. Because of the Empire's size, the light
cavalry and the infantry heavily outnumbered the corresponding

Conclusion

forces in other Hellenistic armies. In fact, however, great numbers of light cavalry were not employed on all occasions owing to constant unrest in the eastern provinces, and, unlike the Ptolemies who gave arms to the native Egyptians, the Seleucids were aware of the importance of not encouraging the military potential of the Syrians and Babylonians, realizing that an uprising at the heart of the kingdom might well undermine its very existence. Another Seleucid advantage was the utilization of Indian elephants, which were obtainable thanks to the position of the Seleucid realm and were superior to the Ptolemies' African elephants.

The tactics and performance of the Seleucid as well as of other Hellenistic armies on the battlefield have been little appreciated by modern historians and regarded as replicas of Alexander's basic disposition without his ingenuity and brilliance of manoeuvre.[1] The only contribution to the art of warfare generally attributed to the Seleucid armies is the deployment of elephants in a mainly defensive role. But this dismissal does some injustice to the Seleucid kings, who in almost all their battles employed different and unexpected manoeuvres. The basic disposition and tactics admittedly followed the scheme of Alexander's army: the phalanx was posted in the centre and was protected by cavalry in the flanks and by lights either in the flanks or front. The main purpose was to drive away the opposing flank and so make it easy for the cavalry to take the enemy's centre in the flank or in the rear. In this, the Seleucids did not have much choice; once their Hellenistic rivals were disposed in this formation they had to adapt themselves accordingly. At Magnesia, however, when facing the Roman legions, Antiochus III was able to deploy cavalry between the phalanx and the <u>argyraspides</u> in order to drive a wedge in the wall of legionaries so that each part could be outflanked separately. Even in the limited framework of conventional Hellenistic warfare the contribution of the Seleucids cannot be ignored: they may be credited with certain innovations in the disposition of the troops, such as the flexible and well-protected structure of the phalanx divisions at Magnesia and Beith-Zacharia, the introduction of a tactical offensive reserve force at Ipsus and against Molon, the blocking of circumventing routes at Panion and Thermopylae, etc. The actual plans

of campaign, while employing varying stratagems, always involved
the element of surprise. At Ipsus and Elasa the army laid a trap
for the strongest flank of the enemy by means of a partial retreat,
enticing the enemy's cavalry away from the battlefield, then
blocking their way back with elephants or cavalry and, in the case
of Elasa, also catching it between two fires; at Cyrrhestica
Demetrius' troops were overwhelmed by the sudden appearance of
Seleucus himself and his elephants from a hidden side route in
their flank; the battle against Molon was decided, almost without
bloodshed, by the surprise appearance from behind the lines of the
reserve force which had hitherto been kept hidden, and a similar
stratagem, performed in this case by elephants, was employed
against the Galatians (Luc. _Zeuxis_ 9). At Raphia Antiochus bypassed the elephants in front of both opposing flanks in order to
outflank the Ptolemaic left-wing cavalry, and carried on the
pursuit with the intention of killing Ptolemy himself and so
deciding the issue.

  The test of an army lies in its performance not only in open
confrontation, but also in marching, storming fortified positions
and blocked passes, and defending strategical routes. The
Seleucids were especially impressive in the utilization of flexible
plans to clear ambushes and blocked routes. The use of a bait
force to locate the enemy's position and the combined efforts of
special units in the defile and the ridges to dislodge the enemy
in the Elburz mountain were remarkable tactical innovations; the
unique composition at Beith-Zacharia of the Seleucid column of
self-contained divisions, each a 'mini-formation' of the
conventional Hellenistic battle line, constituted an offensive
spearhead instead of the ordinary defensive order in long columns;
the attack of the Seleucid 'lights' on the Ptolemaic position at
Porphyrion by climbing the rock while exposed to enemy fire from
above, and the three-fold operation to close in on the defenders
in the pass itself, is an outstanding example of tactical and
personal bravery. Tarn rightly sensed that if more records of
Seleucid military activity were available, significant innovations
in mountain warfare would be brought to light.[2] In the defensive
array forced on Antiochus III at Thermopylae owing to his
considerable inferiority in manpower and cavalry, he was not

content with a static line but deployed his troops in a flexible order which would break the enemy's line and then be able to turn immediately to pursuit.

In view of the Seleucid army's considerable ability, what then was it that hampered it in its campaigns against the Romans? The advantage of the legion over the phalanx in rough terrain was not always relevant since the two main confrontations with the Roman army took place on a flat arena, and, in theory, Antiochus III should have been able to overcome the legionaries as Pyrrhos demonstrated at Heraclea.[3] The main factor responsible for ruining Antiochus' chances at Thermopylae was the low standard of discipline among the phalangites, who took to their heels on observing the capture of the camp and the danger of being taken in the rear. A similar threat of being outflanked caused the dispersal of the phalanx line at Raphia, where the phalangites, had they offered resistance for a while (Antiochus being expected to return from the pursuit), could have saved the day. A considerable improvement in the discipline of the phalanx can be detected at Magnesia. Despite the rather desperate situation, the Seleucid centre formed itself into a 'square' and did not abandon its position until the elephants, confined in the 'square', ran wild. As far as the last battle is concerned, the tendency to extravagance which was customary in contemporary siege and naval warfare and the quality of Antiochus III's leadership must bear the brunt of the blame. First and foremost there was the clumsy attempt to 'jump the gun' by employing scythed chariots against the Roman cavalry, despite the lessons of Cunaxa and Gaugamela and the failure of another exotic weapon, the elephant, in similar circumstances at Zama. The weakness of leadership is also to be seen in other Seleucid battles, especially Raphia. Like most Hellenistic commanders, with the exception of Antigonus at Paratakene and Seleucus I at Ipsus, Antiochus involved himself personally in the battle at the front of the spearhead cavalry, which prevented him from playing his proper role of commander in chief by observing general developments and directing and controlling the entire force. By charging at the head of the picked cavalry he was doing as Alexander had done, but Alexander always chose the right moment, and never charged with the Companions unless he was sure that this would have a decisive effect and that he was not needed in another part of the arena; in any case, he never lost sight of what was happening behind him, and he recognised the importance of altering his tactics when necessary and abandoning the pursuit.[4] Antiochus III, on the other hand, at Raphia as well as at Magnesia, rode at the spearhead of the attack and carried on the pursuit to accomplish his preconceived purposes of killing Ptolemy and capturing the Roman camp, without taking notice of what was happening on the battlefield. If there had been a decline in the Seleucid army in comparison with Alexander's Macedonians, it was evident in discipline and in tactical planning and leadership in battle, rather than in the general standard and performance of the troops.

Finally, a few words for the evaluation of the battles against Judas Maccabaeus. The traditional description of the Jewish few and weak who bravely withstood the royal force is based on the misleading picture presented by the Jewish sources, which for didactic purposes concealed the units and total manpower at Judas Maccabaeus' disposal. But analysis of the sources suggests that the Jews were often superior in number and, though inferior in weapons, they were not unarmed but had phalanx and cavalry units. On the other hand, the well-known explanation that Judas Maccabaeus succeeded from time to time because the Seleucid army degenerated in the second century B.C. and was not able to operate on hilly terrain does not hold water. The Seleucid army, thanks to the organization of the Guard, did not deteriorate prior to the internal crisis later in the forties and the army as a whole was experienced in coordinated operations in uneven battle arenas and in addition included special contingents recruited from among hill people (cf. II Macc. 4.29, 5.24, 12.35). As a matter of fact, most of the Jewish victories were achieved against small detachments organized by local governors. Of the campaigns against royal armies, only the battle of Ammaus can be regarded as a major victory, achieved thanks to careful planning, acquaintance with the terrain, and the element of surprise (I Macc. 3.38-4.25).[5]

NOTES

CHAPTER 1

1 See the detailed discussion of H. Delbrück, <u>Numbers in History</u>, esp. 12-25. On another angle of the question: Polyb. 2.33.17-18.
2 Cf. Antigonus' 88,000 troops in 306 (Diod. 19.73.2).
3 See the figures for the other monarchies in W.W. Tarn, <u>Antigonus Gonatas</u>, 424-8; J. Beloch, <u>Griechische Geschichte</u>, IV.1.348-52.
4 App. <u>Syr</u>. 32(161) - 70,000. The slight discrepancy is explained by Appian's tendency to simplify and generalize figures (see H. Nissen, <u>Kritische Untersuchungen über die vierten und fünften Dekade des Livius</u>, 196). Other sources, not dependent on Polybius, provide much higher figures and are generally worthless. Thus Florus, based on annalistic sources, reports 300,000 infantry and a similar number of cavalry (24.1).
5 P.12 et passim; <u>Geschichte der Kriegskunst</u>, I.367-8.
6 See Kromayer's analysis of the figures in J. Kromayer - G. Veith, <u>Antike Schlachtfelder</u>, II.210-11 (esp. 211 n.5) and cf. a somewhat different view, <u>ibid</u>. 181 n.4.
7 On the defence of the Seleucid camp at Magnesia, Livy 37.43.10-11; App. <u>Syr</u>. 36(184), but no figures are recorded.
8 Appian's version, identifying the <u>argyraspides</u> as cavalry (<u>Syr</u>. 32(164)) is of no value: apart from the many inaccuracies in his list which discredit him, there was no such contingent in Alexander's time nor in the Hellenistic period, while the existence of the infantry <u>argyraspides</u> is well established (see in detail p.59 above). Besides, Livy would not write 'cohors' (see below) for an <u>ilē</u> in Polybius, and he uses 'cohors' regularly of infantry and not cavalry. In the same way as Antisthenes confused the cavalry Guard at Thermopylae with the hypaspists, the infantry Guard (p.64 above), so Appian turned the <u>argyraspides</u> into cavalry (contrary to

Kromayer, Schlachtfelder, II.210 n.1).

9 Their definition as 'regia cohors' does not indicate that they were of the same order as a Roman cohort (amounting to 1,000 in Augustus' time). Livy did not find in Polybius any indication of their strength, and may merely have translated the term tagma, syntagma or systēma usually applied to various corps of differing strengths (e.g. Polyb. 5.53.3; 11.23.1: 16.19.7; 30.25. Cf. Diod. 17.57.2; Plut. Eum. 8.5 etc., and see M. Feyel, RA 6 sér.5 (1935)42-7 esp. 47 n.3; F.W. Walbank, Philip V of Macedon, 253 n.7; Lesquier, 366-7; see also the regia cohors in Curt. 8.6.7, 8.20; 10.7.16, 8.3, for the 50 paides basilikoi (id. 5.42.1; Diod. 17.65.1)).

10 The 20,000 infantry and 12,000 cavalry which are said to have taken part at Ipsus (Diod. 20.113.4; Plut. Demetr. 28.3) must be disregarded as they do not represent the full recruitment potential of later armies: the Seleucid kingdom was at that time confined to the provinces beyond the Euphrates, and the military settlements in the west had not yet been established. The detachment which liberated the Ionian cities from the Galatians in the time of the First Syrian War (Lucian, Zeuxis, 8-11) comprised only a small part of the Seleucid army, which was attached to the seething Syrian front (see in detail B. Bar-Kochva, Proc. Camb. Phil. Soc. N.S. 19(1973)3-5).

11 N.C. Debevoise, History of Parthia, 17 n.69; P. Pédech, REA 60(1958)73 n.1; F.W. Walbank, A Historical Commentary on Polybius, II.236.

12 At least some of the military settlers in Phrygia and Lydia, which had recently been pacified by Antiochus following the execution of Achaeus, were left behind, as can be deduced from Jos. Ant. 12.147.

13 Plut. Alex. 66.2; Curt. 8.5.4, though their reliability is doubtful.

14 Oros. Hist. 5.10.8 (100,000 soldiers and 200,000 followers); Diod. 33.15-17 (300,000 losses); see also Debevoise, 31 n.9; G. Downey, A History of Antioch in Syria, 125 n.28; G. Rawlinson, Parthia, 94.

15 E. Bickerman, Institutions des Séleucides, 90.

16 See the stelai in G. Mendel, Catalogue des Sculptures Grecques,

Romaines et Byzantines, nos.102-8.

17 Among the scholars approving the figures see: C.R. Conder, Judas Maccabaeus and the Jewish War of Independence, 134, 157; E. Bevan, The House of Seleucus, II.298; A. Kahana, The Apocrypha, I.114; S. Zeitlin, The First Book of Maccabees, 100. A different view is taken by B. Niese, Hermes 35 (1900) 283, 300, 460; W.O.E. Oesterley, I Maccabees, 60; F.M. Abel, Les Livres des Maccabées, 65, 79, 116; J.C. Dancy, A Commentary on I Maccabees, 7, 93, 97, 114, etc.; M. Avi-Yonah, Studies and Essays in the Lore of the Holy Land, 63-4.

18 See also I Macc. 4.6, 29, 7.40, 9.5-6; II Macc. 8.1, 16.

19 Abel, Maccabées, p.XXIV; Dancy, 3; C.C. Torrey, The Apocryphal Literature, 73.

20 On the historiographical character of II Macc. see Niese, Hermes 35 (1900) 299-307; E. Bickermann, RE s.v. Makkabäerbücher, col.729ff.

21 See esp. Niese, op.cit. 271-2; Abel, Maccabées, pp.XXII, XXXIV-V; Dancy, 1-2; J. Efron, Historians and Historical Schools, 129-31 et alii. See esp. I Macc. 3.18, 46-60, 4.8-10, 24, 30-2, 5.62, 7.41-2, 9.46, 12.15 etc. II Macc. 3.25-8, 10. 28-9, 31, 11.8-10, 12.15-16, 15.27. The impact of the historiographical doctrine of the two books is also to be detected in the presentation of ambushes carried out by Judas Maccabaeus as straightforward frontal attacks, in the absence of references to the Jewish cavalry, in the excusatory approach to the Jewish defeats, even to the extent in I Macc. of slurring over them, and in the turning of defeats into victories by II Macc. (I Macc. 3.11, 4.11-14,34, 6.47, 13.22; II Macc. 12.37, 13.22, and see pp.175-6, 194-7, 267 n.15 above).

22 A similar disproportion between the forces of both sides, to quote just one example, is reported in the accounts of Timoleon's campaigns in Sicily (see e.g. Diod. 16.77.4, 78.2; Plut. Tim. 25.3). Because he was a favourite with the sources behind the versions of Diodorus and Plutarch (mainly Timaeus, see H.D. Westlake, CQ 32 (1938) 68-72; T.S. Brown, Timaeus of Tauromenium, 83-7) the hero's stature was magnified by the attribution of considerable numerical superiority to the enemy (note Polyb. 12.23-4, 25f7, 25h2 on Timaeus' ignorance of

military affairs, and 25i5, 25k1 on his talent for invention).
23 On the purposes of the eastern expedition to recover Armenia and regain effective control in Persis and Elymais, see O. Mørkolm, Antiochus IV of Syria, 166-7, 178. See the summary of the various theories in: Ed. Will, Histoire Politique du Monde Hellénistique, II.296-8.
24 So Abel, Maccabées, 65.
25 In contrast to Niese, Hermes 35 (1900) 466.
26 II Macc. could possibly have used the obscure term μυρίων (cf. 11.4), and the attached δις was affected by the δισχιλίων in the next verse (8.10 - the Lucianic version reads here δισμυρίων, which is certainly wrong but reflects the probable confusion between the two lines).
27 On the position of Apollonios and Sērōn see Abel, Maccabées, 55-7; B. Bar-Kochva, PEQ 107 (1975, forthcoming).
28 Cf. I Macc. 3.10, 41; cf. the numbers in 10.71, 77, 85 (though they might be exaggerated), and see Abel, Maccabées, 65 on the original reading Edōm instead of Arām (Syria) in 3.41.
29 On the revolt in the eastern satrapies see Ed. Will, Histoire Politique du Monde Hellénistique, II.308-10, and selected bibliography there. The date of Timarchus' death is not known, but a Babylonian cuneiform tablet states that from 151, i.e. between April 161-April 160 B.C. (according to the Babylonian reckoning of the Seleucid era which went back to April 311, see F. Kugler, Sternkunde und Sterndienst in Babel, I.214), Babylonia was controlled by Demetrius (J.W. Strassmaier, Zeitschr. f. Assyr. 7 (1893) 110), and from a combination of data in App. Syr. 47; Polyb. 31.33, 32.2-3; Diod. 31.28, it seems likely that the issue was decided at the beginning of 160 (so W. Otto, RE s.v. Herakleides$^{(32)}$ 467; K. Ziegler, RE s.v. Timarchos$^{(5)}$, 1238; H. Volkmann, Klio 19 (1925) 393). The battle of Elasa took place in the first month of 152 B.C. (I Macc. 9.3). As the expedition of Bacchides is directly connected with the Jews, the chronological basis for its date must be April 311, according to the Babylonian system. (On the two chronological systems employed by I Macc. see E. Bickermann, RE s.v. Makkabäerbücher, cols.781-4; id. Der Gott der Makkabäer, 155-8; I. Schaumberger, Biblica 36

(1955) 426-7 et al.). The expedition to Elasa is, therefore, to be dated in April 160 B.C. The same date is valid even if we assume that I Macc. adopted a 'mixed' system; reckoning years according to the Macedonian starting point of October 312, and months - according to the old Israelitic system commencing the year from Nisan-April (see e.g. I Macc. 4.52, 10.21).

30 See Diod. 31.27a for the support the troops in Media gave Heracleides, the local satrap (Timarchus' brother). It is impossible to say whether the reoccupation of Babylonia meant the pacification of Media as well.

31 App. Syr. 12(48), refers only to 10,000, cf. p.207 n.4 above.

32 See also id. 16(66-7); Livy, 35.42.4-6; 36.7-8, 15.5 etc.

33 See Kromayer, Schlachtfelder, II.208; J.A.O. Larsen, Greek Federal States, 416.

34 Kromayer dated the battle to 24 April 191 (Schlachtfelder, II. 220-7; see also M. Holleaux, Études d'Épigraphie et d'Histoire Grecques, V.403); H. Matzat, Römische Zeitrechnung für die Jahre 219 bis 1 V. Chr., 197, suggested 22 June, and O. Leuze, Hermes 58 (1923) 269-277, prefers 23 May. I am inclined to accept Kromayer's arguments.

35 See L. Casson, Ships and Seamanship in the Ancient World, 270-2. According to Mediterranean Pilot, IV^7 (1941) 10, the waves are usually 3-4 by the Beaufort Table (2.5 m), which is barely above the danger limit for vessels of the trireme class and storms as high as 8 by Beaufort are common even in mid-May, nor must the strong north to northwest winds be disregarded.

36 On the fabrication of the speeches, see Nissen, 180 etc. The dubious character of the speech is obvious from the reference to the landing force as Dahae, Medes, Cadusians and Elymaeans (Livy 35.49.12; cf. 48.5), when these oriental troops actually delayed in Asia too long to come to Thermopylae. The same misrepresentation of the Seleucid army recurs in Glabrio's alleged address to the troops (Livy 36.17.5; cf. p.227 n.110 below).

37 J. Kromayer - G. Veith, Heerwesen und Kriegführung der Griechen und Römer, 183-4, and see Morrison - Williams, 244-9; A.W. Gomme et al., A Historical Commentary on Thucydides, IV. 309-10.
38 Morrison - Williams, 248, 263ff.
39 On these sorts of vessels, W.W. Tarn, Mariner's Mirror 19 (1933) 68; id. Hellenistic Military and Naval Developments, 126, 130 n.1.
40 According to the number of Athenian soldiers and vessels in the expedition to Sicily (Thuc. 6.43): the 6,400 strong landing force were divided between 40 Athenian stratiōtides to which were added no more than 22 vessels of the Allies (at least 12 of the allied triremes were fighting vessels, see Gomme, IV.309). See also Kromayer, Heerwesen, 183; Casson, 93, counts 60 Athenian stratiōtides instead of 40, which distorts his calculation. Morrison - Williams, 248, estimate, with no apparent reason, the number of Greek soldiers in each vessel in that expedition as 72. Their assumption, based on Thucydides 8.74.1-2, that the number of sailors in troop-ships was similar to that of warships and that, therefore, their capacity was not very great, seems to ignore the special circumstances of the occasion. The number of sailors in the vessel sent to Euboea was not changed because the ship did not carry landing troops but patrolled the island, and because the 'four hundred' were anxious to get hold of the paralos and dispose of its crew as soon as possible.
41 See Casson, 82 and 106 n.42. Polybius 1.26.7 mentions 300 sailors and 120 soldiers serving in the Roman quinquireme, but this was an ordinary warship and not a troop carrier (see also J. Kromayer, Philologus 54 (1897) 491).
42 On the indirect acquaintance of Hieronymus with Porphyrios, see E. Taeubler, JQR 37 (1946-7) 13 n.22.

43 See the detailed discussion of Holleaux IV.211-335.

CHAPTER 2
1 Lesquier, Les Institutions militaires de l'Egypte sous les Lagides, 11-29.
2 See especially: Griffith, Mercenaries, 147-170; Bickerman, Institutions, 74-8. Only A. Bouché-Leclerq, Histoire des Séleucides, I.476, regards the settlers as veterans who had served their time.
3 Polyb. 5.53.3, 79.4.5; 10.29.5; 16.18.4; 30.25.3; App. Syr. 18(83), 32(161); Livy 36.18.2; 37.40.1,7. On the argyraspides see in detail above p.59 ff.
4 So Bickerman, Institutions, 74.
5 The significance of this statement has been so far overlooked, because the argyraspides have been erroneously regarded as orientals.
6 See Griffith, Mercenaries, 151-3.
7 See Griffith, Mercenaries, 164; Bickerman, Institutions, 77.
8 Bickerman, ibid. 85-6, regards them as civilian settlers, but service by Babylonian Jews in the Seleucid army appears from II Macc. 8.20, and the same is indicated by Jos. Ap. 2.39; id. Ant. 12.119. See also Bengtson, Strategie^2, II.68; A. Schalit, JQR 49 (1960) 289-318; B. Bar-Kochva, Proc. Camb. Phil. Soc. N.S. 19 (1973) 5-7. The confinement of military settlements to Phrygia and Lydia alone (see p.25) further verifies the historicity of Josephus' account.
9 See Griffith, Mercenaries, 154-5.
10 G. Radet, De Coloniis a Macedonibus in Asiam cis Taurum deductis; A. Schulten, Hermes 32 (1897) 523-37; the same is implied by M. Clerc, De rebus Thyatirenorum, and C. Schuchardt, AM 10 (1885) 1-7. On cleruchs and katoikoi in Ptolemaic Egypt: P Teb. I.545-50; Oertel. RE s.v. Katoikoi, 17-18; Holleaux, II.37-8.
11 Bickerman, Institutions, 102; M. Launey, Recherches sur les armées hellénistiques, I.669-75.
12 See Dittenberger's notes ad loc. (56-7). The document applies the participle οἰκοῦντες to the former Magnesian katoikoi (95, 97-8), although they had two extra kleroi (perhaps

situated nearer to the fortress), because it refers at the
same time to other members of the old garrison who had no
land (ℓ.102). But it may also be that the term katoikoi was
reserved for farmers serving in the reserve, and not used for
active soldiers in permanent garrison as those in Palai-
Magnesia seem to have been, even if they did own lands. For
the latter, the lands were a form of payment. The relatively
large holdings (see $\ell\ell$.102-3; τρεῖς κλήρους ... κλῆρον ἱππικόν)
enabled them to make a reasonable profit by renting the land
to tenants.

13 A. Schalit, König Herodes, 177ff.
14 See also $\ell\ell$.36, 43-4 and $\ell\ell$.46, 49 in comparison with ℓ.37.
15 On the other hand it seems that the second element in Magnesia,
the 'cavalry and infantry under the open sky' (hypaithroi),
are not included among the katoikoi as generally accepted, but
were mercenaries encamped beside the city (so also Launey, II.
671; V. Ehrenberg, The Greek State, 224). This follows from
the syntactical structure of the class list ($\ell\ell$.35, 36, 71,
etc.), and especially from one of its versions (ℓ.14), and the
designations of the emissaries sent to Smyrna (ℓ.21). The
Smyrnean offer to accommodate the Magnesians wishing to settle
in the city would have substance only if some of the soldiers
were not settlers. Finally, it is hard to believe that
soldiers owning allotments nearby should have continued to
reside in camps. Dittenberger's reading of ℓ.49 appears to
undermine this view, but inspection of the inscription in the
Ashmolean Museum, Oxford, revealed that by omitting the τε
there is enough room on the stone to introduce the article τῶν
and read: κατοίκων ἱππέων καὶ πε|ζῶν, τῶν κατὰ πόλιν καὶ τῶν
κατὰ τὰ| | ὕπαιθρα. ℓ.74, being merely a negligent paraphrase,
does not refute my conclusion. Welles, Royal Correspondence,
no.51, which records the grant of lands to |...τῶν| δὲ μήπω
ἐστεγνοποιημένων (ℓ.15), does not reflect an existing situation
but a promise for the future.
16 See for instance: Bevan, Seleucus, I.265; Griffith,
Mercenaries, 151-3; M. Rostovzeff, CAH VII.169; Tarn -
Griffith, Hellenistic Civilization, 148; H. Bengtson,
Griechische Geschichte, 415; Ehrenberg, 150, 228, 265 et al.

17 P. Foucart, BCH 9 (1885) 395; M. Frontrier, Μουσαῖον καὶ Βιβλιοθηκὴ τῆς Εὐαγγελικῆς Σχολῆς, Σμύρνα, 1886, 74; W.M. Ramsay, Cities and Bishoprics of Phrygia, 199, 583, 703; Ed. Meyer, Hermes 33 (1898) 643-4; F. Oertel, RE s.v. Katoikia, 1-2; V. Chapot, La province romaine d'Asie, 97; L. Robert, Études Anatoliennes, 192-3; Rostovzeff, SEHHW, I.477, II.644; Launey, I.366; D. Magie, Roman Rule in Asia Minor, II.1023.

18 W.W. Tarn, The Greeks in Bactria and India, 18; Tarn - Griffith, 147; see also A.H.M. Jones, The Greek City from Alexander to Justinian, 160 (the Hellenistic equivalent for the Athenian metoikoi), and Rostovzeff, Kolonates, 261-2.

19 The only case on record which may fit Tarn's definition is the Jewish katoikia at Hierapolis (CIJ II no.775), but it could also have been a rural settlement attached to the polis by sympoliteia, like the Macedonians mentioned in imperial inscriptions of Hierapolis. (On the status of these Macedonians see Magie, II.988 n.25, in contrast to H. Swoboda, Lehrbuch der griechischen Staatsaltertümer[6], 200 n.13.)

20 See P Teb. 5.180; 27.50; 44.12; 124.2, 7; et pp.545-50; other references in Oertel, 20-6.

21 Diod. 19.27.5; 33.4a: Polyaenus 7.40: Polyb. 5.65.10, 77.7; 15.25.17; 30.28 (in contrast to Robert, loc.cit.; Holleaux, II.37-8; Launey, I.444; Walbank, Polybius I.591). On the Mysian katoikiai see p.228 n.113 below. The Galatian katoikiai may also be regarded in the same context. The Galatians serving perhaps as mercenaries were not military settlers in the strict sense, but their original settlement in Asia Minor by Nicomedes was based on the same principle - lands in return for certain military obligations (see Memnon 11.5(19)) - and it stands to reason that later, when the area was virtually controlled by the Seleucids, they retained the same status. Polybius, who was acquainted with the circumstances of the Galatian settlement, is applying the 'technical' terminology carelessly here. He may also have been distracted by the Galatian military settlements in Macedon (Polyb. 4.67.6; Livy 42.51.4 and see W.W. Tarn, Antigonus Gonatas, 192; Griffith, Mercenaries, 68, 78-9) and in Egypt (Polyb. 5.65.10). See also the conditions imposed by

the Romans on the Galatian envoys which indicate the military character of the Galatian settlements in Asia Minor (Polyb. 30.28).

22 Institutions, 104 n.4, followed by A. Schalit, König Herodes, 178. The occurrence of katoikoi in I Macc. 1.38 is probably due to the influence of the word katoikia, a translation of the Hebrew mōshav, later in the same verse. In any case, for various reasons a military settlement could not have been established in Jerusalem (or the Akra), see B. Bar-Kochva, Zion 38 (1973) 39-44.

23 See H.B. Swete, An Introduction to the Old Testament in Greek, 8-16.

24 See the list in Oertel, 7-8, additions by Magie, II.1022-6, and other references in notes 25,113f below. Obviously settlements whose names are introduced by the participle of katoikein should be excluded.

25 OGIS 338. ℓ.15 certainly refers to soldiers (cf. the settlers at Palai-Magnesia in OGIS 229). The katoikoi recorded in some of Priene's inscriptions (Inscr. Prien. 112.79; 113.42; 118.13) were not necessarily farmers in the chōra as suggested by Oertel (op.cit. 2). They may have occupied one of the fortresses belonging to the city in the northern part of the Maeander valley (on the territory of the city and the fortresses, see Kleiner, RE s.v. Priene, 1184), or even have been originally settled by the Seleucids and attracted to Priene sometime after the battle of Magnesia by a sympoliteia, like that between Smyrna and Magnesia, in order to reinforce the city in face of the constant challenges from Miletus and Samos. A sympoliteia is mentioned in Inscr. Prien. 108.22, but the parties involved cannot be ascertained. Similarly, there is no reason to suspect that the katoikoi in Welles, Royal Correspondence in the Hellenistic Period, no.47, were not military settlers.

26 See Oertel, 20-6.

27 The Lycian Cardaces called οἱ κατοικοῦντες ἐν Καρδάκων κώμῃ (M. Segrè, Clara Rhodos 9 (1938) 190) were not military settlers as has been suggested (Rostovzeff, II.646; E.V. Hansen, The Attalids of Pergamon, 184; Magie, II.1026; Launey,

I.486). The participle form of katoikein, the absence of any
indication of military obligations in this long inscription
and the heavy burden of the poll-tax imposed on them as on the
laoi suggest that in the Hellenistic period they were a
civilian element, although the possibility that they were
initially settled there by the Persians for military purposes
cannot be ruled out. Rostovzeff's view that the Cardaces were
'demoted' by Eumenes (II.648) does not agree with Eumenes'
policy and military needs. Similarly, Launey's conjecture
(I.347) that Selge in Pamphylia and the Carian Mylasa were
Macedonian military settlements from the evidence of the
Macedonian shield on some of their coins has to be rejected.
There is no indication of Macedonian descent for the Selgeans
in the detailed account of their campaign with Pendelissus and
Achaeus (Polyb. 5.72-6), and Macedonian shields could have been
adopted by the city's energetic militia. Mylasa, however, did
not strike the coins referred to, and the name Mylasa does not
appear on them: they were struck by Eupolemus to pay his
troops (see W. Wroth, Num. Chron. 3 Ser. 9 (1891) 136).
Generally, it is doubtful if Macedonian shields or helmets on
coins can be considered decisive evidence as suggested by
Launey.

28 See OGIS 101, 229, 266, 338; Jos. Ant. 12.149-50 and see below
on the various Macedonian settlements in the area (n.32).

29 Stratonikeia in Caria, named after the wife of Seleucus I or
Antigonus, was not 'Macedonian' as claimed by Strabo 14.2.25
(660), and therefore there is no reason to regard the
citizens as military settlers. In the first century B.C. they
referred to themselves as 'Stratonikeians of the autochthonous
metropolis of Caria' (SEG IV. 263), which is certainly more
reliable evidence. Strabo's circumlocutions in referring to
the city's membership in the Chrysaorian League further cast
doubt on his credibility. Bean's suggestion that the city
claimed 'autochthonic' descent because of its location on the
site of an ancient Carian city (OCD^2 s.v. Stratonikeia) cannot
be accepted. The same applies to almost every Macedonian city
in the east, but the settlers in fact emphasize their
Macedonian descent. Strabo seems to have been misled by the

name Stratonikeia. Stephanus' πόλις Μακεδόνων (s.v. Στρατονικεία) originates in Strabo, as can be deduced from the verbal similarity of the second part of this entry.

30 See Rostovzeff, I.500; Launey, I.255-6.
31 Even if A.H.M. Jones is right, and the Ptolemies controlled Pamphylia only for a short while (The Cities of the Eastern Roman Provinces 127), Seleucid supervision may have been only nominal due to its geographical position.
32 The sources: Oertel, 4; Griffith, Mercenaries, 151; Tscherikover, Städtgründungen, 200; Magie, II.1972-4.
33 Cf. C. Préaux, L'économie royale des Lagides, 493-7, on the shortage of lands and the allocation of wasteland to the Egyptian cleruchs in second century B.C. Ptolemaic Egypt.
34 Contrary to Bickerman, Institutions, 82. Other commentators laid too much stress on the danger of the recurrence of a Galatian invasion from the west.
35 For control of the southern route by Korakesion (Alanya) and Perge see Strabo 14.5.3(668); Polyb. 21.42. On Korakesion: Keil-Wilhelm, Jahreshefte, 1915, Beiblatt, 8.
36 The only clear case in which the Galatians turned against a Seleucid king was when they supported Antiochus Hierax against Seleucus II and later joined Pergamon against their former ally (for details see F. Stählin, Geschichte der Kleinasiatische Galater, 18-30, and Launey, I.504-6 and the sources there), but in neither instance did they have to face battle on two fronts.
37 Tscherikover, Städtgründungen, 200: Griffith, Mercenaries, 151; Jones, The Greek City, 9; Tarn, Bactria, 10-11; Tarn-Griffith, 149, but see the reservations of Rostovzeff, I.482; Launey, I.337-8.
38 This information is confirmed by coins from the beginning of the Roman period which show the influence of the emblems of Thessalian Larissa (W. Wroth, Catalogue of the Greek Coins of Galatia, Cappadocia and Syria, pp.LXVIII-LXIX).
39 A.H.M. Jones, The Greek City, 48; id. Cities, 243-4.
40 Cf. Joshua 15.37; Judges 9.21; I.Chron. 7.37.
41 Cf. Steph. Byz. s.v. Ἀντιόχεια. See also J.B. Segal, Edessa, 'The Blessed City', 6.

42 On the history of Adessa, see C.B. Welles, Yale Classical Studies 5 (1935) 121-42.
43 App. Syr. 57; Plin. HN 5.87; Steph. s.v. Ἀμφίπολις and see Jones, The Cities, 442 n.3.
44 Bactria, 6-11.
45 So also, Rostovzeff, I.482, against Tarn-Griffith, 149.
46 Bickerman's doubts about the military obligations of the Seleucid cities, on the grounds of the traditional autonomy of the polis (Institutions, 72ff.), were rightly rejected by Rostovzeff as too formalistic (I.500, III.1437-8). The Seleucids did not treat their foundations in the same way as the old Ionian cities (see Ehrenberg, 191-8; Jones, The Greek City, 98-109; and the detailed discussion of A. Heuss, Stadt und Herrscher des Hellenismus, esp. 245-54). The clearest evidence to this effect is a letter from Antiochus VIII or IX to Seleucia Pieria, dated 109, granting the city autonomy, proclaiming its liberty and offering a treaty (OGIS 257; Welles, Royal Correspondence, no.71-2). The rights of the polis, interpreted in this traditional light, were then conferred only in the years of decline in a desperate attempt to prevent the dismemberment of the kingdom. M. Rostovzeff, CAH VII.185, attributes the 'liberation' of the city to Seleucus II according to Sylloge^3 475, but the last document clearly refers to Athens and not to Seleucia, see A. Wilhelm, Hermes 34 (1899) 233.
47 Cf. Rostovzeff, SEHHW I. 498 on the large population of Apamea at the beginning of the first century A.D.
48 See also A. Downey, A History of Antioch in Syria, 81.
49 See C.H. Kraeling JBL 51 (1932) 137-9. On the Babylonian Jews in the Seleucid army cf. p,213 n.8 above.
50 See also Downey, Antioch, 82; C.B. Welles, Studi in onore di A. Caldevini e R. Paribeni, 81-99.
51 So Rostovzeff, I.481; J. Liebeschuetz, Antioch, City and Imperial Administration in the Later Roman Empire, 149-50, tends (though rather hesitantly) to regard the kleroi as public and not privately-owned estates, but his argument in support of the second possibility is more convincing. On the other hand, his evidence from the context to the contrary does

infer too much from the text, which is not a legal one. All in all, the language of the passage is decisive: there are two occurrences of the word ἰδία and none of κοινη, which would have been applied to these estates had they been public property. On the size of the population in the first century A.D. see Plin. HN 6.122.

52 Not all of them were fugitives from Magnesia (so: Th. Mommsen, Römische Geschichte^4, V.456; Downey, 92-3; Launey, I.267). Apart from Cretans, no mercenaries from the Greek islands took part in Magnesia (see p.51 above).

53 See Droysen, Geschichte des griechischen Kriegswesens, 165 no.3.

54 The correspondence between 'Alexandria, Seleucia and Babylonia' and 'Egyptians, Syrians and Parthians' rules out the alternative identification with Mesopotamian or Persian Seleucia.

55 On the identification of Cyrrhestica as one of the four satrapies, Jones, Cities, 241-2, esp. n.21.

56 On the background: W.W. Tarn, CAH VII.725; H.H. Schmitt, Untersuchungen zur Geschichte Antiochos des Grossen und seiner Zeit, 132, 165. Launey's suggestion of regarding them as Syrians (I.538-9) is unacceptable.

57 W. Wroth, Catalogue, pp. LI, 133.

58 C.B. Welles et al., The Excavations at Doura-Europus, Final Report, V. Part II nos.12, 15 and Welles' notes ad.loc. See further Griffith, Mercenaries, 156-7.

59 Rostovzeff, SEHHW, I.498, but see his reservations there.

60 Diod. 91.1; Amm. Marc. 14.2.3; Plin. HN 5.86; 6.118; Tac. Ann. 6.41; Isid. Char. 1.

61 Plut. Demet. 7; Diod. 19.91.4; Riv. di. Fil. 10(1932) 464; OGIS 254.

62 Tscherikover, Städtgründungen, 159; Griffith, Mercenaries, 150.

63 E.H. Minns, op.cit. 22-65 (see esp. p.52); cf. L. Mitteis, z. Savigny-Stiftung, Röm. Abt. 36 (1915) 428-9; Griffith, Mercenaries, 160, 177; Rostovzeff, SEHHW, I.490; Tarn-Griffith, 146, 159-60; Tarn, Bactria, 8-9.

64 See Minns, 42-5, 59-60.

65 Ibid. 28 ℓ.12: 29 ℓ.28: 30A ℓ.8,B.ℓ.8 (in fact synkleroi).

66 Against Minns, 52 ('perhaps veterans or other servants of the

state'). The size of the kleros can be deduced from its price or rent, see Minns, 30 ℓ.10, etc.

67 So Griffith, Mercenaries, 160, see also Minns, 52 (rather vaguely) and Mitteis, 428: against M.B. Haussoullier, Rev. hist. de droit français et étranger 47 (1923), 539.

68 On the machimoi see especially Lesquier, 19-21, etc. The success of the Egyptian phalanx at Raphia does not argue against my assessment of the military skills of the Egyptians: out of a population of several million (as estimated by M. Segrè, Bull. Soc. arch. Alex. 29 (1934) 258), it would always be possible to find 20,000 men capable of phalanx warfare.

69 Minns, p.28 ℓℓ.6-8 et passim.

70 So A. von Gutschmid, Geschichte Irans und seiner Nachbarländer, 27-8; but see B. Niese, Geschichte der Griechischen und Macedonischen Staaten, II.163.

71 On the background: E. Bevan, Seleucus, I.265, 290-1; S.K. Eddy, The King is Dead, 75ff.; Schmitt, 46-51 and esp. 47; E.T. Newell, The Coinage of the Eastern Seleucid Mints, 280; Ed. Meyer, Blüte und Niedergang des Hellenismus in Asien, 34; F. Altheim, Weltgeschichte Asiens in griechische Zeitalter, 272ff.

72 Despite the striking similarity of the figures quoted in the two consecutive stratagems I am not convinced that the number of surviving settlers was considerably lower: 1,000 Thracians and an unspecified number of Agrianians out of a contingent of 2,000 men, recruited in the eastern military settlements, took part in the battle at Raphia (see p.50 above), and to them must be added the Macedonian settlers in the area who were integrated into the phalanx.

73 Cf. L. Robert, Opera Minora Selecta, 1218-19.

74 Cf. Griffith, Mercenaries, 160.

75 Bactria, 23.

76 See Rostovzeff, SEHHW, I.480.

77 H. Gelzer, Sextus Julius Africanus, I.4, 20, 118, 256ff.; M. Stern, Tarbitz, 33 (1963-4) 336; id. Historians and Historical Schools, 27-8; J. Efron, Memorial Book to G. Allon, 78-86.

78 Dion: Steph. Byz. s.v. Δίον; Gerasa: Germer-Durand RB 4

(1895) 387 n.7, and see also Jones, The Cities, 237, 448 n.15. Gadara: Steph. s.v. Γάδαρα. After mentioning trans-Jordanian Gadara he notes that there is also a village called Gadara in Macedon. The pure Semitic name suggests that the compiler had become confused by knowledge he had about the Macedonian descent of Palestinian Gadara.

79 See also, A. Galili, Molad 52 (1968) 170, 172.
80 See Tscherikover, Städtgründungen, 73-4.
81 The phrase ἔθνη καὶ ἀπὸ Σαμαρείας has been explained in various ways. It seems to me to suggest that ethnē stands for goyim (gentiles), which was used in the time of the Second Temple, inter alia, to denigrate and humiliate the Samaritans (II Kings 17.26, 29.14; Neh. 5.8-9, 17, 6.6, 16, 13.26; Ezra 6.21; Sirach 50.26). The second component ('from Samaria') may then be identified with the inhabitants of the city Samaria, and not of the Samarian hyparchy.
82 B.V. Head, Historia Numorum^2, 716.
83 The arguments of H. Willrich (Urkundenfälschung in der hellen-istisch-jüdischen Literatur, 39ff.) against the authenticity of the document were refuted by M. Stern, The Documents on the History of the Hasmonean Revolt, 104-5.
84 See the list in Bickerman, Institutions, 53 n.3, to which may be added fortresses in Palestine like Acre (Diod. 19.93.7; I Macc. 12.45), Dor (Polyb. 5.66; I Macc. 15.10-14; Jos. Ant. 13.223), Jaffa (Diod. 19.59.2, 93.7; I Macc. 16.75) and perhaps also Iamnia (PCZ 59006; I Macc. 5.58-9; II Macc. 12. 32-5; the Thracian cavalry probably garrisoned the citadel).
85 For the identification of the fortresses see: F.M. Abel RB 34 (1925) 203-8; M. Avi-Yonah, Geographical History of Palestine, 36; id. Atlas of the Period of the Second Temple, the Mishna and the Talmud, 30.
86 Griffith, Mercenaries, 153; Tarn, Bactria, 7. Tarn-Griffith, 148; see also Jones, The Greek City, 44.
87 On Nakrasa, see Griffith, Mercenaries, 151 n.4. But even if Griffith is wrong and OGIS 268 is to be dated in 240, the status of Nakrasa as a polis could also be accounted for by a grant in the crisis years of the Laodicean War, perhaps made not by Seleucus II but by Eumenes I or Attalus I, the

champions of Greek culture. See Bevan, <u>Seleucus</u>, I.200, on the policy of attracting the Greco-Macedonian element in an attempt to win over the settlers in the newly occupied territories. The Attalids are later on recorded as granting citizenship to soldiers (<u>OGIS</u> 338).

88 On the background see C.J. Cadoux, <u>Ancient Smyrna</u>, 114-19. The former hostility between the two cities is indicated in <u>OGIS</u> 229 ℓ.41ff. and perhaps also 228. ℓℓ.8-9.

89 Contrary to Schalit, <u>Herodes</u>, 177, who is probably misled by the recurrence of the word <u>polis</u> with regard to Magnesia in the treaty with Smyrna (<u>OGIS</u> 229); in the Hellenistic period it was applied to various settlements, irrespective of their constitutional status. On the other hand, the Magnesians are not described as <u>dēmos</u>, but by various other terms like <u>plēthos,</u> <u>politeuma</u>, <u>koinon</u>, etc. (ℓℓ.71, 72, 83, 88 etc.; on the meaning of <u>politeuma</u> in this context, see W. Ruppel, <u>Philologus</u> 82 (1936) 295-7), nor is there any allusion to <u>polis</u> officials (see esp. ℓ.21), in sharp contrast to the abundance of terms referring to Smyrnean political institutions and functionaries (<u>dēmos</u> <u>boulē</u>, <u>phylai</u> <u>archōn</u> <u>dēmosion</u>, <u>klērōtērion</u>, etc.). The Magnesian <u>hyparchoi</u> (ℓ.77) were probably officers subordinated, according to the agreement, to the <u>archōn</u> of Smyrna (ℓ.55) who was certainly a military man (see Dittenberger <u>ad loc</u>.). The <u>tamiai</u> are obviously temporary appointments to facilitate the financing of the <u>synoecismos</u> ceremony (ℓℓ.82-3). The Smyrneans are also twice referred to as <u>plēthos</u> (ℓℓ.78-9, 88), but only when mentioned together with the Magnesians. When they are mentioned apart (ℓ.83), the Smyrneans are designated as <u>dēmos</u> and the Magnesians as <u>plēthos</u>.

90 All the epigraphical material indicating the change of constitutional status is from the Roman period (see for instance, J. Keil & A.V. Premerstein, <u>Denkschr. der Akad. der Wiss. in Wien</u>, 54.2 (1911) no.1, etc. See also Strabo 13.3.5 (621); App. <u>Mith</u>. 61). The same applies to the numismatical evidence (B.V. Head, <u>Catalogue of the Greek Coins of Lydia</u>, p.LXIX). The Seleucid royal mint, located according to E.T. Newell, in Magnesia (<u>The Coinage of the Western Seleucid Mints,</u>

271-283) did not strike municipal coins. The inscription of A. Koerte *AM* 24 (1899) 410, which may imply an early recognition of Magnesia as a *polis*, may also be dated after the battle of 190 (*ibid*. 212).

91 On the psychological need for establishing the traditional political institutions for the Greeks in the east, see Jones, *The Greek City*, 24; cf. Alexander's settlers of Bactria-Sogdiana who revolted because they were dissatisfied with conditions (Diod. 18.7).

92 On the separate administrative development see W.W. Tarn, *Proc. Brit. Acad*. 16 (1930) 105; *id. Bactria*, 1-6, 241; Ehrenberg, 144-5; Tarn-Griffith, 130-1; Welles-Rostovzeff, *Yale Class. Stud*., 2 (1931) 48 n.1. For objections to Tarn see Bengtson, *Strategie*^{2}, II.30-7, 55, and 188-193; but see A. Heuss, *Klio* 21 (1949) 307.

93 *The Greek City*, 23. See also Ehrenberg, 149-51.

94 M. Segrè, *Bull. Soc. Arch. Alex*. 29 (1934) 267; Rostovzeff, I.497-8; *id. CAH* VII.169; Tarn, *op.cit*. 70; C. Edson, *CP* 53 (1958) 153-70, and esp. 169, argues that ancient authors from Josephus onwards called the Seleucid kingdom 'Macedonian' because the Macedonians were predominant numerically as well as politically, but the same sources apply even more frequently to the Seleucids the names 'Syrians', 'the kingdom of Syria' or 'the kingdom of Asia'. Edson's answer is that these terms were not official, but the name 'Macedonians' was not official either: it does not figure in contemporary documents and appears only in later historians. The Seleucids were given this name for two main reasons: first, in contrast to the Ptolemies who gave preference to the Egyptian cult even outside Egypt (see for instance *Inscr. Prien*. p.XVI), they promoted the Greco-Macedonian religious tradition; and secondly, having controlled almost the entire east for such a long period, they were entitled to be recognized as the true successors of Alexander.

95 Comparable material is of little value: from Diod. 18.7, it follows that Alexander settled 2,000 infantry and 300 cavalry in each of the Bactrian and Sogdianian cities, provided that the recorded foundations in that region represent the real

total of settlements, which is not necessarily the case. On
the other hand, a Ptolemaic cleruchy like Kerkeosiris
contained only 102 soldiers in a population of about 1,500
(D. Crawford, <u>Kerkeosiris</u>, 122-3). The Roman colonies in
Italy consisted of no more than 300 families in the fourth
century, but 200 years later the settlers numbered 2,000
families per colony (Livy 8.21.9; 34.45.1; 39.55.7-9).

96 Rostovzeff, I.497 et al.
97 <u>Institutions</u>, 81-8. Bickerman argues that there is no
Seleucid parallel to the Ptolemaic practice of naming the
settlers according to their unit which would indicate their
individual obligation to the crown, but he ignores the
detachment of Magnesian settlers represented as belonging to
the 'phalanx' (<u>OGIS</u> 229. ℓℓ.103-4 and see in detail p.56
above), and the soldier in Susa described as belonging to the
'horsemen under Alexander' (<u>SEG</u> VII. no.17) who may well have
been a settler. Bickerman's other points are less convincing:
the possibility that the soldiers in Thyatira (<u>OGIS</u> 101)
consisted of only a fraction of the adult population does not
indicate that the levy was collective. On the contrary: as
the soldiers define themselves as a particular and separate
body, they are obviously a permanent unit and not a temporary
levy. The presence of a physician of the 'Hyrcanian
Macedonians' in Amphissa for 22 years (E. Schwyzer, <u>Dialectorum
Graecarum exampla epigraphica potiora</u>, 369) does not prove that
the settlers were not committed personally to serve in the
army. He was indeed born to a settler's family, whence the
attribute 'Hyrcanian', but he may have been landless either
because his father was still alive or because there were too
many heirs, and was therefore exempt from military service.
It is worth noting that he came to Greece immediately after
the battle of Magnesia, which may also mean that special
political circumstances drove him away from his fatherland.
Finally, the chiliarchies mentioned in the document of
Mnesimachus of Sardis (W.H. Buchler & D.H. Robinson, <u>AJA</u> 16
(1912) 12-13) are not regional units, as Bickerman presumes,
but battalions of the regular army financed by friends of the
king regardless of whether it was Antigonus I or Antiochus

III, in return for lands and villages in Asia Minor (see Jones, Cities, 44; M. Rostovzeff, CAH VII.172). The new interpretation and dating of the document by K.T.M. Atkinson, Historia 21 (1972) 45-74, does not offer another explanation for the chiliarchies mentioned in the inscription.

98   On the collaboration of Achaeus with Egypt, cf. Polyb. 5.57.2, 66.3, 67.12-13; 8.15.1-3, 10. See further, Schmitt, 166-70; E. Badian, Gnomon 38 (1966) 713.

99   On the dimensions of this expedition see also 5.77.1. Nothing seems to suggest that the Mysians or the main army joined only later with Achaeus (against Griffith, Mercenaries, 143 n.1): Achaeus' arrival was anxiously awaited because he would be able to communicate with Logbasis, his old friend (see 5.74.9).

100 Cf. too Molon's troops, 5.54.2. On the loyalty of the settlers to the legitimate regime, see Griffith, Mercenaries, 168. Badian's explanation for this episode (Gnomon 38 (1966) 714), that Achaeus' troops, whom he reckons to be mercenaries, were unwilling to fight Antiochus because they knew they could not win, is not convincing; with the possible help of the dissatisfied settlers of the eastern provinces and the rebels in Cyrrhestica, Achaeus' troops were stronger than the loyal army, and mercenaries would not have described Antiochus in the words quoted above.

101 On the numerical strength of the Pergamene army see Griffith, Mercenaries, 181.

102 Livy 37.40.1, 7 and see pp.9, 168-9 above.

103 See p.18 above. The force did not include oriental auxiliaries of whose absence Antiochus repeatedly complained, and the account of the battle indicates that the light troops, probably mercenaries, were not numerous (see p.161 above).

104 Tarn, erroneously regarding the argyraspides at Raphia and Magnesia as oriental, reckons that the number of phalangites had increased at Daphne in comparison with the earlier campaigns, and attributes the new recruits to cities founded by Antiochus Epiphanes (Bactria, 23, 186, and see also Griffith, Mercenaries, 152-3). But apart from the inaccuracy of Tarn's calculations, it has been already shown by Mørkolm (115-8) that scarcely three of the fifteen cities

usually attributed to Epiphanes can be proved to have been founded by him. Of these three, the Epiphaneias in Armenia and Media (former Ecbatana) were not able, in any case, to contribute manpower to the phalanx. The first was not founded until after Daphne, and the settlers of the second were confined to their own area like other reserve troops in that region. See also Jones, The Greek City, 16, who thinks that all Antiochus did was grant the status of polis to these cities.

105 Cf. Polyb. 5.54.8, and see Schmitt, 133.
106 Livy 37.40 - 6,000 cataphracts, 1,000 agēma and 1,000 regia ala and perhaps 500 Tarentines (on the number of Tarentines see Kromayer, Schlachtfelder, II.211). On the recruitment drive: Livy 35.48.5, 49.8; App. Syr. 12(47); 21(94).
107 Polyb. 30.25 - of the 9,500 cavalry mentioned in this passage only the 1,000 agēma, 1,000 ilē basilikē, 1,000 Nisaeans and 1,500 cataphracts were 'operational'. On the 3,000 politikoi cavalry see above p.30, and p.73 on the philoi and epilektoi.
108 See B. Bar-Kochva, Proc. Cambr. Phil. Soc. N.S. 19 (1973) 4-5.
109 See the various views especially: Jones, The Greek City, 23-4; Bickerman, Institutions, 76; Launey, I.96, 293, 297; II.109; E. Cavaignac, Rev. de Phil. 25 (1951) 294; Ehrenberg, 148; Walbank, Polybius, I.608; cf. the statistics on the Ptolemaic settlers, Griffith, Mercenaries, 243, which indicate that in the third century only one third of the settlers were of Macedonian descent.
110 The pezetairoi described as 'Syrians' in Plut. Flam. 17 were undoubtedly Macedonian military settlers like the regia ala in Livy 37.40.11 (see p.69 above). The cavalry men (lonchophoroi and xystophoroi) also referred to in the same passage as 'Syrians', were allies and subjects from the upper satrapies (see Livy 35.49.8). This description is inspired by Livy's contemptuous attitude to the Seleucid army (loc.cit. and 36. 17.5, all in speeches fabricated by Livy himself, see Nissen, 180, cf. Plut. Moral. 197c, and see further p.211 n.36 above).
111 P.M. Fraser, Ptolemaic Alexandria, 71-2, 6.
112 According to the reference to the Hellenes in OGIS 229 as the civilian element, the soldiers were probably of the same

descent; cf. Ed. Meyer, Hermes 33 (1898) 647; Rostovzeff I.492.
113 The Mysian Katoikiai: Polyb. 5.77.7. The Myso-Macedonians: Plin. HN 5.120; Ptol. Geog. 5.2.13; AM 19 (1894) 102-3, 123-4; cf. the Mysians in OGIS 338 ℓ.15. On the identification of the Myso-Macedonians see Griffith, Mercenaries, 145, 167 n.2, 178-9; Magie, Asia Minor, II.974.
114 Jos. Ant. 12.147-53; CIJ II.775. One of the Jewish settlements can perhaps be identified. Another grave-stone of the third century A.D. found in the area mentions Ἰουδδηνῶν κατοικία (M. Fontrier, Μουσαῖον Εὐαγγελικῆς Σχ. Σμύρνα, 1886, 73-4). As the settlement name was probably Ἰοῦδδα (cf. the various spellings of 'Jews', 'Jewish' in CIJ II. nos.745, 748, 758, 789, 790, 794, etc.), it is impossible to resist the temptation to identify the settlers as Jews. The apparently gentile terminology of the inscription, the Hellenized names and the reference to the hierōtaton tameion were all quite common among Jews in that period (CIJ II. nos.741, 752, 773, 778, 786, 791, 799). Radet's (p.22) and Launey's hesitations (I.551 n.4) are superfluous.
115 Strabo 13.4.13(629). On the Persian impact on the local cult, see M. Foucart, BCH 11 (1887) no.2. See further, Kromayer, Schlachtfelder, II.116 n.4.
116 Macedonians - Livy 36.18.2; Appian, Syr. 32(161); Polyb. 30. 25.5; Polyaenus 4.9.3 (?); phalanx - Polyb. 5.52.3, 79.5; 10.29.5; 16.18.4; Appian, Syr. 18(83); Livy 37.40.1.
117 Bactria, 8.
118 On the development in Egypt see in detail, C. Préaux, L'économie, 468-72; id. Recueils de la Société Jean Bodin, III, La Tenure (1938) 41-57; Crawford, 56-7.
119 See C.B. Welles (ed.), The Excavations at Doura-Europos, Final Report, V. Part I. no.15 (pp.84-91). See also no.12 for the Parthian era. Contrary to Griffith, Mercenaries, 156-9.
120 The inscription of Mnesimachus of Sardis, even if it is to be related to Antiochus III's time (see K.T.M. Atkinson, Historia 21 (1972) 62-9), is irrelevant here (contrary to Atkinson, ibid. 65, 69): Mnesimachus was not a military settler, but, in view of the size of the estate, a military

or civilian beneficiary of fairly high rank (cf. Griffith, Mercenaries, 157 n.3).
121 Mercenaries, 163.
122 On the Ptolemaic Guard see Lesquier, 23-4; Fraser, I.69, II.152 and esp. Polyb. 15.25.17.
123 On their relationship with the Empire, see Strabo 16.1.18(744); Weissbach, RE s.v. Elymais, 2464, designates them wrongly as mercenaries.
124 Walbank, Polybius, I.582-3 and see also Launey, I.39, 253 n.7; Griffith, Mercenaries, 176.
125 The stelai: G. Mendel, Catalogue des Sculptures Grecques, Romaines et Byzantines, I. nos.102, 103; on their dating see Launey, I.41; Bickerman, Institutions, 89-90.
126 See Launey, I.476, 480, 586.
127 Cf. the omission of the Cadusians, 82.12 (cf. 79.7) and especially the confusion in 82.10 (cf. 79.3-4). Walbank (Polybius, I.608, with earlier bibliography) reckons that the Carmanians were divided between the units because they were differently armed. Both units seem to consist basically of light infantry and therefore, however diversified their armament, the distribution of the Carmanians among other nationalities, with all the problems involved, is rather difficult to conceive.
128 So Launey, I.562 n.2; Walbank, Polybius, I.609; not so Griffith, Mercenaries, 144; see Polyb. 5.71.1. For the name Zabdiel cf. I Macc. 11.17; G.A. Cooke, A Text-Book of North Semitic Inscriptions, no.114 p.272; probably in the neighbourhood of Tadmor.
129 See Polyb. 5.55, and Schmitt, 61 and 149, on the status of Atropatene.
130 Kroll, RE s.v. Karmania, 1956, reckons the Carmanians to be mercenaries, but Antiochus would not have spent his money on mercenaries of this sort. Their grouping together with subjects is decisive.
131 So Launey, I.486, 508 n.5; Walbank, Polybius, I.609. They do not seem to have any connection with the Cardaces in Caria who, as has been argued above (p.216 n.27), were not military settlers, and in any case were in Achaeus' realm and therefore

could not be mobilized for Raphia.

132 Other references to Lydian soldiers mentioned by Launey, I.449 are rather doubtful: Curtius 6.6.35 is phrased in terms too vague to allow any conclusion to be drawn (so Launey, ibid.), and the 'Lydian' soldiers in the Hellenistic period are undoubtedly military settlers (Diod. 19.29.2; Livy 37.40.12; 42.52; Mendel, I.263 n.104; and see p.69 above on the regia ala).

133 Genesis 10.21, and see I.M. Grintz, Studies in early Biblical Ethnology and History, 56-7. But Lydia in Asia Minor is clearly referred to in verse 13. See the Assyrian documents in E.F. Weidner, Die Inscriften der Altassyrischen Könige, 58 n.4; M. Streck, Vorderasiatische Bibliothek, VII p.CCCLXX; id. Zeitschrift für Assyriologie 12 (1898) 78; 13 (1899) 167-8; 20 (1907) 456; A. Sånda, Mitteilungen der Vorderasiatisch - Ägyptischen Gesellschaft 7 (1902) 127.

134 For the status of Persis at that time see Schmitt, 46-51; E. Badian, Gnomon 38 (1966) 711.

135 Bickerman, Institutions, 58. On the frequent combination of archers with Agrianians in Alexander's army, see Griffith, Mercenaries, 17.

136 On 'Persians' as a designation of armament and style of warfare rather than of nationality in Ptolemaic Egypt see Lesquier, 106ff.; F.M. Heichelheim, Die auswärtige Bevölkerung im Ptolemäerreich, 13ff.; Griffith, Mercenaries, 250, and see also ibid. 144 on these Thracians as mercenaries from Thrace.

137 Cf. the Persian influence on the Seleucid army in the First Syrian War, Polyaenus 4.15.

138 On the status of the Elymaeans under the Seleucids see Strabo 16.1.18(744).

139 On their status see Griffith, loc.cit. et al. On the state of affairs in Greece, see J.A.O. Larsen, Greek Federal States, 419-33. The Achaeans sided with Pergamon, and the Aetolians, who were granted a six-month truce, had to fend for themselves. Seleucid recruiting officers who were frequently seen in the Ionian markets (Plautus MG 72ff., 75, 974; Polyb. 5.35; 33.18.14) were probably now banned by the hostile Greek cities.

140 Cf. the role of the Thracians at Gaugamela, Arr. Anab. 2.12.5.

141 On the violation of the Apamea treaty, Griffith, Mercenaries, 147, contrary to Launey, I.384.
142 On the identification of the 'Syrians' of the regia ala as Macedonian settlers see p.69 above. The same applies probably to the 'Syrians' assisting in the defence of Thermopylae in 279 (Paus. 10.20.5) and to the 'Syrians' in Plut. Flam. 17 (see p.227 n.110). On Syrians in other Hellenistic armies, Griffith, Mercenaries, 68 n.3, 127; Launey, I.536-9.
143 So Launey, I.536. Cf. Livy 35.49.8; 36.17.5; Plut. Moral. 197c (all in speeches fabricated by Livy himself, see Nissen, 180. The references in Plutarch were inspired by Livy, cf. Plut. Flam. 17.5), probably following the contemptuous attitude to the Babylonians in the Greek literature (on the Babylonians in the eyes of the Greeks, see Eddy, 105-6 and sources there).
144 Mercenaries, 170, though he himself overestimates the number of the Seleucid mercenaries at 23,500 at Raphia (ibid. 144).
145 On the revolt see J.G. Milne, JEA 14 (1928) 226-34; C. Préaux, Chronique d'Égypte, 11 (1936) 522-52.

CHAPTER 3

1 Polyb. 5.52.3, 53.8, 68.11, 79.5; 10.29.5; 16.18.2, 4; 30.25; App. Syr. 18(83), 32(161); Livy 36.18.2; 37.40.1; Plut. Flam. 17; Polyaenus 4.9.3. The term sarissophoroi designates light cavalry armed with long lances in Alexander's army (see W.W. Tarn, Alexander the Great, II.157; A. Spendel, Untersuchungen zum Heerwesen der Diadochen, 22-3; A.M. Snodgrass, Arms and Armour of the Greeks, 114, 120), and disappears in the Hellenistic period. Livy's description of the sarissophoroi in action at Thermopylae (36.18.2) and the parallel version of Appian (Syr. 19(84)) leave no doubt that they really are phalangites. Livy's phrasing ('quos sarisophorus appellabant') may indicate that it was at least a popular nickname for the phalangites, and see also Polyaenus 2.29.2.
2 On the question of length of the sarissa in the Hellenistic period see: Delbrück, Kriegskunst, I.369-74; Kromayer - Veith, Heerwesen, 134ff.; Tarn, Developments, 21; Walbank, Polybius, II.586-8; Snodgrass, 118-9. The best summary of the various problems connected with the sarissa is Lammert, RE

s.v. Sarissa, 2515-30. And see also Tarn, Developments, 14-16; id. Alexander, II.169-71, on the sarissa of Alexander. Polybius' excursus on the phalanx and its equipment (18.29), since it is an appendix to Cynoscephalae, may refer chiefly to the Antigonid phalanx.

3 Kromayer-Veith, Heerwesen, 133, 135; Walbank, Polybius, II.281, contrary to Launey, II.354 n.1; see also Asclep. 5.1; Aelian, Tact. 12; Plut. Aem. 20.2

4 Proc. Camb. Phil. Soc. N.S. 4 (1956-7) 3-10.

5 M. Feyel, RA 6 sér. 5 (1935) 31. On the identification of the soldiers and the application of the code to the army as a whole, and particularly to those engaged on combat missions, and not only to soldiers on garrison duties, see Feyel, ibid. 64; G. De Sanctis, Riv. di. Fil. 12 (1934) 515-21; C.B. Welles, AJA 42 (1938) 245. P. Roussel, RA 6 sér. 3 (1934) 42-3, 45-7, is less convincing.

6 See also Polyb. 11.9.5. Philopoemen did indeed reform the Achaean phalanx along Macedonian lines, but Plutarch's wording does not necessarily imply Macedonian influence in the introduction of breastplates (so Griffith, op.cit. 6).

7 On the use of the coat of mail in the Roman army, see Polyb. 6.23.15; see also Grosse, RE s.v. 'Lorica', 1444-5; Lammert, RE s.v. Thorax, 332-6.

8 Polybius' text has undoubtedly been corrupted and seems rightly emended by Kaibel as follows: Μακεδόνες δισμύριοι <χρυσάσπιδες μὲν μύριοι> καὶ χαλκάσπιδες πεντακισχίλιοι <οἱ> δὲ ἄλλοι ἀργυράσπιδες (see Polyb. ed. Büttner-Wobst (Tübner) VI. 301). Droysen's emendment: Μακεδόνες δισμύριοι <ὧν> χαλκάσπιδες <μὲν> πεντακισχίλιοι <οἱ> δὲ ἄλλοι ἀργυράσπιδες (Kriegswesens, 167 n.1) is less likely. The omission of the καί is not necessary; on the contrary, the argyraspides, being a selected crack force, could not have occupied three quarters of the phalanx. I Macc., in his account on Beith-Zacharia, which took place two years after Daphne, confirms the participation of chrysaspides in the Seleucid phalanx.

9 Polyb. 2.60; Plut. Cleom. 23.1; Aem. 18.3; Livy 42.41.2, 44; Diod. 31.10; see generally: Pollux 1.175, and perhaps Onas. 1.20.

10 Xen. Hell. 7.5.20; Plut. Eum. 14.3; Polyb. 11.4.7, 9; Plut. Aem. 14.8; id. Sulla 16; Onas. 28.
11 Polyaenus 4.16 cannot be considered as indicating an earlier introduction of decorated shields. If there is any historical truth in that episode, it is to be explained by the special circumstances.
12 See Theoc. id. 17.93-4 (Ptolemaic army); Diod. 20.83.2-3 (Demetrius Poliorcetes).
13 The sympoliteia by itself did not provide exemption as the status of polis in the Hellenistic world did not automatically convey exemption from taxes and other levies unless this was officially declared (see Jones, The Greek City, 108-9). On the levies and taxes imposed on the Ptolemaic cleruchs, see Lesquier, 214f., and Schalit, JQR 49 (1960) 309 for the Seleucid and Pergamene katoikoi. Cf. Welles, Royal Correspondence, no.54 ℓℓ.9.16-18; Jos. Ant. 12.151.
14 Dittenberger, ad loc. n.56-57, on the τρεῖς κλήρους.
15 Cf. Polyb. 2.58.1 on the Achaean garrison sent to Mantineia.
16 Spendel, 35-47; Tarn, Alexander, II.137-42 and 153 n.3; id. JRS 31 (1941) 173; Walbank, Philip V of Macedon, 292; id. Polybius, I.274-5; Griffith, Mercenaries, 319; Milns, Historia 20 (1971) 186-96.
17 See Spendel, 44-5; Berve, 128; Tarn, Alexander, II.116-18, 151-2, rejects this reference as anachronistic, and is certainly right with regard to Diod. 17.57.2.
18 On the Antigonid hypaspists see M. Feyel, RA 6 sér. 5 (1935) 63-4; F.W. Walbank, Philip V, 290-2; and see Polyb. 15.25.3 for the Ptolemaic guard.
19 See Griffith, Mercenaries, 119, 319; Walbank, ibid. 292-3; id. Polybius, I.590-1.
20 Polyb. 5.25.1, 65.2, 25, 82.4; Plut. Aem. 18.3; Polyaenus 4.9.3; P Petr. III.12.1.16.
21 See e.g.: Kromayer-Veith, Heerwesen, 109; Spendel, 41; H. Berve, I.125; H.W. Parke, Greek Mercenary Soldiers, 156; J.R. Hamilton CQ N.S. 5 (1955) 218-19. Against them are: Tarn, Developments, 16-17, and Griffith, Proceed. Camb. Phil. Soc. N.S. 4 (1955-6) 5. On the equipment of Philip V's Guard see Walbank, Philip V, 290, 293; R.D. Milns, Historia 16 (1967) 510.

22 So rightly, Walbank, Polybius, I.608.
23 Cf. Griffith, Mercenaries, 164. Josephus may have drawn this information from Diodorus, but it may also be his own interpretation of I Macc.
24 In contrast to W.W. Tarn, Gonatas, 428; Rostovzeff, I.497; Launey, I.313; Bickerman, Institutions, 56; but see Bengtson, Strategie^2, II.68 n.1.
25 On the significance of τούτων οἱ πλείονες see p.64 and esp. p.235 n.37.
26 On Abae in Phocis see RE s.v. Abai, 11.
27 Cf. Photius s.v. πεζέταιροι; Dem. Ol.2.17.
28 See F. Lammert, RE s.v. πεζέταιροι, 1412: N.G.L. Hammond, OCD^2 s.v. 'hetairoi', 513; J.N. Kalléris, Les anciens Macédoniens, 242; Berve, 112ff.
29 Contra R.D. Milns, Historia 16 (1967) 511, who suggests that the infantry Guard, named in his view originally hypaspistes, was established sometime between 356 and 349 B.C. His evidence is the absence of breastplates in the hypaspistes, the later Guard, which, bearing in mind that there was no difficulty in providing defensive armour to the king's Guard, must be explained, according to Milns, by assuming that this unit was formed only after the unarmoured territorial phalanx proved its efficiency at Pangaeus in 356. This, however, is not decisive, and one may argue that the terrain of north Macedon, the battlefield of the Macedonian kings up to Philip, did not favour this sort of heavy armour, and in any case, after the phalanx system had proved itself successful, the cuirass may have been taken away from the Guard to allow them more flexibility. On the other hand, there is no reason why Theopompus should have confused the hypaspistes with the pezetairoi if the two corps existed in his time.
30 On some of the difficulties involved, see Tarn, Gonatas, 190.
31 See some references in Tarn, Alexander, II.149-50; Walbank, Philip V, 292-3.
32 Schlachtfelder, II.151-3, and see Livy 36.18.5.
33 See B. Bar-Kochva, Proc. Camb. Phil. Soc. N.S. 19 (1973) 3-5.
34 Bickerman, Institutions, 52-3; Walbank, Polybius, II.64.
35 On hypaspistes as a personal guard at Philip V's court, see

Walbank, Philip V, 290. The therapeia (Polyb. 5.56.7, 69.6) seems to have been the personal guard of the Seleucids, see Walbank, Polybius, I.536.

36 Cf. Livy 36.19.11. The participation of cavalry in this flight is quite likely, and in view of the defensive character of the battle, the lack of room for manoeuvre, and the prospect of a head-long rout, Antiochus' best plan was indeed merely to observe the battle with the virtually passive cavalry around him.

37 Polybius states that the majority of the picked troops were argyraspides. The smaller group would have consisted of the hypaspistes. But one should not attach too much importance to this division. On the evidence of other references, comparison with Alexander's guard, and the title hegemōn attached to their commander (Polyb. 7.16.2), which implies a subordinate position in contrast with the title stratēgos reserved for commanders of independent contingents (see p.92 above), it seems that the hypaspistes were usually considered to be a part of the argyraspides. At any rate, in practical terms it does not make any difference.

38 Tarn, Alexander, II.148-9, 153.

39 On the equipment of the Antigonid hypaspistes, see Walbank, Philip V, 293; Feyel, RA 6 sér. 5 (1935) 63.

40 Plut. Aem. 19.4; IG II^2.1487 ℓ.96; Lindos II.2.C.XLII; Livy 43.41 (cetrati), and even Polyaenus 4.2.10 referring to the larger type of Philip II's time. Cf. the aspis of the hypaspists at Amphipolis (Feyel, op.cit. 31 ℓ.4).

41 See Lammert RE s.v. Sarissa, 2515-30.

42 See the summary of the different views by G.R. Watson, The Roman Soldier, 62-3. Watson's conclusion that the 60-libra weight equipment attributed by Vegetius to route marches (Epit. rei. milit. 1.19) was carried only in exceptional circumstances does not accord with the emphatic nature of Vegetius' statement and underestimates what could have been required of a well-trained soldier.

43 See Rüstow-Köchly, Geschichte des Griechisches Kriegwesens, 236-7; Lesquier, 62, 103; Kromayer-Veith, Heerwesen, 132; Feyel, op.cit. 46-50; C.B. Welles, AJA 42 (1938) 248-9;

Walbank, Philip V, 293; id. Polybius, II.286, and sources there.

44 Asclep. Tact. 2.1 is too theoretical and is influenced by disposition of heavy infantry in general and Alexander's phalanx rather than by the phalanx of the Hellenistic monarchies.

45 So Bengtson, Strategie^2, II.66; and see OGIS 217, 272, 277; Plut. Demetr. 474; App. Syr. 36; Diod. 33.28; 34.17; Jos. Ant. 13.131.

46 So in the Ptolemaic army, Lesquier, 92-3.

47 On Alexander's subdivisions, see R.D. Milns, Historia 20 (1971) 194.

48 The main contributions to these questions are: Berve, 104, 126, 129; Tarn, Alexander, II.139, 154-67; P.A. Brunt, JHS 83 (1963) 25-45; Griffith, JHS 83 (1963) 68-74; Milns, Historia 20 (1971) 193.

49 I follow on this point Berve, 112; Tarn, ibid., 167, against Brunt, 31, 41; cf. Griffith, ibid. 74 n.17.

50 So rightly, Spendel, 14. At first sight it might appear from Plut. Eum. 7, that Eumenes' agēma was made up of Macedonians: on one hand he is reported to have been aware of the importance of not posting Macedonians opposite Craterus, and on the other it is said that the agēma was deployed on the other flank opposite Neoptolemus. But the Macedonians who were kept out of Craterus' sight may well have belonged to the 20,000 'mixed' infantry which took part in the battle (Diod. 18.29.4, 30.5, and see Griffith, Mercenaries, 41). The identity of the agēma may be deduced from the various references to the development of Eumenes' army: at the time he left Leonnatus, Eumenes took with him 300 cavalry and 200 τῶν παίδων ὁπλοφόρους (Plut. Eum. 3.5); even if they had been Macedonians, later developments would have forced Eumenes to replace them with orientals: shortly after the occupation of Cappadocia he displayed his mistrust of the Macedonians (Plut. Eum. 4.3, admittedly the phalanx put under his command by Perdiccas) and to counterbalance them recruited 6,300 oriental cavalry (the 300 above the round figure of 6,000 were perhaps an agēma? see p.238 n.61 below), and trained them to a standard which aroused the

Macedonians' envy. 5,000 of these cavalry are reported to have fought against Craterus and Neoptolemus. Eumenes' earlier dissatisfaction with the Macedonians, his ever-increasing reliance on the oriental cavalry, their high standard and loyalty, and above all the sympathy and admiration evinced by the Macedonians towards Craterus and their lack of regard for Eumenes as an 'outsider', render it very unlikely that Eumenes would have risked surrounding himself with a Macedonian agēma in the battle against Craterus. See also Diod. 19.27.2; 28.3. The agēma of Antigonus or Demetrius (Diod. 19.29.4, 82.1) is more likely to have been Macedonian but one cannot say for sure. In view of the profound Persian influence upon Leonnatus, his agēma, called 'the agēma of the companions' (The Suda, s.v. Λεοννάτος), may well have been oriental (contrary to Spendel, loc.cit.).

51 Spendel, 12; and see Diod. 18.2.2, 3.4; 19.28.3, 29.4, 82.3; Arr. τὰ μετ' 'Αλέξ.28.

52 Perhaps Diod. 19.82.2 refers to the agēma.

53 Contrary to Bickerman, Institutions, 52, who regards them as two separate units.

54 Cf. the 2,000 man strong βασιλικὸν ἄγημα τῶν ἐπιλέκτων of Pyrrhus at Asculum (Dion. Hal. 20.1.4).

55 On the number of troops under Antiochus' personal command see Walbank, Polybius, I.611 n.9. Walbank's puzzlement in p.613 n.84.1 is unnecessary: the ilē basilikē, numbering 1,000 horse, formed only half of the cavalry posted ἐν ἐπικαμπίῳ.

56 App. Syr. 32(163) defines the agēma as 'the so-called agēma of the Macedonians'. Bickerman, Institutions, 59, prefers Appian, and assumes that Livy is mistaken. But it seems more likely that Appian is only presenting the Seleucid agēma as the successors of Alexander's celebrated agēma without referring necessarily to their nationality, as he does consistently with regard to other corps of the regular army, see e.g. 19(84), 32(161), 34(177), 35(178, 183). A paleographical error cannot be ruled out, but Livy's reference to 'eiusdem regionis ... gentium' and their mistaken definition as auxiliaries (37.42.7-8, see p.170 above) suggest that, in any case, the original reading was Mēdoi. If Appian really

meant to indicate the nationality of the troops, he may well have found Makedones in his MS.

57 Contrary to Launey, I.450, 538-9, and Walbank, Polybius, I. 613-4, who reckon that the 'Syrians, Phrygians and Lydians' were indigenous.

58 The main source is Justin 41.6.6. See the summary of the problem in Will, II.338-9 and bibliography there.

59 Unfortunately, Diodorus' allusion to the agēma is incomplete. Walton in his translation (Loeb ed. vol.12, p.11) supplies the missing words in brackets: '(that they always fought) in the ranks of the first agēma of the cavalry'. He is probably influenced by the preceding sentence 'as allies to the royal line descended from Seleucus Nicator'. But in view of their opposition to Demetrius II (see Strabo 10.16.2(752)), this passage can only refer to Alexander Balas and his infant son Antiochus, who were introduced as the legitimate successors. If both sentences refer to the same period, which is still a possibility, this supports my view that the Larisseans were admitted to the agēma around 148-147 B.C.

60 Diodorus mentions 800 infantry and 200 cavalry while Appian refers to 1,000 infantry and 300 cavalry. Appian may be giving the total number of troops found in his source (800 + 200 = 1,000), as he usually does (cf. p.207 n.4 above), and misunderstanding an accidental reference to the agēma as indicating an additional force, by adding 300 cavalry to make up what was known to him to be the standard strength of that unit in the armies of the Successors (see below). Cf. similar discrepancies between Diod. 19.100.7 and Plut. Demetr. 7.3, as well as between Plut. Caes. 52.2 and Caes. De Bello Africo 2.1-3.1; for the last reference, see W.E. Sweet, CW (1951) 178.

61 See for instance, Plut. Eum. 7; Diod. 19.27.2, 28.3, 29.5, 82.1; Polyb. 2.65.2 (on the last reference cf. Walbank, Philip V, 289), etc. For Alexander's agēma see R.D. Milns, Historia 16 (1967) 167.

62 In any case, the Macedonians of Carrhae contributed only a small number of cavalry (see 92.2) and, as they were pressed into this service could not be trusted to act as a guard.

63 See the summary of the various suggestions in J.K. Anderson,

Military Theory and Practice in the Age of Xenophon, 106-7, 248-9; cf. also H. Droysen, RE s.v. Agema, 771; Kalléris, 80-1.
64 Xenophon, Res. Lac. 11.9, 13.6, does not seem to support this interpretation, cf. Anderson, 248.
65 For the Seleucid philoi see Bevan, Seleucus, II.280; Spendel, 17; G. Corradi, Studi Ellenistici, 318-43.
66 So M.L. Strack, Rhein. Mus. 55 (1900) 161-90, esp. 190; P.M. Fraser, Ptolemaic Alexandria, II.62-6, 183-4.
67 The words οἷς ἐπηκολούθει, probably influenced by the same phrase in par.5 above, must be omitted, together with the figure 1,000 which in the form of ᾳ could easily have been inserted because of its frequent recurrence in this passage. Bickerman, Institutions, 59, considers the epilektoi to be a separate unit.
68 See Tarn, Developments, 76-83, 156-9.
69 Spendel, 10-11; Kromayer, Heerwesen, 138.
70 Launey, I.356; Snodgrass, 122, and see especially: H. Kähler, Der Fries vom Reiterdenkmal des Aemilius Paulus in Delphi, 34.
71 Developments, 77.
72 On the development of the equipment of the cataphracts, see Tarn, Developments, 73-8; R.M. Rattenbury, CR 56 (1942) 113-16.
73 See Walbank, Polybius, II.227; Kromayer-Veith, Heerwesen, 138-9 regards the oulamos as a subdivision of the ilē, which he considers to number 128; and see also Lammert, RE s.v. ἴλαι, 997.
74 Asclep. 7.11; Arr. Tact. 18.2-3; Polyb. 10.23.1-6; Lesquier, 88-91.
75 On the number of the Tarentines see Kromayer, Schlachtfelder, II.211.
76 On the political terms see G. Woodcock, The Greeks in India, 47-9.
77 The allies had to make all haste to the battlefield because Lysimachus might meanwhile have been defeated by Antigonus' superior army (see Diod. 20.109).
78 Cf. the 37 elephants who crossed the Alps with Hannibal in 219 (Polyb. 3.42.11) only one of whom was still alive shortly after Trebia (ibid. 74.11).

79 W.W. Tarn, JHS 40 (1940) 84-9.
80 See the latest discussion on this question in W. Gowers, African Affairs 47 (1948) 173-80.
81 See e.g. Diod. 18.71.4-5; 19.84.1-4; Livy 44.41.4; Zonaras 9.22 (p.269); cf. the anachronistic allusions in Polyaenus 4.3.17; Curtius 4.13.36 (for the last reference see E.W. Marsden, The Campaign of Gaugamela, 41); see on these devices R.F. Glover, Greece and Rome 17 (1948) 7-8.
82 See E.T. Newell, Western Seleucid Mints, III.156.
83 See the text in Sidney Smith, Babylonian Historical Texts, 156.
84 JHS 46 (1926) 157; id. JHS 60 (1940) 87; id. Developments, 96.
85 See in detail B. Bar-Kochva, Proc. Camb. Phil. Soc. N.S. 19 (1973) 3-5. The conclusion on the relative chronology in this article (p.5) is unfortunately not accurate and should be as follows: the 'elephant victory' - after April 273 B.C.; the repulsion of the Egyptian invasion - between April 274 and March 273; the despatch of the elephants from Babylonia - March 273 (year 38 runs from April 274 to April 273).
86 Tarn, JHS 46 (1926) 157ff.
87 See G.M. Allen, Proceed. Acad. Nat. Science Philadelphia, 88 (1936) 25-6; cf. the reduction in the number of Antigonus' elephants from about 200 at Partakene to about 75 at Ipsus, see the calculations in Beloch, Griechische Geschichte, IV.1. 356.
88 See the comment of Gowers, 174, on the origin of this passage in Polybius.
89 For the latter's elephants see W. Gowers & H.H. Scullard, Num. Chron. 6 ser. 10 (1950) 273 n.9.
90 See e.g. Encyclopaedia Brit. (1972) VII.273.
91 Gowers & Scullard's suggestion that he inherited these elephants from Ptolemy I, who acquired them in the last years of the fourth century (op.cit. 274-5), does not take into account that only a few could have survived until the late seventies. I would not regard the account of the procession of Ptolemy II as evidence for the capture of many Seleucid elephants by the Egyptians during the revolt at Apamea (contrary to P. Goukowsky, BCH 96 (1972) 492): the conclusion that the elephants described by Callixenos (ap. Athen. 5.200f.) as

figuring in the procession were actually Indian if they were not dummies is not inevitable, and the date of the procession is uncertain anyway and may have been before the revolt (see W.W. Tarn, JHS 53 (1933) 59; W. Otto, Zur Geschichte des 6 Ptolemäers, 82 n.6).

92 At Raphia they drew up 73 elephants (Polyb. 5.82.7); on the elephant stations on the Red Sea see: M. Cary, The Geographical Background of Greek and Roman History, 206; Tarn-Griffith, 246; W. Gowers, op.cit. 43; W. Krebs, Wissenschaftliche Zeitschrift der Universität Rostock 13 (1964) 212-4.

93 Cf. the corruption of Δ (4) to Λ (30) in I Macc. 6.37 rightly noted by A. Rahlfs, ZAW 52 (1934) 78-9.

94 The elephants captured by Demetrius II according to Ant. 13.120 were obviously Ptolemaic.

95 Jos. Ant. 13.144 is an inexact paraphrase of I Macc. On the use of elephants to storm fortifications see Tarn, Developments, 95-6; Glover, 9.

96 See P. Gardner, Catalogue of Greek Coins, the Seleucid Kings of Syria, 115(Index); E.T. Newell, Eastern Seleucid Mints, 198.

97 On the armour of the elephants and of the archers posted on 'towers' on their backs see P. Goukowsky, BCH 95 (1972) 474-98.

98 Cf. Diod. 19.82.4; τῶν ψιλῶν τοὺς ἱκανούς.

99 Seleucus' heavy force was composed of the following elements: 1,000 troops who accompanied him to Babylonia in 312 (Diod. 19.90.1; App. Syr.273(54); 1,000 troops who deserted from Antigonus' garrison (Diod. 19.91.3); in the battle against Nicanor, the satrap of Media, Seleucus had at his disposal 3,000 infantry (ibid. 91.2) part of whom may have been lights; a substantial number of Nicanor's 10,000 infantry (91.1) joined Seleucus (91.5); some of them were certainly lightly-armed orientals (91.4). The rest probably were Macedonians formerly settled by Alexander and Antigonus in the upper satrapies, but their readiness at this stage to follow Seleucus to Asia Minor is rather doubtful.

100 This actually happened at the eve of Ipsus, see Tarn, CR 40 (1926) 14; id. Developments, 38.

101 See for instance at Cunaxa: Xen. Anab. 1.8.19-20, and Gaugamela: Arr. Anab. 3.135.5-6; Diod. 17.53.2.

102 Daniel 11.40 does not refer to Epiphanes' Egyptian campaigns (against J.M. Montgomery, The Book of Daniel, 464-5; C. Lattey, The Book of Daniel, 107-9) but to the apocalyptic 'end of days' following the religious persecutions, cf. B. Bar-Kochva, Zion 38 (1973) 42 n.56.
103 See other considerations in Abel, Maccabees, 449; Dancy, 65, 114; against Bickerman, Institutions, 60.
104 On the Ptolemaic chariots see Droysen, Kriegswesens, 164 n.2.

CHAPTER 4

1   Ipsus - Plut. Demetr. 19.3; Cyrrhestica - Plut. Demetr. 29.3; Polyaenus 4.9.3; Curupedion - App. Syr. 62(328); Galatians - Lucian, Zeuxis, 8-11, see also OGIS 220; Molon - Polyb. 5.53.7, 54.1; Fourth Syrian War - Polyb. 5.59.1, 60.3 (Seleucia), 69.6 (Porphyrion), 71.7 (Rabatamana), 82.8, 84.1, 8, 11-13 (Raphia); Achaeus - Polyb. 7.16.1-2, 17.6; The Eastern Expedition - Polyb. 10.29, 49; Thermopylae - Livy 36.18-19; App. Syr. 17-19; Magnesia - Livy 37.41.1, 42.7-8, 43; App. Syr. 32-6; Antiochus IV - I Macc. 1.16-20, 3.37; Demetrius I - Jos. Ant. 13.59; Antiochus VII - Justin 38.10.9-10.
2   On this Macedonian tradition see Kromayer, Schlachtfelder, I. 166; Kromayer-Veith, Heerwesen, 84-5.
3   Especially Ptolemy II and IV, see e.g. Polyb. 5.34.4-10, 87.3, etc.; cf. E. Bevan, The History of Egypt under the Ptolemaic Dynasty, 57, 220; G.H. Macurdy, Hellenistic Queens, 119-20. The later Antigonids were not distinguished for bravery either: Philip V evidently tried to escape from the battlefield at Cynoscephalae at an early stage, and Perseus' notorious flight from Pydna is repeatedly dwelt on by ancient historians (Plut. Aem. 19.3, 23; Livy 44.42.1-2, etc.).
4   I Macc. 4.26-35, 6.28-54 (Lysias); App. Syr. 26 (Seleucus); Polyaenus 4.17 (Achaeus); I Macc. 9.1 (Bacchides); Polyb. 5. 42.5, 45.6, 46.6, 59.2 (Xenoetas, Xenon, Theodotus).
5   Otto-Bengtson, Niedergang des Ptolemäerreiches, 185 n.2.
6   Cf. Arr. Anab. 3.5.3 for Alexander's army and Berve, 195, 303; for Ptolemaic Egypt see Lesquier, 99ff.; Schulthess, RE s.v. Γραμματεῖς, 1777; Launey, II.778-9.
7   See Y.H. Landau, IEJ 11 (1961) 125. Landau's conclusion that

he was not Chief Secretary of the whole army but only of an army corps obviously disregards the elements of the title.
8   Strategie^2, II.64, 155.
9   On the use of this term to designate the commander of the army in the west after Alexander's death, see F. Schachermeyr, Klio 19 (1925) 441ff.; W. Ensslin, Rhein. Mus. 74 (1925) 293-307. On its meaning in the Ptolemaic administration: Lesquier, 73, 76-7, 336.
10 On the authenticity of the document, see Niese, Hermes 35 (1900) 297.
11 Antipater - Polyb. 5.79.12; 16.18.7; Livy 37.41.1 (on his kinship to the king see Holleaux, III.195-8); Seleucus the Elder - Polyb. 16.18.5; Antiochus the Younger (later Antiochus IV) - Polyb. 16.18.8; Seleucus III - Livy 37.41.1 (later Seleucus IV).
12 Theodotus - Polyb. 5.40.1-3, 46.3, 61.3, 79.4, 81; 7.16.2; Nicolaus - Polyb. 5.61.8-9, 68.5; 10.29.6, and see Launey, I. 186-7; Lagoras - Polyb. 7.15-18; Hippolochus - Polyb. 5.70.11, 71.11, 79.9; Ptolemy - Polyb. 5.65; OGIS 230; Y.M. Landau, IEJ 16 (1966) 66.
13 Xenoitas - Polyb. 5.45.6; Menedamos - Polyb. 5.69.4, 79.6, 82.11 (and see Robert, Hellenica 7 (1949) 5-22); Lysimachus - Polyb. 5.79.11; Polyaenus 4.17; Nicomedes - Polyb. 10.29.6; Polyxenidas - Polyb. 10.29.6 (on his naval career, Lanschau, RE s.v. 1850-1).
14 Griffith's statistics (Mercenaries, 242-3) refer mainly to officers of the second rank.
15 Lysias - see Beloch, Griechische Geschichte, IV.2.548; Byttacus - Polyb. 5.79.3, and perhaps OGIS 254; Zeuxis - OGIS 235; Menippus - Livy 36.11.6; Andronicus - Livy 37.13.9; Tryphōn - Strabo 16.2.10(752). Tryphōn is said to have been brought up at Apamea and been close to the king, which may indicate that he served in the Guard.
16 Holleaux, III.183-93 argues from his name that he was Lydian, but as the Lydians themselves were no longer a warlike nation by this time, he may have come from one of the military settlements in the area.
17 Xenon - Polyb. 5.42.5, 43.7; Diocles - Polyb. 5.69.5;

Theodotus Hemiolios – Polyb. 5.42.5, 43.7, 59.2, 79.5, 87.1; Hermogenes and Diognetus – Polyb. 5.60.4; Ardys – Polyb. 5.53.3, 60.4; Livy 33.19.10; Themison and Eurylochus – Polyb. 5.79.10, 12; Diogenes – Polyb. 10.29.5; Mendis and Philip – Livy 37.41.1; App. Syr. 33(170).

18 For the opposition to Hermeias see esp. Polyb. 5.41.4, 56.15; cf. W. Otto, RE s.v. Hermeias, 727.
19 Bickerman, Institutions, 64–7; Bengtson, Strategie^2, 155.
20 But he may have been the commander of only 16 elephants (see Asclep. 9.1).
21 Institutions, 64–5, and so Bengtson, Strategie^2, 64–7, 155 etc. though the latter distinguishes three kinds of stratēgoi. See Berve, 202–3 on Alexander's army.
22 See Launey, I.25–6; M. Rostovzeff, REA 33 (1931) 12.
23 OGIS 101, 217; Holleaux, III.285 ℓℓ.23–4, 288 ℓℓ.20–1.
24 Feyel, RA 6 sér. 5 (1935) 54–5; W.F. Walbank, Philip V, 293–4; id. Polybius, I.281; Bengtson, Strategie^2, III.25; see Lesquier's hesitations, p.93; cf. OGIS 738.
25 See e.g. Jos. Ant. 12.261; I Macc. 3.10 (Apollonius the meridarch and stratēgos of Samaria); Polyb. 21.16.4; Jos. Ant. 12.136 (Zeuxis as hyparchos and stratēgos of Phrygia), etc. On the military duties of these governors see Bengtson, Strategie^2, 188–93; see also Heuss, Gnomon 21 (1949) 309.
26 Cf. D. Cohen, De Magistratibus Aegyptiis externas Lagidarum regni provincias administrantibus, 36ff.; Lesquier, 84; Feyel, op.cit. 53.
27 On Susa as the residence of the satrap, see Polyb. 5.46.7; 48.14.

CHAPTER 5

1 See recently: Watson, 54–72; Anderson, 84–100.
2 See Launey, II.869–74.
3 See also Arr. Anab. 3.20–1 for Alexander's forced marches in pursuit of Darius.
4 On forced marches in the Hellenistic period see Tarn, Developments, 40–1; M. Cary, A History of the Greek World from 323 to 146 B.C., 237.
5 E.A. Heyden, Beiträge zur Geschichte Antiochus des Grossen,

29ff.; Kromayer, Schlachtfelder, II.135, 221; L. Robert, Hellenica 7 (1949) 15-6, 25-9; Holleaux, V.401; CAH V. 212.
6   Cf. Pericles' celebrated epitaph, Thuc. 2.39.
7   M. Feyel, RA 6 sér. 5 (1935) 31-3; P. Rousel, RA 6 sér. 3 (1934) 40; I.G. XII. Suppl. 644. And see: S.B. Kougeas, ΕΛΛΗΝΙΚΑ (1934) 177-208; C.B. Welles, AJA 42 (1938) 252-5.
8   Rousel, loc.cit., ℓℓ.1-7; on the Roman fustuarium: Polyb. 6.37.1-6.
9   So G. De Sanctis, Riv. di Fil. 12 (1934) 515-21; Welles, op. cit. 246.
10 So De Sanctis, op.cit. 517-18; Welles, op.cit. 245; G.T. Griffith, Proc. Cambr. Phil. Soc. N.S. 4 (1956-7) 4-5; contrary to Feyel, op.cit. 63-5.
11 Attempts to arrive at a more precise identification of Polybius' source have been made by T.S. Brown, Phoenix 15 (1961) 187-95; P. Pédech, La méthode historique de Polybe, 144; Schmitt, 178-9; Schmitt's argument against Brown, based on Polyb. 5.56.1 (op.cit. 179 n.4), is not decisive.
12 On the standard of discipline of the Galatians cf. Polyb. 5.78.1-5, 111.1-7; Paus. 1.7.2; Diod. 22.9; Polyaenus 4.6.17, etc.
13 See G. Rudberg, Forschungen zu Poseidonios, 11-13.
14 See Reinhardt, RE s.v. Poseidonios[3], 632, for Poseidonius' historical approach.
15 On the humour and irony of Poseidonius, see Rudberg, op.cit. 13-15.
16 Ibid. p.16 and see e.g. the exaggerations of Poseidonius' extracts in Athen. 5.210d,e; 12.540a,c, 549d, 550b, et passim.
17 See Watson, 68, 133-42.
18 H. Berve, II.169, 193; H.W. Parke, Greek Mercenary Soldiers, 207; Rostovzeff, SEHHW I.130.
19 Cf. Frontinus 4.1.6 for the limiting of the number of servants and attendants to one for each 'decade'.
20 On conditions of service in the Hellenistic armies see Parke, loc. cit.; Holleaux, III.15-26; Rostovzeff, I.145-7; III.1345; Launey, II.785-90.
21 Justin, 38.10; I Macc. 4.23; and the trilingual stele on

Raphia, H. Gauthier & H. Sottas, Un décret trilingue en
l'honneur de Ptolémée IV. 66 ℓℓ.10-15; see also Livy 37.44.3.

22 The identification of Sidetes as 'Antiochus who led the
expedition against Arsaces' may perhaps strengthen this view,
although when the same anecdote recurs in 5.210 c-d he is
defined as 'Antiochus son of Demetrius'. Athenaus 5.439e
introduces him again as 'the king who fought against Arsaces'.
In this case the association is obvious; Arsaces, when
burying his enemy, comments on his insatiable desire for
drink.

23 So also, Bickerman, Institutions, 91 n.6.

24 On the wide meaning of aposkeuē see Holleaux, III.15-17.

25 See Parke, loc.cit. (especially the references in n.7), 214;
cf. pp.109,162,200 above.

CHAPTER 6

1 On battle accounts in Plutarch, see J.R. Hamilton's recent
Plutarch, Alexander, A Commentary, p.XXXVII-XLI.

2 See e.g. the bad omens (29.1), the farewell speech of
Antigonus to his guard (28.4-5), his abandonment by all his
troops except Thorax of Larissa (29.5), etc. Plutarch's
approach is summarized in his own words in 28.1: 'the fortunes
and acts of the man whom I am narrating bring me back to the
tragic stage ...' etc. For a recent treatment of Duris'
influence on Plutarch see W.E. Sweet, CW (1951) 179-81; P. De
Lacy, AJP 73 (1952) 168-71; M.J. Fontana, Le lotte per la
successione di Alessandro Magno, 326-33. On Duris as an
historian see: F. Susemihl, Geschichte der griechischen
Literatur, 591; Ed. Schwartz, RE s.v. Duris, 1953-8; R.
Schubert, Die Quellen zur Geschichte der Diadochenzeit, 60-107.

3 On Hieronymus see especially: W. Nitsche, König Philipps
Brief an die Athener und Hieronymus auf Cardia; Schubert, 6-
60; F. Jacoby, RE s.v. Hieronymus, 1540-60; T.S. Brown, AHR
53 (1947) 684-96. On Hieronymus' presence at Ipsus, see
Lucian, Macr. 11; and cf. Nitsche, 4.

4 Cf. e.g. Plut. Eum. 15.3-18 with Diod. 19.32-4, and his
version of Cyrrhestica (see below).

5 See D.A. Russel, JRS 53 (1963) 21-8.

6 For the latest discussion of the 'Einquellenprinzip' in regard
   to Diodorus 18-20 see: Fontana, 259-81; J. Seibert, Untersuchungen zur Geschichte Ptolemaios I, 64-83, who argues for
   five sources, is much less convincing.
7 Other sources have contributed mainly the location of the
   battle, which is not recorded in the two main authorities:
   Diod. 19.55.2-9; Plu. Pyrrh. 4.2-3; App. Syr. 55; Arr. Anab.
   7.18.5; Nep. De regibus 2.3.1-2; IG^2 II.I.657; Polyaenus
   4.7.1-2 (so J.G. Droysen, Geschichte des Hellenismus, II.2.221;
   Schubert, 725; against J. Melber, Jahr. Class. Phil. Suppl. 14
   (1885) 628); 4.12; 9.4; 12.1.
8 E. Honnigman, Byzantion 4 (1935) 647-51; G. Radet, REA 38
   (1936) 263; L. Robert, Hellenica 7 (1949) 216-9 (and see the
   comprehensive bibliography there of earlier identifications);
   C. Wehrli, Antigone et Demetrios, 70.
9 W. Hünerwadel, Forschungen zur Geschichte des Königs
   Lysimachos von Thrakien, 47, who locates Antigonus' winter
   quarters east of Bolu. Had this been so, the battle would not
   have taken place at Ipsus. Antigonus would have been able to
   prevent Seleucus' forces, encamped in Cappadocia, from
   joining their allies.
10 On the plain see Strabo 12.4.7(565); for its identification
   see C. Perot, Galatie et Bithynie, I.43, 54, 56. As winter
   quarters: Diod. 20.109.6, and as the assembling place:
   Beloch, Geschichte, III.1.171 n.2; Ern. Meyer, Die Grenzen der
   hellenistischen Staaten in Kleinasien, 27; Hünerwadel, 50;
   contrary to Niese, Geschichte, I.350.
11 According to Diod., Seleucus brought with him about 12,000
   cavalry. The total allied cavalry is estimated by Plutarch to
   have been 500 more than that of Antigonus, i.e. 10,500, but as
   Lysimachus also must have had some cavalry, I would suggest as
   more appropriate the reading πεντακισχιλίους τῶν ἐκείνου
   πλείονας, and so bring the total up to 15,000 (see a similar
   discrepancy between 500 and 5,000 between Plut. Demetr. 5.2,
   and Diod. 19.85.3, both based on Hieronymus).
12 The 4,000 horse which fled with him to Ephesus (Plut. Demetr.
   30.1) probably belonged to this flank.
13 See the description of his isolation among the phalangites; cf.

Arr. Anab. 4.26.3; Tarn, Developments, 36-7, fails to consider the possibility of the king riding with the cavalry Guard among the phalangites, Cf. Plut. Pyrrh. 17.1.

14 Developments, 35-6.
15 In view of the preceding ἐφόβουν the phrase περιήλαυνον (Plut. Demetr. 29.3) is probably to be understood in the transitive sense, i.e. 'pushed around, harassed', and not in the intransitive meaning ('to ride around'), but, in any case, the attrition of Antigonus' phalanx would have been more effectively accomplished by cavalry who could have carried more ammunition (on Seleucus' mounted archers see Diod. 19.113.4).
16 If my suggestion is accepted, Seleucus' nickname 'the elephantarch' (Phylarchus ap. Athen. 6.261 b-c; Plut. Demetr. 25.4) may be taken at its face value.
17 I do not share W. Whatley's scepticism (JHS 84 (1964) 119-39, esp. 121) about the possibility of reconstructing the tactical planning of ancient battles. Although developments on the battlefield may have led to changes in plan, it would be going too far to suggest that ancient generals had only a vague idea of what they intended to do. Except in this point, I fully appreciate the acuteness of Whatley's observations.
18 So Tarn, Gonatas, 10; id. Developments, 68 et al.
19 Cf. Plut. Eum. 16; Polyaenus 4.6.12-13, and Demetrius' efforts at Gaza to rescue his 'baggage' - Diod. 19.84.7.
20 Cf. the fortification of Lysimachus' camp several months earlier, Diod. 20.108.5.
21 See the massacre of the Autriatai after the battle of Lampsacus (Polyaenus 4.12.1) in 302 (on the chronology, Melber, 639).
22 Developments, 68-9; id. JHS 40 (1940) 87 n.1.

CHAPTER 7

1 See the background in J.G. Droysen, Geschichte, I.409; Hünerwadel, I.68-9; Bevan, Seleucus, 65-7; W.W. Tarn, Gonatas, 99-100.
2 See E. Honnigman, RE s.v. Κυρρηστική 191-8; U. Kahrstedt, Syrische Territorien in hellenistischen Zeit, 30, 48, 104,

112; R. Dussaud, Topographie historique de la Syrie antique et médiévale, 467 (and see Strabo 16.2.8(751); Ptolem. Geog. 5. 14.10). Ptolemy's map, in which Cyrrhestica is separated from the Amanus range by a region called Pieria, which caused Honnigman some doubts (ibid. 191), gives a completely distorted picture: the Amanus range in fact is parallel to the bay of Alexandretta (Iskenderun) and the land in between was called Pieria (Strabo 16.2.8(751)), but Ptolemy charted the Amanus range from the northeast corner of the bay vertically northwards so that no room was left for the Pieria except between it and Cyrrhestica.

3 See Honnigman, loc.cit., and V. Tscherikover, Städtgründungen, 55, on the foundation of the city.
4 The form Κυρρηστοῦ for the citizens of Cyrrhus figures on coins and in literary sources, see W. Dittenberger, Hermes 41 (1906) 190; Honnigman, loc.cit.
5 See Demetrius' attempt to surprise Seleucus at night, Polyaenus 4.9.2; Plut. Demetr. 49; and see Melber, 634, on the sequence of events.
6 Dussaud, 470-1; E. Honnigman, ZDPV 48 (1924) 9. For a good summary of the remains see Hachette Guides, Syria, 427-8.
7 It is true that 11,000 infantry and an unspecified number of cavalry who started on the expedition (46.2) were reinforced by some of Lysimachus' officers (46.4), but a considerable number were drowned in the Lycus (46.5; Polyaenus 4.7.12), 8,000 died in the plague (47.1), and others defected during Demetrius' 40 days' illness (48.3).
8 The only parallel in the Hellenistic period which occurs to me is the 'disappearance' of Antigonus Doson's Illyrians at Sellasia in the bed of the Gorgylos, although this was not a tactical surprise effected in the midst of the battle (Polyb. 2.66.10-11; Plut. Philop. 6.2; id. Cleom. 28).

CHAPTER 8

1 On the satrapies under Molon and the general background see recently Schmitt, Untersuchungen, 123-4; and cf. also Bengtson, Strategie^2, II.85ff.
2 See the various suggestions for his route in E.H. Herzfeld,

Memnon 1 (1907) 126; P. Pédech, REA 60 (1958) 71-2; Schmitt, 144-5; Herzfeld's suggested route, with which Pédech is in accord, is much shorter and seems more probable.

3 F. Sarne and E.H. Herzfeld, Archäologische Reise in Euphrat und Tigris Gebiet, II.83; and see the arguments in Pédech, ibid. 72; Schmitt, 137.

4 See Schmitt's analysis of the sequence of events, 142 n.2.

5 So Pédech, op.cit. 72-3. Schmitt's suggestion of identifying the pass with the Sakaltutan range, the second of the ranges on the way to Chanikin (op.cit. 145), is less reasonable, and his arguments against Pédech are rather weak. Moreover, the Sakaltutan range is much wider than the reported 40 stadia which separated the camps (52.8 and see further below), and one wonders how they could have camped on the slopes of the rough plateau. Furthermore, the 'parallel' march of the two armies suggested by Schmitt (which is the only possibility according to his identification) was out of the question since the range is crossed by only one route that can be considered for military purposes. Besides, Polybius' narrative (52.7-8) suggests that the two sides confronted each other by approaching from opposite directions.

6 See also Molon's night attack on Antiochus' camp from an elevated position, 52.9-14.

7 Contrary to Pédech, op.cit. 73 who locates the battlefield in the plain to the south of the Qyrmyzy-Dereh range, probably assuming that Antiochus crossed the range and the battle took place near Molon's camp. But nothing seems to suggest that Antiochus succeeded in forcing the battle on his opponent in this highly unfavourable arena (despite the nocturnal turmoil in Molon's camp), or that the two sides did not challenge each other in the conventional way by advancing half of the distance between the camps (cf. Livy 37.38.9, etc.).

8 On the topography of Cynoscephalae see Kromayer, Schlachtfelder, II.75-8; W.K. Pritchett, Studies in Ancient Greek Topography, 129-32.

9 Cf. the Greek mercenaries at Raphia, Polyb. 5.84.9.

10 On the use of epitagma for reserve forces, cf. Plut. Pomp. 19; P Grenf I.40; Lesquier, 85.

11 The position of archers and Agrianian akontists on the extreme
    right at the Granikos and at Issos as suggested by J.F.C.
    Fuller, The Generalship of Alexander the Great, 150, 158, is
    not supported by Arrian, but, if Fuller's theory is right, the
    purpose at the Granikos may have been to offer artillery-like
    cover to Alexander's cavalry in the course of its courageous
    attempt to cross the river in the face of the enemy, and, at
    Issos, to give the right flank as much protection as possible
    from the Persian light infantry, which could have taken
    Alexander's army from the rear by way of the overhanging ridge.
12 Op.cit. 177.

CHAPTER 9
1 Ern. Renan, Mission de Phénicie, 510, followed by Dussaud,
   410; E. Honnigman, ZDPV 47 (1924) 33; P. Thomsen, Loca Sancta,
   s.v. Porphyrion.
2 F.M. Abel, Histoire de la Palestine, 77, followed by E.
   Galili, Ma'arachōt, 22 (1954) 60-1; 57 (1968) 53-6.
3 The identification is C. Clermont-Ganneaux's Recueils
   d'archéologie orientale, 4.65-74; cf. Honnigman, op.cit. 32;
   B. Spuler, RE s.v. Platanus, 2338-9. Dussaud's hesitations
   (p.46), on the ground that it would have been wiser to put
   outposts in front of the main blockade at Porphyrion, are not
   justified; there is no indication of any skirmish before
   Porphyrion, and in any case their tactical value is rather
   questionable. See also below on the advantage of the three
   cliffs being within sight of each other.

CHAPTER 10
1 A. Momigliano, Aegyptus 10 (1929) 189; W. Otto, Beiträge zur
   Seleukidengeschichte, 83; and see Walbank, Polybius, I.613;
   cf. also T.S. Brown, Phoenix 15 (1961) 193, who takes the
   middle course suggesting that Polybius used pro-Seleucid as
   well as pro-Ptolemaic sources.
2 See Gauthier-Sottas, p.35 ℓℓ.16,23-5; III Macc. 1.6-7. Cf.
   Momigliano, ibid. 188; J. Gutman, Scholia 3 (1959) 56-7. On
   the attitude of the Jewish aristocracy at that moment see M.
   Stern, Tarbitz 32 (1962-3) 45-6; cf. Jos. Ant. 12.129-44 on

the pro-Seleucid policy of the Jews at the time of the Fifth Syrian War.

3 Another explanation for the hostile characterization of Philopator: see C. Préaux, Chronique d'Égypte, 40 (1965) 364-75; Fraser, Alexandria, II.144 n.180.

4 So, without further comment, C.W. Emmet, The Third Book of Maccabees, p.X.

5 On Ptolemy of Megalopolis see: Susemihl, I.905; Volkmann, RE s.v. Ptolemaios (43), 1762-3; F. Jacoby, FGrH. II B4 p.592. On traces of his work in Polybius see Walbank, Polybius, I.30, 566, II.493.

6 J. Braslvsky, Studies in our Country, its Past and Present, 252-3; I. Margovsky, Archeological News 3 (1969) 44.

7 Polybius' chronology is confirmed by the trilingual stele of Pithom according to which Ptolemy fought on the tenth day after leaving Pelusium (Gauthier-Sottas, p.34, ℓℓ.10-11). Ptolemy's march took five days, and Antiochus arrived at the spot on the same night (80.4). The two armies encamped opposite each other for five days (82.1) before doing battle. The battle seems to have taken place in the late afternoon (85.13, 86.1,3), accounting for the statement that the armies waited five days. Cf. Titus' forced march in four days from Pelusium to Raphia (Jos. Bell. 4.660-3), but that was in winter (ibid. 654, 658), and with a small force, and one of picked troops. Alexander's much smaller and considerably lighter force (accompanied by a fleet which probably carried the baggage) covered the distance from Gaza to Pelusium (205 km) in seven days (Arr. Anab. 3.1.1; Curt. 4.7.2), and Antigonus with his large army in 306 probably in ten days (Diod. 20.73.3).

8 I am obliged to Mr H. Tsoar, of the Geographical Department, Ben-Gurion University in the Negev, who kindly provided me with this information based on his field research in the area. See also id. Sand Dunes of El-Arish, 69-70.

9 Had the 61,000 Ptolemaic phalangites (n.11 below) been deployed in the usual depth of 16 lines (Polyb. 18.30.1 and see p. 66 above), they would have occupied 3600 m (on the basis of 3 feet per phalangite, Polyb. 18.29.2, Arr. Tact.

12-16). The 6,000 semi-heavy Thracians and Galatians, in the 8-line deep formation usual for such troops (see ibid. 14.2; Asclep. Tact. 6.2), with each soldier occupying 3 feet (Arr. Tact. 4.3), required 650 m. The 5,000 cavalry, drawn up in 8 lines, the spacing between the ilai being equal to the front of each ilē, and each cavalry taking up 3 feet (Polyb. 12.18. 3-4; Asclep. Tact. 7.4; Diod. 19.27), occupied 1000 m. These contingents, together with the necessary gaps between them, could have occupied approximately the whole width of the 5.6 km pass.

10 'Cataphracts', who were armoured and equipped with long pikes, could certainly have broken into the phalanx lines, but Antiochus did not have cataphracts at this stage, and even later, at Panion and Magnesia, the cavalry pike was not yet a match for the formidable infantry sarissa (see p. 74 above).

11 25,000 'phalanx', 20,000 Egyptians and 3,000 Libyans trained in the Macedonian style, 3,000 agēma, 2,000 'peltasts' - probably hypaspists (see Walbank, Polybius, I.590), and 8,000 Greek mercenaries (for the latter see Griffith, Mercenaries, 318, and cf. the following note).

12 20,000 phalanx, 10,000 argyraspides and 5,000 Greek mercenaries (see 84.9; note also that the opposing Ptolemaic 'peltasts' were actually phalangites).

13 If the phalanx in the centre, which numbered 45,000, was deployed in 32 lines, the whole Ptolemaic army must have stretched not more than 4.1 km (cf. n.9 above) in the 5.6 km wide pass.

14 On the military application of the term cf. G.T. Griffith, JHS 57 (1947) 77 n.3.

15 The second part of the paragraph is certainly distorted; the conjunction καί should be inserted between καθωπλισμένων and τούς, and the sequence of the sentences altered because Byttacus was in charge of 5,000 oriental 'lights' (see 79.3), and the contingent 'armed in the Macedonian style' was certainly posted next to the 'lights' in the centre (see 82.2).

16 The words παρ' αὐτοὺς τοὺς ἱππεῖς (82.4) must be supplemented by ἐν μετώπῳ (cf. 82.10), otherwise the position of the Cretans in both armies would not make sense (in contrast to

Walbank, Polybius, I.611).

17 'Those equipped in the Macedonian style' (82.10) certainly refers to the argyraspides, see 79.4 and cf. 82.2. Cf. Walbank, Polybius, I.611. On the reconstruction of this paragraph see the previous note.

18 On the rare appearance of 'light' native Egyptians in the Ptolemaic army in the fourth and third century B.C. and their intensive training as phalangites on the eve of Raphia, see Griffith, Mercenaries, 109-10, 120-5, 139-41; W. Parmans, Aegyptus 31 (1951) 218.

19 See also III Macc. 1.2-3. For the value and sources of III Macc. 1.1-8 see A. Tscherikover, The Jews in the Greco-Roman World, 340-1; J. Gutman, op.cit., 54-9 and bibliography there.

20 J.P. Mahaffy, Hermathena, 1899, 140-52; Griffith, Mercenaries, 122-3; followed by W.W. Tarn, CAH VII.730; Rostovzeff, SEHHW, III.1397; M. Cary, A History of the Greek World from 323 to 146 B.C., 403; Launey, I.99-100; Walbank, Polybius, I.590. Against this theory see Permans, op.cit. 214-22; C. Cavaignac, Rev. de Phil. 25 (1951) 292-4.

21 See the various forms of phalanx defensive formations in Kromayer-Veith, Heerwesen, 135-6.

22 See Permans, op.cit., 217-8.

23 See Griffith, Mercenaries, 109-11; M. Segrè's calculations in Bull. soc. arch. Alex. 29 (1934) 267-8 are misleading, as they take the 70,000 Ptolemaic troops at Raphia as a basis for reckoning the European population in Egypt.

24 The 5-7 arourae granted to the Egyptian machimoi, as compared with the Europeans' 30 and 80 arourae, would have been enough only for a starvation diet. See the calculations of Crawford, 123-5.

CHAPTER 11

1 On the purpose of the expedition: W.W. Tarn, JHS 60 (1940) 88; but see E. Badian, Gnomon 38 (1966) 712.

2 So P. Pédech, REA 60 (1958) 76; Walbank, Polybius, II.236.

3 Pédech, ibid. 74-7.

4 See 29.1 where οὔτ' ἄν ἐπιτηδειοτέρους τόπους ... etc. presumably refers to the Parthian cavalry.

5   So Kiessling, RE s.v. Hyrkania, 501.
6   See e.g. the elementary advice of Vegetius 3.6-7.
7   On the Parthian boundaries on the eve of the expedition, see Schmitt, 51; see also Polyb. 10.31.11.
8   Probably the neo-Cretans mentioned on various occasions, so Griffith, Mercenaries, 144 n.2; Launey, I.284.
9   'Acting as a covering force' - Walbank, Polybius, II.241. 'Acting in support' - see Polyb. II.14.1, and the noun ἐφεδρεία - 5.23.3, 4; 18.23.8; 32.5.9; possibly 3.69.10; 23.16.2. The verb ἐφεδρεύειν in Polybius has also some other meanings: 'to protect', 'to keep guard', 'to lie in wait', 'to form the reserve', 'to remain in the reserve' and even to 'control, supervise' (see the references in A. Mauersberger, Polybios Lexicon, s.v., though his interpretations are not always acceptable). The noun ἐφεδρεία also has the meaning of 'an advance guard' (Polyb. 18.21.2,4; 36.8.3 and possibly 3.112.2; 7.17.2; 10.38.8), but the indicated close connection between the operation of the Cretans and that of the mountaineers excludes this possibility.
10 So A. Galili, Ma'arachōt 52 (1968) 52-3.
11 Contrary to Pédech, op.cit. 77, who thinks that their task was to occupy the high ground and clear it of the enemy.
12 Polyb. 10.29.5-6. They may have been Greeks: on thōrakitai in the Achaean army, Polyb. 4.12.3; 11.11.3-4, 14.1, 15.5; and cf. Walbank, Polybius, II.285-6; for thyreaphoroi see IG VII.2716 (despite the conversion to Macedonian armaments in Boetia and Sparta after 245, see J. Beloch, Klio 6 (1906) 44; M. Feyel, Polybe et l'histoire de Béotie, 193-7, and in Achaea - Plut. Philop. 9); but they may also have been Galatians (Droysen, Heerwesen, 167 n.2), known by their traditional thyreos, who adopted the cuirass during the third century (Launey, I.529-33). They may also have been mixed: the thyreophoroi being Galatians and the thōrakitai being Greeks or vice versa.
13 For the typical Greek and Hellenistic march order see Kromayer-Veith, Heerwesen, 79, 82, 114, 141.

CHAPTER 12

1. See Walbank, Polybius, II.421-3; Holleaux, III.311-35; Josephus' chronology, Ant. 12.131 is certainly mistaken, see A. Momigliano, Boll. di Phil. Class. 35 (1928-9) 89-90.
2. See Holleaux, III.320; Walbank, ibid. 523.
3. Hieronymus' statement (ibid. 14) - that Scopas fought against Antiochus before the reoccupation of Jerusalem by the Ptolemies - must not be taken literally (so also E. Taeubler, JQR 37 (1946-7) 14). Had there been any major battle before Panion, one would have expected it to be indicated by the sources. Moreover, it is highly unlikely that the huge Seleucid army stayed in Palestine during the winter season, which was when the Ptolemaic invasion took place (Jos. Ant. 12.135). So Bevan, Seleucus, II.36.
4. See Holleaux, III.317-35.
5. Scopas' operations in Palestine are not recorded in detail. All one may say with certainty is that he was forced into conducting a difficult siege or battle against the Jews around Jerusalem (Jos. Ant. 12.131 and cf. 135, 139, 144), and that Ptolemaic troops garrisoned Samaria, Abila, Gadara, and Batanea (134, 136), although these may have been Ptolemaic military settlers in the area (see p.35 above) who had perhaps remained loyal to their dynasty. De Sanctis' conjecture that Polybius' fragment (?) preserved in the Suda (s.v. ῥεμβωδοῦς and Σκόπας), about Scopas' failure to occupy some unspecified city, refers to an unsuccessful siege of Damascus is based on his surprising suggestion that Damascus was on the way from Abila to Sidon, both of them known to have been occupied by Scopas (Storia dei Romani, IV.1.119, esp. n.10). Obviously he failed to consult the map.
6. On the chronological question see Holleaux, II, pp.312-31.
7. Tyre, the nearest port, probably sided with the Seleucids, cf. Polyb. 5.61.5, 62.2, 70.2 for the campaign of 218. The same applies to Acre-Ptolemais (ibid.). See on the other hand Polyb. 5.69.10 - 70.1 for Sidon's pro-Ptolemaic policy in that same year. The land route to Egypt was ruled out because of the hostility of the Jews and perhaps of other nationalities also, who would have taken the chance to

demonstrate their loyalty to their new master. There were, in addition, the tremendous difficulties facing a retreating army in the Sinai desert.

8   Other reservations are trivial and were raised only for the sake of argument (19.2-3, 7, 8, 9, 10-11). Most of them prove only that Zeno's account was somewhat sketchy, but the same criticism may apply to Polybius' description of certain campaigns.

9   Zeno's failure to mention Antiochus the Elder among those reporting to the camp after the battle (19.9) could not have been the reason for Polybius' suspicion: he must have known that very few battle accounts could be as comprehensive as to contain such trivial details. The argument in 19.9 gives the impression that Polybius was determined to 'tear Zeno to pieces' at all costs, and this casts doubt on his integrity when criticizing other historians (see further below). Furthermore, if Polybius had had positive evidence that Antiochus the Younger was not at Panion, he would not have hesitated to point this out.

10 Walbank, II.524; O. Mørkholm, Antiochus IV of Syria, 38; Holleaux, III.182; G.T. Griffith, OCD^1 s.v. Antiochus IV, 60.

11 See also J.R. Hamilton, Plutarch, Alexander, A Commentary, 23.

12 The identification: Ed. Robinson, Biblical Researches in Palestine, III.350-1; see also: Holscher, RE, s.v. Panias, 599-600; Dussaud, 390-1; cf. Jos. Bell. 1.404-6, 3.509; Steph. Byz. s.v. Πανιάς.

13 For the later Roman road from Panion to Damascus, see P. Thomsen, ZDPV 33 (1917) 33; M. Avi-Yonah, Geography, 83; see also Jos. Bell. 3.510.

14 So also, G. De Sanctis, Storia dei Romani, IV.1.119; Bevan (op.cit. II.37) and Avi-Yonah (Atlas, 21) assume that Antiochus entered Palestine by the somewhat shorter route crossing the Lebanon Valley. But as Panion-Bānyās lies 11 km from that main road which passes along the foothills of Upper Galilee, and the marshes of the Ḥuleh blocked the valley 3 km to the south of Panion (Jos. Bell. 4.1.3 - Daphne is identified with Ḥ. Dufna. For the extension of the marshes see Y. Karmon, The Northern Hūlā Valley, 56 n.9),

they suggested that Antiochus turned aside to invade Batanea
(the Bāshān), southeast of the Golan Heights, as indeed he
did after the battle (Jos. Ant. 12.136). To have made a
detour to the Bashan, with Scopas not far away, however,
would have exposed Antiochus' own territory in the north to
the risk of Ptolemaic invasion, and the advantages of such a
move at that stage seem dubious. In any case, any expedition
from Syria to the Bashan would have been conducted by way of
Damascus. It could have involved Antiochus III's heavy troops
in a decisive battle on an unfavourable, hilly terrain.

15 On the deterioration of the Ptolemaic phalanx, see Griffith,
Mercenaries, 120-5; and see further p.141 above. Scopas'
frequent recruiting campaigns in Greece underline the
Ptolemaic shortage of manpower. As the revolt of the native
Egyptians had not yet been put down (on the duration of the
revolt see Polyb. 5.107.1-3; 14.12.4; C. Préaux, Chron. d'
Egypte (1936) 526ff.), we may assume that the Egyptian
machimoi were kept out of this expedition.

16 The 'left' in 18.8 and 19.4 may at first sight be understood
as 'the left of the whole array', but 18.6 clearly indicates
that the hill was occupied by the right flank of the main
part of the Seleucid army which was deployed 'on the level
ground' or, in other words, it dominated the left flank of
that part of the Ptolemaic army that was posted in the plain.

17 Walbank, op.cit. 524 n.18.6 suggests some other identifications, but he fails to consider the whole topographical
picture; the places he proposed are too far from Panion or
lie in an entirely flat area.

18 The location of the left wing in the 'level ground' (ἐπιπέδους)
mentioned in the same passage seems to indicate this interpretation of ὑπώρεια.

19 Even the summit of Tel-'Azzāziyāt is still lower than Bānyās
Plateau, but the question of the relative heights is actually
irrelevant here; what counts is the view and impression of
the observer and, due to an optical illusion, Tel-'Azzāziyāt
seems, on the spot, to overlook the platform. Moreover,
Zeno's Ptolemaic source (see A. Momigliano, Aegyptus 10 (1929)
189), probably an eyewitness (see p.154 above), was himself

fighting in the 'platform', as may be suggested by the abundance of topographical and military details on this part of the scene. For him and the bulk of the Egyptian army posted there, Bānyās Plateau was 'level ground' (ἐπιπέδους...), but Tel-'Azzāziyāt a steep slope. The view from Bānyās Plateau to the south and southwest shows Tel-'Azzāziyāt to be clearly a slope which constitutes the last terrace of the Golan Heights, while Bānyās Plateau seems, to one standing on the spot, to be entirely separated from the Golan Heights and Mt Ḥermōn.

20 Antiochus the Elder was sent ἐπὶ μὲν τὴν ἑωθινήν (5, MS P). Despite the tautology of ἅμα τῷ φωτί (6), ἑωθινή has to be interpreted as 'early morning' and not 'east'. ἑωθινή - 'early morning', which is an adjective, occurs without the noun (Polyb. 3.83.7 - ἐπὶ...; 1.67.9, 87.7, 3.43.1, 4.78.6 - ὑπὸ τὴν ἑωθινήν), while as 'east' it does not occur in Polybius, and certainly is quite rare without the noun. Polybius may be quoting Zeno, and eloquence is known to have been one of the characteristics of the Pathetics (but there is some verbosity also in 3.83.7 and 4.78.6).

21 See e.g. Livy 37.41.4, the situation admittedly being aggravated by the fog.

22 The Seleucid force had indeed the advantage of height in the southern arena, but the ground in the area is uneven and rolling, and, in any case, a phalanx running downhill was in danger of breaking its close ranks and would have preferred to take the defensive. This limitation of the phalanx was well demonstrated at Cynoscephalae and outlined by Polybius in his excursus on the phalanx (18.31.5).

23 On the size of the Seleucid aposkeuē at Panion see Daniel 11.13.

24 Cf. especially the positioning of the elephants at Magnesia behind the argyraspides and the Roman legions (Livy 37.39.13, 40.6-7). On the use of elephants as a screen against cavalry see Tarn, Developments, 96.

25 Polybius' comment on his treatment of the naval battle at Lade and Nabis' expedition (16.14-17) just proves that Zeno was overcome by patriotic sentiments and was not acquainted with

the topography of the Peloponnese.
26 It is worth noting that Polybius' failure to 'sense' the topographical background and the location of the troops, and to support his arguments with any external evidence, proves that he did not himself describe the battle in his chronological narrative, but only referred to it in a short note.
27 See the account 16.1-17.7. Polybius was tactful enough not to touch on the old historian's patriotic feelings in his letter, and did not refer to Zeno's account of the battle of Chios and Lade, also criticized in the sixteenth book (14.5-15.8).
28 It is worth noting that Polybius' topographical account of Antiochus III's invasion of the Phoenician coast (5.68) is no less distorted (see Walbank, Polybius, I.594 n.8).
29 If the last suggestion holds water, further doubt is cast upon Polybius' integrity and motivation when criticizing other historians (cf. nn.8 and 9 above). Walbank's comment on Polybius' approach seems, therefore, somewhat partisan: 'Such errors should be treated, not with bitterness and virulence ... but with the kind of charitable good nature which led Polybius himself to write to Zeno pointing out his errors χάριν τῆς κοινῆς ὠφελείας' (Polybius, I.11).

CHAPTER 13
1 On the various stages of the 'cold war' see Holleaux, V. 156ff.; E. Badian, Studies in Greek and Roman History, 112-35; H.E. Stier, Roms Aufstieg zur Weltmacht, 163ff.
2 Cf. the strategy of the Greeks in 480 and 279 (Hdt. 7.175ff.; Paus. 10.20ff.) and Antigonus Doson (Polyb. 2.52.7-8).
3 On this route cf. Procop. De Aedific. 4.2.18-21; Plut. Demetr. 23; and see C.B. Grundy, The Great Persian War, 261-4; C. Hignet, Xerxes' Invasion of Greece, 134-41.
4 Although Livy calls them twice castella (17.1, 18.8 but see 16.11, 17.12, 18.8 - caecumen, vertices, iugo), it seems that they were not fortresses but posts in the open field. The detailed accounts of Cato's detour in Plutarch (Cat. Mai. 13-14) and Frontinus (Str. 114.4) do not refer to any fortress, and as there were no fortresses in the range before 207, no

one would have been interested in constructing them between
207-191 (contrary to P. Leake, Travels in Northern Greece,
II.64). Livy may have misinterpreted the word akra found in
Polybius in this context (so App. Syr. 17(77), 18(78,80);
Zonaras 9.19C. On the different usages of akra see
Mauersberger, Lexicon, 45-6). On the identifications see
Leake, ibid. 61-4; F. Stählin, Das hellenische Thessalien,
204; Kromayer, Schlachtfelder, II.139-44; J. Farrel, JHS 30
(1910) 116-17; K.W. Pritchett, Topography, 71-9. The
suggestions based on the false assumption that remains of
Hellenistic fortresses should be sought in the area, all
fail to take notice of the upper trail from Saromata to
Mettdenitza, under the highest summit of the range (Trig.
Point 1372), which could easily have brought the Romans to
the rear of the Seleucid camp. Furthermore, I would think
that the highest summit is the most likely to be called after
the whole range (or vice versa). Finally, this trail is the
only one which was not visible from the stone wall which
climbed up the hill (see above).
5   See further P.A. Mac-Kay, AJA 67 (1963) 241-55.
6   Kromayer, op.cit. 148 and esp. n.1.
7   See Kromayer, ibid. 147-8.
8   See Kromayer, ibid. 150.
9   Kromayer, ibid. 147.
10 P. Bequignon, RA 6 sér. 4 (1934) 20.
11 Kromayer, op.cit. 150.
12 See Kromayer, ibid. 151-2. On the transportation of
    artillery machines to Greece and their operation in Euboea
    and at Larissa, see Livy 35.51.9; 36.10.8.
13 On the various towers see E.W. Marsden, Greek and Roman
    Artillery, 126-63.
14 See Marsden, ibid. 166; Tarn, Developments, 119-21.
15 On the topography see N.G.L. Hammond, JRS 56 (1966) 39ff.
16 On these difficulties see Tarn, Developments, 119-20;
    Marsden, op.cit. 164.
17 Plutarch (or rather Cato himself) does not mention any
    negligence, but it is to be expected that the commander
    would report that resistance was stubborn (cf. Plut. Aem.

16.2 for Nasica at Tempe).

18 Plutarch, who reports that as soon as Antiochus lost control the tide of the battle immediately turned, explains that he was hit by a stone and lost some teeth (Cat. Mai. 14), but I doubt if a slight injury of the sort would have broken such a tough and experienced man (see esp. Polyb. 10.49.14). This derogatory account seems to have its origin in the anti-Seleucid tradition which is so clearly discernible, i.e. in the fabricated story of his infatuation with the girl Euboea (see p. 95 above).

19 Pédech's view (La Méthode Historique de Polybe, 368-9) that Cato was sent only to 'neutralize' the Aetolians is rather curious.

CHAPTER 14

1 App. Syr. 21(95), 27-8, 30(150-1); Livy 37.9.8-11, 17, 31.3, 34-5, 38.1-3. See also Kromayer, Schlachtfelder, II.154-63.
2 On the topographical background see B. Bar-Kochva, Scripta Classical Israelica 1 (1974) 16.
3 So H. Nissen, 195-7; Ed. Meyer, Rhein. Mus. N.F. 36 (1881) 120-6; Ed. Kümpel, Die Quellen zur Geschichte des Krieges d. Römer gegen Antiochus III; Kromayer, Schlachtfelder, II.217-19. Contrary to Th. Mommsen, Römischen Forschungen, II.511-45 (esp. 514-15), followed by Ed. Schwartz RE s.v. Appianus, 219ff.
4 See Nissen, loc.cit.; W.W. Tarn, CQ 20 (1926) 100.
5 On Dio's own claims to be widely acquainted with Roman historians, see F. Miller, Cassius Dio, 34.
6 Schlachtfelder, II.168-71, and see 177 n.2 on the slight deviation in the course of the river in the north, contrary to P. Leake, Journal of a Tour in Asia Minor, 163-79.
7 On the strength of the turma, Polyb. 6.20.9; 25.1; Varro, De Ling. Lat. 5.91.
8 Livy is obviously more accurate in locating the alae on the flanks of the legions, see Nissen, 196; on the conventional Roman battle order see Kromayer-Veith, Heerwesen, 370; Watson, 24-5, etc.
9 On the standard numerical strength of the cavalry attached to

the legions and <u>alae</u>, Polyb. 6.20.9, 26.7.
10 Livy 37.39.10; App. <u>Syr</u>. 31(158).
11 On the standard number of these per legion, Polyb. 6.21.9, and their tactical role, Polyb. 15.12.3; see also Kromayer, <u>Schlachtfelder</u>, II.181.
12 The <u>hastati</u> of the 5400-strong legion (Livy 37.39.7) are to be estimated at about 1500 troops (see Polyb. 6.20.9, 21.6-10), which were divided into ten maniples (<u>id</u>. 6.24.3) of 150 men each. As the maniple was 6 lines deep (Kromayer-Veith, <u>Heerwesen</u>, 287, 357), 25 men were posted in the front line. Each legionary occupied 3 foot (<u>ibid</u>. 358 and see Polyb. 18.29.7-9), and as a space equal to the width of a maniple was left between the maniples (Livy 8.8.5-9; and see Walbank, <u>Polybius</u>, II.588-9), the front of the legion extended over 1500 feet, c. 450 m.
13 For the usual depth and spacing in Roman cavalry see Kromayer-Veith, <u>Heerwesen</u>, 359, 369, cf. Polyb. 12.18.3-5.
14 So rightly Nissen, 196; Kromayer, <u>Schlachtfelder</u>, II.182-3.
15 This assumption probably lies behind Mommsen's running description of the battle (<u>Römische Geschichte</u>[7], 738-9) and G. De Sanctis' (<u>Storia dei Romani</u>, IV.1.200), though only with relation to one flank; Kromayer, <u>ibid</u>. 183 n.2, fails to see the difficulties.
16 One possibility for instance is that Polybius used the verb προτάσσω which may be interpreted also as 'posted on the extreme flank' (cf. Griffith, <u>JHS</u> 67 (1947) 79 n.1 for Alexander's disposition at Gaugamela). On the effect of Livy's patriotism on his version cf. p.170 above.
17 On the authenticity of this division and its tactical significance see Kromayer, <u>Schlachtfelder</u>, 215, who stresses the need for turning the phalanx more flexibly in face of the highly mobile legions (contrary to Delbrück, <u>Kriegkunst</u>, I.368, who describes this order as a <u>Phantasie</u>).
18 Appian recounts that 22 elephants were posted at the side of each <u>meros</u>, probably misinterpreting Polybius' statement that the total of the elephants in the centre stood at 22.
19 Livy's 1200 Dahae are preferable to Appian's 200 (so Kromayer, <u>Schlachtfelder</u>, II.211).

20 Contrary to Kromayer, Schlachtfelder Atlas, 44, who follows Livy's account.
21 See Nissen, 196-7.
22 See the conflicting versions on the role of Attalus, Livy 37.43.3; App. Syr. 36(186).
23 So rightly F. Adcock, The Greek and Macedonian Art of War, 47; cf. Tarn, Developments 20 on Gaugamela.
24 See Kromayer, Schlachtfelder, 189 n.3, who rightly regards Livy as more accurate; cf. the battle between Lucullus and Tigranocerta, Plut. Luc. 26-8.
25 The developments on the argyraspides' front are not recorded, but the reference to the participation of Domitius, the commander of the Roman left flank, in the attack on Antiochus' phalanx (App. Syr. 35(178)) suggests either that, being exposed on one flank, they joined the phalanx 'square', or that they gave way earlier. In view of their high standard and the tendency for them to be generalized as 'phalanx' (e.g. Polyb. 30.25.5), the first alternative seems the more likely.
26 Appian's account of Antiochus' easy repulsion of Attalus' 200 cavalry, who tried to block his way back (36(186)), is more explicit than Livy 37.43.7 (so Kromayer, Schlachtfelder, 194 n.4; Ed. Meyer, Rhein. Mus. 36 (1881) 123).
27 On composition of the army of Pergamon see Griffith, Mercenaries, 176.
28 Contrary to Kromayer, Schlachtfelder Atlas, Röm. Abt. II.44, who attributes only a defensive role to the phalanx.
29 The weather conditions which are said to have hindered the Seleucid light infantry (Livy 37.41.2-5, and with greater exaggeration, Florus and Zonaras), would also have impeded Eumenes' archers who actually decided the battle (see esp. App. Syr. 33(171)). Livy's comment that the Romans suffered less from the fog and mist because they comprised mainly heavy troops is too ridiculous to be attributed to Polybius. Appian refers to the weather conditions without further comment.
    It should be added in this context that Antiochus did not

carry the pursuit more than a short distance, and therefore it was not 'irresponsible', as is suggested by Appian 34(177) – ἐπὶ πολὺ διώκων and Livy (37.42.8 – effuso cursu), both based on Polybius. The Roman camp was just 1 km behind the front line as suggested by the distances quoted by Livy and the nature of the battle area (see Kromayer's map, Schlachtfelder Atlas, Röm. Abt. Blatt 9.m.8). Cf. Polybius' comment on the pursuit at Raphia, p.137.

30 On its authenticity, see Nissen, 196; Ed. Meyer, Rhein. Mus. N.F. 36 (1881) 123-4.

CHAPTER 15

1 See Abel, RB 33 (1924) 510; M. Avi-Yonah, Studies, 60; O. Plöger, ZDPV 74 (1958) 166-9.
2 See Abel's identification, ibid.
3 The sequence of events in I Macc. 6.31, 49-50 is obviously distorted, and 49-50 should follow immediately on 31 (so Dancy, 138, against Abel, Maccabées, 124). A similar distortion occurs in I Macc. 9.34 (see 9.43ff.) and 3.52 (see 4.3-4; and cf. Jos. Ant. 12.306). Josephus in Ant. 12.368, 375, follows I Macc., but in II Macc. 13.22 and in Bell. 1.41, for which Josephus did not use II Macc. (see Niese, Hermes 35 (1900) 518-21 et al.), the occupation of Beith-Sour preceded the battle. The same reason which led Lysias to spend his time in besieging Beith-Sour in the first place must have prevented him from advancing northward before occupying the fortress. The distortion in I Macc., which might have been made by a later editor, was probably caused by the resemblance between the siege of Beith-Sour and that of Jerusalem and the difficulties imposed on both by the Sabbatical year (6.50-4). Some verses referring to the evident surrender or occupation of the quarters outside the temple may have been omitted between verses 49 and 51.
4 See Abel, RB 33 (1924) 211.
5 See for instance Abel, Maccabées, p.XXIV; Dancy, 3; C.C. Torrey, The Apocryphal Literature, 73.
6 Significantly, Josephus in Bell., based on a different source, does not mention the death of the elephant, although his

account concentrates on this episode relatively fully
(1.42-4).

7 See Ed. Meyer, Ursprung und Anfänge des Christentums, 164-5;
H. Willrich, Juden und Griechen vor der makkabäischen Erhebung,
107; E. Schürer, Geschichte des jüdischen Volkes[4], I.196 n.30;
E. Bickermann, RE s.v. Makkabaerbücher, 796; Niese, Hermes 35
(1900) 514-518; Abel, Maccabées, XII; E. Büchler, REJ 32 (1896)
199; 34 (1897) 93; Dancy, 30; but see V. Tscherikover, Hellen-
ism and the Jews, 392-5; id. The Jews in the Greco-Roman World,
135-45.

8 Cf. the Byzantine excerpts of Diodorus' account of Ipsus which
seem to be too interested in the role of the elephants - Diod.
21.2.

9 See e.g. Grimm, Handbuch, XXVII-XXX; H. Bloch, Die Quellen des
Flavius Josephus, 80-2; Momigliano, Tradizione, 27-30; E.Z.
Melamed, Eretz Israel 1 (1951) 122-30, et al.

10 Cf. e.g. Josephus' addition to I Macc. 4.3 in Ant. 12.306 -
'leaving many fires in the camp' etc. (cf. App. Sam. 16;
Polyaenus 4.15).

11 C.R. Conder, PEF (1875) 67, suggests Ras-Sherifeh northeast
of Beith-Zacharia; Abel, Maccabées, 117 and S. Wibbing, ZDPV
78 (1962) 163 - the saddle of Balloutat el Yerza; A. Avishar,
Judas Maccabaeus' Campaigns, 237 - lat. 1635/long. 1199 (a
part of the modern road which is obviously recent and arti-
ficial).

12 The description ἀπέναντι τῆς παρεμβολῆς τοῦ βασιλέως (I Macc.
6.32, a translation of the vague Hebrew mineged - opposite)
does not necessarily indicate that the Jewish camp could be
seen from Beith Sour, and that the Jews did not set an
ambush.

13 P. Thomsen, ZDPV 40 (1917) 81, 82 (referring only to the
western route), and PEF maps, sheets 17, 21.

14 I Macc. 6.33b refers only to the preparations of the Seleucid
army before the march and cannot be taken to indicate that
both armies were drawing up their lines in front of each
other. The word αἱ δυνάμεις recalls the expression τὸ ὅρμημα
τῶν δυνάμεων (47), and is perhaps a translation of the
Hebrew gdudim (battalions, cf. LXX at I Chron. 12.18; II

Chron. 25.9, 10, 13) which may refer to the 'elephant divisions'. Jos. Ant. 12.370, describing a conventional confrontation, is just an inaccurate paraphrase of I Macc.
15 On the nature of the first campaigns we have the comment of II Macc. 8.6-7, which probably refers also to the battle against Apollonius (I Macc. 3.10-12; so Bevan, Seleucus, II.238). The circumstances of the battle of Ammaus (I Macc. 3.46-4.25) do not allow for the possibility of a conventional confrontation: the selection of the Jewish force before the battle (3.55-6, quite acceptable, despite the literary influence of Deut. 20.5-9, in view of the difficulties of controlling a large force on a night march in rough terrain, see 3.57, 4.1), their night march, their view of the fortified camp (4.7), and above all the timing of the march when the Seleucids expected Gorgias to surprise the Jewish camp (4.1-3), all suggest that Judas counted on reduced alertness on the part of the Seleucids and burst into the camp. The description of 4.14 is obviously obscure and misleading.
16 See Conder, PEF 4 (1875) 67; Abel, RB 34 (1925) 214.
17 Cf. the strong impact on their enemies produced by the appearance of the Hellenistic armies, Onasan. 28; Plut. Aem. 14, 18; Sulla 16; Luculus 27, et al.
18 The Hebrew original of I Macc. undoubtedly used the word 'phalanx' in transliteration (cf. 9.12, 10.82) as it usually does with regard to military terms (e.g. 13.43). Cf. I. Bäer, Zion 33 (1968) 105 n.9 on ritual terms.
19 3 feet for each phalangite and for each horseman, the phalanx being up to 16 lines deep and the cavalry 8 lines (see the references p.168, and p.252 n.9 above).
20 It is perhaps worth paying attention to the similarity of the description καὶ ἤρχοντο ἀσφαλῶς καὶ τεταγμένως (I Macc. 6.40) to παραπορευομένων <ἐν> τάξει καὶ βάδην (Polyb. 10.30.9), which refers to the 'bait force' of the Cretans in the Elburz (see p.144 above). It may indicate the application of the same tactics, but admittedly can also be taken as describing the ordinary routine of the phalanx march (cf. e.g. Arr. Anab. 2.10.3).
21 Cf. the effectiveness of the elephants against the Galatians,

Luc. Zeuxis, 10-11, and in Pyrrhos' Italian expedition, Plut. Pyrrh. 21.7; Justin 18.2. On the effect of the coloured shields cf. p.233 n.10,12 above.

22 The Jews might perhaps have been ignorant of the practice of the Seleucid king to fight among the cavalry, but, however unacquainted with external events, they would have known the age of the king, and would therefore not have expected him to ride on the back of the elephant in the front 'division'. The tradition about Eleazar's motive, preserved in two independent versions, reaffirms the prevailing tendency of contemporaries to glorify the Hasmoneans.

23 On this region as the possible traditional sanctuary of Judas Maccabaeus, see Avi-Yonah, Studies, 57 and cf. I Macc. 2.28, 3.10-11; II Macc. 15.1. Despite the anachronistic name of Gophnitis-Gōfnā (Avi-Yonah, Geography, 52; id. The Holy Land, 96), I tend to regard the information on the flight to Gōfnā as genuine: Judas and his close supporters probably did not seek refuge in the temple; otherwise I Macc. would not have failed to refer to their role in the heroic defence of the holy place (I Macc. 6.48-54). In these circumstance one of the mountainous regions to the north of Jerusalem was a reasonable alternative. Josephus or his source had no reason to invent this as they did not apply this sort of criticism to I Macc., and the region is not named in any other instance as a refuge of the rebels. The anachronistic name Gōfnā is perhaps due to the possible use Josephus made of Nicolaus in whose days the old 'Afarayim was renamed Gōfnā.

CHAPTER 16

1 See Avi-Yonah, The Holy Land, 47.
2 The victory over Nicanor at Adasa is not dated by the sources, which refer only to the annual celebration in 13 Adar (March) to commemorate the event (I Macc. 7.45; II Macc. 15.36; Megillat Ta'anit, 13 Adar). It was preceded according to I Macc. by the accession to power of Demetrius I at the end of summer or autumn of 162 B.C. (on this dating see H. Volkmann, Klio 19 (1925) 388; E. Bickermann, Der Gott der Makkabäer, 738; J. Schaumberger, Biblica 36 (1955) 426). The battle of Elasa

took place on April 160 (see p.210 n.29 above). If we accept that the despatch of the Jewish delegation and the negotiations with Rome took place between the battles of Adasa and Elasa, as can be assumed according to the chronological sequence of I Macc. (7.39-9.1) and the internal and external circumstances, some months must have elapsed between the two battles (I Macc. 7.50 must not, therefore, be taken literally), and the battle of Adasa cannot be dated later than March 161, i.e. about a year before the battle of Elasa. And indeed, a document preserved in Ant. 14.233 indicates that the negotiations were terminated in 161 (see B. Niese, Orientalische Studien Theodor Nöldeke gewidmet, II.817-29; M. Stern, The Documents, 76-7, 83). Timarchus' revolt came to an end only at the beginning of 160 (see p.210 n.29 above).

3 On the authenticity of the document and the background see M. Stern, The Documents, 74-82; T. Liebmann-Frankfort, L'antiquité classique 37 (1969) 101-20. The suggestion of W. Wirgin, PEQ 101 (1969) 15-20, that the treaty was signed 4-5 years earlier, cannot be supported. See also Justin 36.3.9 and n.2 above. On the negotiations of Timarchus with Rome see Will, II.309.

4 The treatment of Nicanor's corpse, which contravened the basic rules of the Greco-Hellenistic world, may perhaps also have prompted the Seleucid determined reaction. For the treatment of the dead in the Greek Code of War see: C. Phillipson, The International Law and Custom of Ancient Greece and Rome, 275-9; R. Lonis, ap. J.P. Vernant (edit.), Problèmes de la guerre en Grèce ancienne, 231-43; cf. I Macc. 9.19; Jos. Ant. 12.432 interprets this verse in light of the usual custom.

5 On Bacchides' rank see Avi-Yonah, The Holy Land, 47; Abel, Maccabées, 131; Bengtson, Strategie^2, II.181-5, believes he was military commander of Seleucis, the great concentration of Macedonian settlers in North Syria.

6 On the identification of the fortresses see Abel, RB 33 (1925) 203-8; Avi-Yonah, The Holy Land, 53-4.

7 Studies, 63-4.

8 The possibility that I Macc. deliberately exaggerated the

number of the Jewish casualties in order to demonstrate that only the Hasmonean family was able to lead the people (which might be assumed from 5.61-2) must be discounted: from II Macc. it seems clear that the defeat in Marisa was on an especially large scale. While II Macc. turns even the Jewish collapse at Beith-Zacharia into a victory (though in laconic phrasing) without any indication of Jewish casualties, with regard to the battle at Marisa he admits that Jewish troops were killed (12.34) and that there was a critical stage in the battle (12.36), and tries to blame the casualties on pagan idols found later in their clothing (12.40). Furthermore, to support the argument that the casualty rate cited in I Macc. is designed to serve the politico-dynastical purpose mentioned above would require decisive evidence from another episode that the author is in fact ready to distort the truth for the sake of this purpose, but no such parallel episode exists. On the contrary, for one of Jonathan's battles, I Macc. reports that two sub-commanders saved the day while Jonathan's men took to their heels, and the stand of Jonathan himself at the moment is passed over in discreet silence (11.70-1).

9 See e.g. Diod. 19.82, 85.3 (Gaza); Polyb. 5.79.13, 86.5 (Raphia). Livy's numbers for Magnesia (37.43.1) are certainly wrong, and the figure of 1,400 captives may perhaps represent the number of captured horsemen, while the 50,000 losses, if the figure is to be trusted and derived from Polybius and not from an annalistic source, must have included prisoners, see App. Syr. 36(189).

10 On the identity of the episodes in I Macc. 5.55-62 and II Macc. 12.32-45, see Abel, Maccabées, 441.

11 See p.222 n.85 above on the authenticity of the document.

12 This figure has been preserved because it does not apply to actual fighting: most of the Jewish soldiers had been sent home before Jonathan was trapped by Tryphōn. The disclosure of the real number did not affect the author's didactic purpose (see below). On the other hand, there is no reason to assume that the author, who had accurate information on Jonathan's period, exaggerated the number of Jewish troops

involved. The number of potential Jewish mercenaries mentioned in the document of I Macc. 10.36-7 (see above) further supports the credibility of this figure.

13. See D.J. Crawford, Kerkeosiris, 122-31.
14. The refutation of the 800-men figure further undermines the widely accepted hypothesis about the 'internal crisis' in the Jewish conservative party (esp. A. Geiger, Urschrift und Übersetzungen der Bibel, 24ff.), which has already been refuted on other grounds by J. Efron, Historical Schools, 117-49.
15. See esp. S. Klein, The Land of Galilee, 9-16; cf. e.g. Avi-Yonah, The Holy Land, 66. The evidence for the existence of a large Jewish population in Galilee does not pertain to the generation of the rebellion and therefore cannot prove that the evacuation was only partial.
16. E.g. Klein, ibid. 11-12. Bacchides' route to Arbēl from the north could not have been named after Bēt Gilgāl. Even if such a locality is to be identified in the area (which is rather doubtful), it could not have been known sufficiently well or of sufficient topographical significance to justify naming the road after it (on the biblical application of the term 'road' with a place name, see Y. Aharoni, The Land of the Bible, 49-57), and Maisalōt (routes, tracks, in Hebrew, as Klein rightly says) could not refer to the steep slopes of Arbēl. The only way to occupy the rock was from the plateau on the southwest, but the word is meaningless when referring to this flat area because mobility from this direction is not confined to certain routes. Abel, Maccabées, 160, suggests the reading Galil instead of Gilgāl. In addition to the arguments raised above against the 'northern' identification, it could be added that the substitution of a well known district like Galilee for Gilgāl, which was almost unknown in the time of the second temple, is rather unlikely. In Joshua 12.23 the occurrence of a substitution is more likely because of the predominant position of Gilgāl in the stories of the conquest of Canaan.
17. K.L.M. Grimm, Das erste Buch der Maccabäer erklärt, 132-3; Oesterley, 96.

18 I.M. Grintz, Zion 12 (1946-7) 6, identifies Maisalōth with the village Messilya near Jenin, and Galgala with the village Jaljiliya, 28 km to the north of Jerusalem, but, as according to the sequence of events in the verse, the Gilgāl Road led to Messilōth, the road from the north to Messilya (or to any other point on the way to Jerusalem) would not have been named after Jaljiliya, a small, unimportant, and remote village 50 km to the south of Messilya and 5 km off the main road to Jerusalem. The same applies to the modified suggestion of Z. Vilnay, Judaea and Samaria, 169.

19 See PEF map, sheet 17. The route has two names in the Bible - Joshua 8.15; Jud. 20.42 (so Y. Aharoni, 56). The present road, which lies 1 km south of the biblical route, follows the route cut by the Romans (see P. Thomsen, ZDPV 40 (1917) 75).

20 On the identification of Gilgāl near Jericho, see recently O. Bachli, ZDPV 83 (1967) 64-71.

21 Cf. C.R. Conder - H.H. Kitschner, The Survey of Western Palestine II.1.292-3.

22 The Arbeēl listed by the dubious Midrash Va-yis'aū in the description of the legendary battles of the sons of Jacob in the Sichem area (see R.H. Charles, The Testament of the XII Patriarchs, 235-8), is as suggested by Klein, a distortion of 'Akrābā or 'Akrābel (ZDPV 57 (1934) 96). The Book of Jubilees (34.8) and the Testaments of the Patriarchs (Judas 3), the older versions of the legend, read Rôbel and Ιωβηλ.

23 Cf. I Macc. 5.23 for the plural ending. The form ἐν 'Αρβαττοις is probably a corrupt version of Ναρβαττοις referring to Narbatta, the district west of Samaria (see Grintz, op.cit. 12).

24 The first source may so be read by changing the vocalization of the Massorah in Joshua 16.1 (cf. LXX ad loc.).

25 Klein, Galilee, 11, 12; Avi-Yonah, Geography, 146; Abel, RB 33 (1924) 380.

26 The expression παρενέβαλον ἐπὶ 'Ιερουσαλημ (I Macc. 9.3) does not necessarily indicate that Bacchides first tried to besiege the city before moving northwards to face Judas Maccabaeus, as some scholars maintain. The word ἐπί stands

for the Hebrew mūl ('opposite', etc.; see LXX Josh. 9.1, 22.11 and elsewhere), which in Hebrew does not necessarily have implications of distance but of sight. In this context it may only indicate that he encamped within sight of Jerusalem. And indeed the Bēt-El mountains, being the highest of the Judaean mountains, offer a good view to the south as far as Jerusalem. Moreover, such an interpretation would not fit in with the location of Judas' and Bacchides' camps (see below), which suggests that Bacchides tried to reach Jerusalem from the north.

27 For the identification of Adasa and Kefar Salama, the battle-fields against Nicanor (I Macc. 7.31, 40), in the plateau to the north of Jerusalem near Givʻon, see Abel, Maccabées, 139, 142; id. RB 33 (1924) 377-8; Wibbing, ZDPV 88 (1962) 165.

28 RB 33 (1924) 382-3. Perhaps the Biblical Beērā, see I Chron. 7.37 and Jud. 9.21. On the geographical character of this genealogy of Asher see S. Yeivin, Biblical Encyclopedia, I.779. Abel, ibid. and Avi-Yonah, Geography, 160, who prefer the form Beērōt, ignore the difficulties that arise out of the suggested identity between this locality and the Gibeonite city, which should be placed further to the south (on its identification see Z. Kalai, Eretz Israel, 3 (1954) 111-15). Nevertheless, I would not deny the possibility that the location was named Beērōt in the Hellenistic period, and had no connection with the Gibeonite city. There is indeed no doubt that at least one MS of the Hebrew Text of I Macc. reads Beērōt (see the following note).

29 Abel, ibid. 383-4; and see I Chron. 2.39-40, 8.37 (Elʻāsā). Ḥirbet La'asa on the Bēt Ḥorōn Ascent suggested by C.R. Conder, 157, and S. Klein, The Land of Judaea, 63-4, is only the remains of an Arab building and cannot comply with any identification of Βερεα. Βηρζητω, specified by Josephus as the site of Judas' camp (Ant. 12.422), is obviously wrong, and the word itself is corrupt (contrary to S. Yeivin, BJPES 8 (1941) 83-4, and Avi-Yonah, Atlas, 30, who suggest the identification with Beēr Zayit, 8 km north of Ramallah). As is commonly accepted, for his paraphrase of the campaign's descriptions in Antiquitates Josephus did not use any source

other than I Macc. (see p.176 n.9 above). His version does not, therefore, have the value of an independent source and must be understood either as his own invention or, what is more likely, the result of the textual transformations of I Macc. Indeed, the Lucianic group and one MS of the Syrian translation which is influenced by it, have the identical form Βηρζητω instead of Berea and the like, the camping place of the Selucid army according to the main MSS of I Macc. This change is probably due to the paleographical similarity between Beērōt and Beēr Zayit in Hebrew. The Lucianic and the pre-Lucianic version, which was based on the Alexandrian version and consultation of the Hebrew original (see Swete, Introduction, 81ff.; S. Jellicoe, The Septuagint and Modern Study, 157-71), used a Hebrew MS, which read Beēr Zayit. Josephus, who used the pre-Lucianic version (H.St.J. Thackeray, Josephus, the Man and Historian, 85), copied this incorrect form and altered the camping place of the Seleucids to the camping place of Judas Maccabaeus. This conclusion is supported by the absence of any reference in Antiquitates to the location of the Seleucid camp, a detail which Josephus does not neglect in descriptions of other campaigns. At any rate, Josephus' reading cannot be taken to indicate that the Seleucids camped at Beēr Zayit as suggested by Schürer (Geschichte des Jüdischen Volks[4], I 222 n.36); the armies had a good view of each other from their camps (9.5), but Beēr Zayit cannot be observed from Elasa.

30 Ibid. 286-7.
31 See e.g. I Macc. 4.36, 6.48 (τὸ ὄρος Σιων).
32 J.C. Michaelis, Deutsche Übersetzung des ersten Buchs der Maccabäer mit Anmerkungen, 193-4; Yeivin, loc.cit.; Abel, Maccabées, 162-3. Yeivin is mistaken in identifying ashdōt ha-Hār with the approach to the Gōfnā valley. The author of I Macc., who was well acquainted with biblical terminology, would not have used the term ashdōt to refer to the gentle slopes nor to an internal valley of the central mountain range (see below on the meaning of ashdōt).
33 C.C. Torrey's revised reading ἕως ἄνω τοῦ ὄρους (JBL 53 (1934) 32) cannot be accepted because the letters Άζ, being found

also in Josephus (Ant. 12.429), are undoubtedly original in the Greek text of I Macc.

34 The correct reading in verse 15 is keras as suggested by a group of MSS and not meros (see v.16 - ὅτι συνετρύβη τὸ δεξιὸν κέρας). But it may well be that in order to diversify the style the translator took the liberty of using the word meros for the Hebrew keren (wing, keras), esp. as the Hebrew word behind meros in 9.4 was probably ṣad (see LXX to I Sam. 23.23), which in Hebrew means also wing.

35 Abel's answer to this difficulty is that ἕως 'Αζωρου ὄρος means only 'in the direction of' (RB 33 (1924) 386-7), but this interpretation does violence to the Greek ἕως, as well as to the Hebrew 'ad which underlies it. For a similar pursuit by cavalry for a distance of 30 stadia cf. Diod. 19.30.7-9.

36 On the synaspismos see: Kromayer-Veith, Heerwesen, 135-6 and e.g. Diod. 16.3; Arr. Tact. 11.4; Plut. Tim. 27, etc.

37 Cf. the employment of helepolis by Simon in 140 (I Macc. 13.43).

38 I Macc. 12.35. On the reading of the MSS see Abel, Maccabées, 442; and also see W. Kappler's apparatus ad loc.

39 See PCZ no. 59003, 59004.

40 Some scholars suggest that Hyrcanus died only in the seventh year of the reign of Antiochus IV; see Momigliano, 193; Abel, Maccabées, 339; M. Hengel, Judentum und Hellenismus, 501.

41 On the possible participation of Jews from abroad in the battles, though not on the basis of battle accounts, see Hengel, 32, 501: S. Appelbaum, The Jews in Cyrene, 118, and perhaps Avi-Yonah, Essays and Studies, 79.

42 On Jewish soldiers (including cavalrymen in Egypt) see V. Tscherikover, The Jews in Egypt, 32-5; Launey, I.544; for the existence of Jewish units in the Ptolemaic army at an early date see A. Kasher, The Civil Status of the Jews in Egypt and their Rights in the Hellenistic and Roman Period, 11-22.

CONCLUSION

1 See e.g. W. Rüstow - H.A.J. Köchly, Geschichte des griechischen Kriegswesens, 160-1; Droysen, Kriegswesens, 177-84; Niese, Geschichte, I.323; Beloch, Geschichte, IV.1.358; Kromayer-Veith, Heerwesen, 141-6; Tarn, Developments, 61; Cary, History,

238; Adcock, Art of War, 54.
2 Developments, 23.
3 On this and other successes of phalanx formations against legions see Tarn, ibid. 26-7.
4 See Tarn, ibid. 30-1, 69; G.T. Griffith, JHS 67 (1947) 85-9.
5 On the evaluation of Judas Maccabaeus' campaigns and especially the dubious success at Beith-Sour (I Macc. 4.26-35), see further in detail: B. Bar-Kochva, The Campaigns of Judas Maccabaeus (forthcoming, Hebrew).

BIBLIOGRAPHY

Abbot,F.F. & Johnson,A.C. Municipal Administration in the Roman Empire. Princeton, 1926.

Abel,F.M. Géographie de la Palestine. Paris, 1933.
- Histoire de la Palestine. Paris, 1952.
- Les Livres des Maccabées. Paris, 1949.
- 'Les Confins de la Palestine et de l'Egypte sous les Ptolemies', RB 49 (1940) 55-75.
- 'Topographie des campagnes Maccabéennes', RB 32 (1923) 495-521; 33 (1924) 201-17, 371-87; 34 (1925) 194-216; 35 (1926) 206-22, 510-33.

Abrahams,J. Campaigns in Palestine from Alexander the Great. London, 1927.

Adcock,F.E. The Greek and Macedonian Art of War. Berkeley, 1957.

Aharoni,Y. The Land of the Bible. London, 1971.

Allen,G.M. 'The Forest Elephant of Africa', Proc. Acad. Nat. Scien. Philadelphia. 88 (1936) 15-44.

Altheim,F. Weltgeschichte Asiens in griechische Zeitalter. Halle, 1947.

Anderson,J.G.C. 'A Summer in Phrygia', JHS 17 (1898) 81-128.

Anderson,J.K. Military Theory and Practice in the Age of Xenophon. California, 1970.

Atkinson,K.T.M. 'A Hellenistic Land-Conveyance', Historia, 21 (1972) 45-74.

Avishar,S. Judas Maccabaeus Campaigns. Tel-Aviv, 1957 (Hebrew).

Avi-Yonah,M. Atlas of the Period of the Second Temple, The Mishnah and Talmud. Jerusalem, 1966 (Hebrew).
- Essays and Studies in the Lore of the Holy Land. Tel-Aviv, 1964 (Hebrew).
- Historical Geography of Palestine from the End of the Babylonian Exile up to the Arab Conquest[3]. Jerusalem, 1962 (Hebrew).
- The Holy Land from the Persian to the Arab Conquest, A Historical Geography. Michigan, 1966.

Aymard,A. 'Du nouveau sur la chronologie des Séleucides', REA 57
(1955) 102-12.
Bächli,O. 'Zur Lage des Alten Gilgal', ZDPV 83 (1967) 64-71.
Badian,E. Studies in Greek and Roman History. Oxford, 1964.
- (Review) Schmitt. Untersuchungen zur Geschichte Antiochos'
des Grossen und seiner Zeit. Gnomon 38 (1966) 709-16.
Bäer,I. 'The Persecution of the Monotheistic Religion by Antiochus
Epiphanes', Zion 33 (1968-9) 101-24 (Hebrew).
Bar-Kochva,B. 'On the Sources and Chronology of Antiochus I's
Battle against the Galatians', Proc. Camb. Phil. Soc. 119,
N.S. 19 (1973) 1-8.
- 'On the Status and Nationality of the Garrison in the Akra on
the Eve of the Religious Persecutions', Zion 38 (1973) 33-47
- 'Hellenistic Warfare in Jonathan's Campaign near Azōtos',
Scripta Classica Israelica 2 (1975, forthcoming).
- The Campaigns of Judas Maccabaeus, Cathedra of the
History of Eretz-Israel and its Settlement
(forthcoming, Hebrew).
- 'Sēron and Cestius Gallus at Beith-Horon', PEQ 107 (1975)
(forthcoming).
Bean,G.E. Stratonikeia. OCD^2, 1019.
de Beer,G. Alps and Elephants. London, 1955.
Beloch,J. 'Griechische Aufgebote', Klio 6 (1906) 33-78.
- Griechische Geschichte^2. Berlin, 1922-7.
Bengtson,H. Die Strategie in der Hellenistischen Zeit^2. Munich,
1964.
- Griechische Geschichte. Munich, 1950.
Bennet,B.B. 'The Search for Israelite Gilgal', PEQ 104 (1972)
111-22.
Bequignon,Y. 'Recherches archéologiques dans la vallée du
Spercheios', RA 6 sér. 4 (1934) 14-33.
Berve,H. Das Alexanderreich auf prosopographischer Grundlage.
Munich, 1926.
Best,J.G.P. Thracian Peltasts and their influence on Greek Warfare.
Groningen, 1969.
Bevan,E.R. A History of Egypt Under the Ptolemaic Dynasty. London
1927.
- The House of Seleucus. London, 1902.

Bickerman,E. Der Gott der Makkabäer. Berlin, 1937.
- Institutions des Séleucides. Paris, 1938.
- 'Makkabäerbücher', RE XIV 1. 779-805.
Blinkenberg,C. Lindos, Fouilles de l'acropole, 1902-1914, Inscriptions. Copenhagen, 1941.
Bloch,H. Die Quellen des Flavius Josephus. Lepizig, 1879.
Bouche-Leclerq,A. Histoire des Séleucides. Paris, 1914.
Brand,C.E. Roman Military Law. Texas, 1968.
Braslvsky,J. Studies in our Country, its Past and Present. Tel-Aviv, 1954 (Hebrew).
Brown,T.S. 'Apollophanes and Polybius, Book V', Phoenix 15 (1961) 187-95.
- 'Hieronymus of Cardia', AHR 53 (1947) 684-96.
Büchler,A. 'La Source de Flavius Josèphe dans ses Antiquités (XII. 5.1-XIII)', REJ 32 (1896) 179-99; 34 (1897) 69-93.
Buchler,W.H. & Robinson,D.H. 'Greek Inscriptions from Sardis', AJA 16 (1912) 11-82.
Buresch,K. Aus Lydien, Epigraphisch-Geographische Reisefrüchte. Leipzig, 1898.
- 'Zur Lydischen Epigraphik und Geographie', AM 19 (1894) 102-32.
Cadoux,C.J. Ancient Smyrna. Oxford, 1938.
Cary,M. The Geographic Background of Greek and Roman History. Oxford, 1949.
- A History of the Greek World from 323 to 146 B.C. London, 1932.
Casson,L. Ships and Seamanship in the Ancient World. Princeton, 1971.
Cavaignac,E.M. (Review) Launey, Recherches sur les armées hellénistiques. Rev. de Phil. 25 (1951) 292-4.
Chapot,V. La province romaine proconsulaire d'Asie. Paris, 1904.
Charles,R.H. The Greek Version of the Testaments of the Twelve Patriarchs. London, 1913.
Clerc,M. De rebus Thyatirenorum. Paris, 1893.
Clermont-Ganneaux,C. 'Platanus de Phenicie', Recueils d'archéologie orientale, 8 vols., Paris 1888-1924, vol.6, 65-74.
Cohen,D. De magistratibus Aegyptiis externas Lagidarum regni provincias administrantibus. 's Gravenhage, 1912.
Conder,C.R. Judas Maccabaeus and the Jewish War of Independence. London, 1894.
- 'The Hill Country of Judaea - Fifth Campaign', PEF 4 (1875)

66-72.

Conze,A. Die Attischen Grabreliefs. Berlin, 1900.

Cooke,G.A. A text-book of North-Semitic Inscriptions. Oxford, 1933.

Corradi,G. Studi Ellenistici. Torino, 1929.

Crawford,D.J. Kerkeosiris. Cambridge, 1971.

Cumont,F. Fouilles de Doura-Europos. Paris, 1926.

- 'Nouvelles Inscriptions Grecques de Suse', Comptes Rendus de l'Acad. des Inscr. et Belles-Lettres. 1931, 233-50, 278-92; 1932, 271-86.

Dancy,J.C. A Commentary on I Maccabees. Oxford, 1954.

Debevoise,N.C. A Political History of Parthia. Chicago, 1938.

De Lacy,P. 'Biography and Tragedy in Plutarch', AJP 73 (1952) 159-71.

Delbrück,H. Geschichte der Kriegkunst^3. Berlin, 1920.

- Numbers in History. London, 1913.

Dittenberger,W. 'ETHNIKA und Verwandtes', Hermes 41 (1906) 78-102; 161-219.

- Orientis Graeci inscriptiones selectae (OGIS). Leipzig, 1903-5.
- Sylloge inscriptionum Graecarum^3(Sylloge). Leipzig, 1915.

Downey,G. A History of Antioch in Syria. Princeton, 1961.

Droysen,H. 'Agema', RE I. Col. 771.

- Heerwesen und Kriegführung der Griechen. Freiburg, 1888.

Droysen,J.G. Geschichte des Hellenismus. Gotha, 1877-8.

Ducrey,P. 'Aspects juridiques de la victoire et du traitement des vaincus', ap. J-P. Vernant (edit), Problèmes de la guerre en Grèce ancienne, 231-45.

Dussaud,R. Topographie historique de la Syrie antique et mediévale. Paris, 1927.

Eddy,S.K. The King is Dead. Lincoln (USA), 1961.

Edgar,C.C. Zenon Papyri. Catalogue général des Antiquités egyptiennes du Musée du Caire, 79. 4 vols. Cairo, 1925-31.

Edson,C. 'Imperium Macedonicum: the Seleucid Empire and the Literary Evidence', CP 53 (1958) 153-70.

Efron,J. 'Simon son of Shetaḥ and Janaeus', Memorial book to G. Allon (1970) 69-132 (Hebrew).

- 'The Revolt of the Hasmoneans in Modern Research', Historians and Historical Schools (Lectures delivered at the seventh convention of the Historical Society of Israel). Jerusalem, 1962, 117-43 (Hebrew).

Ehrenberg,V. The Greek State. Oxford, 1960.
Emmet,C.W. The Third Book of the Maccabees. London, 1918.
Ensslin,W. 'Die Gewaltanteilung im Reichsregiment nach Alexanders Tod', Rein. Mus. N.F. 74 (1925) 298-308.
Farrell,J. 'Notes on the Position of Rhoduntia', JHS 30 (1910) 116-17.
Feyel,M. Polybe et l'Histoire de Béotie. Paris, 1942.
- 'Un nouveau fragment du règlement militaire trouvé à Amphipolis', RA 6 sér. 5 (1935) 29-68.
Fontana,J.M. Le Lotte per la Successione di Alessandro Magno dal 323 al 315. Palermo, 1959.
Fontrier,M. ΕΠΙΓΡΑΦΑΙ ΛΥΔΙΑΣ. Μουσεῖον καὶ Βιβλιοθήκη τῆς Εὐαγγελικῆς Σχολῆς, Σμύρνα, 1886, 73-5.
Forbiger,A. Handbuch der Alten Geographie. Leipzig, 1842.
Foucart,M.P. 'Exploration de la plaine de l'Hermus per M. Fontrier', BCH 11 (1887) 79-107.
- 'Inscriptions d'Asie Mineure', BCH 9 (1885) 387-403.
Frankel,M. Die Inschriften von Pergamon (Inschr. Perg.). Berlin, 1890.
Fraser,P.M. Ptolemaic Alexandria. Oxford, 1972.
Frey,J.B. Corpus Inscriptionum Judaicarum (CIJ). Rome, 1936-52.
Fuller,J.F.C. The Generalship of Alexander the Great. London, 1958.
von Gaertringen,F. Hiller. Die Inschriften von Priene (Inschr. Prien.). Berlin, 1906.
- Historische Griechische Epigramme. Bonn, 1926.
Galili,E. 'The Seleucid Invasion of Palestine', Ma'arachot 22 (1954) 35-73 (Hebrew).
- 'The Enemies of the Hasmonaeans', Ma'arachot 52 (1968) 50-8 (Hebrew).
Gardner,P. Catalogue of Greek Coins, the Seleucid Kings of Syria. London, 1878.
Gauthier,H. & Sottas,H. Un décret trilingue en l'honneur de Ptolémée IV. Cairo, 1925.
Geiger,A. Urschrift und Übersetzungen der Bibel. Frankfurt, 1928.
Gelzer,H. Sextus Julius Africanus. Leipzig, 1880.
Germer-Durand,R.P. 'Exploration Épigraphique de Gerasa', RB 4 (1895) 374-400.
Geyer,F. 'Lysimachus', RE XIV. 1-39.

Glover,R.F. 'The Tactical Handling of the Elephant', Greece and Rome 17 (1948) 1-11.

Gomme,A.W. Andrews,A. Dover,K.J. A Historical Commentary on Thucydides. Oxford, 1945-70.

Goukowsky,P. 'Le roi Poros, son éléphant et quelques autres', BCH 96 (1972) 474-502.

Gowers,W. 'The African Elephant in Warfare', African Affairs 46 (1947) 42-9.
- 'African Elephants and Ancient Authors', African Affairs 47 (1948) 173-80.

Gowers,W. & Scullard,H.H. 'Hannibal's Elephants Again', Num. Chron. 6 ser. 10 (1950) 271-80.

Grenfell,B.P. An Alexandrian Erotic Fragment and other Greek Papyri (PGrenf. I). Oxford, 1896.
- & Hunt,A.S., Smyly,J.G. The Tebtunis Papyri (PTeb.). London, 1902.

Griffith,G.T. 'A Note on the Hipparchies of Alexander', JHS 83 (1963) 68-74.
- 'Alexander's Generalship at Gaugamela', JHS 57 (1947) 77-89.
- 'ΜΑΚΕΔΟΝΙΚΑ: Notes on the Macedonians of Philip and Alexander', Proc. Camb. Phil. Soc. N.S. 4 (1956-7) 3-10.
- The Mercenaries of the Hellenistic World. Cambridge, 1935.

Grimm,K.L.W. Das erste Buch der Maccabäer erklärt. Leipzig, 1853.
- Kurzgefasstes exegetisches Handbuch zu den Apokryphen des Alten Testament. Leipzig, 1851-60.

Grintz,Y.M. 'Cities of Nabhrakhta', Zion 12 (1946-7) 6-26 (Hebrew).
- Studies in Early Biblical Ethnology and History. Tel-Aviv, 1969 (Hebrew).

Grosse. 'Lorica', RE XIII. 444-9.

Grundy,G.B. The Great Persian War. London, 1901.

von Gutschmid,A. Geschichte Irans und seine Nachbarländer von Alexander den Grossen bis zum Untergang der Arsaciden. Tübingen, 1888.

Gutman,J. 'The Historical Value of III Macc.', ΣΧΟΛΙΑ 3 (1959) 49-72 (Hebrew).

Hamilton,J.R. Plutarch, Alexander, A Commentary. Oxford, 1969.
- 'Three Passages in Arrian', CQ N.S. 5 (1955) 217-21.

Hammond,N.G.L. 'Pezetairoi', OCD^2 513.

Hammond,N.G.L. 'The Opening Campaigns and the Battle of the Aoi
Stena in the Second Macedonian War', JRS 46 (1966) 39-54.
Hansen,E.V. The Attalids of Pergamon. Ithaca, 1947.
Hatch,E. & Redpath,H.A. A Concordance to the Septuagint. Oxford,
1897.
Haussoullier,M.B. 'Un loi grecque inédite sur les successions ab
intestat', Rev. hist. de droit français et étranger 47 (1923)
515-53.
Head,B.V. Catalogue of the Greek Coins of Lydia. London, 1901.
- Historia Numorum. Oxford, 1911.
Heichelheim,F.M. 'Die auswärtige Bevölkerung im Ptolemäerreich',
Klio, Beiheft 18 (1925).
Hengel,M. Judentum und Hellenismus. Tübingen, 1969.
Herschfeld. 'Abai', RE I. 11.
Herzfeld,E. & Sarne,F. Archäologische Reise in Euphrat und Tigris
Gebiet. Berlin, 1920.
- 'Untersuchungen über die historische Topographie der Landschaft
am Tigris, kleinen Zab und Gebel Hamrin', Memnon 1 (1907) 126.
Heuss,A. (Review) Bengtson, Die Strategie. Gnomon 21 (1949) 304-18.
- 'Stadt und Herrscher des Hellenismus', Klio, Beiheft 26 (1937).
Heyden,E.A. Beiträge zur Geschichte Antiochos' des Grossen.
Emmerich, 1873.
Hignett,C. Xerxes' Invasion of Greece. Oxford, 1963.
Hill,G.F. Catalogue of the Greek Coins of Lycia, Pamphylia and
Pisidia. London, 1897.
- Catalogue of the Greek Coins of Lycaonia, Isauria and Cilicia.
London, 1900.
Hogarth,O.G. 'Notes on Phrygia Paroreus and Lycaonia', JHS 11 (1890)
151-67.
Holleaux,M. Études d'Epigraphie et d'Histoire Grecques. Paris, 1942.
Hommel. 'Metoikoi', RE XV. 1413-57.
Honnigman,E. 'Historische Topographie von Nordsyrien im Altertum',
ZDPV 47 (1923) 149-93; 48 (1924) 1-64.
- 'Κυρρηστική', RE XII. 191-8.
- 'Sur Quelques Évêches d'Asie Mineure', Byzantion 4 (1935) 643-
54.
- 'Orontes', RE XVIII. 1. Col. 1163-4.
Hünerwadel,W. Forschungen zur Geschichte des Königs Lysimachus von

Thrakien. Zürich, 1900.
Jalabert,L. & Mouterde,R. Inscriptions grecques et Latines de la Syrie. Paris, 1929.
Jellicoe,S. The Septuagint and Modern Study. Oxford, 1968.
Jones,A.H.M. The Cities of the Eastern Roman Provinces. Oxford, 1971.
- The Greek City from Alexander to Justinian. Oxford, 1940.
Kahana,A. The Books of the Apocrypha. Tel-Aviv, 1956 (Hebrew).
Kähler,H. Der Fries von Reiterdenkmal des Aemilius Paulus in Delphi. Berlin, 1965.
Kahrstedt,U. Syrische Territorien in hellenistischen Zeit. Berlin, 1918.
Kallai,Z. 'An Attempt to Determine the Location of Beeroth', Eretz Israel 3 (1954) 111-15 (Hebrew).
Kalléris,J.N. Les anciens Macédoniens. Athens, 1954.
Kappler,W. Maccabaeorum Liber I. Göttingen, 1936.
Karmon,Y. The Northern Huleh Valley. Jerusalem, 1956 (Hebrew).
Kasher, A. The Civil Status of the Jews in Egypt and their Rights in the Hellenistic Period. Tel-Aviv, 1973 (Diss. Hebrew).
Kawerau,G. & Rehm,A. Das Delphinion in Milet. Berlin, 1914.
Keil,J. & Premerstein,A.V. 'Bericht über eine dritte Reise in Lydien', Denk. Akad. Wiss. Wien. 53. 2 (1908); 54. 2 (1911); 57.1 (1914) 1-122.
- 'Melampagos in Sipylosgebirge', Jahr. Österr. Arch. Instit. Wien. 1913, Beiblatt, 164-7.
- & Wilhelm,A. 'Vortäufiger Bericht über eine Reise in Kilikien', Jahreshefte, 1915, Beiblatt, 5-59.
Kiepert,H. A Manual of Ancient Geography. London, 1881.
- Formae Orbis Antiqui. Berlin, 1893.
Kiessling. 'Hyrkania', RE IX. 454-526.
Klein,S. 'Palästinisches in Jubiläenbuch', ZDPV 57 (1934) 7-27.
- The Land of Galilee. Jerusalem, 1938 (Hebrew).
- The Land of Judaea. Tel-Aviv, 1946 (Hebrew).
Kleiner,G. 'Priene', RE Suppl. IX. 1182-222.
Koerte,A. 'Inschriften aus Bithynien', AM 24 (1899) 398-450.
Kougeas,S.B. 'Διάγραμμα Στρατιωτικῆς Οἰκονομίας ἐκ Χαλκίδος', ΕΛΛΗΝΙΚΑ 6 (1934) 177-208.
Kraeling,C.H. 'The Jewish Community at Antioch', JBL 51 (1932) 130-60.

Krebs,W. 'Elefanten in den Heeren der Antike', Wissenschaftliche Zeitschrift der Universität Rostock, 13 (1964) 205-20.

Kroll. 'Karmania', RE X. 1955-6.

Kromayer,J. 'Die Entwicklung der römischen Flotte von Seeräuberkrieges des Pompeius bis zur Schlacht von Actium', Philologus 54 (1897) 426-91.

- 'Hannibal und Antiochus der Grossen', N. Jahr. Klass. Alt. 10 (1907) 681-99.
- & Veith,G. Heerwesen und kriegführung der Griechen und Römer. Munich, 1928.
- Antike Schlachtfelder in Griechenland. Berlin, 1903-31.
- Schlachtfelder Atlas zur Antiken Kriegsgeschichte. Leipzig, 1922.

Kümpel,E. Die Quellen zur Geschichte des Krieges der Römer gegen Antiochus III. Hamburg, 1893.

Kugler,F. Sternkunden und Sterndienst in Babel. Münster, 1907.

Lammert,E. 'Ἴλαι', RE IX. 997.

- 'Πεζέταιροι', RE XIX. 1412-4.
- 'Sarisse', RE IA. 2515-30.
- 'Thorax', RE VIA. 332-6.

Landau,Y.H. 'A Greek Inscription from Acre', IEJ 11 (1961) 117-26.

- 'A Greek Inscription found near Ḥefzibah', IEJ 16 (1966) 54-70.

Larsen,J.A.O. Greek Federal States. Oxford, 1968.

Lattey,C. The Book of Daniel. Dublin, 1918.

Launey,M. Recherches sur les armées hellénistiques. Paris, 1949.

Leake,W.M. Journal of a Tour in Asia Minor. London, 1824-6.

- Travels in Northern Greece. London, 1835.

Lesquier,J. Les Institutions militaires de l'Egypte sous les Lagides. Paris, 1911.

Leuze,O. 'Die Feldzüge Antiochus' des Grossen nach Kleinasien und Thrakien', Hermes 57 (1923) 269-77.

- Die Satrapieeinteilung in Syrien. Halle, 1955.

Levick,B. Roman Colonies in Southern Asia-Minor. Oxford, 1967.

Liebeschuetz,J.H.W.G. Antioch,City and Imperial Administration in the Later Roman Empire. Oxford, 1972.

Liebmann-Frankfort,T. L'antiquité classique 38 (1969) 101-20.

Lonis,R. Les usages de la Guerre entre Grecs et Barbares. Paris, 1969.

Lumbroso,G. Recherches sur l'Economie Politique de l'Egypt sous les Lagides. Turin, 1870.

Mac-Kay,P.A. 'Procopius' De Aedificiis and the Topography of Thermopylae', AJA 67 (1963) 241-55.

Mac-Shane,R.B. The Foreign Policy of the Attalids of Pergamon. Illinois, 1964.

Macurdy,G.H. Hellenistic Queens. Baltimore, 1932.

Magie,D. Roman Rule in Asia Minor. Princeton, 1950.

Mahaffy,J.P. 'The Army of Ptolemy IV at Raphia', Hermathena 13 (1899) 140-52.

- The Flinders Petrie Papyri. Dublin, 1891-1905.

Marcus,R. 'Antiochus III and the Jews'. Josephus (Loeb. ed.), Jewish Antiquities (trans.). London, 1943, vol. VII, 743-66.

Margovsky,I. 'The Survey at Raphia', Archeological News 3 (1969) 40 (Hebrew).

Marsden,E.W. Greek and Roman Artillery. Oxford, 1969-71.

- The Campaign of Gaugamela. Liverpool, 1964.

Matzat,H. Römische Zeitrechnung für die Jahre 219 bis 1 v. Chr. Berlin, 1889.

Mauersberger,A. Polybios Lexicon. Berlin, 1956-.

Melamed,E.Z. 'Josephus and I Maccabees: A Comparison', Eretz Israel 1 (1951) 122-30 (Hebrew).

Melber,J. 'Über die Quellen und den wert der Strategensammlung Polyäns', Jahr. Class. Phil. Suppl. 14 (1885) 415-688.

Mendel,G. Catalogue des Sculptures Grecques, Romaines et Byzantines. Constantinople, 1912.

Meritt,B.M. 'An Athenian Decree', Studies presented to D.M. Robinson. II. 299-303. St Louis, 1953.

Meyer,Ed. Blüte und Niedergang des Hellenismus in Asien. Berlin, 1925.

- 'Die Maked. Militärcolonien', Hermes 33 (1898) 643-7.

- 'Die Quellen unserer Überlieferung über Antiochus des Grossen Römerkrieg', Rhein. Mus. 36 (1881) 120-6.

- Ursprung und Anfänge des Christentums. Berlin, 1923.

Meyer,Ern. Die Grenzen der hellenistischen Staaten in Kleinasien. Göttingen, 1925.

Michalis,J.D. Deutsche Übersetzung des ersten Buchs der Maccabäer mit Anmerkungen. Göttingen, 1778.

Michel,Ch. Recueil d'inscriptions grecques. Brussels, 1896-1900.
Miller,F. Cassius Dio. Oxford, 1964.
Milne,J.G. 'Egyptian Nationalism under Greek and Roman Rule', JEA 14 (1928) 226-34.
Milns,R.D. 'Philip II and the Hypaspists', Historia 16 (1967) 509-11.
- 'The Hypaspists of Alexander', Historia 20 (1971) 186-95.
Minns,E.H. 'Parchments of the Parthian Period from Avroman in Kurdistan', JHS 35 (1915) 22-65.
Mitteis,L. 'Zwei griechische Rechtsurkunden aus Kurdistan', Z. Savigny-Stiftung, Röm. Abt. 36 (1915) 425-9.
Momigliano,A. Filippo il Macedone. Florence, 1934.
- Prime linee di storia della tradizione Maccabaica. Torino, 1931.
- 'U decreto trilingue in onore di Tolomeo Filopatore e la quarta guerra di Celesiria', Aegyptus 10 (1929) 180-9.
Mommsen,Th. Römische Geschichte. Berlin, 1888-94.
- Römischen Forschungen. Berlin, 1864-79.
Montgomery,J.M. The Book of Daniel. Edinburgh, 1927.
Mørkolm,O. Antiochus IV of Syria. Copenhagen, 1966.
Morrison,J.C. & Williams,R.T. The Greek Oared Ship. Cambridge, 1968.
Müller,C.O. Antiquitates Antiochenae. Göttingen, 1839.
Nellen,D. 'Zur Darstellung der Schlacht bei Sardes in den Quellen', AS 3 (1972) 45-54.
Newell,E.T. The Coinage of the Eastern SeleucidMints. New York, 1938.
- The Coinage of the Western Seleucid Mints. New York, 1941.
Niese,B. Geschichte der griechischen und makedonischen Staaten seit der Schlacht bei Chaeronea. Gotha, 1893-1903.
- 'Kritik der beiden Makkabäerbücher', Hermes 35 (1900) 268-307, 453-527.
- 'Eine Urkunde aus der Makkabäerzeit', Orientalische Studien Thoedor Nöldeke gewidmet II, 817-29. Gissen, 1906.
Nissen,H. Kritische Untersuchungen über die Quellen der vierten und fünften Dekade des Livius. Berlin, 1863.
Nitsche,W. König Philipps Brief an die Athener und Hieronymus von Kardia. Berlin, 1876.
Nussbaum,M. Observationes in Flavii Josephi Antiquitates (Diss, 1875).
Oertel,F. 'Katoikoi', RE XI. 1-26.

Oesterley,W.O.E. 'I Maccabees', ap. R.H. Charles, The Apocrypha and Pseudepigrapha of the Old Testament. Oxford, 1913.

Otto,W. 'Beiträge zur Seleukidengeschichte', Abh. d. Bayer. Akad. d. Wiss. Philos.-philol. Abt. hist. Klass. 34.1. Munich, 1928.

- 'Herakleides'(32), RE VIII. 1. 465-8.
- 'Hermeias' (1)', RE VIII. 1. 726-30.
- 'Hippolochos', RE VIII. 1862-3.
- Priester und Tempel im hellenistischen Ägypten. Leipzig, 1905-8.
- Zur Geschichte des Zeit des 6 Ptolemäers. Munich, 1934.
- & Bengtson,H. 'Zur Geschichte des Niederganges des Ptolemäerreiches', Abhand. d. Bayer. Akad. d. Wiss. Phil.-hist. Abt. N.F. 17 (1938).

Parke,H.W. Greek Mercenary Soldiers. Oxford, 1933.

Pédech,P. 'Deux campagnes d'Antiochus III chez Polybe', REA 60 (1958) 67-81.

- La Méthode Historique de Polybe. Paris, 1964.

Permans,W. 'Notes sur la bataille de Raphia', Aegyptus 36 (1951) 214-22.

Plöger,O. 'Die Feldzüge der Seleukiden gegen den Makkabäer Judas', ZDPV 74 (1958) 158-88.

Possenti,C.B. Il re Lisimacho di Tracia. Torino, 1901.

Powell,J.U. Collectanea Alexandrina. Oxford, 1925.

Préaux,C. L'économie royale des Lagides. Brussels, 1939.

- 'L'évolution de la tenure clerouchique sous les Lagides', Recueils de la Société Jean Bodin, III, La Tenure (1938) 41-57.
- 'Esquisse d'une histoire des revolutions égyptiennes sous les Lagides', Chronique d'Égypte 11 (1936) 522-52.
- 'Polybe et Ptolomée Philomator', Chronique d'Égypte 40 (1965) 364-75.

Pritchett,W.R. Studies in Ancient Greek Topography. Berkeley, 1965-9.

Radet,G. De coloniis a Macedonibus in Asiam cis Taurum deductis. Paris, 1892.

- 'Ipsos et la bataille de 301', REA 38 (1936) 263.

Rahlfs,A. 'Die Kriegselefanten im I.Makkabäerbuche', ZAW 52 (1934) 78-9.

Ramsay,W.M. The Cities and Bishoprics of Phrygia. Oxford, 1897.

- 'Contributions to the History of Southern Aeolis', JHS 2

(1881) 44-56, 271-308.
- The Historical Geography of Asia Minor. London, 1890.

Rattenbury,R.M. 'An Ancient Armoured Force', CR 56 (1942) 113-16.

Rawlinson,G. Parthia. London, 1883.

Reinech,A.J. 'Les mercenaries et les colonies militaires de Pergame', RA 12 (1908) 174-218, 364-89; 13 (1909) 102-19, 363-77.

Reinach,Sal. 'Eléphant foulant aux pieds un Galate', BCH 9 (1885) 485-93.
- La nécropole de Myrina. Paris, 1887.

Reinach,Th. Papyrus grecs et démotiques. Paris, 1905 (P Rein.).

Reinhardt,K. 'Poseidonios', RE XXII. 1. 558-826.

Renan,Ern. Mission de Phenicie. Paris, 1862.

Robert,L. Études Anatoliennes. Paris, 1937.
- Etudes épigraphiques et Philologiques. Paris, 1938.
- 'Inscriptions Seleucides de Phrygie et d'Iran', Hellenica 7 (1949) 5-29.
- 'Le Culte de Caligula à Milet et la province d'Asie', Hellenica 7 (1949) 206-38.
- Opera Minora Selecta. Amsterdam, 1969.
- Villes d'Asie Mineure. Paris, 1935.

Robinson,E. Biblical Researches in Palestine. London, 1838-41.

Rostovzeff,M. 'A Parchment Contract of Loan from Dura Europus on the Euphrates', Yale Class. Studies 2 (1931) 1-77.
- 'Angariae', Klio 6 (1906) 249-58.
- Studien zur Geschichte des römischen kolonates, Archiv für Papyrusforschung Beiheft I. Leipzig, 1910.
- The Social and Economic History of the Hellenistic World. Oxford, 1940 (SEHHW).

Roussel,P. 'Décret des Péliganes de Laodicée-sur-mer', Syria 23 (1942-3) 21-32.
- 'Un règlement militaire de l'époque Macedonienne', RA 6 sér. 3 (1934) 39-47.
- Alexandre et l'hellénisation du Monde antique (Histoire Grecque IV). Paris, 1938.

Rudberg,G. Forschungen zu Poseidonius. Uppsala, 1918.

Ruge. 'Synnada', RE IV.A. 1410-12.

Ruppel,W. 'Politeuma-Bedeutungsgeschichte eines staatsrechtlichen Terminus', Philologus 82 (1926-7) 268-312, 431-51.

Russel,D.A. 'Plutarch's Life of Coriolanus', JRS 53 (1963) 21-8.
Rüstow,W. & Köchly,S. Geschichte des griechischen Kriegwesens. Leipzig, 1852.
Sachs,A.J. & Wiseman,D.J. 'A Babylonian King List of the Hellenistic Period', Iraq 16.2 (1954) 202-12.
de Sanctis,G. 'Il regolmento militaire dei Macedoni', Riv. di Fil. 12 (1934) 515-21.
- Storia dei Romani. Torino, 1923.
Sânda,A. 'Untersuchungen zur Kunde des Alten Orients', Mitteilungen der Vorderasiatische Gesellschaft 7 (1902) 1-79.
Schachermeyr,F. 'Zur Geschichte und Staatrecht der frühen Diadochen Zeit', Klio 19 (1925) 435-61.
Schaefer,H. 'Paroikoi', RE XVIII^4, 1696-1707.
Schalit,A. König Herodes. Berlin, 1969.
- 'The Letter of Antiochus III to Zeuxis regarding the establishment of Jewish Military Colonies in Phrygia and Lydia', JQR 49 (1960) 289-318.
Schaumberger,J. 'Die neue Seleukidenliste BM 35603 und die makkabäischen Chronologie', Biblica 36 (1955) 423-35.
Schmitt,H.H. Untersuchungen zur Geschichte Antiochus' des Grossen und seiner Zeit (Historia, Einzelschr. VI). Wiesbaden, 1964.
Schubert,R. Die Quellen zur Geschichte der Diadochen Zeit. Leipzig, 1914.
- Die Quellen Plutarchs in den Lebenschreibungen des Eumenes, Demetrius und Pyrrhus. Leipzig, 1878.
Schuchardt,C. 'Makedonischen Colonien zwischen Hermos und Kaikos', AM 10 (1885) 1-17.
Schulten,A. 'Die Makedonischen Militärcolonien', Hermes 32 (1897) 523-37.
Schulthess. 'Γραμματεῖς', RE VII, 1708-79.
Schunk,K.D. Die Quellen des I und II Makkabäerbuches. Halle, 1954.
Schürer,E. Geschichte des jüdischen volkes im Zeitalter Jesu Christi^4. Lepizig, 1901-11.
Schwartz,Ed. 'Appianus', RE II. 216-337.
Schwyzer,Ed. Dialectorum Graecarum exempla epigraphica potiora. Leipzig, 1923.
Segal,J.B. Edessa, 'the Blessed City'. Oxford, 1970.
Segrè,M. 'Iscrizioni di Licia', Clara Rhodos 9 (1938) 181-208.

Segrè,M. 'Popolazione e superficie dell' Egitto nell' eta greco-
romana', Bull. Soc. Arch. Alex. 29 (1934) 257-305.
Seibert,J. Untersuchungen zur Geschichte Ptolemaios' I. Munich,
1969.
Seyrig,H. 'Décret de Seleucie et ordonnance de Seleucus IV', Syria
13 (1932) 255-8.
Smith,Sidney. Babylonian Historical Texts. London, 1907.
Snodgrass,A.M. Arms and Armour of the Greeks. London, 1967.
Spendel,A. Untersuchungen zum Heerwesen der Diadochen. Breslau,
1915.
Spiegelberg,W. 'Beiträge zur Erklärung des neuen dreisprachigen
Priesterdekretes zu Ehren des Ptolemaios Philopator', S.-B.
München, 1925, Anh. 4, pp.1-30.
Spuler,B. 'Platanus', RE XX. 2. 2338-9.
Stählin,F. Das Hellenische Thessalien. Stuttgart, 1924.
- Geschichte der Kleinasiatischen Galater. Leipzig, 1907.
Steinwender,Th. Die Sarissa und ihre gefichtmässige Führung.
Danzig, 1909.
Stern,M. 'Josephus' Historiographical Method'. Historians and Historical
Schools (Lectures delivered at the seventh convention of the
Historical Society of Israel), Jerusalem, 1962, 22-8 (Hebrew).
- 'Notes to the Story of Joseph, Son of Tobiah', Tarbitz 32
(1962-3) 35-47 (Hebrew).
- The Documents on the History of the Hasmonaean Revolt. Tel-
Aviv, 1965 (Hebrew).
- 'The Political Background of the Wars of Alexander Janaeus',
Tarbitz 33 (1963-4) 325-36 (Hebrew).
Stier,H.E. Roms Aufstieg zur Weltmacht und die griechische Welt.
Cologne, 1957.
Strack,M.L. 'Griechische Titel im Ptolemäerreich', Rhein. Mus.
N.F. 55 (1900) 161-90.
Strassmaier,J.N. 'Zur Chronologie der Seleuciden', Zeitschr.f.
Ass. 8 (1893) 107-13.
Streck,M. 'Das Gebiet der heutigen Landschaften Armenien,
Kurdistan und West Persien nach den babylonisch - assyrischen
Keilinschriften', Zeitschr. f. Ass. 12 (1898) 57-115.
- 'Labbunal und Laban', Zeitschr. f. Ass. 20 (1907) 456-60.
Summer,G.V. 'The Legion and Centuriate Organization', JHS 55 (1970)

67-78.

Susemihl,F. Geschichte der griechischen Literatur. Leipzig, 1891-2.

Swartz,Ed. 'Duris', RE V. 1853-8.

Sweet,W.E. 'Sources of Plutarch's Demetrius', CW 44 (1951) 177-81.

Swete,H.B. An Introduction to the Old Testament in Greek (Revised by R.R. Ottley). New York, 1968.

Swoboda,H. Lehrbuch der griechischen Staatsaltertümer. Tübingen, 1913.

Tarn,W.W. Alexander the Great. Cambridge, 1948.
- Antigonus Gonatas. Oxford, 1913.
- Hellenistic Military and Naval Developments. Cambridge, 1930.
- 'Polybius and a Literary Commonplace', CQ 20 (1926) 98-100.
- 'The Date of Milet, I. III. no. 139', Hermes 65 (1930) 446-54.
- 'Seleucid Parthian Studies', Proc. Brit. Acad. 16 (1930) 1-33.
- The Greeks in Bactria and India. Cambridge, 1938.
- 'The First Syrian War', JHS 46 (1926) 156-62.
- 'The Oarage of Greek Warships', Mariner's Mirror 19 (1933) 52-74.
- 'The Proposed New Date for Ipsus', CR 40 (1926) 13-15.
- 'Two Notes on Seleucid History', JHS 60 (1940) 84-9.
- Review. F.W. Walbank, Philip V of Macedon, JRS 31 (1941) 172-3.
- & Griffith,G.T. Hellenistic Civilization. London, 1952.

Taubler,E. 'Jerusalem 210 to 199 B.C.', JQR 37 (1946-7) 1-30, 249-64.

Thackeray,H.St.J. Josephus the Man and Historian. New York, 1929.

Thomsen,S. 'Die römischen Meilsteine der Provinzen Syria, Arabia und Palaestina', ZDPV 40 (1917) 1-103.

Torrey,C.C. The Apocryphal Literature. London, 1963.
- 'Three Troublesome Proper Names in First Maccabees', JBL 53 (1934) 31-3.

Tscherikover,V. Die hellenistischen Städtgründungen von Alexander dem Grossen bis auf die Römer Zeit. Philologus Suppl. - IX.1. Leipzig, 1927.
- Hellenistic Civilization and the Jews. Philadelphia, 1961.
- The Jews and the Greeks. Tel-Aviv, 1963.
- The Jews in Egypt. Jerusalem, 1963.
- The Jews in the Greco-Roman World. Tel-Aviv, 1961.

Tsoar,H. Sand Dunes of El-Arish Area. Jerusalem, 1970 (Diss. Hebrew).

Vernant,J.P. (edit.) Problèmes de la guerre en Grèce ancienne. Paris, 1968.
Vilnay,Z. Judaea and Samaria. Tel-Aviv, 1968.
Volkmann,H. 'Demetrios I und Alexander I von Syrien', Klio 19 (1925) 373-412.
- 'Ptolemaios (43)', RE XXIII^2, Coll. 1762-3.
Walbank,F.W. A Historical Commentary on Polybius. Oxford, 1957-67.
- Philip V of Macedon. Cambridge, 1940.
Watson,G.R. The Roman Soldier. London, 1970.
Webster,G. The Roman Imperial Army. London, 1969.
Wehrli,C. Antigone et Demetrios. Geneva, 1969.
Weidner,E.F. Die Inschriften der altassyrischen Könige. Leipzig, 1926.
Weissbach. 'Elymais', RE V. 2458-67.
- 'Kyros', RE Suppl. IV. 1128-77.
Welles,C.B. 'New Texts from the Chancery of Philip V of Macedonia and the Problem of the "Diagrama"', AJA 42 (1938) 245-60.
- Royal Correspondence in the Hellenistic Period. New Haven, 1934.
- 'The Constitution of Edessa', Yale Class. Studies 5 (1935) 121-42.
- 'The Greek City', Studi in onore di A. Calderini e R. Paribeni. Milan, 1956, 81-99.
- & Fink,R.D., Gilliam,J.F. The Parchments and Papyri. Doura Europos, Final Report, V. 1. New Haven, 1959.
Westlake,R.H. 'The Sources of Plutarch's Timoleon', CQ 32 (1938) 65-74.
Whatley,W. 'On the Possibility of Reconstructing Marathon and Other Ancient Battles', JHS 84 (1964) 119-39.
Wibbing,S. 'Zur Topographie einzelner Schlachten des Judas Makkabäus', ZDPV 78 (1962) 159-70.
Wilcken,U. 'Ein Beitrag zur Seleukidengeschichte', Hermes 29 (1894) 436-50.
Will,É. Histoire Politique du Monde Hellénistique. Nancy, 1966.
Willrich,H. Urkundenfälschung in der hellenistisch-jüdischen Literatur. Göttingen, 1924.
Wirgin,W. 'Judah Maccabee's Embassy to Rome and the Jewish-Roman Treaty', PEQ 101 (1969) 15-20.
Woodcock,G. The Greeks in India. London, 1966.

Wroth,W. Catalogue of the Greek Coins of Galatia, Cappadocia and
    Syria. London, 1899.
 - 'Eupolemus', Num. Chron. 3 ser. 11 (1891) 135-9.
Yeivin,S. 'Ashdod Ha'har', BJPES 8 (1941) 83-4 (Hebrew).
 - 'Asher', Biblical Encyclopaedia (Jerusalem, 1955) I. 777-86
    (Hebrew).
Zeitlin,S. The First Book of Maccabees. New York, 1950.
Ziegler,K. 'Timarchos'[5], RE VI. AI. 1237-8.

ADDENDA

Addenda are keyed by the sign † in the margin of the relevant page.

14 According to a Babylonian cuneiform chronicle Antiochus
Epiphanes died in Persia sometime during the first half of
November or December 164 (see: A.J. Sachs & D.J. Wiseman, Iraq
16.2 (1954) 308). The expedition to Beith-Zacharia took place
no earlier than April 162 (I Macc. 6.20, according to the
Babylonian systems, see p.210 n.29 below). As more than two
years elapsed between Antiochus' death and this expedition it
seems likely that some of the troops came back to Antioch long
before the expedition, and the force under Philippos which
threatened the capital (I Macc. 6.55-6) comprised garrison
troops who were left behind to control the rebelious eastern
regions and perhaps even military settlers of the Upper
Satrapies. At any rate, even if security in these regions
deteriorated considerably after Antiochus' death, Lysias, the
regent, would not have allowed himself to confine the bulk of
the imperial army to the eastern satrapies for another two
years in the first years of his effective rule, and had he lost
control of them and had they actually refused to come back, he
could hardly be expected to endanger Antioch by trying to over-
power the Jews before settling the more urgent internal crisis.
It must be added that the date given by II Macc. 6.21 for the
battle of Beith-Zacharia (year 149 i.e. April 163 - April 162),
being also an 'internal' one, cannot be reconciled with that
of I. Macc. (contra J. Schaumberger, Biblica 36 (1955) 430).
The dates in II Macc. for events after the purification of the
temple are generally incorrect, see e.g. 9-10, 11.23-6, 14.1.
Note also that the effects of the sabbatical year mentioned in
I Macc. 6.53, which began in the autumn of 164 (see Schürer,[4] I
35-6), were strongly felt in besieged Jerusalem only in spring
162. I Macc. 6.49,53 do not necessarily indicate that the

Addenda

page

14 expedition took place in the sabbatical year.

40 The possibility that the military settlements were manned also by 'lights' was rightly discounted. It would have been redundant to settle troops of this sort, who could easily be acquired from among the native populations of the Empire. At any rate, an examination of the population of military age in the settlements of Syria and Mesopotamia suggests that it was equal in number to the available phalangites from these regions (see p.44) and therefore does not allow for any 'lights' from these settlements. The OGIS 229 inscription provides a good illustration: the settlement in Magnesia was occupied by settlers who belonged to phalanx and cavalry units (see pp. 26,56-8 above) while mercenaries who resided 'under the open sky', i.e. on the fringe of the settlement, did not own land there (p.214 n.15 above). The latter are certainly identical with the Persians, presumably archers, who were not allotted lands even at the time of the great crises of the Laodicean War (p.57 above).

41 The numerical estimate of the military settlers based on the heavy troops includes the 10,000 argyraspides, the infantry Guard, and 2,000 cavalry Guard, both composed of the younger generation of the settlers (see pp.60-2,70 above). Consequently the number of kleroi can be arrived at by deducting the number of Guardsmen.

45 Examination of the nationalities in the Seleucid phalangites south of the Taurus indicates that local elements of oriental origin were not included in the heavy infantry. This practice undoubtedly derived from the fear of turning the Empire's pride and joy, the symbol of Macedonian strength, over to the local population, which might have encouraged internal ferment as happened in Ptolemaic Egypt after the battle of Raphia. On the other hand, in Asia Minor we find Jews and Persians who may well have been phalangites, but they were alien corn among the locals and consequently identified more with the central government and could be trusted. For this reason, the 'Myso-

Addenda

page

45 Macedonians' referred to in these regions (see p.228 n.113) are more likely to have been Macedonians settled in Mysia than native Mysians. This policy was reversed by the second half of the second century B.C. at the time of the internal struggle at Antioch, when the pretenders to the throne were short of manpower and therefore allowed local orientals to form phalanx contingents (see e.g. I Macc. 10.71,82, and in detail: B. Bar-Kochva, Scripta Classica Israelica 2 (1975, forthcoming)).

52 It is difficult to decide whether the Jews who repulsed the Galatians at Babylonia in 235 B.C. (II Macc. 8.20, see B. Bar-Kochva, Proc.Cambr.Phil.Soc. N.S. 19 (1973) 5-7) were 'lights' or military settlers serving as phalangites. As has already been stated the Seleucid phalangites in Daphne were almost equal in number to the Greco-Macedonian settlers in Syria and Babylonia (p.44 above), but it might be suggested that Jewish settlers were not mobilized at that time due to the revolt in Judaea. The possibility that they were phalangites is supported by the absence of any contingent of Jews in the 'light' national contingents at Raphia and Magnesia. On the other hand, this absence can be explained by their involvement in routine security assignments in Babylonia (for which phalangites would not have been left behind).

129 Momigliano's suggestion that Zeno of Rhodes should be seen as Polybius' source for Raphia must be discounted in view of Polybius' sharp criticism of Zeno's work, and his lack of regard for the latter as a describer of battles.

134 Exposing the Seleucid cavalry wings to a possible charge by the Ptolemaic elephants would have been much more significant to the outcome of the battle than leaving the light infantry unprotected against phalangites. As the horses could have overtaken the elephants and confrontation of cavalry troops would have been decided much faster than duels between elephants, owing to their speed and mobility, it means that Ptolemy actually 'neutralized' Antiochus' superior elephant-force by forcing him to deploy them in front of the wing's cavalry.

Addenda

page

156 On the various meanings of the term 'phalanx' see H. Droysen, <u>Geschichte des griechischen Kriegswesens</u>, 171 n.3, and cf. e.g. Polyb. 1.33.6, 2.37.7, 115.12.

177 (a) According to II Macc. Judas Maccabaeus even followed the Seleucid army before it climbed up Mt Hebron (12.14-15) and stayed some time near Beith Sour to help the besieged population (12.19-20).

177 (b) In determining the site of the battle and the route to the battlefield it must be remembered that I Macc. is invariably precise as to topographical descriptions. Despite his tendency towards biblical associations he locates the first battle against Nicanor in the hamlet of Kefar Salama (7.31), despite the fact that Giv'on, which is so well known from biblical times and the victories of the early Israelites, is situated nearby on the opposite hill to the south. On the identification of Kefar Salama see Abel, <u>Maccabées</u>, 138-9.

185 The rejection of the low figures attributed to the Jewish force is based on several considerations. The exaggerated figures given for the Seleucid armies (see pp.12-15 above) themselves suggest that the strength of the Jewish army might be underestimated. The Books of the Maccabees do not differ in this respect from other ancient historians who, even when accurate in their battle descriptions, always tended to distort the relative strengths of the contenders. In order to arrive at a more reasonable estimate, attention must be paid to demographical data, documents, 'slips of pen' in the sources and analyses of the battle descriptions (provided they can be trusted) combined with features of the terrain. These methods are applicable to the battles of the Maccabees. As far as battle descriptions are concerned, I Macc. can be regarded as one of the most accurate works of ancient military historiography. The features of the terrain fit in with the course of the battles, and, furthermore, the data on the tactical composition of the Seleucid detachments, their commanders, arms, deployment and tactical methods can be established. I

Addenda

page

185 Macc. is unreliable only with regard to battles about which he evidently did not have any real information (see the brief narrative of 3.10-12, 4.34-5). His general reliability is reinforced by comparison with the dubious descriptions of II Macc. on the one hand, and the independent version of the battle of Beith Zacharia in <u>Bell</u>. 1.41-6 (see p.176 above) on the other. The abundance of biblical phrases and associations does not discredit the reliability of the military information because they almost always have a factual basis. Nevertheless, it must be stressed that, like those of other historians, the narrative of I Macc. is elliptical and selective, never covers the whole battlefield, and from time to time deliberately omits information which might interest the historian. Likewise, I Macc. is indistinguishable from his contemporaries in reports of speeches attributed to military leaders: they are always the author's pure invention and contribute only to the understanding of his historiographical purposes and religious beliefs.

186 When this book was already in proof it came to my attention that Avi-Yonah, in a recent publication, expressed the view that the Jewish force after the purification of the temple numbered 22,000 men, although he does not elaborate on this and is content with saying: 'Judah set out for Gilead with eight thousand men, while his brother Simeon headed for Galilee with three thousand. Since we know that the two other commanders, Joseph ben Zechariah and Azariah remained in Judaea, and since it is not likely that the Hasmonean brothers withdrew more than half their men out of Judaea, it may be assumed that they had 22,000 men at their disposal at a time', see M. Avi-Yonah, 'The Hasmonean Revolt and Judah Maccabee's War against the Syrians', <u>ap</u>. A. Schalit (ed.), <u>The Hellenistic Age</u>, The World History of the Jewish People (Jerusalem 1972), p.167.

197 The arguments raised above about the deliberate 'silence' of the Book of Maccabees about the real figures of the Jewish army and its tactical composition may seemingly be challenged

Addenda

page

197 by the description of Simon's battle against the governor Kendebaios in the Ayālōn Valley in 140 B.C. which refers to 20,000 Jewish combatants who also included horsemen (I Macc. 16.4). But it must be borne in mind that the character of the narrative changes from ch. 14 onwards, after the proclamation of independence. Thereafter the emphasis is on Simon's royal (or rather presidential) pomp, his extension of the borders, diplomatic relations, the development of ports, and general affluence and security. Simon is said to have been appointed as <u>stratēgos</u> whose duty was to see to manpower, armaments and fortifications (14.42), and the author is eager to show that he performed his duties satisfactorily. Nonetheless I do not rule out the well known suggestion (based on other considerations) that ch. 14-16 of I Macc. are a later addition. The deployment of cavalry in the Jewish army among the infantry (I Macc. 16.7), a procedure which deviates from stereotypical Hellenistic tactics, further suggests that by the time of Simon the Jews were well acquainted with cavalry warfare.

INDEX

Afrin(river),114
Abae,61
Achaeans,55,74,86,142,166,233 n.15
Achaeus,18,31,41-2,94,208
Acre,128,222 n.84,256 n.7
Adasa,27,184,194-5,268 n.2
adekateutoi,57-8
Aegae,36
Aegean(sea),16,158,163
Aetolians,19,30,51,100,146,148, 150,153-4,156-8,160
Agathocles,111
agēma,21,33,42,58-9,64-5,67-75, 134,166,168-70,180,202
Agrianians,50,221 n.72
akontists,50,108,119,251 n.11
akra,261 n.4
Akra(Jerusalem),128,175
akrophylakitai,32
alae(Latin),165-8,170-1
Alcimos,192
alertness,97-9,100
Alexander(army of),1,7,10,34-5, 54-5,58-9,63-4,67,72,74,96, 138,148,205-6
Alexandria(stelae of),111
Amanus,112,200,206
ambush,142,179,209 n.21
Ammaus,13,100,267 n.15
Amphipolis(Macedon),55,97,235 n.40
Amphipolis(Mesopotamia),28
Amyzon,92
Ancyra,92
Andromachus,139
Andronicus,148
Anthedon,27
Antigonids(army of),58,63,68, 71,92-3,105-16
Antigonos Monophthalmos,29,77, 105-10,201,207 n.2,252 n.7
Antioch(Syria),29-30,39,71,81
Antiochus I,55,58,63,78,107
Antiochus III,3,8,9,10,15-19, 35,41,43,49,56,64,74-6,79,80, 82,85,89,95,117,121-2,124,127, 135-8,142,155,161,170-5,180, 200,203,205,206
Antiochus the Elder(son of Antiochus III),148,152,155
Antiochus IV,13,14,56,80,83,85, 87,89,118,149,151,155,226 n.103
Antiochus V,148,174,257 n.9
Antiochus VII(Sidetes),9-11,30, 85-7,100
Antiochus VIII(Grypus),97
Antiochus Hierax,86,218 n.36
Antipater,30
Apollonia,Apollonitis,117,119
apoikia,35
aposkeuē,8,100-2,109,145,153, 162,200,206
Arabs,49,136
Arbēl,188-91
archers,55,108-9,126,144,155, 161,167,172,251 n.11,264 n.29
Ardys,88
Arethusa,27
argyraspides,9,20-1,40-1,46,58- 62,64-6,73,88,90,135-7,140, 161-2,166,168-9,172,202-3,207 n.8,213 n.5
Ariarathes,48,51
armour(breastplates,cuirass), 54-6,59,66,74-5,144-5,180
Arsaces,142
artillery,75,161,261 n.12
Asia Minor,11,18,26,30,37-8,41-5, 50,52,69-70,111,129,138,142
Aspasianus,87
ateleia,57
Athenians,29,212 n.40
Attalus I,41,264 n.26
Autriatai,248 n.21
auxiliaries,48-53,122,169,170,172
Avroman,32
Axios,27
Azōtos,193,196-7

Ba'al Ḥaṣōr,189,191,193,195,199, 200
Babylonia,37,52,78,117,184,195
Bacchides,15,86,184-200

Bactria,10,62-3,69,77-8,85,224 n.95
Balas(Alexander),31,61,70,81, 85,148
Bānyas Plateau,153
Bataneia,35,258 n.14
Beēr Zayit,273 n.29
Beēra,27,192
Beith Sour,73,174-5,177,179
Beith Zacharia,14,19,55,73,75, 80,82,174-83,197,199,203-4, 232 n.8
Bēt El,187,189-92
booty,197
Bouplagos,93
Brochoi,149
Brundisium,158
Byttacus,88

Cadusians,50,212 n.36
Callidromus,160,162
camp,91,100-1,109,133-4,150-1, 153,162,165,171,191-2,200, 207 n.7,267 n.15
Cappadocians,18,76,166,169
Cardaces,50,217 n.27,229 n.131
Carians,51
Carmanians,49,50
cataphracts,69,74-5,148,155-6, 166,168,170-1,227 n.106,253 n.10
Cato,96,102
cavalry,33,42-3,67-75,89-93, 107-9,129,132-4,136-8,148, 153-4,168-9,171,181,183, 194-5,263 n.13
Chalchanlyan Pass,142
chalkaspides,56
Chandragupta,76,79
chariots,73,83-4,107-8,169, 171-2,205
Cheronesus,27
chiliarchies,65,68,71,92,98
chōra,216 n.25
chōrion,37-8
chrysaspides,56
Cilicia,Cilicians,36,49,51-2
cleruchies,cleruchs,43,47,87, 213 n.10,218 n.33
cohors,207 n.8,208 n.9
Coile Syria,13,35-6,86,124, 128-9,146
condition of service,100-1
Cophanis,33
Craterus,236 n.50
Cretans,18,25,30,48-9,51,71,82,
90,132,134,144,166,171
Cunaxa,205
Curupedion,85,163
cursus honorum,89-90
Cynoscephalae,119,172-3,259 n.22
Cyrrhus,Cyrrhestica,27,29,30-1, 39,41,64-5,85,87,100,111-16, 129,204
Cyrtians,48,51,117-18

Dahae,49,51,166,168,170,212 n.36
Damascus,149, 257 n.12
Damouras,149
Daphne,7,9,13,14,30,40-3,48,52, 55-6,59,60,68,73-5,80-1,84
dekas,66-7
Demetrias,16,158,160
Demetrius I,15,36,77,85,184
Demetrius II,21,28,30,59,60,70, 89,148
Demetrius Poliorcetes,35,83,105-16
Diadochs,Successors(armies),7, 58,64,68,71,74,100
Diocles,88
Diogenes,88
Diognetus,88
Diophanes,99
Diophantus,61
Dor,222 n.84
doryphoroi,98
Dositheus,194,197
Doura Europos,31,39,43
Duris(of Samos),105

Ecbatana,32
Edessa,27
Edomaeans,13,174,210 n.28
Egypt,24,45-7,58,93,201,213 n.10
Egyptians,65,87
Elasa,14,184-200,210 n.29
Elburz,59,62,85,90,142-5,182, 204,267 n.20
Eleazar,83,175,182-3
elephants,55,73,75-83,107-9,119, 133-4,137,148-9,154-6,158,161, 167,171,175,177,180-1,183, 203-4,236 n.50
elephantarch,88,90-1,248 n.18
eleutheroi,30
Elymaeans,48,50-1,119,212 n.36
emergency appointments,91
Epaminondas,56
ephodos,97
epigonoi,141
Epigenes,121

epilektoi,67,73,180
Euboea,95
Eumenes(of Cardia),56,58
Eumenes II,171,217
Eupolemus,217 n.27
Europos(Media),32
Eurylochus,88

Flamininus,Titus Quinctius,16, 74
flight,pursuit,rout,96,108-9, 136-8,170-1,193,195,200, 205-6

Gadara,35
Galatians,18,19,26,34,44,51-2, 63,78,99,119,132,166,169,204, 208 n.10,215 n.21
Galilee,185,188,257 n.14
Gaugamela,7,205,230 n.140
Gaza,68,82,85,107,128-9,132-4, 270 n.9
Gazigöl Hammam,108
Gerasa,35
Gerrha,119
Giladitis,35,185,189
Gilgāl,188-91
Gofnitis,Gōfnā,176,183
Golanitis,35,150
Gorgias,74,185-6,194,267 n.15
Granikos,251 n.11
Greek(officers,mercenaries),18, 48-9,87,119,135
Guard: infantry,55,58-66,88,94, 96,140,202;
  cavalry,67-75,85,107, 135,207 n.8
Gurob(papyrus),30,92
gymnasium,94

Halūṣā sands,131
Hannibal,142,172,239 n.78
hastati,263 n.12
hegemōn,91-3
Heraclea(Media),32
Heracleides,211 n.30
Heracleon(of Beroea),97,101
Hermeias,89,98,121
Hermogenes,88
hetairoi(Companions,regia ala, hippos hetairikē,ilē basilikē), 62,64,67-75,92,119,134,153, 166,169,180
Hierapolis,215 n.19
Hieronymus(of Cardia),76-7,105, 112

hipparchia,75,93
hipparchos,91-3
Hippos,35
Hippolochos,88-9
hoplitagōgai,17-18
Ḥuleh valley,150,152,257 n.14
hypaithroi,57,214 n.15
hyparchoi,93,223 n.89
hypaspists,58,64-5,73,116,207 n.8
Hyrcanian Plain,225 n.97
Hyrcanus(son of Joseph),197

Iamnia,222 n.84
ilē,72,75,168,207 n.8
India,77-9,154,203
instructors(military),94
Ionian cities,25-6,37,111,163
Ipsus,58,72,76-8,82-3,85,105-10, 137,203,204-5,208 n.10,266 n.8
Iranians,33,42,45,202
Issos,251 n.11

Jaffa,222 n.84
Jerusalem,174-5,179,184,187
Jews(Diaspora),29,34,36,43,45, 48,80,83,87,197-8,213 n.8,251 n.2
Jonathan,186,194,196-8,270 n.8
Judaea,13-14,80-1,86,174-200
Justinian,160

katoikia,katoikoi,22-6,29,33-4, 39,41,43,45-6,57-8,213 nn.10, 12,214 nn.15,19,215 n.21,216 nn.22,25
Kefar Shan,131
keras,154-5,275 n.34
Kerkeosiris,43,224 n.95
kleros,land allotments,21-2,29, 31-2,34-5,37-8,46,57-8,60,201, 226 n.97
komē,23,33,37
Korakesion,218 n.35
Kurdaruz Pass,119

Lagoras,88,90
Laodicea,32
laoi,217 n.27
Larissa(Syria),21,27-8,70,238 n.59
Larissa(Thessaly),180
Leon,93
Lebanon(mountain),128
Lebanon(valley),149,257 n.14
Leonnatus,237 n.50

Lepidus,Marcus Aemilius,170
leukaspides,56
Libyans,21,45
light infantry,'missile troops',
   48-53,55,63,107-8,119,121,
   131,132-4,144-5,160-1,180,
   196,204
lochos,66
luxury,96,99,100,128
Lycians,51
Lydia,21,25-6,37-8,43-4,63
Lydians,50,69-70
Lysias,13,81,84,86,177,179
Lysimachus,106-7

Maccabees,Hasmoneans,2,12-15,19
Maccabaeus,Judas,15,19,36,81,
   174-200,206,209 n.21
Macedonian style(arms,tactics),
   59,63,138,237 n.50,253 n.15,
   254 n.17
Macedonians,20-2,25,27-8,30-4,
   36,39,40,44-5,54,56,59,60,
   62,69,71-3,86-8,171,201,215
   n.19,217 nn.27,29,237 n.55
machimoi,136,139-41,221 n.68,
   254 n.24,258 n.15
Magnesia(ad Sipylum),7,8-9,21-
   3,38-40,44,57-8,214,225 n.97
Magnesia(battle of),30,48,51-2,
   59,68-9,74-5,80,82-3,85,96,
   163-73,205-6,207 n.7,270 n.9
Magnesia(on the Maeander),28
maintenance(arms),97
maniple,263 n.12
marches(route),65,69,75-6,95,
   129,191,204
Marisa,186,194
Marsyas valley,124
Medes,44,50,69,70,74,122,212
   n.36
Media,10,11,32,37,42-3,45,50,
   69,70,72,111,114,117,132,202
Megalopolis,157
Megara(Syria),29
Megasthenes,76
Mendis,88
Menedamus,88,127
Menippus,88
mercenaries,48-53,57,64,72,101-
   2,119,201,270 n.12
meridarchēs,93
meros,155,167,193,275 n.34
Mesopotamia,21,31,42-4,52,117
metoikoi,215 n.18
Miletus,25

Mişpa,73
Mnesimachus,225 n.97,228 n.120
Molon,18,31-3,42,59,70,74,79,83,
   85-8,94,98,117-23,132,203-4
morale,101,165,172
mounted archers,167-8,182,248
   n.15
Mygdones,27
Mylasa,217 n.27
Mysians,34,41,45,51-2
Myso-Macedonians,228 n.113

Nabis,157
Nakrasa,44
Naolaos,121
Nasica,261 n.17
Neoptolemus,236 n.50
Nicanor,15,81,91,184,187,192,195
Nicarchus,88,91,136
Nicolaus(of Damascus),14,176
Nicolaus(Aetolian),88,144
Nicomedes,215 n.21
night watch,96-7,100,162
Nisaeans,42,74,227 n.107

Oborzos,33
ochloi,30,95
Octavius,Gnaius,81
oulamos,75
outflanking,encircling,etc.,108-9,
   116,122-3,133,135-8,153,169,
   172,199,251 n.11

paides basilikoi,208 n.9
Palai Magnesia,29,32,35,57-8,60
Pamphylians,51
Panion,18,20,35,64,69,74,80,82,
   85,90,108,146-57,169,203
Paralos,212 n.40
Paratakene,205
Parthians,11,21,34,75,142
Parthia,74,81
Pathetics,12,259 n.20
patrols,100
Pella(Trans Jordan),27,35
peltasts,58,60,62-5,136,161-2,
   166-9
pelte,65
Pelusium,129
Pericles,245 n.6
Persepolis,34,50
Perseus,243 n.3
Persia,11,33-4
Persians,45,50,57
Persis,33-4,42,50,210 n.33
pezetairoi,54,62,227 n.110

phalanx,phalangites,15,20-1,34,
  40-1,45-7,54-67,82-3,96,107-9,
  119-21,129,132-41,148-9,153,
  156,166-7,170-2,176,180-1,
  195-9,201,203,252 n.9,264
  n.25
Philip II,66,95,100
Philip V,15,19,55-6,63,97,158,
  161
Philistines,13
philoi,67,71,73
Philoteria,35
phrourion,29,37
phrouroi,34
Phrygia,21,25-6,37-8,43-5
Phrygians,69-70
Phrygios,165
Pieria,27
Pisidians,48,51
Platanus,126
plēthos,167
plunder,97-8
polis,23,25,31,34,37-9,43,45-6,
  202,219 n.46,233 n.13
polishing(arms),99
politeuma,23
politikoi,227 n.107
Polyxenides,17,88,90,144
Pompeius Trogus,10,163,170
Porphyrion,85,124-7
Porphyrios,146,212
Porus,76
Poseidonius,11,99,100,101
Priene,25,30,216 n.25
prodromoi,182-3
promachoi,skirmishers,9,90,161,
  166,171,182,193,195-6
Ptolemies,Ptolemaic(army),20-3,
  26,35,40,45,47-8,53,58-9,65,
  71,77,79,80,85-6,88-9,92,
  124-41,203
Ptolemy I,35,71,240 n.91
Ptolemy II,84,240 n.91
Ptolemy IV,82,128-9,132,138-9,
  146,204
Ptolemy V,146
Ptolemy VI,81
Ptolemy,son of Aeropos,155
Ptolemy,of Megalopolis,129
Ptolemy,son of Menestheus,88
punishment,97
Pyrrhos,79,205,237 n.54

quinquireme,17-18,212 n.41

Rabatamana,85

Raphia,7,9,19,34,40-2,45,47-51,
  59,60,69,73-4,82,85,87,96,100,
  128-41,169,205-6,270 n.9
Ras el Sadiyatt,124-6
Ras Nebi Younes,124-5
regia cohors,59
reserve,epitagmata,116,122-3,168
right flank,wing,85,121,134,155,
  161,166-7,193,199
Rinocolura,131
Romans,Roman(army),16,51,96,100,
  158,162,165-6,169,170,172,205,
  224 n.95
'Roman'contingent,41,55-6,60,97,
  180,181-3

Sabun-Suyu,114
Salonian plain,107
Samaria,36,256 n.5
Samaritans,222 n.81
Sardis,37,63-5,85,163,165,171
sarissa,54,65,75,162
sarisophoroi,54
Scopas,146,148,150,153,155-7
secretary,chief,86-7
Seleucia(ad mare),29,30,44,85,
  219 n.46
Seleucia(on the Tigris),31,117
Seleucia(upon the Eulaeus),34-5
Seleucis,21,88
Seleucus I,29,30,33,35,71,76,83,
  105,110-16,241 n.99
Seleucus II,38,57-8,86
Seleucus III,34
Selge,41-2,217 n.27
Sellasia,249 n.8
semaia,66
semi-heavy troops,64,129,156,171
Sērōn,210 n.27
settlement,settlers(military),18,
  20-48,56,59,60-1,70-2,74,86,89,
  94-5,99,101-2,111,121,132,135-
  6,144,202
shields,54-6,65,74,144-5,175,180,
  183-4,196-7,217 n.27,233 nn.10,
  12
Sidon,126,146,149,156-7,256 nn.5-
  6
Sidon(stelae of),11,48
siege,98-9,174
Simon,194,196
Sinai desert,129
Sipsin,107
slingers,117,121,126,161
Smyrna,21-2,38,57-8,214
Sosibius,139

speira,66
square(formation),171,205
stratēgia,65-6,92,193
stratēgos,13,87,80-3,184
stratēgos autokratōr,87
stratiōtides,17,212 n.40
Stratonikeia,217 n.29
surprise attack,99,191,267 n.15
Susa,21,35,93,225 n.97
Susiana,11,35
symmachoi,48
sympoliteia,215 n.19,216 n.25, 233 n.13
synaspismos,196
Synnada,109
syntagma,208 n.9
systēma,208 n.9
Syria,28-31,41-2,217 n.27
Syrians,69-70,227 n.110
Syrian War I,78,111,208 n.10
Syrian War IV,85,87,89,149

tacheiai,17
tacticians,55,75
tagma,66-7,208 n.9
Tapurians,142
Tarentines,90,108,155,169,227 n.106
taxes,57,217 n.27
Tel 'Azzāziyāt,150-5
Tel Fakhr,150-5
tetrarchy,66
Theodotos(Aetolian),90,124, 126-7,138
Theodotos Hemiolios,86,88
Thera,61
therapeia,235 n.35
Thermopylae,8-10,15-18,41,48,51, 53,63-4,75,80,82,85,95-6,101, 158-62,172,203-5,207 n.8,212 n.36
Thorax,246 n.2
Thracians,33-4,42,50-1,55,132, 134,171,222 n.84
Timaeus,209 n.22
Timarchus,14,70,184,210 n.29, 211 n.30
Timoleon,57-8
Titus,257 n.7
Tobiah,35,197-8
training school,94
Trallians,51,166,171
Trans-Jordan,35,197
trap,108,198-200
trireme,17-18
Tryphon,70,81,88,92,270 n.12

Tychon,86
Tyre,256 n.7

upper satrapies,eastern provinces,18,19,72,82,85,129, 132,174,184,227 n.110

velites,166

Wadi Sheḥēt,177,179
winter quarters,95-6,107,128,146

Xenoitas,86-8,98
Xenon,87-8
xyston,xystophoroi,74-5,119,227 n.110

Zabdiel,87
Zagrus,119
Zama,80,172,205
Zeno of Rhodos,128,146,157
Zeuxis,88,170,244 n.25

CENTR

| 10,000 argyraspides | 20,000 phalangite |

25,000 'Macedonian' phalangites | 20, p

CENTR

LIBRARY OF DAVIDSON COLLEGE